Studies in Regional and Local History

General Editor Jane Whittle

Previous titles in this series
Founding Editor Nigel Goose

Volume 1: *A Hertfordshire demesne of Westminster Abbey: Profits, productivity and weather* by Derek Vincent Stern (edited and with an introduction by Christopher Thornton)

Volume 2: *From Hellgill to Bridge End: Aspects of economic and social change in the Upper Eden Valley, 1840–95* by Margaret Shepherd

Volume 3: *Cambridge and its Economic Region, 1450–1560* by John S. Lee

Volume 4: *Cultural Transition in the Chilterns and Essex Region, 350 AD to 650 AD* by John T. Baker

Volume 5: *A Pleasing Prospect: Society and culture in eighteenth-century Colchester* by Shani D'Cruze

Volume 6: *Agriculture and Rural Society after the Black Death: Common themes and regional variations* by Ben Dodds and Richard Britnell

Volume 7: *A Lost Frontier Revealed: Regional separation in the East Midlands* by Alan Fox

Volume 8: *Land and Family: Trends and local variations in the peasant land market on the Winchester bishopric estates, 1263–1415* by John Mullan and Richard Britnell

Volume 9: *Out of the Hay and into the Hops: Hop cultivation in Wealden Kent and hop marketing in Southwark, 1744–2000* by Celia Cordle

Volume 10: *A Prospering Society: Wiltshire in the later Middle Ages* by John Hare

Volume 11: *Bread and Ale for the Brethren: The provisioning of Norwich Cathedral Priory, 1260–1536* by Philip Slavin

Volume 12: *Poor Relief and Community in Hadleigh, Suffolk, 1547–1600* by Marjorie Keniston McIntosh

Volume 13: *Rethinking Ancient Woodland: The archaeology and history of woods in Norfolk* by Gerry Barnes and Tom Williamson

Volume 14: *Custom and Commercialisation in English Rural Society: Revisiting Tawney and Postan* edited by J.P. Bowen and A.T. Brown

The World of the Small Farmer

Tenure, Profit and Politics in the Early Modern Somerset Levels

Patricia Croot

University of Hertfordshire Press
Studies in Regional and Local History

Volume 15

First published in Great Britain in 2017 by
University of Hertfordshire Press
College Lane
Hatfield
Hertfordshire
AL10 9AB
UK

British Library Cataloguing in Publication Data
A catalogue record for this book is available from the British Library

ISBN 978-1-909291-86-7 hardback
ISBN 978-1-909291-87-4 paperback

Design by Arthouse Publishing Solutions Ltd
Printed in Great Britain by Charlesworth Press, Wakefield

Contents

Maps

Tables

Publication grant

Publication has been made possible by a generous grant from the Marc Fitch Fund.

Studies in Regional and Local History

General Editor's preface

In 1978 Patricia Croot made a brief but incisive contribution to the 'Brenner Debate', arguing for the importance and dynamism of small farms in the development of capitalism. Here, for the first time, we have the pleasure of publishing her detailed research into this topic, focused on the early modern farmers of the Brent Marsh region in the Somerset Levels. It presents a powerful argument for the significance of small farmers in the development of agrarian capitalism. Croot argues that such farmers were commercially orientated and eager to innovate. Landlords played little role in these communities and the farmers valued their political and religious independence as well as their economic agency. These views stand in contradiction to much that has been written about economic development in rural England. The Marxist model argues that the peasantry were thrown off the land so that landlords could engross their farms and replace them with large farmers with insecure tenures who were forced to increase profits in order to pay high rents. The non-Marxist Smithian model offers a remarkably similar story. Agrarian capitalism was located on large enclosed farms, fostered by short leases and high rents. The great agricultural 'improvers' were all gentleman farmers with money to invest: this was where the source of progress and innovation lay. Both models have the large arable farms of the Midlands and East Anglia in mind, and largely ignore other types of agriculture. Yet pastoral farming based on cattle breeding, dairying or sheep-raising was not a specialist concern confined to peripheral areas: it dominated much of the western half of England from the Scottish border to the Dorset coast, as well as Wales, Scotland and Ireland. We need to know how these types of farming systems became more commercialised, as well as the story of the large arable farms of the Midlands and East Anglia.

The classic models of agrarian development have come under increasing criticism in recent years: the medieval economy has been shown to be more commercialised, and to have achieved higher crop yields, than was previously appreciated; tenants rather than landlords have been identified as the main enlargers of farms in the late fifteenth and sixteenth centuries; Robert Allen has argued strongly that it was yeoman farmers who achieved significantly improved crop yields in the late seventeenth century. In this context, Patricia Croot's work on Somerset provides an important addition to our understanding of rural England's economic development in the early modern period, offering a fresh and original perspective. The drained 'moors' or marshes of the Somerset Levels offered rich pasture land to the farmers of the region, and only limited opportunities for growing arable crops. Manorial lords had a limited influence on the functioning of these communities, and no gentlemen managed to accumulate large estates in the region. Yet what emerged during the early modern period was a strongly market-orientated form of farming enterprise, much more akin to small businesses than to subsistence-orientated peasant farms. Animals, dairy products and specialist crops such as teasels were produced for sale. Improvements in productivity were driven by a desire for increased profits. Leasehold developed within the farming community with farmers both leasing out their secure copyhold tenures and renting extra pieces of land. Their proud independence led to strong political and religious identities, rather than economic 'backwardness' or disconnection from national trends and changes. In order to understand the outlook and attitudes of small farmers, Patricia Croot provides a holistic study of society and economy. For instance, she demonstrates that income was determined by renting and leasing as well as agriculture and farm size: all these issues are explored. Manorial structures and land tenures are examined, but also inheritance patterns, wills and pre-mortem transfers. Women's rights and roles as landholders and farmers are considered. And, importantly, the book considers not only settlement patterns and landscape but the structure of society: the distribution of wealth, religious views and grass-roots politics – factors that both united and divided sections of particular village communities.

Ultimately, like all the best local studies, this book is more than just a detailed study of a particular locality, fascinating though that is. It presents a strong argument against assuming that early modern England's small farmers were the passive victims of economic development, or an obstacle to change that had to be swept away before progress could take root, instead demonstrating that small farmers were agents of economic development. In doing so it suggests there was not one route to agrarian capitalism, or indeed a single form of agrarian capitalism. Farms, and agricultural economies, could become commercialised and specialised in a number of different ways. While this has previously been acknowledged via international comparisons, the point has never been so effectively made for England itself – so often seen as the template for the development of capitalism – as it is in this detailed local study.

Jane Whittle
October 2016

Acknowledgements

I have benefited from much help in the genesis of this book, and it is a pleasure now to be able to acknowledge and thank those who have assisted and encouraged me in this work. The initial research was carried out with the support of the Economic and Social Research Council, and I would like to thank not only my supervisor at the University of Leeds, Gordon Forster, for all his help and advice, but also his colleagues at Leeds, Christopher Challis and David Parker, for their assistance in various ways. In London, Jack Fisher's pithy insights helped me get to the heart of the issues I was tackling, and his Pre-Industrial Economic History seminar at the Institute of Historical Research provided unparalleled opportunities for intellectual discussion and enjoyable dinners with so many other historians. John Broad, David Underdown and David Hey made helpful comments on various sections, and Peter Earle and Peter Edwards also kindly made their research notes available. In Somerset I received much help from the staff, past and present, of the former Somerset Record Office, now the Somerset Heritage Centre and part of the South West Heritage Trust, and also from the archivist of Corpus Christi College Oxford, regarding the college's estates, and the Chancellor of Wells Cathedral, who made available manuscripts in the Chapter Library at Wells. Dr Katherine Wyndham searched out documents on Edingworth manor that were still then at Orchard Wyndham, and entertained me at Orchard to view them. Robert Dunning, editor of the *Victoria County History of Somerset*, and local historian Mrs Pamela Slocombe also drew my attention to some valuable source material. Creating a monograph out of my research was a tortuous process, and I owe an enormous debt of gratitude to Penelope Corfield for her generous help and kindness in the development of the initial version of the book. Alan Crossley read the final draft and made many helpful suggestions, and Henry French also read the text and gave me encouraging advice. I would like to thank the Advisory Council of the Institute of Historical Research in the University of London for the Senior Research Fellowship that gave me indispensable access to materials I required, and am grateful to Cath D'Alton for drawing the maps and patiently carrying out the many changes I made. My heartfelt thanks also go to the Series Editor, Jane Whittle, for the interesting and stimulating suggestions she has made. Lastly, I would like to acknowledge my love for and gratitude to my late aunt and uncle, Phyllis and Gerald Norman, who gave me first-hand experience over many years of a mixed dairy family farm in Somerset.

Abbreviations

AHEW4	J. Thirsk (ed.), *The Agrarian History of England and Wales*, IV, *1500–1640* (Cambridge, 1967)
AHEW5	J. Thirsk (ed.), *The Agrarian History of England and Wales*, V, *1640–1750*, i, *Regional Farming Systems* (Cambridge, 1984); ii, *Agrarian Change* (Cambridge, 1985)
BAHS	The British Agricultural History Society
BL	British Library
CCC	Corpus Christi College, Oxford
DNB	*Dictionary of National Biography*
HMC	Historical Manuscripts Commission
ODNB	*Oxford Dictionary of National Biography*
OED	*Oxford English Dictionary*
SHC	Somerset Heritage Centre (formerly Somerset Record Office)
TNA	The National Archives
VCH	Victoria County History

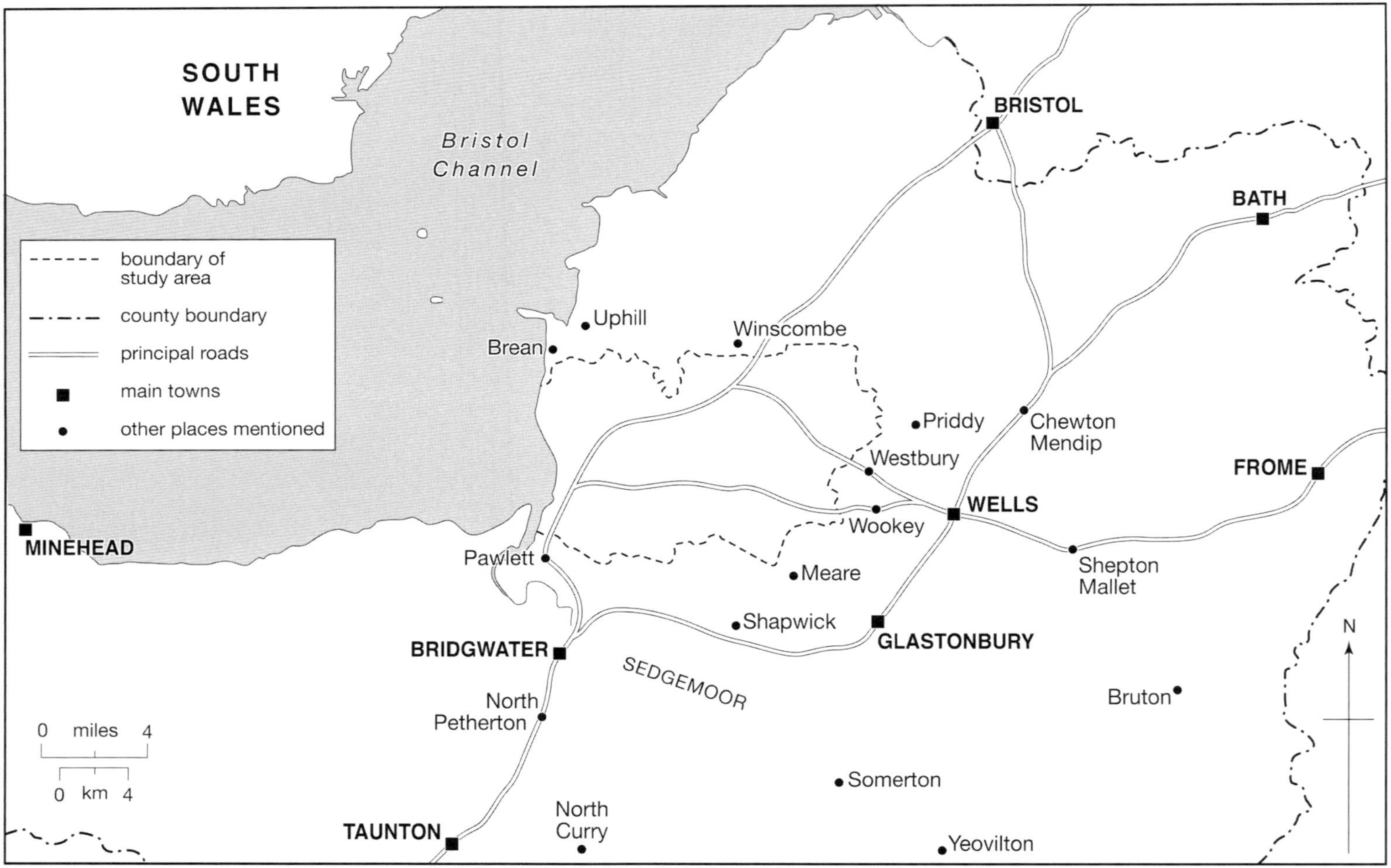

1 Central Somerset and the study area.

Chapter 1

Introduction

My interest in the small family farmer began many years ago, at a time when the image of early modern farming, in both general agricultural histories and detailed local studies, was very different from what I knew about farming in Somerset. The history of the sixteenth to the eighteenth centuries revolved around the agricultural revolution, with the changes which took place in tenure, farming practices and farm sizes, and many conclusions about those aspects were often based on limited local studies.[1] Copyhold tenure was seen as weak, with copyholders at the mercy of manorial lords, who were removing them to reorganise their land into large farm units.[2] Small landholders and cultivators were seen as economically backward and a block to the increase in agricultural production which was necessary to make possible the industrial revolution and the creation of a workforce no longer involved in agriculture but free to work in industry. Small cultivators were not big enough to specialise and could not afford important innovations to increase production; therefore, they could not contribute to the country's output and were regarded as little more than subsistence peasants who were in the process of disappearing.

At that time Robert Brenner published his Marxist-based analysis of the transition from feudalism to capitalism in Europe to explain why agricultural capitalism, leading to an industrial revolution, happened first in England rather than elsewhere. It provoked much criticism and many published responses, eventually gathered together with Brenner's original article and rebuttal as *The Brenner Debate*.[3] The limitations of his evidence made it easy to criticise him: with the vast variety of landscapes, manorial types and economies in England, one can always find a manor or parish somewhere to support or destroy almost any model of change, and there was not enough evidence to show which (if any) was the most common or influential model for the country as a whole. However, his work had the effect of focusing much subsequent attention by medieval and early modern historians on both this period of transition and the emergence of agrarian capitalism – attention which included several substantial

---

1 e.g. J.D. Chambers and G.E. Mingay, *The Agricultural Revolution 1750–1880* (London, 1966); E. Kerridge, *The Agricultural Revolution* (London, 1967). A handful of studies of individual parishes, such as W.G. Hoskins, *The Midland Peasant* (Chichester, 2008), and M. Spufford, *Contrasting Communities: English Villagers in the Sixteenth and Seventeenth Centuries* (Cambridge, 1974), are constantly cited to support national trends.

2 R.H. Tawney, *The Agrarian Problem in the Sixteenth Century* (New York, 1967 reprint of 1912 edn).

3 T.H. Aston and C.H.E. Philpin (eds), *The Brenner Debate: Agrarian Class Structure and Economic Development in Pre-Industrial Europe* (Cambridge, 1985).

works on the nature of agrarian society and economy in the early modern period,[4] though again using studies of one parish or a limited area as an illustration.

A significant element of the argument in Brenner's original article was the insecurity of peasant tenure in England, based largely on the work of Tawney[5] and firmly directed at the sixteenth century as the period of change. When challenged by historians who could show, for example, that legal security for copyholders existed in the sixteenth century,[6] he dismissed this as a later development after the 'damage' had been done, and asserted that the real period of insecurity for customary tenants was in the fifteenth century, before copyhold had developed fully and received legal protection from the common law and equity courts. The insecurity of customary tenure was important to his argument because it implied that manorial lords were able to turf out customary tenants, seize their lands, adding it to the demesne, and change their tenure willy-nilly,[7] in line with the Marxian model of the dispossession of the peasantry by the landowners. Demesne was widely let on commercial leases in the fifteenth century, and Brenner identified this as the central pivot of change that led to agrarian capitalism, by allowing subsequent landlords (300 years later) to use the classic capitalist leasing structure for a large portion of the land of each manor; he thus pushed back the origins of the transition to capitalism into the Middle Ages. Although lords were reluctant to move to commercial leasing, the process is still seen as a typical class struggle in Marxist terms, with the lords oppressing the peasantry and destroying their chances of establishing legally secure, freehold rights over their land (unlike the situation Brenner identifies in France).

The difficulty is that there are no comprehensive figures for any of this. For example, Brenner's figure for the amount of demesne land as just under a third of all agricultural land in England is based on Kosminsky's work on the Hundred Rolls of 1279, which cover only a band of manors across the south Midlands from Suffolk to Warwickshire (784 vills).[8] This demesne total was subsequently augmented by Campbell to cover 800 vills, but it is still only perhaps 6 per cent of the total number of vills in England, and, as Kosminsky pointed out, they all belong to a somewhat economically and socially homogeneous part of the country. Campbell, who also considered figures for lay-owned demesne derived from early fourteenth-century inquisitions *post mortem* covering most of England, concluded that demesne land may have formed from a fifth to a third of lowland England, but his figures do not include the sizeable holdings of the Church.[9] The actual amount of demesne land involved is, perhaps, only important

4 e.g. H.R. French and R.W. Hoyle, *The Character of English Rural Society: Earls Colne, 1550–1750* (Manchester, 2007); J. Whittle, *The Development of Agrarian Capitalism: Land and Labour in Norfolk, 1440–1580* (Oxford, 2000).

5 Tawney, *Agrarian Problem*.

6 e.g. P. Croot and D. Parker, 'Agrarian Class Structure and the Development of Capitalism: France and England Compared', in Aston and Philpin, *The Brenner Debate*, pp. 79–90.

7 Aston and Philpin, *Brenner Debate*, pp. 293–6.

8 E.A. Kosminsky, *Studies in the Agrarian History of England in the Thirteenth Century* (London, 1956), p. 74.

9 B.M.S. Campbell, *English Seigneurial Agriculture, 1250–1450* (Cambridge, 2000), pp. 37, 57–8.

in relation to France (which had much less), but, even so, the smaller the area the less the significance of the 'large demesne farms' in relation to the English economy and economic change.

The other assumption, though, about how much customary land was taken by lords and added to their demesne, is based on even shakier ground: about half a dozen studies of limited areas or individual estates in which it can be shown that this occurred.[10] With such a sweeping generalisation, it is not possible to know how much land was involved or whether this was a new and major change in tenures or just the kind of pattern of change in tenure (both from *and* to customary tenure) that was observed, for example, by Kosminsky in the thirteenth century and has been studied in detail for southern England more recently, where again leased land at times changed back to heritable (customary) tenure.[11] A variety of tenurial adaptations emerged in the fifteenth century, as lords sought tenants, tenants sought better terms and customary tenure devolved into copyhold. In some manors demesne was actually added to the amount of copyhold in the fifteenth century, and often left a legacy of difficulties for subsequent copyholders, who did not have the protection of custom for those holdings when, in the later sixteenth century, manorial lords wanted to make further changes.[12]

The Marxian model of the change from feudalism to capitalism, involving the dispossession of the agrarian population from the land, is accepted by an ideologically diverse range of historians as being the major element of change in England's economic history, but Marx's analytical modelling is not very helpful to historians trying to describe how, why or what actually happened in the changes in agrarian society and economy that we can observe in the evidence from the fourteenth century onwards. Marx had no good sources for English medieval history available to him, one reason why his account of the transition is so difficult to accept, especially for medievalists,[13] and his sketchy treatment of feudalism, taken by him and others to include serfdom, has left a wide field for Marxist historians to disagree about the important aspects of medieval development.[14] Clearly the disappearance of feudal land relationships is an important change, but it neither happened as Marx thought nor was its outcome what he anticipated. Subsequent research, especially the detailed work that has been carried out in the last few decades

---

10 Aston and Philpin, *Brenner Debate*, p. 294 n.

11 M. Bailey, 'The Transformation of Customary Tenures in Southern England, c.1350 to c.1500', *Agricultural History Review*, 62 (2014), pp. 225–6. Also M. Bailey, *The Decline of Serfdom in Late Medieval England: From Bondage to Freedom* (Woodbridge, 2014), p. 24; he points out the great variety of tenures and experiences found across England.

12 R.W. Hoyle, 'Tenure and the Land Market in Early Modern England: or a Late Contribution to the Brenner Debate', *Economic History Review*, 2nd ser. 43/1 (1990), p. 4. In the Glastonbury manors demesne was parcelled out as 'overland' but without customary appurtenances: below, Chap. 3, n.55.

13 West, F.J., 'On the Ruins of Feudalism – Capitalism?' in E. Kamenka and R.S. Neale (eds), *Feudalism, Capitalism and Beyond* (London, 1975), p. 60.

14 J. Hatcher and M. Bailey, *Modelling the Middle Ages: The History and Theory of England's Economic Development* (Oxford, 2001), pp. 71–2.

on medieval cultivators and landholders, as well as on their relationships with the urban economy,[15] has shown us a far more complex and interesting medieval society than is encompassed by feudalism alone, particularly in countering the picture of the stereotypical medieval 'peasant', trapped on a manor and in subsistence farming. As a recent survey of medieval economic developments suggests, what we are looking at in the earlier period is the development of a more widespread commercial economy in farming, industry and trade, ready to take advantage of technical changes that made large-scale capitalism both possible and necessary.[16]

The whole concept of an 'agricultural revolution' is equally, if not more, problematic in understanding the process of economic and social change. This revolution is seen as a set of interdependent strands that inevitably worked together to lead to rural capitalism, partner of the Industrial Revolution, but it has become a straitjacket in the assessment of the early modern agrarian economy, limiting the way in which agricultural change is viewed. This monolithic model is not the only possibility, however: Robert Allen's study of the south Midlands, for example,[17] shows that the strands making up the 'revolution' can be separated out, and that any one strand may not be necessary for all the others. For example, increased grain yields, essential to support a non-agricultural population, were not dependent on enclosure or the engrossing of holdings into large farms: yeomen and peasants using better seeds were largely responsible (and this increase occurred all over north-western Europe). The increased efficiency of large farms, achieved by shedding labour, was not necessary to provide labour for industry in the eighteenth century: the increased labour availability came a hundred years before industry was ready to absorb it. And, importantly, the increased income that landlords received from tenurial and land-use changes in the eighteenth century was not part of a symbiotic change that funded agricultural improvements, but, rather, came at the expense of farmers and labourers, with the latter increasingly under- or un-employed and dependent on poor relief. The traditional agricultural revolution often reads like an apologia for the landowning class, a justification for their expropriation of agricultural profits as being necessary for economic and industrial development, but most of the profits seem to have been spent on luxury housing and goods, flamboyant display and gambling rather than on rural investment. The presence of large landowners has been shown to be unnccessary for agricultural progress and productivity in some modern peasant/smallholder societies, while the creation of large farms is not the only model of efficiency and economic progress that can be found.[18]

---

15 Much of this surveyed and analysed in C. Dyer, *An Age of Transition? Economy and Society in England in the Later Middle Ages* (Oxford, 2007).

16 *Ibid.*, p. 42.

17 R.C. Allen, *Enclosure and the Yeoman: The Agricultural Development of the South Midlands 1450–1850* (Oxford, 1992).

18 F. Ellis, *Peasant Economics: Farm Households and Agrarian Development* (2nd edn, Cambridge, 1993), pp. 201–21; R. McC. Netting, *Smallholders, Householders: Farm Families and the Ecology of Intensive, Sustainable Agriculture* (Stanford, CA, 1993), pp. 27, 147–51; Allen, *Enclosure and the Yeoman*, pp. 307–1.

Another strand commonly seen as an essential part of the agrarian and commercial revolution in this period is specialisation, both in agricultural output and in economic activities generally. That this is necessary to achieve economic progress and material enrichment has now been challenged, however, by detailed analyses of probate inventories in two counties between 1600 and 1750. Thus, whereas in Cornwall agricultural specialisation reflected increasing poverty, particularly when household production such as spinning declined, in Kent the opposite was true: production did not become specialised and by-employment continued alongside a growth in material wealth, as in that county by-employment was not an indicator of self-sufficiency or a desperate search for a living but an indication of 'entrepreneurial drive' and greater market involvement.[19]

Attitudes towards the 'peasantry'

The main drawback of the classic 'transition to capitalism' model from my point of view is the concomitant attitudes, held by Marx and by both supporters of Brenner and those challenging him, towards the so-called peasants, passive victims of the march towards capitalism: that the medieval and early modern English 'peasantry' were happy to stay as subsistence farmers; that they had to be forced to become market orientated; that only large-scale producers would be market-orientated and make a worthwhile contribution; that changes to leasing were forced on peasants, who were only interested in staying on their own little plot.

'Peasant' must be one of the most ambiguous and misused appellations in all of historical writing, but, though its use is frequently criticised, it has become all-pervasive: it is widely used to describe the average old-fashioned cultivator, holding land by customary tenure and farming in traditional ways, to distinguish them from tenant farmers holding by rack-rent tenures and more modern arrangements. The use of 'peasant' in relation to English agrarian history is vague and general – the *Oxford English Dictionary* defines 'peasant' as any country-dweller from farmer to labourer – but peasants are usually taken to mean small pre-industrial owner-occupiers who were rarely more than subsistence farmers.[20] Since most peasants were supposed to have disappeared in England in the face of agrarian development in the seventeenth century,[21] it follows that they were economically backward and an obstacle to progress.

The use of the term peasant in medieval and early modern English history was challenged many decades ago by Alan Macfarlane, who defined peasant societies as having the following economic features: property owned by the household or family and not individuals, with the head of the household acting as 'manager' for the family; farm labour supplied primarily by family members, with wage labour rare; the family

19 M. Overton *et al.*, *Production and Consumption in English Households, 1600–1750* (Abingdon, 2012), pp. 170–74.

20 A. Macfarlane, *The Origins of English Individualism: The Family, Property and Social Transition* (Oxford, 1978), p. 10, gives examples of this use.

21 J. de Vries, *Economy of Europe in an Age of Crisis: 1600–1750* (Cambridge, 1976), pp. 82–3.

producing almost all its needs, both goods and services; specialist craftsmen and rural industries correspondingly limited; the absence of cash, local exchange and markets, and in particular no land market, as the family tried to hold onto their piece of land; relatively little geographical mobility.[22] He criticised the use of this peasant model for histories of English rural society in any period, as even in the thirteenth century the English were 'highly mobile, both geographically and socially, economically "rational", market-orientated and acquisitive'. John Beckett's examination of the use of 'peasant' has shown that the word itself appeared in the sixteenth century, referring to labourers and anyone you did not like the look of, and was generally a class of people usually found abroad. To this was later added a Romantic usage from the eighteenth century, to mean any small-scale rural cultivator from an Arcadian past whose disappearance began to be deplored. Its modern use by historians, however, can include small freeholders, copyholders, small tenant farmers, yeomen, anyone who farms only or mainly with family labour, and labourers with grazing rights.[23] Being both pejorative and socio-economically inaccurate, it is a term best avoided, but is handy for historians who want to underline the perceived differences between backward small cultivators and progressive large farmers. What all the definitions have in common is that they are economically pejorative (peasants are not part of the capitalist system, therefore are backward). Using 'peasant', which is no longer applied in England to rural cultivators, underlines the difference between past cultivators and the modern world, and makes it easier to dismiss them.

Mark Overton has pointed out that we can only guess at the proportion of the population in the early sixteenth century engaged in agriculture, but thinks it may be around three-quarters, so that on average each producer must feed his own family and meet one-third of the needs of another. As farm sizes varied so greatly, he suggests that 'quite a high proportion [of producers,] perhaps 80 per cent[,] were living at subsistence levels'.[24] This is a very broad assumption and, since the figure will include a great many 'semi-farmers' – those who were principally craftsmen or labourers living on their wages but also with a little land or grazing rights, a group more readily identifiable in later periods – the figure for those actually wholly dependent on farming becomes even more approximate. Nevertheless, this whole disparate collection of small cultivators and landholders can be readily summarised and disparaged *en masse*. Firstly, as their acreage was too small to produce a worthwhile surplus, so the argument goes, they can be producing only for home use; the assumption is that small farm units will always be worked as subsistence units, marketing very little produce and therefore making a negligible contribution to feeding a non-agricultural

22 Macfarlane, *Origins of English Individualism*, pp. 18–25, 163.

23 J.V. Beckett, 'The Peasant in England: A Case of Terminological Confusion?', *Agricultural History Review*, 32 (1984), pp. 113–23, discusses in detail its etymology and misuse; Allen, *Enclosure and the Yeoman*, pp. 81–5, also discusses various definitions of its usage, particularly in relation to the disappearance of small landholders and/or cultivators.

24 M. Overton, *Agricultural Revolution in England: The Transformation of the Agrarian Economy 1500–1850* (Cambridge, 1996), p. 22. His argument does depend on his figures being accurate, of course.

population, and having little to do with new developments in agriculture. While such producers were not completely self-sufficient, in that they needed to buy some goods and find cash for rent or taxes, their aim was subsistence-orientated, producing for home needs first and foremost and consuming most of what they produced from a mix of crops and livestock determined by local tradition and custom as well as by subsistence needs: 'Subsistence farmers produced no more than was necessary for their subsistence and were not producing food for its exchange value in the market.'[25] The market, therefore, did not have much influence on their production decisions, whereas 'larger, profit orientated, farmers', though facing the same constraints of soil, climate and local traditions, 'also had an eye to the market as to which crop and livestock combinations would make them most money'. How on earth can anyone, especially anyone living 400 years later, tell what farmers have in their minds, though? This is simply an assumption based on the size of the holding; no evidence is ever produced to show small cultivators turning their backs on the market.

Linked to size is the second reason: that, as small farmers maintained a mixed farm production, they were obviously attempting self-sufficiency rather than being market-orientated. They were not interested in profits, and therefore not interested in making changes to increase production, nor in specialising in one or two crops and buying what they did not produce. However, the prevalence of a mixed farm output, so often noted as part of old-fashioned and uncommercial farming, is one of the reasons why smaller producers were so successful and survived despite everything that seems against them. Historians are quick to point out how vulnerable is the small husbandman who in years of poor harvests can barely cover his home needs (seed and food) and cannot take advantage of the higher prices that are likely to ensue, unlike the larger farmer with the bigger surplus.[26] But mixed farming provided the small husbandman with alternative crops to sell, and why should he not sell all his wheat at the higher price, and buy a cheaper grain to eat?

This assumption about subsistence has been taken further by others in asserting that the vast majority of producers in the early sixteenth century were *happy* to be subsistence-orientated: they listened to sermons telling them that greed was bad and that they should be happy with their lot, just labouring to stay alive;[27] they then went home presumably determined to make as little money as possible. If commentators and parish priests were banging on about being satisfied with your lot and eschewing greed, however, it can only be because there was a lot of it about.

Overton also argues that the high density of markets in England in the sixteenth century is an indicator that producers were largely subsistence-orientated (because it indicates the lack of a national marketing network),[28] although to me it rather suggests that producers were desperate to sell wherever they could: the lack of a marketing network is the product of low demand rather than the subsistence outlook of the

25 *Ibid.*, pp. 21–2.

26 *Ibid.*, p. 20; French and Hoyle, *Character of English Rural Society*, p. 29.

27 K. Wrightson, *Earthly Necessities: Economic Lives in Early Modern Britain, 1470–1750* (London, 2002 edn), pp. 28, 57.

28 Overton, *Agricultural Revolution*, p. 22.

producers. Furthermore, even the small farmers of the *nineteenth* century, it seems, 'were more concerned with family needs and neighbourhood obligations than with profits from trade in agricultural products'.[29] Everyone who works, even in the twenty-first century, works for their own or family needs first, and neighbourhood obligations are often heaviest on the better-off in the community, but what is really being said here is that small farmers always farm for their own food first.

The outlook of small farmers

There is nothing intrinsically 'backward' or subsistence-orientated about a small farmer, however. None of the evidence put forward for the existence of subsistence farmers – small size of holdings, density of markets, lack of demand by the comparatively small non-agricultural population – is evidence for a subsistence *attitude*. Producers required opportunity, and only the demand for products, whether industrial – such as wool – or food, from a rising population made increased output worthwhile. The argument seems to be that, because there were only a limited number of families not engaged in farming and therefore needing to buy food from the agricultural sector, the producers in that sector were not interested in *selling* more if they could.

This is evidently not true, because when demand increased with population growth and prices rose in the sixteenth century farmers large and small responded by producing more and selling more. This willingness and ability to respond to market demand led to noticeably greater profits for small owner-occupiers as well as large.[30] It is hard to see how England could have fed itself in the early modern period, with a growing non-agricultural population, if it had to rely solely on the output of 'large' farms, which were not all that common; the total output of thousands of small farms is not a negligible contribution. As Allen has pointed out in relation to Oxfordshire crop yields, all the increase in wheat yields and half the yields for barley that were realised by enclosed capitalist farmers in the early nineteenth century had already been achieved by yeoman farmers (whom he equates with peasants) in open fields by the late seventeenth century, probably as a result of new and better seeds.[31]

My main argument against the idea that small farmers must be subsistence-orientated is that it flies in the face of both the practicalities of farming and, indeed, human nature. If a farmer is not completely self-sufficient then he always has to consider the market in planning his output. Harvests are always uncertain, disease and other problems affect livestock and, if a producer wants to be sure to be able to meet all his needs, both in food and in cash, he has to plan an output that is not only spread between products but also fetches the best possible prices. Otherwise he cannot be sure he will be able to get money when he needs it. Leaving it to chance after you have finished eating everything you want is hardly part of the careful traditional farming way attributed to the early sixteenth-century outlook.[32]

29 *Ibid.*, p. 178.

30 Wrightson, *Earthly Necessities*, pp. 139–41.

31 Allen, *Enclosure and the Yeoman*, pp. 206–8.

32 Wrightson, *Earthly Necessities*, p. 57.

The assumption that cultivators were happy to stay as subsistence farmers can also be dismissed on rational grounds. While there will always be a few individuals who have eccentric or nonconformist ideas about life, if a majority of the English population was content just to grow enough to eat and restock we would still be living in caves. The desire for material betterment, whatever the form it takes, seems to me to be a fundamental of human existence and the engine that has always driven the economy. Acquisitiveness, the desire for goods, often dismissed as 'greed', is evident in probate inventories, and even farmers who do not want carpets and pictures for the home will still strive for a better horse, cow or plough, and, while cooperating in their farming activities within the community, they still want to compete with their neighbours (bigger yields, fatter steers, more land, new house), all of which becomes more apparent in evidence from the later sixteenth century. Indeed, the fact that small cultivators in the early sixteenth century show great inequality in landholdings and in taxed wealth demonstrates that they were already striving and competing in the previous century.[33] Studies of modern societies also reveal that smallholders can be just as acquisitive and competitive as large farmers (or anyone else), even between relatives, building up holdings and making investments both in farming and in property elsewhere, and creating the same inequalities that are found in late medieval England.[34]

Self-sufficiency and/or subsistence farming may be forced onto people in various conditions: political or social ideology (such as serfdom); poor or non-existent access to markets or severely reduced demand, either structural or temporary (as in warfare); holdings too small to support a family with problems of obtaining additional land; no access to other income. However, this still does not mean that cultivators are subsistent from choice, and modern studies show how important is the role played by the market. Peasant households are defined by a number of characteristics, which, while they distinguish peasants from other rural producers, rural and urban workers, and capitalist enterprises, do not necessarily distinguish peasants from other kinds of family farmers. What does distinguish them from the latter, however, is their relationship with the market, in their varying commitment to it, depending on how much they need to use at home and how much they need to buy, but also the incomplete character of that market: that is, they do not have easy and free access to credit at national rates of interest controlled by market forces, to necessary products such as fertiliser or seed at open market prices or to information about prices or farming practices, all of which makes them in some degree dependent on their own produce for survival. Peasant societies are, however, seen as transitional rather than fixed in a traditional way of life, in the sense that when certain conditions, such as those found in a reasonably open and efficient market, are present, the farmers cease to meet the definition of peasant and become commercial family farmers instead. The reverse can also occur when a country's national economy collapses.[35] In all cases it is the access to a wider, freer market, for buying and selling both produce and land and obtaining information

33 Whittle, *Development of Agrarian Capitalism*, pp. 209–12; below, Chap. 6, Wealth in the Levels.

34 Netting, *Smallholders, Householders*, pp. 202–7.

35 Ellis, *Peasant Economics*, pp. 9–11, 13.

and credit, that makes the difference. Though markets in early modern England were not completely 'free' in the economic sense, having controls imposed by government, especially in relation to grain and to the activities of middlemen, buyers and sellers could travel where they wished and private marketing was also possible.[36]

Commercially orientated cultivators

So, rather than assuming that small producers held back agricultural change and had to be disposed of, we should see them as cultivators who were themselves held back by the economic and tenurial structure in which they operated, and that, rather than having to be forced into producing for the market by being dispossessed from customary holdings and given commercial leases, they actually welcomed the possibility of making greater profits. Their drive for profits and for the bettering of their lives and those of their children was just as significant in economic and agricultural change as the landlords' drive for higher rents. This is the context in which some recent work on rural history has produced a more sophisticated view of aspects such as the relationship between large landlords and tenants, which has expanded to include relationships between petty-landlords and tenants and between tenants and subtenants.[37]

More recent work on the medieval economy also shows plenty of evidence for a market-orientated attitude among small cultivators, with the market playing an important part in the agrarian economy even in the thirteenth century, long before the widespread introduction of commercial leasing: small producers supported a good-sized urban population as well as rural craftsmen; they invested in technological changes, such as acquiring horses, which also enabled them to use markets further afield; and they adapted to the needs of the market place.[38] Much of this work also shows that the initiatives for change lay with the cultivators: the manorial lords seem to have been forced into adopting commercial leases for their demesne on a widespread scale by their customary tenants, who refused to provide labour any longer. The tenants were clearly happy to have the opportunity to get their hands on more land, especially when it might be among the best in the manor; the emergence of these farmers, most of whom were customary tenants, demonstrates the hunger for land and the necessity to acquire it to increase their profits. Rather than protecting customary tenants, feudalism (that is, serfdom) had in fact held them back.

The desire for profit also applies to those who might make only small surpluses, not just to the larger producers: in many ways more so, as the smaller producer had to work harder than the larger to make money. Many customary tenants did accept changes to their tenure, and because it seems to us to be risky and counter-intuitive for tenants to give up hereditary customary tenures in return for commercial leaseholds so the assumption is that they must have been forced to do it; however, changes

---

36 Overton, *Agricultural Revolution*, pp. 135–6.

37 J. Whittle (ed.), *Landlords and Tenants in Britain, 1440–1660: Tawney's Agrarian Problem Revisited* (Woodbridge, 2013), pp. 216–17.

38 Dyer, *Age of Transition?* pp. 24–5, 27–9.

in tenure seem to be largely related to conditions in the land market, in prices and in availability of land, rather than to compulsion by landlords. Medieval customary tenants may also have accepted leaseholds in place of hereditary villein tenures to avoid villein status and the possibility of the reimposition of labour and other dues: they were not to know that labour dues had gone for good.[39] Whatever the reasons, though, the simplistic class explanation of large-scale dispossession by landlords no longer holds much weight, for the medieval period as well as the early modern.

These new appraisals and understandings of medieval cultivators are important to any assessment of changes in the sixteenth and seventeenth centuries, and early modern historians need to be aware of them, as the rural society of the early sixteenth century must be a continuation from the fifteenth, with its inhabitants looking for better economic opportunities rather than being the subservient and unambitious peasantry so often depicted for the early sixteenth century. These new views of medieval cultivators also undermine the idea that acquisitiveness is a *result* of the transition to capitalism, with a new commercial attitude, growing economic rationality and individualism emerging only in the later seventeenth century, rather than being a contributory *cause*. Alexandra Shepard's study of the change in how individuals expressed their worth concluded that the compulsion to acquire and consume was as strong in the mid sixteenth century as in the later seventeenth; that it was not so much that a consumer society was born but, rather, that consumption priorities were reorientated by changing investment strategies; and that what seems to be a turning point towards modernity was, rather, just an adaptation to the changing economy in which they lived.[40]

Despite the considerable amount of work on fifteenth-century cultivators and on several aspects of early modern rural society,[41] and some new ways of viewing the agricultural revolution, not a lot has changed in the attitudes of many agricultural historians towards small cultivators, who are still seen as 'peasants'. Economic history overall and the model of the change to agrarian capitalism still assume that small cultivators make a negligible contribution to the total agricultural output, that they are a block to progress and that they gradually 'disappeared', rather than that they continued to make a living, contributed to the market and survived alongside the larger capitalist farms that later emerged.

The dual economy

One of the problems with the feudalism/capitalism discussion is that it concerns social–property relationships rather than the economy as a whole. The emphasis placed (understandably given its importance in the modern world) on discovering the

39 Bailey, 'Transformation of Customary Tenures', pp. 223–6. Early sixteenth-century customals in the Somerset Levels still mention labour dues, though there is no evidence of them being exacted: SHC, DD\SG/22.

40 A. Shepard, *Accounting for Oneself: Worth, Status and the Social Order in Early Modern England* (Oxford, 2015), p. 312.

41 Whittle, *Landlords and Tenants*.

roots and processes of rural capitalism permeates all the examinations of change in the countryside and leads historians to dismiss or ignore anything that does not fit the path to large-scale capitalist farming. However, the English economy did not simply change from feudal and customary tenures to large capitalist-funded enterprises. Rather, this transition took place alongside a completely different set of commercial relationships and enterprises, large and small, that were not only present in the Middle Ages but can be seen in our economy today. For medieval cultivators, only their relationship with the manorial lord was 'feudal'; all their other relationships were commercial: leasing land from other holders; letting land to others; buying and selling in the market place; hiring labour. This commercialisation, which permeated most of medieval society and has received much attention,[42] is not encompassed by the feudal model and, indeed, is challenging the latter as an overall model for change in the Middle Ages.[43] Eventually the main exactions of feudalism were abolished by law, followed sometime later by customary tenures,[44] but the large-scale capitalist model is not the whole picture of our economy even in the twenty-first century. Although capitalism both in agriculture and in industry developed along the lines of the Marxian model, with the separation of the ownership of assets from the labour employed, owner–workers such as owner–farmers and small craftsmen were never just swept away and replaced by the capitalist system. If the classic capitalist model is the tripartite one of owner of assets and capital – tenant or manager – hired labour force, where do the numerous small businesses of the modern day fit in? Our modern economy is without doubt market-orientated, and our world is dominated by large capitalist businesses, but 96 per cent of all UK businesses in 2014 were classified as micro-businesses, having fewer than 10 employees, and they accounted for 33 per cent of employment and 19 per cent (in the region of £0.6 trillion) of the annual turnover of the UK private sector; 76 per cent of all UK businesses had no employees at all.[45] Therefore, a significant proportion of our GDP comes from small owner-run businesses, many sole traders or partnerships, sometimes using only family labour, sometimes with a small workforce, and including owner-occupied farms, many of which had been bought by tenant farmers in the early twentieth century when large landed estates were being broken up for sale.[46] These businesses, which populate every town and many villages today, have far more in common with the medieval tailor working at home with family labour, an apprentice and perhaps a journeyman or two than they have with the great global capitalist enterprises of today, but no-one suggests that they are an obstacle to progress which ought to be swept away (unlike the attitude towards the small family farms of the early modern period). They may be

42 e.g. R.H. Britnell, *The Commercialisation of English Society, 1000–1500* (2nd edn, Manchester, 1996).

43 Hatcher and Bailey, *Modelling the Middle Ages*, Chap. 4.

44 Feudal dues in 1660, copyhold in 1925: A.W.B. Simpson, *An Introduction to the History of Land Law* (Oxford, 1961), pp. 22, 258.

45 House of Commons Libr., Business Statistics, Standard Note SN/EP/6152, 28 Nov. 2014.

46 Owner–farmers bought a quarter of all agricultural land 1914–27, to take their share to 36%: F.M.L. Thompson, *English Landed Society in the Nineteenth Century* (London, 1971 edn), p. 332.

an obstacle to market control and greater profits for the global players, but that is not necessarily progress.

This duality and its long history has been recognised by some historians. In his study of the nineteenth century rural social structure, Dennis Mills defines the two systems, the equivalents of the modern 'big business' and the 'self-employed': the estate system of large capitalist farms owned by major landowners, on the one hand, and, on the other, the smaller independent property owners and rural entrepreneurs, including non-farming rural inhabitants, which he for want of a better name calls the peasant system, but the term is not used in the pejorative sense of a backward system in the process of disappearing.[47] The longevity and importance of the dual system needs to be more consistently recognised and incorporated into economic history. The fortunes of small landowners, for example, are not a simple story of gradual disappearance: there are ups (late sixteenth century) and downs (early nineteenth century), and then ups again (early twentieth century). Michael Thompson recognised the irony: 'Within the lifetime of the generation of social historians [R.W. Tawney; A.H. Johnson] who in the 1900s had examined the historical problems of the disappearance of the small landowner this character made a dramatic reappearance.'[48]

The small farmers of Brent Marsh

This book challenges the basic premise that small farmers failed to contribute to the productivity and commercialisation of the early modern economy. It examines the small landholders and cultivators of some parishes in the Somerset Levels, looks at their mixed farm production and their attitudes, and tries to show how different was their experience from that of the small 'peasant' farmers of so many general histories. The emergence of large capitalist farms is an important development, increasing production by improving under-producing or marginal land that needed expensive treatments, and improving labour productivity,[49] but these developments were added to the production of existing cultivators rather than replacing them. In assessing the activities of small farmers, however, the basic difficulty lies in defining a small farm. Calculations were made regarding the theoretical income of a small sheep–corn farmer and the minimum acreage necessary to support a family,[50] but income and costs are harder to compute for farms involved in other types of agriculture. Some studies, using manorial surveys to show how farm sizes have altered, have demonstrated the disappearance of a middle size, leaving fewer larger farms and a handful of very small and largely uneconomic units.[51] However, while this may indeed have happened in some areas, the manorial surveys used for this book do not actually cover farm sizes; rather, they list tenurial units and, even if those holdings change, there is no certainty about the sizes of the farms where sub-letting and annual tenancies are

47 D.R. Mills, *Lord and Peasant in Nineteenth Century Britain* (London, 1980), pp. 15–16.

48 Thompson, *English Landed Society*, p. 333.

49 Allen, *Enclosure and the Yeoman*, pp. 218–22.

50 *AHEW4*, pp. 653, 658.

51 e.g. Spufford, *Contrasting Communities*, pp. 65–72.

prevalent, so there is very little evidence, and certainly very little systematic evidence, for actual farm sizes.[52] Obviously, the minimum size of a viable farm unit increased over the centuries as the cost of living rose and cultivators' needs and desires for material goods increased,[53] leading to different definitions of 'small' in different periods, but each period will still have some farms that are relatively smaller and some relatively larger. This whole problem has been examined by Leigh Shaw-Taylor, who has avoided the problem of finding out the sizes of farms by defining farms in terms of their labour. Since a major element of a capitalist farm is the use of mainly paid labour, he has defined a capitalist farm as those employing two or more paid adult farm workers to each farmer, while family farms are those employing fewer than one paid worker, with a small area of uncertainty between the two groups. This method also avoids having to distinguish between commercial and subsistence orientation.[54] Land ownership, however, is a different matter, with small lifehold estates being more likely to continue as entities: though some might not be viable as farm units they were still capital assets that could be sublet or used to fund better opportunities elsewhere. Thus the disappearance or otherwise of small landholdings has a different trajectory and chronology from those of farm units. For the parishes covered in this book there is some incidental evidence for the sizes of seventeenth-century farm units, and where possible I mention them, though this will still not necessarily represent household income or be the only source of income for the farmer of that unit. However, the financial value, whether in agricultural output or in rent, of the landholdings, most of them comparatively small, can be assessed.

The Somerset Levels in the sixteenth and seventeenth centuries exemplified the largely pastoral economy and society of small family farmers, who, with good markets within reach, were able to diversify their production, develop the livestock farming to which the region was suited and avoid the periodic depressions in corn prices and other problems that seriously affected small farmers in arable economies. This study examines the inhabitants of a group of 16 contiguous parishes in the central Somerset Levels, forming and bordering an area known for several centuries as Brent Marsh. It focuses largely on the landholding and farming population, with only incidental treatment of other groups. The parishes have been chosen for their geographical unity and manorial and economic interdependence, though naturally there were many other links with adjacent parishes and nearby towns. The topography of Brent Marsh – in particular, the large areas of moors and other common grazing – is the major influence in both landholding and farming. Those farmers who held their land by customary tenure had security and suffered relatively little control by manorial lords. The manorial structure and the customary tenure of the area — copyhold for lives – is studied in detail, showing the increasing sophistication in the way it was used and the increasing financial strength and dominance in local society of copyholders, with some even forming a rural middle-class of gentry and professional men by the end

52 Below, Chap. 4, The income of small farmers: Actual farm sizes.

53 French and Hoyle, *Character of English Rural Society*, pp. 30–31.

54 L. Shaw-Taylor, 'The Rise of Agrarian Capitalism and the Decline of Family Farming in England', *Economic History Review*, 65 (2012), pp. 44–6, 49.

of the seventeenth century. The rich and plentiful grazing of the moors and coastal pastures supported small farmers, who did not need industrial by-employments to supplement an income derived from both agricultural output and rents. The way in which land was used, the kinds of agricultural produce commonly found here and the strength of small mixed farms is examined, showing both their flexibility in output and how small producers could alter their farming strategies to suit both their resources and market conditions. These advantages also extended into aspects of family relationships, which are also explored: the ways in which parents could provide for their children, especially in the use of copyhold and leasehold for lives, as well as the roles played by women as successors to their husbands and generally in the economy and the social life of the community. Tenurial and economic freedom and the nearly total absence of county gentry in the area gave the small landholders and farmers independence in their political and social outlook as well, and some events of the seventeenth century throw light on both the political and religious self-determination of rural inhabitants here.

So, welcome to the world of the successful small farmer!

Chapter 2

The Brent Marsh parishes and their inhabitants

An unpopular vicar of East Brent in the early eighteenth century, who had offended his parishioners and had had a difficult time with them in consequence, retaliated by publishing a satire on Brent describing

> The bleak knoll, and all the marshes round,
> A fort of chaos and unfashion'd ground;
> 'Twere made in winter we may safely swear,
> For winter is the only season here.[1]

His comments, though strongly biased, are valuable for their rarity: the travellers of the sixteenth and seventeenth centuries who left written accounts of their journeys rarely traversed the area, nor gave much detail. Leland travelled from Wells to Glastonbury and described only the moor along his road, as a 'great plain of meadow';[2] Camden saw the moors for the difficulty they presented in winter for travellers and cited the monks of Glastonbury, who translated 'Brentmersh' as 'the habitation of fen frogs' and 'Brentknol' as 'the little hill of frogs'.[3] In the later eighteenth century the absence of gentlemen's houses was attributed to the stagnant waters and unwholesome air around the unenclosed moors.[4] However, a visitor in the 1630s did refer to the land around Glastonbury as 'those fertile and pleasant Moores',[5] and Defoe, while also pointing out the difficulties that the Bristol road across Brent Marsh presented for strangers, and the occasional serious flooding from the sea, drew attention to the richness of the grazing used for oxen for the London market, to the cheese, especially that from Cheddar, and to the large number of colts bred on the moors.[6] Some eighteenth-century agricultural improvers were highly critical of the moors, but Richard Locke of Burnham, himself a promoter of improvement and a founder of the Bath and West Society, thought the poor reputation of the area had

---

1 R. Locke, 'An Historical Account of the Marsh-Lands of the County of Somerset', *Letters and Papers of the Bath and West of England Society*, VIII (Bath, 1796), p. 200.

2 L. Toulmin Smith (ed.), *The Itinerary of John Leland in or about the years 1535–1543*, vol. I (parts I–III) (1907), p. 147.

3 William Camden, *Britannia* (1806 edn), I, pp. 77, 82.

4 John Billingsley, *General View of the Agriculture of the County of Somerset* (2nd edn, Bath, 1798), p. 167.

5 L.G. Wickham Legg (ed.), 'A Relation of a Short Survey of the Western Counties … in 1635', in *Camden Miscellany* 16 (Camden Society 3rd ser. 52, 1936), p. 80.

6 Daniel Defoe, *A Tour Thro' the Whole Island of Great Britain*, 2 vols (1927 edn), vol. I, pp. 270–71.

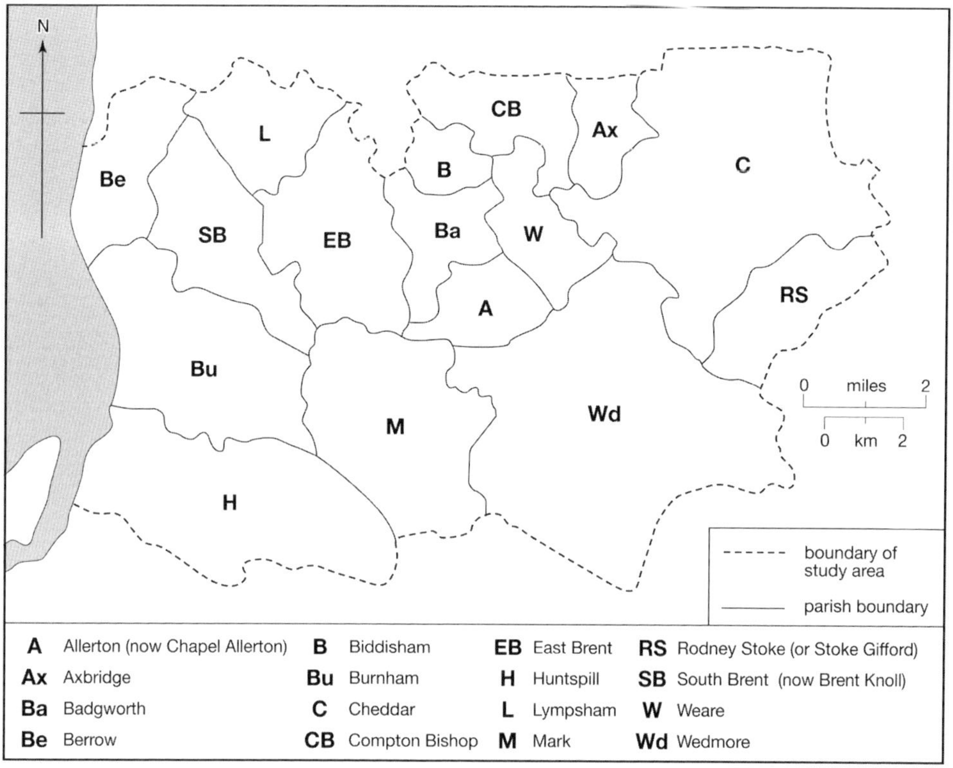

2 The parishes of Brent Marsh.

been generated by the inhabitants themselves, to keep strangers away and rents down.[7] The battle with sea and river floods was not settled (largely) in favour of man until the Second World War,[8] but this did not mean that man could not cultivate and otherwise use the area successfully through the centuries, and the inhospitable image that put off visitors did not deter the inhabitants.

The 16 contiguous parishes of this study, covering 53,066 acres in the nineteenth century,[9] are bounded by the Mendips to the north, the Poldens to the south, the Bristol Channel to the west and the Wells and Glastonbury area to the east.[10] Low-lying and relatively flat, the region was, and still can be, subject to flooding from its rivers, the Axe and the Brue, and from the Bristol Channel. The coastal clay belt is some 20 feet higher than the peat moors inland, so that, instead of draining away

7 R. Locke, 'A History of Brent Marsh', in *Letters and Papers of the Bath and West of England Society*, V (Bath, 1793), p. 200.

8 M. Williams, *The Draining of the Somerset Levels* (Cambridge, 1970), p. 240 and *passim*. Even so, some flooding still takes place in exceptionally bad winters.

9 W. Page (ed.), *Victoria County History of Somerset*, vol. II (London, 1911), pp. 341, 345, 351–2. Acreage for each parish is given in Table 1.

10 See Maps 1 to 3.

easily into the sea, surplus water tended to remain concentrated on the moors, parts of which are below sea level. Reclamation of the moors to provide grazing was undertaken on a large scale by the monks of Glastonbury Abbey in the Middle Ages, using rhynes,[11] sea walls and sluice gates to keep the seawater out and to channel away river water.[12] A large part of the area was divided into manors held by the Abbey, whose tenants were obliged to maintain the walls and rhynes as part of their customary works. Drainage activity appears to have slackened off between 1400 and 1600, though some new land may have been reclaimed around Wedmore island and south of Compton Bishop. Moreover, after the dissolution of Glastonbury Abbey it proved difficult to keep the drainage system as a whole in good repair, as it was left to commissions of the sewers and presentments at local manorial courts to get tenants to keep their ditches clear.

As in other parts of England, speculators in the seventeenth century attempted to enclose the moors and remove common rights, but met with little success, partly because so many manors, manorial lords and commoners had rights in each moor. Even the enclosure and drainage of Sedgemoor, south of the Poldens, the one common moor owned solely by the Crown, failed through distrust and jealousy between Crown, agents, manorial lords and commoners. One moor, Alder or Aller moor near Street, was drained in this period, probably because it was smaller and involved far fewer tenants than Sedgemoor.[13] In Brent Marsh the number of commoners was large: by the 1770s Mark moor was commonable by 1215 separate holdings in 14 parishes,[14] and, as rights were attached to tenements that were indivisible, this number is probably close to the sixteenth-century figure. Only in the late eighteenth century were the moors finally enclosed (by Act), and Mark moor was divided into plots of about one acre per holding, poor compensation for the free grazing the commoners had hitherto enjoyed over 1600 acres.

Because of its intimate association with flooding, including complete inundations by the sea,[15] the area not only acquired the reputation of being unhealthy for human habitation[16] but was also considered rather poor for agriculture.[17] Early settlers did not share this view, however: farming settlements were established on the higher ground surrounding the marshes from Neolithic times, and by the early Roman period the

11 Rhyne or rhine, pronounced reen: the local term for the deep man-made ditches and watercourses used for drainage and as field boundaries; main ones were eight feet wide at the surface and five feet deep.

12 Material on drainage of the moors taken from Williams, *Draining of the Somerset Levels*, esp. chaps 3 and 4.

13 Williams, *Draining of the Somerset Levels*, pp. 96–100, 102.

14 SHC, D\P\b.on.s/23/15.

15 One flood in 1607 was the subject of a tract: Williams, *Draining of the Somerset Levels*, p. 87.

16 Like other riverine or coastal marsh areas in England, it was considered to have endemic malaria, referred to as marsh ague or fever: M.J. Dobson, *Contours of Death and Disease in Early Modern England* (Cambridge, 1997), pp. 321–2. I have found no contemporary reference to this in Brent Marsh, however.

17 Undeserved even in an earlier period: in 1327 the coastal and inland parishes formed the second wealthiest area in Somerset in the lay subsidy: Williams, *Draining of the Somerset Levels*, p. 78.

river Brue, including Badgworth, was a centre of salt production. By the later Roman period the marshes west, north and east of Brent Knoll had been reclaimed and a villa settlement established on low ground east of the knoll.[18] Post-Roman settlement is more obscure before the tenth century, when Axbridge was a *burh* with a royal mint, but there is evidence for settlements at Brent Knoll and Cheddar before AD 700.[19] All the main settlements in each parish existed by 1086,[20] situated either on the higher coastal clay belt, on the slopes of the Mendips or on Wedmore island. Four of the parishes studied here – Compton Bishop, Axbridge, Cheddar and Stoke Gifford or Rodney Stoke – are situated on the springline of the southern slope of the Mendips and contained both rough grazing on the hill above and moorland grazing stretching to the river Axe.[21] Six parishes – Allerton (now Chapel Allerton), Badgworth, Biddisham, Mark, Weare and Wedmore – lie entirely in the levels, though the contours of the land within each parish vary a good deal, and the contrast with the surrounding moors makes some appear quite hilly. The remaining six – Berrow (formerly Berghes), East Brent, South Brent (now Brent Knoll), Burnham, Huntspill and Lympsham – lie along the coastal belt, adjacent to or near the Bristol Channel.

A settlement pattern of both nucleated and dispersed villages reflects the topographical constraints of the area. The most concentrated settlements lay in the four Mendip parishes, where dwellings were built near the small arable fields, sandwiched between the steep upper slopes of the hill above and the meadows and river Axe below. On the other hand, Wedmore parish, most of which lies on an island of slightly higher ground within the moors, had a much greater degree of dispersal. A large settlement existed around the church, forming the borough of Wedmore, but dotted about the island were several villages and hamlets that had cleared their own arable fields and meadow at an early date. A few, such as Allerton and Weare, formed separate parishes, but most were part of Wedmore, which had in all about 12 separate settlements.[22]

Virtually the only buildings of note or substance in the 16 parishes were the churches: nearly all were large; all except Allerton church had towers, generally of the type for which the county is justly famous, with the Perpendicular Somerset tracery, pinnacles and battlements; and nearly all had been rebuilt or altered in the Perpendicular style of the late fourteenth to early sixteenth centuries.[23] In addition, 14

---

18 M. Aston and C. Gerrard, *Interpreting the English Village: Landscape and Community at Shapwick, Somerset* (Oxford, 2012), pp. 70–71, 79–91, Chap. 4, *passim*; S. Rippon, *Landscape, Community and Colonisation: the North Somerset Levels* (York, 2007), pp. 68, 73.

19 Aston and Gerrard, *Interpreting the English Village*, fig. 5.2; T. Scrase, *Somerset Towns: Changing Fortunes 800–1800* (Stroud, 2005), p. 8.

20 H.C. Darby and R.W. Finn (eds), *The Domesday Geography of South-West England* (Cambridge, 1967), p. 165 fig. 40.

21 B.M. Swainson,'Rural Settlement in Somerset', *Geography*, 20 (1935), pp. 112–17.

22 See Map 3.

23 Unless noted, descriptions of buildings are taken from A. Foyle and N. Pevsner, *Somerset: North and Bristol* (London, 2011), pp. 81–4, 439–42, 475, 593–4; J. Orbach and N. Pevsner, *Somerset: South and West* (London, 2014), pp. 101–2, 115–16, 130–32, 167–70, 187, 280–82, 414–16, 420–22, 634–5, 653–7, 674–5.

of the churches had new interior fittings in the early seventeenth century: Jacobean pulpits are particularly common, and Axbridge and East Brent obtained their rare Gothic plaster ceilings with elaborate decoration in the 1630s. The paucity of substantial secular buildings surviving from the period arises from the non-residence of the largest landowners. The Rodneys' seat at Stoke Gifford and Glastonbury Abbey's house at East Brent were the only two manor houses inhabited by manorial lords in the early sixteenth century: the Rodneys remained until the mid seventeenth century, but their house was in ruins in the eighteenth, and the fifteenth-century manor house at East Brent built by Abbot Selwood (d. 1493), with its chapel, kitchens, guest house and outbuildings, does not appear to have housed anyone of note after the Dissolution, and was dismantled in 1708.[24]

Even so, the financial success of some local inhabitants by the seventeenth century led to new or rebuilt houses of stone that still survive: the manor farmhouse at Compton Bishop that came into the Prowse family of Axbridge merchants in the late seventeenth century;[25] Hanham Manor, a medieval house with seventeenth-century additions, and a nine-bay house in Cheddar built in the early seventeenth century; and, most notably, the Great House at Theale in Wedmore, built by the Boulting family in the late seventeenth century, of five bays with an outstanding staircase, wall paintings and woodwork. These are the survivors from a great deal of piecemeal improvement to farms and houses at that time, which is hard to date and often obliterated by later alterations. Nevertheless, in the early modern period generally only the parish churches stood out in the villages of Brent Marsh, and the groups of farmhouses, perhaps built of stone and roofed with reed or stone, contained few outstanding houses that could reinforce social divisions between farmers and gentry.

The moors

Considerable effort has been made to define the agricultural regions of England, refining the traditional descriptions of sheep–corn or wood-pasture by using techniques such as the broad analysis of probate inventories to establish the specialisms of a region. However, when detailed research into an area uncovers the existence of several sub-types within an overall region the resulting map of England becomes impossibly diffuse. Research also shows that sometimes the social structure of a particular manor or parish can be the determining factor in the survival of small farms or the type of produce grown or reared, rather than the general agricultural type of the region. A more simplified classification based solely on the landscape type provides a better starting point,[26] to which local research can add any necessary refinements, rather than assuming that the production matches that usually associated

---

24 J. Collinson, *The History and Antiquities of the County of Somerset*, 3 vols (Bath, 1791), vol. I, p. 197; III, p. 605; BL, Egerton MS 3034, f. 106d. John Brent of Cossington, esq., held the manor house as a free tenant 1607, but did not live there: TNA, LR 2/225, f. 53.

25 TNA, PROB 4/8771.

26 J. Thirsk, *Agricultural Regions and Agrarian History in England, 1500–1750* (Basingstoke, 1987), pp. 23–30, 32–3, 38 and Map IV; Overton, *Agricultural Revolution*, pp. 50–56, 62.

3 Brent Marsh: topography, settlement and the moors.

with a particular land type. The part of the Somerset Levels occupied by Brent Marsh falls into two landscape categories: Pastoral Vale along the coastal belt and Fenland inland. The destruction of much of the local probate material has made a statistical assessment of the farming system impossible, though Chapter 4 presents the evidence that does exist.[27] This and other material shows some differences between the regional types as evident in Brent Marsh and elsewhere, particularly in respect

27 Below, Sources: Note on probate sources.

of the fenland; that of Brent Marsh does not necessarily share all the aspects found in the fenland of Lincolnshire and East Anglia, particularly with regard to the social structure and the use of the common land, the moors.

The moors – the large expanses of open pasture that covered much of north and central Somerset – determined not only the field pattern of the region but also the husbandry, because the large amount of grazing available for most of the year – well-watered to provide an early bite for stock – relieved pressure on the cultivated land, especially the arable fields, and allowed flexibility in land use and rotation. The name 'moor' derives from the Old English word meaning marshland and its usage is now almost solely confined to Somerset;[28] so, although called moors, they bore no resemblance to the upland moors of Exmoor or Dartmoor, nor those of the Pennines or North Yorkshire. These latter consisted mainly of rough grazing on poor soil at relatively high altitudes, and remained undercultivated because the climate was generally unsuitable for crops and the soil quickly became exhausted. The Somerset Levels, on the other hand, were undercultivated because of their poor drainage and the nature of the peat subsoil, but produced good grazing on silt-enriched soil. Williams has pointed out that 'the Levels were far from being the unproductive, desolate and dangerous morasses they have sometimes been supposed to be', but had a range of more or less useful resources: pools and watercourses with fish and reeds; the peat turbaries, often inundated but providing fuel; the moors, used for pasturing and also subject to flooding at times; and the improved land of arable, meadow and pasture.[29]

John Billingsley, an ardent improver of the late eighteenth century, complained greatly about these watery, unenclosed moors. In a note he stated that 'Ten Thousand sheep have been rotted in one year in the parish of Mark, before the inclosing and draining took place',[30] but ignores the fact of the obvious value of the grazing, if so many sheep were kept there at all. Sheep rot was always a hazard at certain seasons, even in well-drained regions, but if such an epidemic had ever occurred it was undoubtedly an exception, as farmers would hardly risk their sheep year after year. It is true that some parts of the moors were wet and could be used for only part of the year; indeed, even today they will be flooded in bad winters. However, some winter flooding was deliberate because the silt thus deposited enriched the land and the water kept the soil warm, promoting an early growth of grass.

The open moors of Brent Marsh covered between 10,600 and 13,900 acres, in which tenants of nearby manors had common of pasture and of turbary – the right to dig peat.[31] The largest moors, according to the survey of 1638, were Theale or Tadham moor, with 1802 acres, in which the tenants of Mudgley were commoners, and

---

28 *OED*.

29 Williams, *Draining of the Somerset Levels*, p. 25.

30 Billingsley, *General View*, p. 168. The parish of Mark included Thurlmore.

31 TNA, LR 2/202, ff. 255–68, 1638 survey for the lower figure; the upper figure is the area of moors enclosed in the 18th- and 19th-century enclosure Acts, listed in W.E. Tate, *Somerset Enclosure Acts and Awards* (Frome, 1948). The moors may not be exactly the same in both sources, as several lay partly in parishes outside the scope of this study, and this may account for the large discrepancy in the two totals. The moors are shown on Map 3.

Thurlmore or Mark moor, with 1596 acres, in which Mark tenants were commoners. The hamlets and parishes on the Wedmore 'island' or adjoining it, such as Mark, were well served, with access to about ten common moors,[32] but the coastal manors were not so fortunate. Part of Burnham known as Burnham moor lay adjacent to Mark moor, and Huntspill had two moors, Huntspill moor (641 acres) and Cote Little moor (88 acres), but otherwise there was no common moor within the coastal parish boundaries, and for this reason various manors in those parishes had early in their history acquired intercommoning rights in the inland moors.[33] The manors of East Brent, South Brent, Berrow and Lympsham paid a rent of 'moremeat', either in cash or in kind, as in 1539, when East Brent bought three quarters of oats to give to the lord of the manor of Moore as rent for common pasture in Thurlmore.[34]

Some of the tenants of Huntspill, Burnham and Tarnock also paid for the privilege. In 1525 the eight tenants of customary land in Huntspill de la Haye had common pasture in Thurlmore for a certain number of beasts each, ranging from 6 to 16.[35] The tenants of the sub-manor of Tarnock had common of pasture without stint in Thurlmore for all animals except geese and swine, as well as in Binham moor and Oxmoor, and in Elizabeth's reign tenants of the head manor of Tarnock had common of pasture without stint in the same three moors, the lord paying 2s to Allerton and Mark for the rights in Binham and Thurlmore respectively.[36] The tenants of Biddisham had common without stint in Oxmoor ranging into the adjoining moors.[37]

Periodically, usually once a year in the summer, each moor was 'chased' by officers of the manor in whose jurisdiction the moor lay. The moorwardens or other tenants appointed by the reeve would make a drift of strays, which meant that they rounded up all the animals on the moor and impounded those whose owners had no right of common, charging the owners from a few pence to a few shillings to recover them. Legitimate commoners were supposed to collect their animals at the same time, without charge, but if the reeve had to keep them in custody overnight he would also make a charge of a few pence.[38] The different moors were separated only by watercourses, either natural or man-made, and when in one hard winter the rhynes froze, animals were able to trespass from Thurlmore into Tealham moor.

Sheep, mares, farrowing sows and geese were all kept on the moors; kine were milked there morning and evening, and 'unprofitable' cattle, such as dry cows and young stock, were grazed there. The quality and dryness of the moors varied, occasionally leading to the illegal construction of sleights or enclosures for sheep, such as in Thurlmore, where some commoners were accused of driving away other

---

32 SHC, DD\SAS/C795/PR/462, f. 57.

33 Williams, *Draining of the Somerset Levels*, p. 90, gives a map showing the extent of the intercommoning links for all the Levels.

34 TNA, SC 6/HENVIII/3163, m. 15; E 134/34Eliz/East21. In 1592 the four manors paid £3 6s 8d for their rights.

35 TNA, E 315/385, ff. 90–95d.

36 SHC, T\PH\vch/38, pp. 91–101; TNA, LR 2/191, f. 31.

37 SHC, DD\CC/B/110001, vol. 1, f. 88.

38 TNA, E 134/34Eliz/East21.

men's sheep from a place in the moor called Hust, and keeping their own – about 60–80 sheep, mainly ewes – there for several days. The reason suggested for this antisocial behaviour was that the place was dry and the ewes could lamb there without danger, but the lack of regard for other men's stock, also near to lambing, was considered unusual. Despite the dangers of flooding and sheep-rot, sheep at least were grazed there through the winter.[39]

There is no real evidence that the moors were overstocked or overgrazed in this period, but orders limiting their use, particularly by 'foreigners', were made from time to time, and show a valuable right being jealously guarded, possibly with the fear that its value might be damaged. In general only sheep and unringed pigs had restrictions placed on them, presumably because they tended to leave little for other stock to eat. In Biddisham in 1510 sheep were ordered to be taken off the marsh from the end of March,[40] while in Allerton the homage, the body of manorial tenants who attended the manor court, ordered in 1567 that no tenant was to put sheep into Binham moor between June and Michaelmas and in 1593 that no-one was to keep any sheep in Binham or Allerton moors for three days at a time;[41] presumably the owners would have to graze their sheep on their own pasture or rent grazing elsewhere. The homage of Moore made an order, reported in 1592, that no foreigner should graze sheep on Thurlmore from Ladyday to Midsummerday,[42] but by 1623 the order seems to have applied to everyone.[43] Similar orders were made in Blackford, where sheep were banned from Tealham between Ladyday and Midsummer in 1637 and unringed pigs were not allowed after 3 March,[44] while in 1658 no sheep were to be grazed on Blackford moor indefinitely.[45] The tenor of these orders suggests, in fact, that more emphasis was being put on grazing for cattle, and the grass was being protected for their benefit, but there may have been increased pressure to graze sheep because of a greater emphasis on keeping the latter for meat rather than wool.

The right of common was attached to the free and customary tenements of each manor, and, in some of the manors at least, the tenant of such a holding enjoyed that right only while he was resident on the tenement. If the holding was sub-let with its appurtenances, including common of pasture, the right passed to the undertenant, and leases, even for a short period of years, generally did include the appurtenances. The right was a valuable one and raised the economic possibilities of even a small customary holding: in the manor of Compton Bishop Jeremy Waters felt that it was a matter of some importance that 'although his tenement … was but small, yet his comons were verie good'. Common rights also had a commercial value. William Hixe

39 TNA, E 134/20Jas1/Hil8; SP 16/165, no. 56.

40 SHC, DD\CC/B/131907/8, Biddisham 23 Apr. 2 Hen. VIII.

41 SHC, DD\CCB/131925a/2, Allerton 25 June 9 Eliz.: wording gives 'nativity' but obviously meant nativity of St John the Baptist, 24 June; DD/CC/B/131925a/10, Allerton 17 July 35 Eliz.

42 TNA, E 134/34Eliz/East21. A 'foreigner' meant a person who was not a tenant of the manor of Moore.

43 TNA, E 134/20Jas1/Hil8.

44 SHC, DD\SE/64/1, court roll 26 Feb. 1637/8.

45 SHC, DD\SE/63/1–2, presentments 2 Nov. 1658.

of the manor of Moore grazed some stock of Edward Davys in the commons towards the repayment of a debt he owed him, marking them with his own mark to avoid accusation of trespass, while another commoner also grazed sheep not his own and paid the reeve 13s 4d to overlook the trespass.[46]

The demand for grazing, whether in the moors or elsewhere, is made evident in the grazing of 'foreign' cattle, and produced a smattering of bylaws and orders in the manorial courts. In 1577 the tenants of Biddisham were ordered not to give or sell their common in the manor to anyone from outside any longer, on pain of a fine of 20s, but in 1583 it was necessary to repeat that none of the tenants should sell his common to any outsider if another tenant would give as much for it as the stranger.[47] Blackford tenants were ordered in 1662 not to take any 'foreign' or outsiders' sheep for grazing on the fields of the manor.[48]

Disputes over whether certain inhabitants had the right to graze various moors were regularly taken to the royal courts for arbitration,[49] but it is hard to tell whether this indicates a new pressure on grazing or a new desire to reinforce legal rights; equally acrimonious disputes had been carried on between the abbey of Glastonbury and the bishop and chapter of Wells, and their respective tenants, over moorland rights in the thirteenth and fourteenth centuries.[50] The *villages* did not take each other to court over intercommoning rights, as occurred in other areas of lowland England where grazing was scarce, principally because the moors were controlled on a manorial basis which cut across villages, whose inhabitants did not have any grazing rights unless they were customary tenants. The seventeenth-century cases seem to indicate both the tenants' appreciation of the value of the grazing and a desire on the part of non-commoners to share in this resource.

Common meadow and other grazing rights

At the edges of the moors were the cultivated areas of meadow and pasture, which included some common meadows shared by customary tenants from which stock was excluded until after haymaking: in 1638 the moors and low grounds of Brent Marsh included 4235 acres of common meadows. Although referred to as 'common' meadows, they were not common in the sense that the moors were. The survey lists the moors and manors whose tenants were commoners in them – that is, those who had common rights of pasture and turbary in a moor. The meadows, however, were listed as being in the tenure of named persons, which may be interpreted as meaning that the common rights appurtenant to a customary holding did not include rights

---

46 TNA, E 134/27and28Eliz/Mich21; E 134/20Jas1/Hil8.

47 SHC, DD\CC/B/131911a/2, Biddisham 25 June 19 Eliz.; DD\CC/B/131923/1, *ibid.* 20 Apr. 25 Eliz.

48 SHC, DD\X\HMD, 30 Sept. 1662.

49 e.g. the Exchequer Court has several cases: TNA, E 134/27and28Eliz/Mich21, Compton Bishop, 1585; E 134/34Eliz/East21, Thurlmore, 1592; E 134/37and38Eliz/Mich2, Compton, 1595; E 134/20Jas1/Hil8, Thurlmore, 1623.

50 Williams, *Draining of the Somerset Levels*, pp. 34–8.

over the meadow unless the tenement included a specified holding there.[51] Some meadows had names such as 'dolemead', but there is no evidence that the open meadows were still being shared out anew each year, as happened in Puxton and Congresbury, north of the Mendips.[52] Richard Locke suggested that parcels of the meadows were permanently attached to a holding: a full day's mowing was called a mead, and when tenements came to be identified and boundstones set up they were always estimated as five acres each, although Locke found many of them to be from three to three and a half acres.[53] Some meadows were common in the sense that they were open for grazing by all the tenants between certain dates, and were usually stinted.[54] In other meadows the grazing was controlled and the aftermath of the hay crop was let by the lord: in East Brent in 1516 the reeve held half the aftermath of 21½ acres of meadow in Langmede, and four other tenants rented part of the aftermath of three acres for a few pence a year.[55]

Other forms of grazing were available in some manors. Tenants along the coast and rivers were able to make use of pieces of reclaimed land called warths and hams. In Berrow nearly all the customary tenants in 1516 had as part of their holdings the right to pasture on land outside the sea walls called wall and warth, the sea walls being large banks that could be grazed upon, especially by sheep. Some tenants also had certain quantities of grazing on the New wall, which, as a late reclamation, was part of the overland or demesne of the manor.[56] Similarly, a few Lympsham tenants had grazing in warths and on the walls or along certain paths or droveways among the fields, and five tenants also had grazing stints in Whelpesham, a pasture of 37 acres in which the lord had pasture for 37 beasts and the lord of Lympsham Parva had pasture for three.[57] Some men owned stints in a pasture that was held in severalty by another tenant: one man had the rights to graze 48 sheep on a 100-acre warth in Huntspill belonging to another to whom he sold this right in 1673.[58] By the 1620s some tenants of Berrow had shares in Berrowsham, also a later reclamation. The grazing in the hams was particularly rich and valuable, which led to disputes between lords and their tenants. In Burnham a large pasture of about 100 acres called the Broadwarth was regarded by the tenants as a common pasture where they could graze sheep all year round, whereas the lord, Richard Fynes, began to assert his claim that the land was part of the overland of the manor, and he issued new copies from about 1540

51 TNA, LR 2/202, ff. 255–68.

52 Tate, *Somerset Enclosure Acts*, p. 27. The doles were given symbols marked on apples and drawn out for distribution among the tenants each year.

53 Locke, 'History of Brent Marsh', pp. 191–2.

54 SHC, DD\CC/B/131925a/4, Allerton (?16) July 27 Eliz.

55 BL, Egerton MS 3034, ff. 111, 112d, 126d.

56 *Ibid.*, ff. 172–88. Overland was non-customary land often parcelled out among customary tenants and included their holdings, but did not have customary rights attached. Some was demesne land; it may also be applied to assarted land, but detailed locations usually show it intermingled with customary land, so it was unlikely then to be assarts.

57 BL, Egerton MS 3034, ff. 132–47.

58 SHC, DD\SAS/C82/16, no. 1.

with a clause excluding grazing in this pasture. The tenants brought suits in Requests and Chancery, and Fynes in Chancery and the common law courts. The outcome is unknown, but the clause excluding grazing the warth was still put in copies and leases in the seventeenth century.[59] Lastly, the Mendip hills also had large tracts of grazing – though not nearly as rich – known as sheep sleights or enclosures, taken out of the rough common grazing. Berkeley sleight, belonging to the manor of Cheddar Berkeley, was 100 acres in extent and in 1671 was used for pasturing 200 sheep.[60]

Communications and markets

Though the bleakness of the turbaries can give the Levels a remote air, Brent Marsh formed the hinterland to flourishing markets and had good communications for both local and more distant requirements. The main highway from Bristol to Exeter ran through the western part of Brent Marsh, including Huntspill and East Brent, and at Crosse in Compton Bishop connected with a road from Wells linking the parishes of the southern edge of the Mendips. South of Brent Marsh, the main road from Glastonbury to Bridgwater ran along the Polden ridge, and a local road linked several villages in and around Wedmore with Wells. These roads carried much traffic and, as roads everywhere in this period, were prone to decay.[61] Decay of bridges was another problem. The many watercourses crossing the area necessitated all kinds of bridge, from important stone-built ones to simple wooden footbridges, and demands for their repair, made at quarter sessions as well as in the manorial courts, testify to the importance, as in the case of roads, of having freedom of movement and access to markets.[62] Water transport was a convenient alternative, and in the medieval period seems to have been the principal means by which officials of Glastonbury Abbey travelled to Brent. Quite apart from the major port of Bridgwater, on the river Parrett to the south, the river Axe contained the medieval port of Rackley, below Axbridge, formerly used by merchants of Wells for trade between England and Gascony, Bayonne and Lisbon, and thereafter used for local transport into the nineteenth century.[63] Glastonbury had a similar port at Rooksbridge in East Brent, on the Pilrow Cut, which was still being used for coastal traffic in 1547, when a Bristol merchant took delivery of 20 barrels of butter at Wyngods Pill (creek) there.[64] Uphill, at the mouth of the Axe, was one of several embarkation points along the Somerset

59 I.S. Leadam (ed.), *Select Cases in the Court of Requests AD 1497–1569* (Selden Society XII, 1898), pp. 62–4; TNA, C 1/1158/26–7; C 1/986/70–72; DHC, D-SHC/KG/2669 (copy Oct. 1599); SHC, DD\ARN/12 (lease 1619). Papers re. sale of manor 1650 do not refer to it, either as land or as grazing right.

60 SHC, DD\PO/9, lease Popham to Clipson, 31 Jan. 22 Car. II.

61 e.g. SHC, Q/SR/66/116 and 67/4, presentments of the road between Pawlett and Huntspill market.

62 e.g. SHC, Q/SR/67/4, footbridge from Huntspill to Mark over the rhyne at Notham.

63 Williams, *Draining of the Somerset Levels*, pp. 65n, 68; R.W. Dunning, *A History of Somerset* (Bridgwater, 1978), 21.

64 J.Vanes (ed.), *Ledger of John Smythe, 1538–50* (Bristol Record Society 28, 1974), p. 292.

coast for the frequent traffic with south Wales. Although the coastal ports could be used for transport to London as well as to overseas markets, the transportation of goods to London and other inland centres seems usually to have been by road in the seventeenth century. A regular carrier service to London from several Somerset towns existed by 1637, the nearest such town to Brent Marsh being Wells, from which two carriers went to Holborn and to the City each week.[65]

These transport links, both local and distant, were vital for the inhabitants because they stimulated good markets for the area. Good markets not only allowed farmers to sell their produce but also made it possible for them to buy necessities such as corn, thus freeing them from the need for self-sufficiency and allowing them to specialise in husbandry more suited to the area than arable farming. No seventeenth-century toll books survive for the market towns of the area, but other evidence indicates the goods bought and sold. Weekly markets were held in Axbridge, Wells, Bridgwater and Huntspill, and probably in Wedmore borough as well, at which inhabitants bought and sold beef, mutton, corn, vegetables and wool, as well as livestock, and traders from larger centres such as Bristol also operated there.[66] All the Berrow tithe wheat in the 1620s was taken to Axbridge market, while barley, beans and oats were taken to Bridgwater market.[67] Axbridge, Bridgwater and Wells had large non-agricultural populations that created a steady demand for food and other goods and services – especially Wells, with its ecclesiastical and legal inhabitants – and this ensured that a strong market network would remain in operation. Most parishes also had at least one fair each year, and, taking the 16 parishes as a whole, January appears to be the only month without a fair.[68] The fairs were principally intended for sales of livestock, but other goods, such as textiles, leather goods and small trinkets, were also sold.

Not all buying and selling was done in the open market. Farm produce was also sold by private arrangement, and contracts were made to ensure the supply of food in towns. John Coxe of Axbridge, possibly a victualler, made a contract with Thomas Edwards of Stoke Lane in eastern Somerset *c.*1540 for the supply of 40 quarters of barley malt and 52 bushels of wheat malt, at the rate of three quarters and one bushel respectively a week;[69] the rector of Huntspill sold his tithing corn from 75 acres of mixed grains to a Huntspill butcher in 1541, at a flat rate of 8d an acre;[70] and the farmer of the Berrow tithes sold the corn in the sheaf to two men from Yeovilton in south Somerset *c.*1620.[71] Middlemen from Brent Marsh also operated in the marketing of butter and

65 J.A. Chartres, 'Road Carrying in England in the Seventeenth Century: Myth and Reality', *Economic History Review*, 2nd ser. 30 (1977), pp. 73–94, *passim*; John Taylor, 'The Carriers' Cosmography' (1637), in E. Arber (ed.), *An English Garner*, vol. I (1895), pp. 241–2.

66 SHC, Q/SR/81/62.

67 TNA, E 135/5/45.

68 N.F. Hulbert, 'Survey of the Somerset Fairs', *Proceedings of the Somerset Archaeological Society*, 82 (1936), pp. 83–159; I.F.H. Jones, 'Somerset Fairs', *Proceedings of the Somerset Archaeological Society*, 91 (1945), pp. 71–81; SHC, Q/SR, *passim*.

69 TNA, C 1/973/67–8.

70 TNA, C 1/973/74.

71 TNA, E 178/4467, deposition of Robert Hitchcocke.

cheese: a cheesemonger was living in Wedmore in the 1540s,[72] and local inhabitants were licensed at early seventeenth-century quarter sessions as badgers of butter and cheese, to buy locally and sell at Taunton or in neighbouring counties.[73] Long-distance trade in butter and cheese was growing in the late sixteenth century, with exports from the Bristol Channel ports,[74] while a good deal of the specialised produce of the area was also sold much farther afield, either by middlemen or by the individual producers. In 1598 a Wedmore husbandman took a wain-load of butter and cheese to Andover, where there was a specialised cheese fair, acting as a middleman for his neighbours as well as selling his own produce,[75] while several horse-breeders from the marsh regularly sold their colts at the annual Magdalen Hill horse fair at Winchester in the seventeenth century.[76] Bristol naturally attracted much trade: John Smythe, a Bristol merchant, was supplied by the regular carriers that brought goods from Wells and the neighbouring villages in the first half of the sixteenth century, and corn, butter and cheese were bought in Somerset by Bristol merchants.[77] Even rabbits from the Mendip conigars were being sold in Bristol in the 1640s.[78] Many butchers resident in the area were also graziers, and bought livestock from their neighbours, but beef cattle were also sold to butchers in the towns such as Axbridge and Wells, as well as for the London market: a Huntspill yeoman sold 10 or 12 oxen in 1623 to a man from South Somerset who was well known to him and who subsequently drove the beasts to London.[79]

As a whole, the evidence for the trade and markets of the area gives a picture of a flourishing network of outlets for produce and opportunities to purchase food and other goods, and bears out Defoe's impressions of the produce of the marsh a century later.[80]

Population

Population and its rate of growth or decline are important influences, particularly on the local economy and attitudes towards the inheritance of property. Brent Marsh differed from many pastoral areas principally because the common rights of grazing and turbary in the moors were attached to holdings and were not open to all inhabitants;

72 D.O. Shilton and R. Holworthy (eds), *Medieval Wills from Wells* (Somerset Record Society 40, 1925), p. 81.

73 E.H. Bates Harbin (ed.), *Quarter Sessions Records for the County of Somerset*, vol. I, *James I, 1607–1625* (Somerset Record Society 23, 1907), p. 91; SHC, Q/SR/6/81, 27/217, 52/52, 55/34, 71/222.

74 J. Broad, 'Regional Perspectives and Variations in English Dairying, 1650–1850', in R.W. Hoyle (ed.), *People, Landscape and Alternative Agriculture: Essays for Joan Thirsk* (BAHS, 2004), p. 97.

75 SHC, D\D\cd/28, 'detection' v. Henry Meade, dep. of John Kinge, 10 July 1598.

76 I am very grateful to Prof. Peter Edwards for allowing me to use his transcripts from the Magdalen Hill fair toll books (in Winchester Cathedral Library) and other similar material.

77 Vanes, *Ledger of John Smythe, passim*; T.G. Barnes, *Somerset 1625–1640: A County's Government During the 'Personal Rule'* (Oxford, 1961), p. 10.

78 TNA, SP 28/242, part 1, f. 136.

79 TNA, E 134/20Jas1/Trin11.

80 Defoe, *Tour Thro' Great Britain*, I, pp. 170–71; see above.

only the tenants of the manors could make use of the moors, which meant that these parishes, though mainly pastoral in their economy, were no more 'open' or favourable to poor migrants than were tightly controlled arable parishes. This contrasts with most pastoral areas in England in this period, which either attracted a great deal of immigration or suffered from mortality crises: the northern border counties were especially prone to the latter owing to insufficient harvests and the inability of a large part of the population to buy grain. Poor harvests could affect the death rate in most areas to some extent,[81] but pastoral areas farther south generally suffered more from increases in population, because looser manorial control, the presence of large expanses of commons or woodlands and rural industries there all attracted the poor and landless from less favourable areas.[82]

Estimates of the population and rates of change in Brent Marsh are hard to provide, however. The chantry certificates of 1548 give the numbers of communicants for only four of the 16 parishes,[83] and the Episcopal Returns of 1563 also give the households for four only. Both the 1603 returns and the Compton census of 1676 recorded totals only for the whole diocese and not for individual parishes.[84] Brent Marsh parishes also lack good series of parish registers from which the rate of population change can be assessed: most registers start only in the mid to late seventeenth century. The two exceptions, with full series from the mid sixteenth century, are Axbridge and Wedmore, and neither can be called typical for the area: Axbridge was a long-established market town and Wedmore was two or three times the size of most of the parishes, had several villages and a borough within its bounds and, like Axbridge, attracted numbers of adult craftsmen and servants.[85] In addition, figures for any parish after 1660 were affected by the numbers of dissenters in the area, and Wedmore registers show an abrupt drop in baptisms and marriages which never recovered to pre-Civil War totals.[86]

Taxation returns also give an indication of population, and the muster and subsidy returns of 1522–25 can be particularly useful in this regard, since the muster return included all men over the age of 16 and the subsidies of 1524–25 included all men over the age of 16 with £1 or more in land, movable goods or wages, and occasionally some women, presumably widows or singlewomen who were householders. Since the 1522 muster was ostensibly made for military purposes rather than taxation, and included men without any wealth, it forms both the fullest list and one with more richer people indicated than the two taxation lists. Where all three lists survive, however, a

---

81 A.B. Appleby, *Famine in Tudor and Stuart England* (Liverpool, 1978), pp. 192–3, and *passim*.

82 *AHEW4*, pp. 38–9, 107.

83 E. Green (ed.), *Somerset Chantry Certificates* (Somerset Record Society 2, 1888), pp. 61, 71, 73, 77.

84 BL, Harley MS 594, f. 51; A.A. Dyer and D.M. Palliser (eds), *The Diocesan Population Returns for 1563 and 1603* (British Academy, 2005), pp. 24–5; A. Whiteman (ed.), *The Compton Census of 1676* (British Academy, 1986).

85 Below, Non-Agricultural Occupations.

86 S.H.A. Hervey (ed.), *Wedmore Parish Registers: Marriages 1561–1839* (Wells, 1888); *Baptisms, 1561–1812* (Wells, 1890); *Burials 1561–1860* (Wells, 1890); below, Chap. 6, Political attitudes in the later seventeenth century.

Table 1
Population figures

Parish and acreage	(1) Taxpayers 1524–5	(2) Communicants 1548	(3) Households 1563	(4) Taxable individuals 1660	(5) Hearth Tax No. of houses 1665
Allerton (1169 a.)	17		24	123	47
Axbridge (528 a.)	62			*c.*205 [(c)]	99
Badgworth (1815 a.)	21				[inc. in Weare]
Berrow (2221 a.)	51			193	
Biddisham (572 a.)	33 [(a)]		14	111 [(a)]	41 [(a)]
East Brent (3037 a.)	109			241	
South Brent (3426 a.)	82			246	
Burnham (3907 a.)	68			274	80
Cheddar (6998 a.)	102	70			90
Compton Bishop (2536 a.)	29			*c.*159 [(c)]	100
Huntspill (5944 a.)	105	506		109 [(b)]	151
Lympsham (2082 a.)	52			149	
Mark (4354 a.)	88	450	103	397	139
Rodney Stoke (2345 a.)	28				72
Weare (2146 a.)	20			107	53
Wedmore (9986 a.)	162	1000	206	713	235

Notes: (a) Tithing of Biddisham included Tarnock (in Badgworth parish, Winterstoke H.); (b) only Alston tithing (in Bempstone H.) extant; (c) some amounts or names illegible for these parishes.
Sources: (1) TNA, E 179/169/171; 169/182; 169/169; 169/175.
(2) Green (ed.), *Somerset Chantries*, pp. 61, 71, 73, 77. (3) BL, Harl. MS. 594, f. 51.
(4) TNA, E 179/172/416; 171/336, pt 30; 256/7. (5) TNA, E 179/256/16/11, 14, 19.

comparison shows that any one of the three lists is likely to contain only about two-thirds of a conflation of all three lists, with the shortfall being mainly of people below the £2 level. Overall, a study of population using this source suggests that by the 1520s some 20–25 per cent of the rural population may have formed a category of virtually landless men.[87] Unfortunately not all counties have all three lists, and Brent Marsh has only the return for 1524, but this does give a fair indication of the population above the level of the very poor. Hearth tax returns of the late seventeenth century giving the number of households are often used to compare with the subsidy figures, and exist for 11 parishes in Brent Marsh. Several parishes also have Poll Tax returns for 1660, and these have also been used here to obtain figures for the later seventeenth century.[88] Both, of course, have their drawbacks, and it is clear that there was also inconsistency between parishes in how the taxes were assessed and collected;[89] the figures obtained are listed in Table 1. Three of the parishes for which 1563 figures are available show increases over the 1524 figures of between 17 and 41 per cent, which are similar to the estimates of growth in national population, but do not reach the extremely high rates of growth found in some areas, such as Cambridgeshire fen villages in this same period.[90] The fourth parish, Biddisham, apparently shows a decrease, but this may be a distortion caused because the tax figures included the large hamlet of Tarnock, which lay on the boundary with East Brent, and was later in Badgworth.

A comparison of the number of taxpayers in 1524 and in 1660 shows widely varying rates of increase: 230 and 310 per cent in Axbridge and Compton Bishop (which included part of Axbridge town) respectively, down to 86 and 88 per cent in East Brent and Wedmore; the last two compare closely with Willingham in the Cambridgeshire fens, which had a total increase in taxpayers of 83 per cent between 1524 and the hearth tax of 1664.[91] However, bearing in mind the limitations of tax figures used for population estimates, too much reliance should not be placed on figures that seem to show a trebling of the population in agricultural parishes, where there is no other evidence to support heavy increases.

Incidental evidence also suggests that there was growth in the population, but that it was not so high that it was commented on or led to visible tensions in the community, and it is this, the result of population change, rather than any particular rate of change, that is significant. Reference was made, for other reasons, to an increase in the houses in one hamlet in Wedmore: Heathhouse had two houses *c.*1580, four by 1587, and 'more' had been built by 1597;[92] similarly, references occasionally occur to a barn converted into a house, newly built dwellings, or one

87 J.C.K. Cornwall, *Wealth and Society in Early Sixteenth Century England* (London, 1988), pp. 210, 277–9; Whittle, *Development of Agrarian Capitalism*, pp. 203–7.

88 TNA, E 179/172/416, Brent and Bempstone hundreds; E 179/256/7, Winterstoke hundred. Assessment for Huntspill hundred has not survived.

89 Below, Chap. 6, Wealth in the Levels.

90 Spufford, *Contrasting Communities*, 18.

91 *Ibid.*

92 SHC, D\D/cd/51, Hodges & others v. Tincknell, deps. of Andrew Luccock and Isabel Penn, 15 Jan. 1638.

or two cottages allowed on the waste, inhabited by day-labourers or craftsmen. The increase seems mainly indigenous, and the immigration that occurred was apparently of craftsmen or husbandmen who rented holdings, and not the subsistence poor; no comments have been found regarding poor squatters or an uncomfortably large increase in population. The hearth tax returns of 1665 indicate a number of houses which were empty or put to other uses,[93] which again does not suggest that overcrowding was rife.

Non-agricultural occupations

The occupational structure followed closely the sources of income: most wealth came from the land, and agriculture employed the greatest proportion of those whose occupations can be ascertained. The occupation or status given for male witnesses in the ecclesiastical courts have been compiled into Table 2, which shows that husbandmen and yeomen account for two-thirds of the witnesses, other occupations only a quarter; witnesses whose occupations were not given were also likely to have been husbandmen. The table also gives the occupations of testators, which follow a similar pattern. The term 'husbandman' covered widely differing economic positions, from men who farmed their own holdings to covenant servants in husbandry, but their number in relation to other occupations underlines the overwhelming importance of agriculture in the area.

However, occupations other than farming can be found in every parish, most of them the usual wide range of crafts and services that were required by the farming community and others, but also including a commercial community based on Axbridge. This ancient borough was always overshadowed to some extent by Wells, only a few miles to the east, which had become the largest town in Somerset by the fourteenth century, if not before.[94] Nevertheless, Axbridge had some importance in the Somerset woollen industry in the fourteenth century,[95] as it lay near the Cheddar fulling mills; it was also well placed in regard to the lead, silver and calamine mines on Mendip,[96] and became an important local distribution and marketing centre. By the early seventeenth century it had three companies or guilds – drapers, leathermen and firemen (metal-work) – one of which all householders who kept a shop or stall or resided and kept their family within the borough had to join from 1624; a mayor and aldermen to manage the affairs of the Corporation; and its own justices and sessions.[97] Nearly all the mercers, drapers and other leading tradesmen of the area were based in Axbridge, and the borough probably controlled the activities of the

93 Below, Chap. 6, Table 12.

94 Dunning, *History of Somerset*, 23.

95 H.L. Gray, 'The Production and Exportation of English Woollens in the 14th Century', *English Historical Review*, 39 (1924), p. 30.

96 H.C. Darby (ed.), *A New Historical Geography of England Before 1600* (Cambridge, 1976), pp. 108–9.

97 HMC, *Third Report*, Appendix (MSS of Corp. of Axbridge), p. 302. It is not clear whether it included female householders. A man without a trade could choose which company to join.

Table 2
Occupational structure

Male occupations	From ecclesiastical courts 1549 to 1684		From wills and inventories 1505 to 1693	
	No.	%	No.	%
Husbandmen	165	60.2	213	27.7
Yeomen	18	6.6	136	17.7
All other	69	25.2	109	14.2
Not given(a)	22	8.0	310	40.4
Totals	274		768	

Notes: (a) Mainly at the beginning of each period.
Sources: SHC, D\D/cd, deposition books 1549 to 1638, plus five causes 1661–84; Wills and inventories, PCC and local.

few weavers found in the nearby lowland parishes and the fullers living in Huntspill and Cheddar. Some cloth was consumed locally, since several tailors worked in the area, but much was probably sold elsewhere, as cloth merchants were among the wealthiest men in the district and, like other leading citizens of Axbridge, by the end of their lives had put their money into the purchase of freehold, copyhold and life leasehold land, with which they endowed their children. They also put out money in secured loans, mortgages and other financial dealings, but there was difficulty in this period of finding secure investments other than land.

Although dual employment was commonplace in some similar agricultural regions, the pastoral farmers in Brent Marsh do not seem to have engaged in industrial by-employments.[98] The wives and daughters of husbandmen and labourers did engage in spinning wool and lace-making, but this aspect of women's employment was not confined to pastoral economies. Little evidence of cloth-making, for example, occurs in the admittedly small sample of inventories: no looms, for instance, or even spinning wheels, and only occasional references to wool, yarn or cloth and even then in an inconclusive manner. This is in striking contrast to the equally small sample of surviving inventories for East Harptree, on the Mendips in north Somerset, which included at least one clothier and several references to looms and large stocks of cloth and yarn.[99] Axbridge was well placed to conduct commercial activities in the Mendip area as well as the lowlands, and no doubt this was where the bulk of the wool and cloth handled by Axbridge merchants came from. In the 1530s a Wedmore mercer, William Fereford, had supplied money and wares to the value of 42s to a

98 J. Thirsk, 'Seventeenth-Century Agriculture and Social Change', in *idem* (ed.), *Land, Church and People*, pp. 171–2.

99 Inventories in SHC, D\D/ct. Harptree had been an important cloth-producing village, producing 100–200 cloths a year in the fourteenth century: Gray, 'Production and Exportation of English Woollens', p. 31.

weaver in Devon, probably stock to be made up for Fereford.[100] So, though there was a commercial network for cloth-producers in Brent Marsh that part-time farmers could have taken advantage of if they wished, they do not appear to have done so to any visible degree.

Most of the 51 non-agricultural occupations that appear in sources for the area are those that usually occur in any agricultural economy, processing farm products to meet the basic needs of the population: food, clothing, household goods, farm equipment and buildings.[101] It was an economy typical of pre-industrial England, dependent to a great extent on the countryside, dominated by agriculture and mainly engaged in producing directly for the consumer. Of the occupations found, only tanners, fullers and weavers were probably not selling directly to the consumer, but even in those trades strict craft demarcations were being broken and the craftsmen would sell as well as make the goods.[102] Although the boroughs of Axbridge and Wedmore had the largest concentrations of craftsmen, such men were spread throughout all the parishes studied, rather than settling only in the main towns of the area – Axbridge and Wedmore, or Wells and Bridgwater nearby. Tailors seem to have been particularly numerous and widely spread: 23 tailors occurred in 12 parishes between 1620 and 1657, and even a tiny parish such as Biddisham – 572 acres with only 14 households in 1563 – had two tailors mentioned within three years of one another, in 1620 and 1623. A craftsman's work was not confined to his parish of residence, of course, and some men settled where they had inherited houses or even large copyholdings.[103]

The number of craftsmen such as tailors does suggest that the demand for goods and services was fairly high, arguing a healthy level of agricultural wealth. Other indications of high demand also exist: the large number of weekly markets and seasonal fairs; tradesmen from Bristol who took stalls at Bridgwater market;[104] the hatter from Bruton in the south-east of the county who found it worthwhile to take a stall at St Andrews fair in Wells, in competition with local hatters from Axbridge;[105] and the indications of a wide network of trade links for selling agricultural produce.[106] In a sample of 54 tradesmen and craftsmen in Brent Marsh between 1572 and 1676, 21 were resident in the parish of their birth, 17 came from within 10 miles, five came from large towns or cities and 11 from elsewhere in Somerset and beyond.[107] Of the 54, 21 lived in Axbridge but only a third of these were born there, the rest having migrated into the town, several at apprenticeship age. Another 17 of the sample lived

---

100 TNA, C 1/787/37.

101 Among the less common occupations are silkweaver, brasier, pewterer (all Axbridge), plateworker (Weare), barber-surgeons (Axbridge, Mark, Wedmore), houndkeeper (Huntspill).

102 D.C. Coleman, *Industry in Tudor and Stuart England* (London, 1975), pp. 12, 21; W.G. Hoskins, *Provincial England: Essays in Social and Economic History* (London, 1963), pp. 94–6.

103 e.g. John Adams, a carpenter, held 21 acres of customary land in E. Brent in 1516; his occupation was only recorded to distinguish him from another tenant of that name: BL, Egerton MS 3034, f. 113.

104 SHC, Q/SR/81/62.

105 SHC, Q/SR/72/133.

106 Above, Communications and Markets.

107 Taken from SHC, D\D\cd, ecclesiastical court deposition books.

in Wedmore and seven of these had been born elsewhere, while, of the craftsmen in the other parishes, only a quarter lived in the parish of their birth, compared with a sample of 180 husbandmen and yeomen from the same source, of whom 60 per cent lived in their parish of birth. Because the sample is small, and figures for emigration out of the area are not available, conclusions must be tentative, but certain aspects of this immigration indicate that Axbridge and Wedmore in particular offered a good opportunity to make a living. Three of the migrants came from towns which themselves might be expected to provide good opportunities.[108] One of these migrants was Jasper Wrentmore, who came from Taunton about 1572 when 12 years old, probably as an apprentice, became a woollen draper, was mayor of Axbridge in 1620 and founded one of Axbridge's leading families of the seventeenth century.[109] The area also seems to have attracted men in the clothing trades from old-established cloth areas: both Devon and the town of Frome provided weavers and glovers; another weaver came from North Petherton, south of Bridgwater, while another came from as far away as Herefordshire. The existence of a strong market in goods was important for the economic role of small farmers, because the possibility of buying various goods and services meant that the farmers did not have to engage in those activities themselves. The availability of goods was also, of course, an incentive to them to make greater profits.

Tradesmen here sold their goods or services in a number of different ways. One was to take goods to the weekly markets or the fairs; other sales took place in the tradesman's premises, or 'shop'. Francis Tuthill, a mercer, sold lace and other cloth from his shop in Axbridge.[110] Others worked at the homes of their customers. William Hedlon, a tailor living in Axbridge, 'wrought at his trade of taylor ... for wages' in the house of William Wall at Weare in 1612, making a suit of clothes valued at 40s for Wall's stepson.[111] Men engaged in building work might stay weeks or months at the house of their customer. In the 1570s Thomas Galway, an Axbridge mason, worked on the house of Christian Hopkins in East Brent for three years, during which time he boarded in her house. When he had nearly completed his work, a carpenter, also from Axbridge, was hired by Christian and worked daily on the house while also boarding there.[112] Craftsmen also worked over a wide area: two tilers from Axbridge, two masons from Congresbury (north of the Mendips), two carpenters from Loxton and Congresbury and a mason from Bristol were called on to give estimates for work at Loxton, which lay between Lympsham and Compton Bishop.[113]

Though farmers apparently did not engage in industrial by-employments, some craftsmen did engage in farming. Thomas Looke, a tailor born in Butleigh, south of Glastonbury, had come to Wedmore when 15 years old and lived there and in

108 Bristol, Taunton, Wells.

109 SHC, D\D/cd/54, 'detection' v. Thomas Mooreton, 10 Mar. 1619/20.

110 SHC, Q/SR/34/47.

111 SHC, D\D/cd/76, Horte v. Wall, dep. of William Hedlon, 17 Dec. 1633.

112 SHC, D\D/cd/25, Gee als. Hopkins v. Hopkins, deps. of William Lascombe and Thomas Galway, 13 May 1572.

113 SHC, D\D/cd/71, Englefield v. Gawler, dep. of Nicholas Maies, 9 Nov. 1631.

neighbouring parishes for 30 years. While living in Weare he rented 16½ acres of meadow, most of which he mowed for hay, and continued to mow 13 acres after moving to Mark, but there is no information on whether he had stock or on what he did with the hay.[114] A plateworker living in Weare pastured beef cattle or young stock in the 1660s,[115] while a Wedmore glover rented land which included two acres of arable and kept at least two dairy cows and their calves in the 1670s.[116] Richard Thomas, a Wedmore tanner, left corn, hay and two plough horses at his death in 1640, in addition to all his tanning equipment.[117] Craftsmen also grazed animals on the moors, presumably to take advantage of common rights attached to customary messuages.

The involvement of craftsmen in farming might be interpreted as indicating that the economy of the area could not support full-time crafts, forcing men to supplement their income with by-employments, but the other economic indicators discussed above do not bear this out. Furthermore, a recent detailed study of household production has also come to a different conclusion about by-employment, and shows that the simple model of specialisation equalling greater market involvement and greater material prosperity is not always appropriate in rural households. Specialisation in production can also be associated with increasing poverty, while multi-employment is associated with increasing material wealth and is more indicative of entrepreneurial drive than a retreat into self-sufficiency.[118] Occupational specialisation was never very rigid in the countryside: even most professional men farmed some land. John Westover, father and son, were barber-surgeons in the seventeenth century who farmed inherited land in Wedmore and Allerton; Edmund Bower, a lawyer, farmed his demesne land as well as the parsonage glebe he held on lease, and many parsons farmed their glebe themselves. Naturally, these men did not put a hand to the plough themselves, but the principle – of obtaining income from farming as well as other sources – was the same. Craftsmen were ready to take advantage of any land they held with their dwelling, or could obtain, but possibly they too did not work the land themselves, but left the farming side to their wives or family: a tucker and a blacksmith, both of Wedmore, kept dairy cattle in Blackford moor which were milked by their wives, dairying usually being left to women at this time.[119]

So, although the area supported a number of craftsmen and offered attractive prospects for the usual range of rural craftsmen and tradesmen, agriculture remained the most important source of wealth and work, and industrial activity never became of more than minor significance. When husbandmen took on extra work to supplement their farming income it always seems to have been connected with agriculture, such as helping out neighbours in busy seasons, driving beasts to fairs or looking after stock for non-residents. In fact, industrial craftsmen also turned to casual farm work to

---

114 SHC, D\D/cd/51, Hill v. Counsell, dep. of Thomas Looke, 28 Oct. 1633.

115 TNA, E 134/19Chas2/Mich16.

116 TNA, E 134/29Chas2/Mich2.

117 SHC, D\D/ct, inventory of Richard Thomas, 1640.

118 Overton *et al.*, *Production and Consumption*, pp. 170–71.

119 SHC, D\D/cd/51, 'detection' v. Henry Lange, deps. of Eliz. Petherham and Kath. Napper, 3 Apr. 1623.

supplement their incomes: John Trott, a weaver of Berrow, threshed the tithing corn and did other odd jobs for the sequestrators of Berrow parsonage between 1620 and 1625.[120] It was farming that was the source of most of the casual employment, rather than rural industry.

The economy of the area was thus based deeply on the land, but the land produced two different types of income: that from rents and the profits of land sales and that from agriculture. Two different groups of residents thus benefited from the land and, though the personnel of the groups overlapped, each has to be considered separately. First in importance here, as everywhere at this time, were the owners and holders of land, and these are considered in the following chapter.

120 TNA, E 178/4467; E 135/5/45.

Chapter 3

Landholding and local society

The manors

In the early modern period the manor and its court was still the most prevalent unit in the organisation of land and freehold estates, despite variations in the vitality and usefulness of the courts from place to place. In the Somerset Levels the manors retained their importance for the tenants because customary tenure still flourished and the manor court provided a simple and relatively cheap method of conveying land and registering title, even though in other respects the courts were no longer very effective and manorial jurisdiction had a declining influence over the affairs of the tenants. The manorial structure in the Levels was a complex one, which also limited the control that the owners of manors had over their estates and their ability to make changes. The complexity had been brought about by the creation of sub-manors and by the tendency of freeholders to 'manorialise' their acquisitions of land, which in turn has made it hard to establish the actual number of manors or their acreage. Though customary tenure remained important, the manors varied considerably in size, vitality and unity in the course of the sixteenth and seventeenth centuries, and where manorial records have not survived very little can be said about quite large and important manors; this is particularly true of those owned by laymen, whose surviving records here are very patchy.

Altogether around 50 manors appear in various sources covering the 16 parishes of this study: 40 of those can be considered legal manors for which a court was held at some time in the period, while the remainder have only, perhaps, a single reference to their name,[1] and may not have been legal manors.[2] Since information concerning them is patchy, it follows that their ownership is likewise not always clear: many manors were held by ecclesiastical bodies at the beginning of the sixteenth century and underwent frequent changes in ownership during the next 200 years. Table 3

---

1 e.g. Sir John Couper's holding as a free tenant of the dean and chapter of Wells, in their manor of Allerton, was also called the manor of Allerton in the extent for the sale of the wardship in 1610, and may have included his freehold in Weare and elsewhere: M.J. Hawkins (ed.), *Sales of Wards in Somerset, 1603–1641* (Somerset Record Society 67, 1965), p. 16.

2 The term 'manor' should actually be applied only to those in existence before the Statute of Quia Emptores (18 Edw. I c. 1): W.H. Aggs, *Wharton's Law-Lexicon* (11th edn, 1911), p. 539. A manor required the existence of copyhold land to exist *de facto,* and included the right to holds courts baron and customary. Properly the court baron was the assembly of the lord and his free tenants, but the term was generally applied here to the court at which customary tenants and their lands were dealt with, since they all met together. The *OED* summarises various legal definitions of 'manor'.

Table 3
Ownership of manors

Type of lord	No. of manors held		
	c.1500	c.1600	c.1700
Glastonbury Abbey	6	-	-
Diocesan Clergy	16	8	8
Corporations (Oxford Coll., Hsp., Boro.)	-	1	3
Nobility	8	4	3
Gentry	15	23	19
Crown farmers (often gents from o/s Som.)	-	6	1
Divided (mostly sold to tenants)	-	2	7
Unknown	-	1	4
Total manors	45	45	45

summarises the ownership of 45 manors or so-called manors for which enough information is available.

Where a manor was held by an individual rather than an institution, only rarely did it remain in the same family (by inheritance or marriage) throughout the period from 1500 to 1700. Manors belonging to the diocesan clergy had rather more stable histories: the dean and chapter of Wells, the rector of Huntspill, the prebend of Compton Bishop and the vicars choral of Wells kept their manors throughout the period, apart from brief interruptions during the Edwardian Reformation and the Interregnum. The bishop of Bath and Wells, however, lost the three manors and some small rents he held in the area,[3] while the substantial holdings of Glastonbury Abbey, which were acquired as a whole by the duke of Somerset in 1547, were divided into their component manors and passed to several different owners after the duke's attainder in 1552.

Most lords of the manor, both lay and ecclesiastical, were absentees: the Rodney family were the only holders of a significant manor to live on their estate and, though a few other manorial lords belonged to Somerset gentry families, none attempted to establish a family seat on their manors in the Levels. Manors here in lay hands tended to be small items on a large noble or gentry rent-roll and, being far from the lord's seat, were the first to be handed over on marriage, sold to pay debts or disposed of to tidy up estates; the lord of the manor might not even be the principal beneficiary of the profits, because the manors were often farmed out in entirety and the court held by the farmer. This changed only during the seventeenth century, when some local freeholders built up small, self-styled 'manors' out of their holdings.

The lack of interest shown by the lords in their manors here may have been a result of the manorial structure, which contributed to the lords' weak position in regard to their tenants. Manors in England are usually considered to be one of two types, linked to the landscape and husbandry of each. Some lowland areas, generally on the

3 P. Hembry, *The Bishops of Bath and Wells, 1540–1640* (London, 1967), p. 107.

heavier clays of the Midland plain, tended to be highly manorialised, with a nucleated open-field village and communal agriculture controlled by the manor court; typically the parish contained only one manor or very nearly so, and the manor only one settlement, giving the lord control over inhabitants, immigrants, squatters and parish affairs generally, helped by the fact that the lord usually held a large proportion of the land in demesne, which gave him economic influence as well. This type of manor, often regarded as typical of agrarian organisation in England, is found, for example, in the vales of Yorkshire and Lincolnshire as well as in the Midlands.[4]

The other type is associated with pastoral areas, the uplands, forests and wood-pasture economies, where settlement tended to be spread out in several hamlets and single farms, and the parishes might commonly contain half a dozen manors or more. Manors in the wood-pasture areas of East Anglia were of this type, as were those in most of the northern border counties, parts of the West Midlands, and Devon and Cornwall.[5] In some manors common grazing brought tenants together, in others there were no communal farming activities at all, and it has generally been thought that the control exercised by the court or the lord in this type of manor was weak, and those manors existed chiefly for their financial and legal functions. However, more recent work suggests that there is little evidence that wood-pasture areas were always, or even usually, associated with weak lordship: some such areas were just as heavily manorialised as the Midland manors. Thus within the two broad categories there are many variations. Wood-pasture areas could also include open-field arable, while the non-residency of the lord or the break-up and leasing out of the demesne in parcels to the tenants weakened control in some Midland manors, as did the large number of freeholders in some manors in East Anglia.[6]

The manors in Brent Marsh certainly bear out the hybrid nature that has been found to characterise many manors and the role played in this by the topography.[7] Though it lay in a wood-pasture region, the settlement in the area was mainly in nucleated villages because of the topography and open-field arable still played a significant part in the husbandry, but nearly all the 16 parishes had more than one manor within their bounds, and the way that many sub-manors were formed gave the Levels another layer to its manorial character.

The formation of sub-manors

The existence of one or more smaller manors in a parish alongside the principal manor was fairly common: most pastoral parishes in England that have been studied in detail have been found to contain more than one manor, and even a parish with a nucleated settlement and strong manorial organisation might include another small

4 *AHEW4*, pp. 8, 14, 33.

5 *Ibid.*, pp. 8, 14, 48.

6 *Ibid.*, pp. 8, 92–3; T. Williamson, *Shaping Medieval Landscapes: Settlement, Society, Environment* (Macclesfield, 2003), pp. 180–85.

7 *Ibid.*, p. 180.

manor within its bounds.[8] Those lesser manors might be sub-manors created and held from the head manor, or they might be additional manors whose origins are unknown, either because they had lost a former connection with another manor or because they had been created independently of the principal manor. Additional manors in wood-pasture areas tended to be formed as assarts from unsettled land; they were usually enclosed and held by freeholders, and their lands were physically separate from other manors in the parish.[9] In some forest areas, hamlets that had their own common fields also developed into separate manors,[10] and the manors in Brent Marsh that lay within the parish of Wedmore may have followed this pattern, as several hamlets – Mudgley, Blackford, Crickham, and Cocklake – had their own open fields.[11]

Some sub-manors in Brent Marsh were formed in the usual way, whereby an individual freeholding of one manor became a manor in itself sometime in the Middle Ages, a process which was probably very common throughout England. In Brent Marsh, as in the West Country generally,[12] the number of freehold tenants, where known, was very small, as there were not the many small freeholders holding by socage that had existed, for example, in East Anglian manors by 1086.[13] However, the sub-manors formed from the freeholdings show that the acreage concerned could be quite significant.[14] At Cheddar, where the head manor, Cheddar or Cheddar Episcopi, had about ten free tenants,[15] the lands of five of those had formed sub-manors by the early sixteenth century, all with customary lands that shared the same customs and practices as the head manor.[16]

However, many other sub-manors had a more complicated origin, especially in the four Brent manors and in Badgworth, Tarnock, Allerton and Burnham. Here the sub-manors were formed from freeholdings in several different manors that had come together in the hands of one tenant. A similar process was quite common for monastic estates in the Middle Ages, where tenements and rents scattered over several

8 e.g. Chippenham in Cambs.: Spufford, *Contrasting Communities*, pp. 58, 60.

9 D.G. Hey, *An English Rural Community: Myddle under the Tudors and Stuarts* (Leicester, 1974), pp. 29, 70–71.

10 V. Skipp, *Crisis and Development: An Ecological Case Study of the Forest of Arden 1570–1674* (Cambridge, 1978), p. 7.

11 Below, Chap. 4, Land use in the Levels: Inland parishes. By the sixteenth century, however, some tenants held strips in the fields of one of the other manors, which confuses the likely origins.

12 Tawney, *Agrarian Problem*, pp. 24–5.

13 *AHEW4*, p. 45; A.R.H. Baker and R.A. Butlin (eds), *Studies of Field Systems in the British Isles* (Cambridge, 1973), p. 306.

14 e.g. freeholds in S. Brent, 1516, were 5 ferdels plus 20 acres (formed part of Northgrove); a half yardland plus 2½ acres (part of S. Brent Huish); a half yardland; 5 acres; 60½ acres: BL, Egerton MS 3034, ff. 149d–150d. Freeholds in Lympsham, 1516, were a half yardland, 8 ferdels plus 17 acres (formed the manor of Lympsham Parva, *c.*222 acres); 1 ferdel; 1 ferdel: Egerton MS 3034, ff. 132d–133d.

15 SHC, DD\SE/17/6, Estreat roll, manor of Cheddar, 3 Jas I.

16 *Cheddar Hanhams*: SHC, T\PH\vch/38; *C. Parsonage*: DD\CC/B/131910a/2; *C. Vicars Choral*: DD\CC/L/116013; *C. Fitzwalters*: DD\SAS/H143/4; *C. Berkeley*: DD\PO/1.

parishes and acquired by a religious house at different times were grouped together in an artificial manor for administration. Some of these manors included demesne, and courts were also held, though this probably depended on the existence of customary land: for an estate consisting of freehold rents only, no court would be necessary.[17]

Lay owners, too, probably created 'manors' for the same reason of convenience, and for some the process can be traced quite fully. South Brent Huish, for example, was a distinct manor by 1547, when it was granted to the duke of Somerset, and it had the alternative name of Dawbeney Huish.[18] Henry, Lord Dawbeney, had been a freeholder of Glastonbury Abbey's manors of South Brent and East Brent in 1516, and the reserved rents he had to pay to the Abbey tally with sums payable in 1567 from the manor of South Brent Huish to the lord of South Brent and the former ministers of Glastonbury.[19] Other sums listed in 1567 were due to the lord of the manor of Huish, for which the amount tallies with the freehold rent due to the manor of Huish in 1650,[20] and to the lords of South Brent Rectory and Burnham; no lists of freeholders have been found for those two manors. Thus, sometime in the Middle Ages the manor of South Brent Huish was formed from freeholdings in the five manors of South Brent, East Brent, South Brent Rectory, Burnham and Huish. In the sixteenth century South Brent Huish consisted predominantly of customary land, which was granted out by copy of court roll. It seems likely, therefore, that when the lord of the head manor granted out the freeholdings from which the sub-manors were formed, most if not all their lands were already occupied by customary tenants rather than being demesne, and continued to be granted under custom in the same way. As the rights accruing to the lord of the manor were now transferred to the freeholder, he had to hold a court to administer the property, thus forming a new manor. Even the lands appertaining to various rectories in the area were managed in the form of a manor, since most included a few customary tenements in addition to glebe land and other perquisites,[21] and were themselves sub-manors that had been granted out by the lords of the chief manors.

The way in which these sub-manors were formed had important consequences. Not only did each parish contain several manors, with many of the manors being distributed over several parishes, which considerably weakened the position of the manorial lords and diminished their influence in parish affairs, but also the strips of open-field land of different manors, perhaps three or four, were physically mixed, sometimes inextricably, in the fields, making the consolidation of large demesne

---

17 *AHEW4*, pp. 308–9.

18 *Calendar of Patent Rolls, Edward VI*, vol. 1, pp. 126, 131. Usually called S. Brent and Huish in this period. In 1626 it was called S. Brent Huish alias S. Brent Dawbeney: Hawkins, *Sales of Wards*, p. 64.

19 BL, Egerton MS 3034, ff. 149d., 107; C.R. Straton (ed.), *Survey of the Lands of William First Earl of Pembroke*, 2 vols (Oxford, 1909), II, p. 485.

20 SHC, DD\CC/P/114099.

21 e.g. Rectory Manor of Huntspill, which contained the parsonage house etc, 62 acres glebe land, 12 oxen lease, 8 or 9 tenements containing *c.*24 acres, and same common of pasture as tenants of the head manor of Huntspill: SHC, D\D/rg/201, glebe terriers 1613, 1639. The rector held a manor court roughly twice a year: D\P\hun/3/1/1, court bk, 39 Eliz. to 14 Jas. I.

estates almost impossible, even where the sub-manor included any demesne, thus reducing the lords' economic influence and opportunities for rental improvement through large-scale agricultural changes as well. However, this complex manorial structure is by no means unique to Brent Marsh or to Somerset; it existed even for Midlands manors in the thirteenth century, where the 'typical' coincidence of manor with vill in the classical manorial structure was found to be not typical at all,[22] and is also common in manors in eastern Norfolk, where none was confined to one village, no village fell within a single manor, and some were head manors from which other local manors were held. However, the complexity did not result in lax administration or extra freedoms for tenants in Norfolk, but that may partly be because far more lords in Norfolk were resident on their manors.[23] What is interesting is that the Norfolk manors differed considerably from Brent Marsh in having copyholds of inheritance and a lot of freeholders, whereas Brent Marsh had copyhold for lives and very few freeholders, so the manorial structure does not apparently depend on the factors governing the local tenures.

Though the sub-manors referred to above were formed before the end of the fifteenth century, and probably much earlier, a similar process of manorialisation continued in the early modern period. Freehold estates formed by local gentlemen out of holdings in several different parishes, or perhaps of parcels of former manors which had been sold off piecemeal,[24] were often managed as manors, while even in the late seventeenth century leases for lives in some estates still required suit of court at the owner's residence.[25] Some court rolls are extant for one of those artificial manors in Brent Marsh, belonging to George Hodges, one of the few residents in this area to have social prominence, bearing arms in 1623.[26] A view of Hodges's tenants in 1602 showed that the estate included four tenements formerly part of the manor of South Brent and one formerly of the manor of Wedmore, all granted out by copy of court roll, and five other tenements in Weare and South Brent granted out by leases for lives. Records of the court of George Hodges and his wife Eleanor survive for the years 1605 to 1607, though their 'manor' does not have a name: not much business was carried on – just a few land transactions and presentments for not ditching, the most usual business for manors in the area.[27] No further evidence concerning the subsequent history of George Hodges's court has come to light, and his property here and elsewhere was divided between his granddaughters in 1662.[28] Since not only copies but leases for lives stipulated attendance at court twice a year, Hodges

---

22 Kosminsky, *Studies in the Agrarian History of England*, pp. 73–9.

23 Whittle, *Development of Agrarian Capitalism*, pp. 34–6.

24 e.g. Northgrove: Cal. MSS of Corpus Christi College, Oxford (NRA), vol. 28, f. 63, vol. 30, f. 691; BL, Egerton MS 3034, ff. 149d, 106d–107; Rooksbridge: TNA, C 142/41/28; BL, Egerton MS 3034, f. 107; Straton, *Survey*, II, p. 471; SHC, DD\AH/11/9.

25 SHC, DD\SAS/C61/6; DD\WY/84.

26 F.T. Colby (ed.), *Visitation of the County of Somerset in the Year 1623* (Harleian Society 11, 1876), p. 53. For Hodges's family see Chap. 6, Increase in the gentry.

27 SHC, DD\SH/23.

28 SHC, DD\SH/18.

probably held a court for the purpose,[29] and if the estate had remained intact and the court become permanent the manor might have taken the name of his residence or that of a hamlet on the property.

This apparent desire to manorialise real property even as late as the seventeenth century may be explained in two ways: either men who acquired freehold lands had an attachment to the traditional manorial concept, both for the recognisable status it conferred and the familiarity of its method of managing land and agrarian relations; or the legal strength and convenience of customary tenure made the use of a manor court essential. It would be natural for freeholders to be deeply influenced by the tradition of valuing land for the status and power it gave and the additional social cachet of being a lord of the manor. Practical reasons also made a change from manorial management to direct farming or commercial leasehold less feasible in this area, in addition to the complex manorial structure outlined above: most manors had little or no demesne that could be held and farmed in one unit or could form the nucleus for direct farming. In Glastonbury's manors, for example, the non-customary and former demesne land, called overland in the Levels, had been parcelled out among the tenants well before 1516 and, although it did not include appurtenant customary rights, it was listed with their customary holdings.[30] It was, therefore, the tenants who were in a position to exchange strips, consolidate their holdings and enclose, to carry out rational farm management or changes in farming practice; for the lords it was not possible on a scale large enough to make the effort worthwhile. As far as commercial leasing was concerned, again there were no large blocks of land to attract farmers who would take expensive leases, nor was it easy to exploit land in a way that kept pace with rapidly changing rental values without constant supervision, and few lords lived in or near their manors here.

On the positive side, moreover, the manor did provide a regular fixed income and the form of tenure allowed the fines for copies and leases to be increased to a certain degree without requiring a possibly difficult change in administration that would be bound to arouse opposition among the tenants. This ability to increase income without radical change may have made the lords amenable to keeping the customary tenure here, while elsewhere they were forced to try to change the tenure as the only way to increase their manorial income.

However, even when these factors are taken into account, it is clear that the strength of customary tenure should not be underestimated. Elsewhere in England manors *were* broken up, tenures changed and copyholds turned into rack-rented leaseholds when the tenants' title and custom were not strong enough to prevent it. Examples of more commercial estate exploitation existed, and some men who held manors in this area were merchants from London and Bristol, who are assumed to have brought a more capitalistic outlook to land ownership.[31] More than the negative

---

29 They held two (legal) manors elsewhere in Somerset, possibly encouraging them to treat all their land the same way.

30 BL, Egerton MS 3034, passim.

31 e.g. Thomas Gardiner, citizen and goldsmith of London; Hugh Smythe of Long Ashton, of Bristol merchant family.

factors mentioned, it is the strength and acceptance of the accustomed land tenure above and beyond the limits of common law that seems to be the vital factor in the continuance of the manorial system and the position of customary tenants here, so that even when copies became leases for lives many of the same customary rights were included in the tenants' holdings and continued to be enjoyed by them. The strength of customary tenure may well be a reason why several manors here were broken up and partially or wholly sold to the tenants, such as Wedmore in the 1570s, South Brent in the 1580s, Mudgley *c.*1610, Burnham *c.*1650, Huntspill Mareys from the 1690s and Huntspill in the 1700s.[32]

Customary tenure

Most manorial tenants in sixteenth-century Brent Marsh were copyholders. In South Brent in 1516 93 per cent (72) of the tenants were copyholders; in Huntspill de la Haye 91 per cent (33) were copyholders in 1525; in South Brent Huish 53 per cent (28) were copyholders and 34 per cent life leaseholders in 1567; in Tarnock 60 per cent (15) were copyholders and 8 per cent leaseholders in the late sixteenth century; and in East Brent 84 per cent (98) were copyholders and 7 per cent leaseholders in 1607; the remainder in each case were freeholders.[33] This preponderance of copyholders was common throughout manors in the Somerset Levels.[34]

The work of Charles Gray and Eric Kerridge demonstrated the legal security of customary tenants,[35] whose rights under the custom of the manor were protected in the courts of equity and common law, and this has been borne out by more recent work on agrarian relations in areas where the customary tenure was predominantly copyhold of inheritance, widespread in Eastern England.[36] Customary tenure in the Levels, however, was predominantly copyhold for lives, which was very common in the western half of England: in the West Midlands also, for example, this was generally the form taken by customary tenure.[37] It was in some ways less attractive than copyhold of inheritance, where a holding was granted to the tenant and his heirs forever, so that when a tenant died his heir had the right to succeed him on payment of an entry fine. Since those fines, like the rents, were usually fixed at the very low, early sixteenth-

32 *Wedmore*: BL, Add. MS 33828, f. 364; S.W. Bates Harbin (ed.), *Somerset Enrolled Deeds* (Somerset Record Society 51, 1936), pp. 125–6; *South Brent*: SHC, DD\WM/45; TNA, C 66/1335, m.17; *Mudgley*: S.H.A. Hervey, *The Wedmore Chronicle*, 2 vols (1887, 1898), II, p. 41; *Burnham*: TNA, C 107/114, pt 1; *Huntspill*: R.W. Dunning (ed.), *Victoria County History of Somerset*, vol.VIII (London, 2004), pp. 98–9.

33 BL, Egerton MS 3034, ff. 149d–168d; Straton, *Survey*, II, pp. 471–86; TNA, E 315/385, ff. 90–95d; LR 2/191, ff. 29–31; LR 2/225, ff. 53–114.

34 Dunning, *VCH Som.* III, *passim.*

35 C.M. Gray, *Copyhold, Equity, and the Common Law* (Harvard Historical Monographs 53, Cambridge, MA, 1963); E. Kerridge, *Agrarian Problems in the 16th Century and After* (London, 1969).

36 French and Hoyle, *Character of English Rural Society*, pp. 8–10; Whittle, *Development of Agrarian Capitalism*, pp. 74–81.

37 Overton, *Agricultural Revolution*, p. 35; Hey, *English Rural Community*, p. 70.

century level, this tenure became tantamount to freehold in most respects. Copyhold for lives was granted to the tenants named in the copy for the duration of their lives, usually holding the property successively in the order named in the copy, the next life succeeding on the death, forfeiture or surrender of his predecessor by paying a heriot to the lord, usually either the best beast or goods or a small fixed sum of money.[38] These customary holdings were known in the Levels as 'old austers', and the customary rights, such as grazing in the moors, turbary (or the digging of peat for fuel) and widow's right, and obligations to maintain drainage ditches and sea and river walls, were attached to the dwelling on the holding or its site if decayed. Although the division of holdings was not specifically prevented in any of the local customals, holdings were not apparently divided nor lost small parcels, as far as the manorial surveys indicate, and the right to grazing could not be divided anyway and remained attached to the dwelling.[39] Though the annual rent was fixed and low, the entry fines paid for these copies were generally variable, having to be renegotiated when a new copy was required, and so copyhold for lives is regarded by most writers on the subject as very insecure both legally and financially, as well as restricting the participation of the holders in the land market and their inheritance strategies in providing for their children.[40]

However, despite implications in many works that the level of these variable fines was completely arbitrary at the will of the lord, and so could be used to drive the tenants off the land altogether, local studies have produced little evidence to show that this in fact happened, suggesting that either such fines were not in fact arbitrary, or that the legal position was not quite so straightforward. Two factors may be involved here: one is the body of customs of the manors, which were in most cases upheld in the central law courts, and the other seems to have been a customary right by which a tenant was regarded as having a supra-legal right to his holding, so that he would still remain in possession even when he had in theory forfeited the protection of customary law, perhaps a customary equivalent of the equity of redemption that developed in common law. The reason why the Crown began in the late fifteenth century to uphold custom in the equity and prerogative courts may have been largely political, but that in itself suggests that custom had a force that a body of opinion

38 Wording of the copy specifies this, the most usual form, though occasionally a copy is granted to the purchaser for lives without the right to hold; unless otherwise noted, all copies mentioned below are held by those named in them. Successive holding is the most common form found, though sometimes the first two lives hold jointly, particularly when husband and wife. Occasionally a grant is made for the minority of the lord of the manor by his guardian: e.g. a grant to Richard Nelne and his son William in the manor of Edingworth for the minority of Thomas, son and heir of Ralph Jenyngs: SHC, DD\WY, uncalendared Orchard Wyndham MSS, court roll 31 Mar. 16 Eliz.

39 Williams, *Draining of the Somerset Levels*, pp. 120–21; T.J. Hunt and P.N. Dawe (eds), *Notes and Queries for Somerset and Dorset*, 29 (1968), pp. 157–8.

40 Kerridge, *Agrarian Problems*, p. 37; J. Whittle, 'Individualism and the Family–Land Bond: A Reassessment of Land Transfer Patterns among the English Peasantry', *Past and Present*, 160 (1998), pp. 52–9.

thought should be upheld. The protection that copyholders acquired in the equity courts was also extended in the sixteenth century to the common law courts: initially used by manorial lords as freeholders in dealing with their copyholders and others, the acceptance that 'land held according to the custom of the manor' had a legal force led copyholders to sue their lords in Common Pleas against eviction, though it was not until the later sixteenth century that the common law recognised their right against that of the freeholder.[41]

Customs varied even between adjacent manors, and many practices were taken for granted and never recorded, making them difficult to uncover now, but the customaries that do exist for manors in Brent Marsh can be supplemented with practical examples from court rolls and information from legal cases.[42] The manors held by Glastonbury followed a common custom, which was listed in a customal drawn up in 1494, 'uppon the vewes of old records as also uppon the presentment of the tenauntes within the manors', in the first year of the abbacy of Richard Bere.[43] In these manors copyholds were taken for a maximum of two lives according to the customal, and this is supported by a few examples in equity cases concerning the Brent manors and Northlode (near Glastonbury),[44] but in one such case a copy had apparently been granted for three lives in East Brent in the late sixteenth century, and by the seventeenth there was confusion over how many lives were permitted: East Brent was held by a succession of Crown farmers and stewards and perhaps a new steward had been unaware of the correct number.[45] Northgrove, a sub-manor formed from holdings in East and South Brent, also had a limit of two lives,[46] but in other sub-manors of the Glastonbury manors a maximum of three lives was being granted by the beginning of the sixteenth century, and three lives was the custom in most other

---

41 H. Garrett-Goodyear, 'Common Law and Manor Courts: Lords, Copyholders and Doing Justice in Early Tudor England', in Whittle (ed.), *Landlords and Tenants*, pp. 35–51; Simpson, *Introduction to History of Land Law*, pp. 153–5.

42 Various customs and legal aspects of copyhold in general are discussed in several works from the early eighteenth century onwards, including *The Compleat English Copyholder*, 2 vols (1735); J. Scriven, *Treatise on the Law of Copyholds* (6th edn, 1882); T.E. Tomlins, *Law Dictionary*, vol. I (1835), under 'Copyhold'; Aggs, *Wharton's Law-Lexicon*, pp. 222–5. Copyhold tenure was finally abolished in 1925. None of these works say much about copyhold for lives or its legal implications.

43 SHC, DD\SG/22; this is a copy made in 1592, probably as a result of dispute over custom. There are 40 customs, and against all but five the word 'allowed' is written in a similar hand, but it is not clear whether this was taken from the 1494 original or added when the copy was made. Four of the exceptions concern haymaking and carrying services by cottagers and tenement holders, the only labour services mentioned; probably by the late fifteenth century these were a dead letter anyway. The fifth concerns the rights of the last wife of a tenant. The active role of the tenants in drawing up the customal shows both their interest in preserving custom and its importance to them, as well as their importance for the vitality of the manor.

44 TNA, C 2/Eliz/D2/21; REQ 2/22/99; REQ 2/109/2.

45 TNA, C 2/Eliz/M8/5; E 134/13Chas2/East17 and Mich15.

46 CCC Oxford, Northgrove MSS, Fn 13, survey 1609.

manors for which evidence exists;[47] this was carried over into leasehold for three lives as well, as is the case in manors elsewhere with a similar tenure.[48]

Copies were usually taken for named and living people, but two other possibilities are quite commonly found: a copy to a named woman and her next husband, and one to a named man, his wife, and their first or next child. Sometimes the purchaser of a copy was given time in which to name the lives,[49] or a man would take a copy for himself and his wife and named a relative until such time as the couple had a child. Copyhold for two or three lives was only specified as such from the late fifteenth century: terriers and court rolls of an earlier date are much less informative and usually mention only the holder and his wife, without recording the names of those with future rights in the property. Until the number and ages of the lives in being were of importance in assessing the level of the fine for a new copy, there was no reason to mention in a survey those who were not actually in possession, since in any case the assumption was that the next of kin would have first refusal if the holding became vacant.[50] However, by the sixteenth century the succession to a holding had become formalised in most manors by grants of reversions for the same numbers of lives in addition to the copy in possession. When the last life in the current copy had died or surrendered the reversion came into force and the first life named took possession of the property. Sometimes the number of reversions allowed was limited,[51] sometimes it was 'as many copies in reversion as lord and tenant can agree for':[52] the practice differed widely from manor to manor. The Glastonbury manors and South Brent Huish did not specify a limit to the number of copies in reversion,[53] while some other manors did not allow reversions at all and made provision for the holder to add new lives by

47 (Glastonbury), *S. Brent Huish*: Straton, *Survey*, II, 485, the earliest copy is dated 34 Henry VIII: p. 473; *Lympsham Parva*: SHC, T\PH\vch/38, pp. 103–10, earliest 18 Hen. VII; *Tarnock*: *ibid.*, pp. 91–101, earliest 19 Hen VII. (Other manors), *Cheddar manors*: SHC, DD\CH/4, customs 1757; *Allerton*: Prebendary Coleman, 'Manor of Allerton and its Tenants, 1530–1866', *Proceedings of the Somerset Archaeological Society*, 46 (1900), part II, 81; *Mudgley*: SHC, DD\SAS/C795/PR/462, customs 1558 (this manor was once part of deanery of Wells, and its customs were probably common to other former deanery manors – Mark, Moore, Wedmore); *Blackford*: DD\SE/65/1–2, survey 1657; *Huntspill Rectory*: D\P\hun/3/1/1; *Burnham Rectory*: DD\CC/B/110001, vol. 1, f. 124.

48 Hey, *English Rural Community*, p. 70.

49 e.g. John Keene of Wedmore noted in his will that he had paid his landlord the fine for his 'bargain' and the lord had to add another life when Keene's wife demanded it: TNA, PROB 11/68/153. A landowner, Maurice Rodney esq., left instructions to his executors that George Cade of Rodney Stoke was to hold his bargain for any two lives that he should name, if Rodney's wife and son thought them convenient: PROB 11/72/713. The first name seems always to have been a named and living individual, but the next two could be unknown.

50 See below.

51 Allerton allowed three copies with three lives in each: Coleman, 'Manor of Allerton', p. 81; Northgrove allowed one reversion of two lives: CCC Oxford, Fn 13.

52 Burnham Rectory manor: SHC, DD\CC/B/110001, vol. 1, f. 124.

53 SHC, DD\SG/22, *passim*; Straton, *Survey*, II, 485.

surrendering the old copy and taking a new one.[54] This formalisation had implications for the land market, as it made valuing a holding easier, but the sale of reversions was also a way in which the landowner could even out the income flow from his manor.

The rights of reversioners, however, were complicated by the existence of widow's right, the custom whereby the widow of a copyholder could retain all the customary tenements that her husband held at his death as long as she remained unmarried and lived chastely.[55] As far as can be seen, the custom applied to all manors in the area, though in Cheddar only the widow of the last life in the copy enjoyed this right.[56] The custom irked some copyholders – or rather their heirs – in cases where the next name in the copy was the eldest son, who had to wait for possession while his father's widow, possibly his third or fourth stepmother and younger than he, enjoyed the profits of the holding. Undoubtedly in many such cases widows were bought out directly, sometimes before the death of the tenant. Thus Richard Evans of Lympsham made an arrangement with his wife whereby she agreed to surrender her widow's right in the tenement so that Evans's son John (already married with four children) would have it immediately on Evans's death; in return she received money and goods, and an acknowledgement that part had already been handed over was entered in Evans's will.[57] Alternatively the next heir might employ the kind of arrangement that John Hide of Biddisham made. His stepmother Joan was left in possession of three tenements and 42 acres when his father died about 1580, and Robert Kinge offered to marry Joan in return for 20 marks and the profits of the holdings for six months. Later, however, John found he had been duped, as Joan was already with child by Robert when the bargain was struck, so the property should have been forfeited to John in any case.[58] Widow's right may have been a reason why copyholders agreed to switch to leasehold for lives, as omission of widow's right was a major difference between the two tenures, although there was no strong indication here in the seventeenth century of a dislike of giving the widows control of their husbands' property, and most testators regarded their wives as their natural successors.[59]

Widow's right was modified by some of the other customs governing the rights of copyholders and reversioners. The widow was not entitled to the customary holding if a reversion had been granted before her marriage to the tenant.[60] If a woman bought a reversion for herself and her next husband, but died before the tenement came into her possession, then her widower would have no further claim on the tenement.[61] The husband of a tenant in possession, however, had the right to hold the tenement, but

---

54 Cheddar manors: SHC, DD\CH/4; Mudgley: DD\SAS/C795/PR/462.

55 Overland, which was not customary land, passed straight away to the next life on the death of the holder.

56 SHC, DD\CH/4.

57 SHC, DD\SAS/C795/SE/30.

58 TNA, REQ 2/58/37. Hide brought the case to recover his 20 marks.

59 Below, The switch to leasehold for lives; Chap. 5, Roles of women in rural society: The effects of widow's right.

60 SHC, DD\SG/22, no. 31; Straton, *Survey*, II, 485.

61 SHC, DD\SG/22, no. 33.

on most manors only during her lifetime.[62] These legal refinements, which might take effect without the knowledge of the parties concerned – for example, when a widow knew nothing of reversions granted before her marriage – led to a great many legal wrangles as widows and widowers claimed land they believed they were entitled to, and, as many had probably married with the prospect of the land as a consideration, they were unwilling to let it slip away.

A further apparent injustice was created by the right of the 'taker' of the copy or reversion – that is, the one who had paid for it, who was not necessarily named in the copy – to change the names or dispose of the property without consulting those who were named. This also led to numerous cases, such as that in 1576 of Henry Bailie of Compton Bishop, whose father had paid the fine for a copy for himself, his wife and his son Henry in 1555, but had surrendered the property in 1560 while Henry was still a boy. Henry claimed a custom whereby the copyholder could not grant away the property without a surrender by those, like himself, who would inherit,[63] but all the other evidence is against such a custom when the holder had paid the fine. Scores of similar cases occur in court records and on many occasions the plaintiffs were totally ignorant of who had paid the fine.

The grants of reversions or the ability to add new names as required meant that rarely did a holding become vacant: there were always one or two copies waiting to 'fall in'. It also gave security for the holder's family, who could establish several individuals in succession to the holding. This is contrary to the usual view of copyhold for lives as being of limited value because of the limited timespan, in that the lord would regain the property after the three lives had ended or, if the manor allowed the purchase of a new life following every death or surrender, the lord could then sell it to whoever he liked.[64]

Besides the security of being able to purchase the holding for future lives, the copyholder was also protected by the custom under which the lord would not sell the reversion away from the holder's kin without offering it to them first, an example of the assumption that seems to have governed customary tenure, that the next of kin had a 'right' to inherit parallel to common law rights. This customary right to inherit is bound up with the difficult problem of rights of renewal of copies. In view of the fact that this form of copyhold is regarded as inferior because of its variable fines, it is important to establish whether there was right of renewal, because this would affect the fines permitted in law. Kerridge tried to show that 'any fine, however high, would have been reasonable with holding for term of life',[65] because, unlike a high fine on copyhold of inheritance, there was no right of the heir that could be defeated thereby, the main legal objection to arbitrary fines. However, Scriven, in his *Treatise on Copyholds*, declares that fines for copyholders of inheritance *and* for lives *renewable* must be 'reasonable' – that is, a maximum of two years' improved value.[66] The main difficulty

62 SHC, DD\SG/22, no. 36.

63 TNA, REQ 2/121/35.

64 French and Hoyle, *Character of English Rural Society*, p. 8.

65 Kerridge, *Agrarian Problems*, p. 40.

66 Scriven, *Treatise on Copyholds*, p. 155.

now lies in establishing whether a manor granted a right of renewal. The Glastonbury customal states 'that the children and the next of his keine shall have the reversion of the fathers Tenementes before other person or persons, yf they will seeke it of the lord and geve for it to him as any other will geve at such tyme as the lord will sell it, or els other may buy it'.[67] This is open to differing interpretations, however: a fine equal to that anyone else would give could be seen as unlimited, if the lord found someone willing to offer an exorbitant amount, and 'such tyme as the lord will sell it' could be taken to imply that the lord could withhold the reversion altogether.[68] However, the true meaning may be that exemplified in the custom of the manors of Wedmore and Churchland – which is very similar in wording to the Glastonbury customal – that if any copyhold tenement fell vacant by the death of the tenant 'then the next of the kynde [of that tenant] shall by custom have the same for life paying so much for a fine as any other tenant of the manor would reasonably give without fraud' and agreement of the next of kin had to be given before a copy was granted to a stranger.[69]

This seems, more or less, to have been the practice throughout the manors in Brent Marsh. In Northgrove a tenant in possession had three years or three court days to nominate the reversioner before the lord could grant it away.[70] The tenants of the manor, the homage, were the best protection against the lord attempting to sell away a holding, as grants of copies were supposed to take place in open court,[71] and on occasions when they did not, or when reversioners thought they had been wronged, complaints were made in the manor court or cases brought in the equity courts.

Other sources also suggest that the agreement of the holder was required for the grant of a reversion: a daughter took the reversion of her father's tenement 'by the assent and goodwill' of the said tenant,[72] and in several copyholders' wills the testator nominated the lives to be bought in a reversion or copy or instructed his executors to buy his tenement for a certain person.[73] The entries in the court rolls record when copies were bought through instructions by will,[74] and the book of 'Proposals for Grants' for the dean and chapter's manors also contains a note when a reversion was granted through the nomination of the current holder to someone else.[75] The delicate

---

67 SHC, DD\SG/22, no. 8.

68 I have found no examples of this happening though, nor any cases at law.

69 TNA, REQ 2/21/11; or at least the lord should obtain the agreement of the tenant in possession: REQ 2/32/8.

70 CCC Oxford, Northgrove MSS, Fn 4, court book 1698–1726: a complaint was being made that this custom was often ignored now.

71 TNA, REQ 2/21/11.

72 TNA, C 2/Eliz/D2/21.

73 e.g. Dr William Barker held a reversion in Biddisham in which some of his children were named, and his other two children were to be put in reversion after them: TNA, PROB 11/118/491; John Whitinge's two sons were to enter his tenement and hold according to custom of the manor: PROB 11/149/615.

74 e.g. SHC, DD\CC/B/131926/7, Allerton, 9 Aug. 15 Car. I, reversions taken by Elizabeth, daughter of Walter Bower, gent., deceased, on nomination in his will.

75 SHC, DD\CC/B/114068.

balance of wills between the lord and the tenant is illustrated by the process by which the Crown granted a copyhold tenement on a lease for lives in 1616: the customary holding of William and Robert Grove in East Brent was to be leased to Adrian Bower for three lives, if Bower could come to an agreement with William Grove; if not, the lease was to be granted to Grove for three lives, at half the rent and heriots that Bower would be charged.[76]

In effect, then, customary tenure in this area was defined and supported by quite precise customs that were legally binding on both the tenants and the lord and gave security to the copyholders.

The level of fines

The customs cited show that, though fines were variable, and would therefore rise higher than the fixed fines on copyholds of inheritance, they were by no means arbitrary and would not rise to the level where they would defeat the right of the sitting tenant to buy a copy for his children. Whatever the tenants of the manor thought a reasonable fine was, it would clearly bear a relationship to the rents or produce that the holding could deliver, and only mismanagement by the tenant or a severe financial loss would leave him unable to pay a fine to buy the reversion for his heirs, especially as some manors gave as much as five years or more in which to pay. Furthermore, as shown above, the lord could not legally dispose of the property as he chose in defiance of the wishes of the tenant in possession, a restriction that would help to prevent the fines for copies being pushed up beyond the economic value of the land by outsiders looking for landed investments in copyholds, something that was increasingly common by the late sixteenth century.

However, on a practical level it is not easy to establish whether or not fines were raised beyond a 'reasonable' amount, and therefore whether copies can be considered renewable here. Though some manors have very full series of court rolls with which to examine fines, several unknown factors could affect the amount of the fine: advantageous grants to local officials or the surrender of a previous copy with one or two lives still in being meant a lower fine, and possibly the number and ages of lives in the copy were taken into account when calculating sixteenth-century fines, as they certainly were by the mid seventeenth.[77] Then again, when a tenant failed to take a reversion of his holding for his children there is rarely evidence to show why: he may have had other property for them, he may have sold his right in order to invest elsewhere, or he may have been in financial difficulties.[78]

---

76 TNA, E 310/23/128, f. 30.

77 SHC, DD\SE/65/1–2, survey 1657, lists the ages of the lives in being, as do some of the parliamentary surveys of church lands, the first to do so in the area.

78 References in wills when testators left sums or instructions to buy their holdings indicate that they had just not got around to doing it themselves, possibly not wishing to tie up that amount of money before it was necessary: e.g. John Hide left £100 because he had not bought his Biddisham copyhold for his daughter; he was a well-to-do freeholder and could have afforded it: below, Free and copyhold land in the provision for children: Copyhold.

The strongest support for the view that fines were not beyond the means of the tenants comes from negative evidence: the lack of cases brought by tenants against lords claiming unreasonably high fines. Given that the customals state fines must be a reasonable market level, it is unlikely that tenants would have been slow to bring cases in the equity courts if they were being asked for fines much higher than they could afford, especially since some tenants, or would-be tenants, brought cases in connection with other customs even where they had no grounds at all for their complaints.

Two manors for which the fines have been examined show a widely differing pattern in the amount charged. In the dean and chapter's small manor of Biddisham fines, generally for copies for three lives in reversion, were low considering the acreage and quality of land there,[79] and were affected by a large number of grants to the canons of Wells and their relatives, presumably at a favourable rate. Even ignoring these, the fines levied in the late sixteenth and early seventeenth centuries were still low. For a holding consisting of a tenement and 14 acres, a cottage and seven acres, and two and a half acres of overland meadow, £12 was paid in 1569 for a reversion for three lives, and £13 6s 8d in 1610, both sets of lives being related to the tenant in possession, and in 1620 £8 was paid for a second reversion for the three children of a Chewton (north Somerset) man who had no known connection with the tenant.[80] For two tenements with 28 acres £10 was paid in 1552 for a reversion for two lives, £5 in 1579 for a second reversion for three lives, all connected with the tenant, and £12 in 1572 for a reversion for three lives not connected with the tenant, which was surrendered to the tenant's family five years later.[81] Where new tenants, often Bristol merchants or officials from Wells, took copies, their fines were no higher than those of local families.

In the manor of Edingworth, situated on the valuable coastal pastures and held by a series of gentlemen, fines were much higher, especially from the middle of Elizabeth's reign, when the tenure was changed to leases for 99 years determinable on three lives. For a holding of 18 acres a fine of £63 6s 8d was paid for a copy for three lives in 1587, £115 in 1605 for a lease for three lives, £145 in 1628 and £35 for a reversion for one life in 1689. For a holding of 16 acres the tenants in possession paid £5 for a reversion in 1558, and a fine of £95 was paid in 1594 for a lease for three lives with a change of one name in 1604, and £70 in 1682 for a lease for two lives. New tenants without any apparent connection with the holder did seem to pay more than those related to the tenant, but as these new tenancies mainly followed the surrender or death of the tenant in possession the copies or leases were for three lives in possession, and consequently of greater value than a reversion. Thus, after the death in 1654 of the last holder of 34 acres, valued at £24 a year, a lease for 99 years or three lives was granted in 1657 to William Phippen, yeoman, of Wedmore for the

79 Biddisham was an area of level, well-drained meadow and pasture beside the river Axe.

80 SHC, DD\CC/B/131923/5; DD\CC/B/131925/7; DD\CC/B/131925/2.

81 SHC, DD\CC/B/131922/1; DD\CC/B/131907/20; DD\CC/B/131907/21.

lives of his three grandchildren at a fine of £320,[82] and for a roveless[83] cottage and tenement and 60 acres surrendered by the tenant a fine of £300 was paid in 1596 by John Reeve senior, a Cheddar husbandman, for a lease for three lives.[84]

An assessment of the level of fines presents a difficult problem; too many variables were apparently taken into account when fixing the fines. However, none of the evidence available on tenurial arrangements suggests that manorial lords put up the fines beyond the means of the copyholding class even though the amounts were more than two years' value, and the amounts do seem to be linked with what the market would bear: the levelling off, or even reduction, of fines in the 1680s in Edingworth indicates this. The lords wished to let their land conveniently and profitably, and had no desire to drive off their tenants. The stewards' notes available for some of the manors show that the arrangement of a tenancy was a bargain between two parties, rather than a benefit conferred by the lord.

Forfeiture

The secure position of customary tenants also emerges in cases where they had committed an offence against custom, by which, in theory, they could lose their estate and title in the holding. According to the Glastonbury customal the following actions would lead to the forfeiture of a holding: the selling of trees or fuel without licence; making waste; not repairing any decay of tenement or lands after sufficient warning; keeping an undertenant without licence; dwelling away from the tenement without licence; not serving the lord in war if he was called on by the king.[85] In all manors a widow holding by widow's right forfeited her estate if she remarried or lived unchastely, and in Mudgley she forfeited her estate if she married without the lord's licence.[86] In effect these regulations were designed to protect the lord's lands and the interests of the next tenant from waste or spoil, and they were enforced by presentments of the homage, the body of the tenants of the manor, in the manor court. For example, a tenant would be presented for having a house or barn in disrepair, or for not living on his tenement. An order would be made to rectify the fault, usually by a certain feast day or the next court, and in some courts one or two members of the homage were appointed to see the job was carried out. A penalty was set, generally a fairly low amount varying between 3s 4d and 10s, depending on the manor and period; if the order was not carried out the penalty was forfeited at the next court and a new penalty, generally double, was set.

Clearly the mechanism was a reasonable one, and though obviously forfeiture for a transgression was not likely in the first instance – even the setting of penalties was

---

82 SHC, DD\WY/70; DD\WY, uncalendared Orchard Wyndham MSS, seventeenth-century MS book, Edingworth manor, ff. 63, 65d., 66d.

83 Literally 'roofless', used for sites of old auster tenements without dwellings but still separate holdings.

84 SHC, DD\WY, uncalendared Orchard Wyndham MSS, seventeenth-century MS book, f. 64–d.

85 SHC, DD\SG/22, nos 15, 17, 18, 19, 25, 27.

86 SHC, DD\SAS/C795/PR/462.

rare at the first presentment – the lord had the means of justifiably ejecting a tenant and taking the holding into his own hands. Varying series of court rolls for ten manors have been examined for cases of offences that could lead to forfeiture of the holding.[87] Setting aside forfeiture by widows who remarried, dealt with separately below, there are few cases of such forfeitures even being mooted, although all the offences listed above occur other than not serving the lord in war.

Offences for which forfeiture was actually mentioned in these ten manors were for not residing on their land (two cases) or for alienating the premises (four), all without licence, or for disrepair (three), but forfeiture was invoked more as a threat than with the objective of removing the tenant. In Blackford Ralph Senox and Thomas Hill were presented in October 1655 for not living on their respective tenements, and ordered to do so under pain of £5 each. In October 1656 they were presented again and this time forfeited the £5 and their respective estates in their copyhold tenements 'according to the custom of the manor'. However, at the court held in November 1658 they were still in possession of their tenements and were presented once more for not living there and for having let them to others, and they were ordered to return and reside there. There is a gap in the court papers until 1661 and no more is heard of them, though they were still in possession in 1663.[88]

Short-term alienation – letting the premises for three or seven years – was allowed in most manors without requiring a licence, but the alienation of a tenement for life brought the threat of forfeiture. In one of the four cases found Lewes Symonds had demised his tenements in Edingworth for 60 years or his lifetime, but the outcome of the case is unknown.[89] Of the other three cases, one in 1586 concerned Joan Scott, a joint tenant who sold her right in 15 acres to her co-tenant without licence and so forfeited, but was still presented as joint tenant at her death the following year.[90] Thomas Roche, a Biddisham tenant, alienated a messuage and 13 acres 'against custom' and so forfeited, paying his heriot, but the admission of the next holder, Benjamin Griffen, was respited as he was a minor; Roche was still in possession four years later, when he made a formal surrender to Griffen.[91] In the third case Thomas Swayne forfeited his tenement in 1509 for alienating for life without a licence and paid his heriot. However, at the next court, held in April 1510, he paid a fine of 10s for a new estate in the forfeited

87 Allerton, Biddisham, Blackford, Burnham Rectory, Edingworth, Huntspill Rectory, Lympsham Parva, Northgrove, Tarnock. See MSS sources for dates and refs of court rolls used.

88 SHC, DD\SE/63/1, Blackford court papers; only presentments survive for 1654–8. The holdings were apparently held in right of their wives, according to surveys of 1657 and 1663: Dorothea wife of Thomas Hill held a messuage, 18 acres and 1 cottage; Anne wife of Ralph Senox held a messuage, 21 acres and 8 acres: DD\SE/65/1–2.

89 SHC, DD\WY, uncalendared Orchard Wyndham MSS, Edingworth court bk, 1597. The man to whom the tenements were demised held a cottage of 2 acres pasture sometime before 1605, but there is no other evidence that this is the holding meant.

90 CCC Oxford, Fn 1, Northgrove court rolls, 8 Aug. 28 Eliz., 17 Aug., 29 Eliz.

91 SHC, DD\CC/B/131925a/4, Biddisham, 16 July 27 Eliz., DD\CC/B/131924/4, Biddisham, 14 May 31 Eliz.

tenement for himself and his wife.[92] Though gaps in the series of court rolls make it hard to be conclusive, in all four cases the entries concerning forfeiture for alienation seem to be the first reference to the case, and do not appear to have caused much distress. In fact the presentments appear as the best way for the lord to get his dues on a change of tenant, with legal and official recognition of a *de facto* change.

Failing to make good any decay to land or buildings could also provide grounds for forfeiture, but only after considerable time and many warnings. In Allerton John Collins held two tenements containing a total of 29 acres and was presented in July 1597 for a decayed roof. This was repeated in 1598, 1599 and 1600, during which time penalties of 10s and 20s were forfeited. In July 1601 he was presented yet again for the unrepaired roof and forfeited his estate in the premises, but this was respited by grace of the steward without any reason. He was not presented again and continued in possession of his holdings, dying sometime between 1606, when he was foreman of the homage, and 1609, when his widow surrendered the property.[93] A case in Lympsham Parva ran on even longer than this: Joan Biddle, widow, and her next husband John Broke were presented nine times between August 1582 and September 1602, and at the last of these presentments were ordered to repair on pain of forfeiture. However, by the following April Joan had died and the tenement came into the lord's hands in any case.[94]

Cases mentioning forfeiture were rare considering the number of times similar grounds occurred. In Northgrove a tenant was presented for disrepair in 1576, 1578 and 1579, and, after a gap in the series, was presented for living outside the property in 1583. He died in 1600 and his widow was presented for disrepair.[95] In Huntspill a tenant was presented from 1598 until 1617 and then for living outside as well. Two other tenants were also presented over a four-year span.[96] In Edingworth six tenants were presented over four, five and six years,[97] and this is found in most manors. Disrepair was often linked with living outside without a licence, and the usual outcome of such cases was that the offending tenant paid a fine for a licence. In Biddisham Richard Day was first presented for living outside and for disrepair in 1592, and again in 1593, 1599, 1600 and 1601, when he was also in default for suit of court. In 1602 he was foreman of the homage, paid a fine of £5 for a special licence to live outside and let the property for his lifetime.[98]

---

92 SHC, DD\CC/B/131907/8, Allerton, 10 Oct 1 Hen.VIII; Allerton, 23 Apr. 2 Hen.VIII.

93 SHC, DD\CC/B/131925a/12, Allerton, 29 July 39 Eliz.; DD\CC/B/131924/1, Allerton, 7 Sep. 40 Eliz.; DD\CC/B/131924/6, Allerton, 24 July 41 Eliz.; DD\CC/B/131907/12, Allerton, 22 July 42 Eliz.; DD\CC/B/131907/19, Allerton, 15 July 43 Eliz.; DD\CC/B/131907/14, Allerton, 21 July 4 Jas. I; DD\CC/B/131925/7, Allerton, 14 Aug. 7 Jas. I.

94 N.Yorks. RO, ZJX 3/19/110, Lympsham Parva court bk.

95 CCC Oxford, Fn 1, Northgrove court rolls.

96 SHC, D\P\hun/3/1/1, court bk of Rectory manor.

97 SHC, DD\WY/70, Edingworth court rolls.

98 SHC, DD\CC/B/131909/15, Biddisham, 15 Mar. 34 Eliz.; DD\CC/B/131925a/10, Biddisham, 17 July 35 Eliz.; DD\CC/B/131924/6, Biddisham, 23 July 41 Eliz.; DD\CC/B/131907/12, Biddisham, 21 July 42 Eliz.; DD\CC/B/131907/19, Biddisham, 14 July 43 Eliz.; DD\CC/B/131910a/1, Biddisham, 4 Aug 44 Eliz.

Forfeiture, then, was not used to get rid of unsatisfactory tenants, and indeed it was not really possible for a lord to use forfeiture to obtain holdings for himself: the forfeiture was of a tenant's right in a holding, so that, though the transgressor lost possession, the next life in the copy or reversion took over, not the lord.[99] It was more a safeguard for the lord so that he could obtain his rightful dues for transfer of holdings, prevent waste and get the services he was entitled to. Thus, though the letter of the custom appears baldly and rigidly explicit, the tenant's position was in reality far stronger than the customal suggests.

Forfeiture by widows holding customary land for their widowhood was extremely common, but is in a different category, as it was not strictly for an offence as such. The widow received her husband's customary lands for her support, and if she remarried the need for support was theoretically removed. The custom was strictly enforced because there was generally a tenant waiting eagerly to take over. Where there were no further lives, a widow who remarried sometimes took a copy for the property in her own name and that of her new husband. Agnes Swaine forfeited her widow's estate in a tenement and 21 acres in Allerton when she remarried, but the year before this a copy had been bought for the man she married and her son by her first marriage.[100] In a case concerning a tenement in Burnham Rectory there were apparently no children by the first marriage so the widow, Alice Mower, paid a fine for a copy for herself and her new husband.[101] Similarly, on some manors the lord granted a licence to marry to the widow, who could then keep the holding for life if she remarried.[102] These sorts of case show that being in possession of a holding, even if only under widow's right, gave at least an opportunity to buy an estate in the property, if not first refusal. For example, Grace Deane forfeited her holding of 17 acres in Allerton to the next heir, an outsider and no relation, but the next reversion was bought by her new husband, Thomas Hatch, for himself, a kinsman (possibly the son) of her former husband, and Hatch's son.[103]

The role and value of the manor courts

The penalty of forfeiture, therefore, was a final resort for the lord trying to collect his dues, and it illustrates the role of the manor court, which was primarily a protection for the tenants and their successors and generally only indirectly aided the interests of the lord. A study of manors from the point of view of agrarian history has sometimes implied that the court was the instrument of the lord's control, and that where the lord had left the manor and sold off his demesne the manor collapsed, or at least was subject to partition and alienation of holdings, an influx of squatters and other manifestations of

---

99 'John Collins has not sufficiently repaired, … *his estate in* the said tenement is therefore forfeit' (my emphasis): SHC, DD\CC/B/131907/19, Allerton, 15 July 43 Eliz.

100 SHC, DD\CC/B/131925a/7, Allerton, 28 June 18 Eliz.

101 SHC, DD\CC/B/131925a/1, Burnham Rectory, 27 Aug. 2 Eliz.

102 SHC, DD\CC/A/13324, p. 136.

103 SHC, DD\CC/B/131907/12, Allerton, 22 July 42 Eliz.; DD\CC/B/131910a/1, Allerton, 5 Aug. 44 Eliz.

weak control.[104] This situation, though, is likely to be exceptional: even in the Middle Ages villagers were quite capable of organising themselves outside the structure of the court. For most manors the manor court remained important to the lords as the means of administering the manor and collecting their revenues, and also to the tenants in supporting their customary rights and carrying out the organisation of village life.[105] While in some cases there might be a link between the absence of a lord and the breakdown of manorial organisation, generally the decline of a manor court occurred when it ceased to have an active role in local administration. This might be as a result of the amount of subletting, which meant that the occupiers and residents of the village were not represented in the court,[106] or where commercial leasing of larger farms became important, mainly from the eighteenth century, so that the jury of the manor court, made up of customary tenants, no longer included the wealthiest farmers. The manor court was left only with matters concerning decay and waste of property, while bodies such as the vestry became of greater significance in organising village life.[107]

As the examples below will show, the involvement of Brent Marsh courts in village and farming life certainly declined, but, though most lords were absentees, demesnes were usually parcelled out and agricultural control was reduced to grazing matters and the upkeep of ditches, this did not result in the total collapse of the manors, partition of holdings or other ills. The courts continued to play a vital role in the legal and customary rights of the tenants, and this role ensured the continuation of most of the courts (even though sometimes as meetings out of court); most of the manors remained intact until the nineteenth century and the enfranchisement of copyholds by Act of Parliament. The nature and efficiency of manorial administration did vary, though: in the dean and chapter's manors, notably Allerton and Biddisham, the 1570s marked a period of better administration, with a survey in 1571 of all manors and the introduction of a book to record proposals for grants in about 1576;[108] an increased number of orders and bylaws in this period also suggests that some effort was made to tighten up on infringements. In the manor of Blackford, owned by Sexey's Hospital, Bruton, the advent of a new steward, a lawyer, in 1653 brought better recording and attention to detail: he deleted a casually worded heading and brief date on a court roll and substituted the correct formal style.[109]

The manor courts examined here were courts baron only:[110] leet business, including much local administration and criminal matters, was taken to the hundredal

104 *AHEW4*, pp. 48, 69, 86, 92–3.

105 Whittle, *Development of Agrarian Capitalism*, pp. 82–4; L. Shaw-Taylor, 'The Management of Common Land in Lowlands England, c.1500 to c.1850, in M. de Moor, L. Shaw-Taylor and P. Warde (eds), *The Management of Common Land in North West Europe, 1500–1850* (Turnhout, Belgium, 2002), p. 68.

106 French and Hoyle, *Character of English Rural Society*, p. 295.

107 Shaw-Taylor, 'Management of common land', p. 66.

108 SHC, DD\CC/B/110002, March 1570/1; DD\CC/B/114066.

109 SHC, DD\SE/63/2, 12 May 1653.

110 Not all the Brent Marsh manors, particularly those lay-owned, have surviving court rolls, so some may have had leet jurisdiction.

courts of Brent and Wrington, Bempstone, Winterstoke, or Huntspill and Puriton,[111] though some local matters, such as clearing ditches or communal grazing, which in manors elsewhere might be covered by leet courts,[112] were included. The business of the Brent Marsh manorial courts falls roughly into four categories:

- Land and tenurial matters: grants and surrenders of copies; presentation of deaths; admission of new tenants; licences to live outside the property and to let for years or life.
- Supervision and enforcement of the obligations of tenants and lord: repair of tenements; rhyne and seawall works; repair of pounds (the lord), bridges (the lord), fences, gates, roads.
- Regulation of activities in the manor: orders and bylaws; grazing the open fields; election of officials; strays; driving the moors; exchanges of land and enclosures; trespass; miscellaneous licences.
- Arbitration: views on land, etc., in dispute between tenants, or a tenant and another manor; decisions by the homage; publication of custom.

Listed in this way, these four categories might seem to indicate a good deal of control exercised over the tenants, but in fact not only were practically all items of court business, apart perhaps from licences, more directly in the interests of the tenants than in those of the lord, but also most originated from the tenants themselves. The court, in fact, was of far greater importance to the tenants, who benefited from the customs and could use the court to uphold them and to regulate the behaviour of their neighbours when it impinged on them. The role of the tenants in the functioning of the manor court was proactive even in the Middle Ages and, although by no means egalitarian or democratic, and undoubtedly dominated by the wealthiest customary tenants, the villagers were capable of acting together both in regulating village life and in countering perceived threats to their rights and livelihoods by their lords;[113] although a determined manorial lord in the sixteenth and seventeenth centuries could try to use the court to uphold his rights and control the inhabitants, his success was often limited in the face of concerted tenant opposition.[114] The weakness of the lords' position in the manorial courts is underlined by the fact that lords in the early sixteenth century began suing their customary tenants in the common law courts for the first time, citing custom of the manor, because they could not rely on the manorial court, with its jury of customary tenants, to uphold the lord's rights; the acceptance of the legality of manorial custom in common law marked a significant turning point for customary law and opened the way for tenants also to seek support from common law.[115]

111 Few rolls or other documents survive apart from rolls for Brent up to the 1530s (belonging to Glastonbury).

112 e.g. Earls Colne (Essex): French and Hoyle, *Character of English Rural Society*, pp. 163–71.

113 C. Dyer, 'The English Medieval Village Community and its Decline', *Journal of British Studies*, 33 (1994), pp. 407–29, pp. 427–9; Shaw-Taylor, 'Management of Common Land', pp. 66–8.

114 e.g. French and Hoyle, *Character of English Rural Society*, pp. 149–53.

115 Garrett-Goodyear, 'Common Law and Manor Courts', pp. 40–45.

Much of the business of the court arose from presentments drawn up by the homage and put forward by the foreman; those surviving among court papers are unfortunately rather late in date, when the breadth of court business was declining, but still give an idea of the matters put forward by the tenants. At the court for Biddisham held on 9 August 1639 the homage presented the death of Agnes Griffin since the last court, the heriot paid, and that they supposed Mrs Eleanor Barker to be the next tenant; Mr Tristram Towse and Mrs Eleanor Barker were presented for not dwelling on their tenements; Richard Jervis requested a view upon an encroachment by a tenant of the manor of Churchland, ordered to be carried out on 19 October by the tenants living in the parish on pain of ?12d each; the names of three tenants for election as reeve for next year were put forward from whom the steward could make his choice.[116] Presentments for Blackford for 31 October 1654 show a similar range: the deaths of two tenants with the heriots taken and the names of their successors; an order to clean a watercourse by St Andrew's day on pain of 6d a rope,[117] and the two men to oversee it; the repair of the pound, some gates and a ditch; nominations for the reeve and appointment of a hayward; four tenants that 'do not make their abode on their tenements as they ought'; four tenants for not repairing gates; an order that on reasonable warning all tenants were to send one person from each household to help drive the chase (to round up all the animals on the moor and impound those that should not be grazing there); and two buildings in decay, to be repaired.[118] Orders like those mentioned above came from the tenants, but others might come from the lord or his steward. However, most dealt with agricultural matters or drainage and were of more benefit to the tenant than of concern to the lord. Though licences were granted by the lord, where the other tenants were affected their agreement was obtained, as in the case of a licence to erect a cottage on the waste in Blackford, granted to two day-labourers in 1637 and signed by the lord (the feoffees of Sexey's Hospital) and 19 tenants, with 'we the tenants likewise agree'.[119]

The registration of title to land was the prime function of the manor court, so, naturally, despite variations in the amount and type of business carried out by the court, transactions concerning land, including the swearing in of new tenants and grants of licences, always formed a large proportion of the business, and its proportion increased as land changed hands more often and other business declined. Court business for ten of Brent Marsh's manors is analysed in Table 4. The figures show the proportional increase in land transactions between the sixteenth and seventeenth centuries, and, where court rolls exist for both early and late periods in the sixteenth century (Allerton, Biddisham, Burnham Rectory, Huntspill Rectory, Northgrove), there was a considerable increase in land transactions between the early and late sixteenth century as well.[120] The change in the court's

116 SHC, DD\CC/B/110233, Biddisham court papers.

117 A 'rope' was 30 feet in length: Williams, *Draining of the Somerset Levels*, p. 187.

118 SHC, DD\SE/63/2.

119 SHC, DD\SE/63/1.

120 More detailed figures and dates of court rolls used in P.E.C. Croot, 'Aspects of Agrarian Society in Brent Marsh, Somerset, 1500–1700', PhD thesis (University of Leeds, 1981), p. 483, Table 7.

Table 4
Percentage breakdown of manor court business

Manor & owner	*Date*	*No. of courts*	*No. of entries*	*Land transactions* %	*Tenants' obligations* %	*Agri. regs & arbitration* %
Allerton	16th C	52	284	30	29	42
(D & C)	17th C	39	118	65	15	20
Biddisham	16th C	61	313	38	34	29
(D & C)	17th C	27	101	86	9	5
Burnham Rectory	16th C	26	55	47	38	15
(D & C)	17th C	16	23	83	17	0
Blackford	17th C	29	282	36	53	11
(Sexey's Hsp.)						
Huntspill Rectory	16th C	27	133	26	54	20
(Rector)						
Northgrove	16th C	22	229	70	17	13
(CCC, Oxford)	17th C	29	280	81	10	9
Edingworth	16th C	16	94	44	45	12
(nobility, gentry)	17th C	6	12	33	67	0
Lympsham Parva	16th C	11	26	54	27	19
(nobility, gentry)	17th C	10	26	73	23	4
Tarnock	17th C	13	54	44	41	15
(nobility, gentry)						
Mark (East)	16th C	25	105	80	3	17
(nobility, gentry)	17th C	35	296	55	31	14

Notes: Percentages are rounded to nearest whole number. The samples are taken from all available court rolls dated between 1500 and 1700. Lay-owned manors have only very short series, or (as in Edingworth) are later compilations of court business.

function is particularly marked in the dean and chapter's manors, where in the early seventeenth century there was a great deal of speculation in reversions and the disappearance of practically all other business. In these manors there was also a high proportion of gentry copyholders, generally non-resident, who therefore had little interest in making presentments concerning the upkeep of the manor or farming regulations. In Blackford, on the other hand, most of the tenants lived in the parish of Wedmore, where the manor was situated, and many farmed their land themselves, producing a greater concern with the obligations of the tenants, particularly the proper maintenance of ditches and fences, and repairs to buildings, roads, bridges and the pound: those four items made up just over half of all court business in the extant court rolls, 1635–53 and 1661–88.[121] In the course of the seventeenth century business in most manor courts became limited to land transactions and

121 SHC, DD\SE/64/1; DD\SE/63/1; DD\X\HMD.

decay to buildings and rhynes. The type of farming in Brent Marsh also contributed to the decline in the role of the manor court, with large acreages of pasture held in severalty and closes being carved out of the common arable fields, making the need for rigid regulation of common land less important. The orders that do occur tended to concern the moors, for example, which were still grazed in common.

The decline in the scope of the manor court can be seen in other ways. In Biddisham, admittedly an extreme example because so many tenants were non-resident, presentments for July 1664 were drawn up by only two out of the 16 customary tenants, who stated that as there were not three present to be nominated for reeve according to the custom, the old reeve was to stand again.[122] A year later the entries were headed with the note that only three tenants appeared at the court, and seven were presented for living outside without licence, while in 1671 the aggrieved steward noted that no tenants at all had appeared at the court, and they were all to be fined 10s each if they did not appear next time.[123]

Furthermore, the court's transition from arbiter in all areas of manorial life to that concerned solely with land transfer and the obligations of tenure is reflected in its remoteness from the serious physical events in the area. Years of high mortality are not reflected in the deaths presented in the manor courts, but even more significant – copyholders were, after all, generally among the better-off and therefore less likely to die from disease or famine – is the absence of references to flooding, even the catastrophic inundation of 1607, when the sea was said to have reached Glastonbury Tor, east of Brent Marsh. The waters left their mark on many parish documents, those that survived at all, and drowned large numbers of animals, yet not a single reference occurs in the extant rolls, and the floods were not followed by increased orders to improve rhynes or seawalls even in the worst-hit parishes, such as Burnham. The references that do occur in this connection appear rather in the quarter sessions rolls and in comments about the commissions of sewers, and the latter had in fact taken over responsibility for waterways and drainage systems.[124] The multiple nature of the manorial structure had much to do with the manors' lack of influence or involvement in this regard, and, similarly, the augmentation of local powers at parish level was necessary to overcome the limitations of administration on a manorial basis, where the lands of three or four manors were intermingled. The social and political power of manorial lords was seriously reduced by this bypassing of the manors and their lack of an effective role in the wider community, while the power of the most substantial tenants within the parishes was thereby increased. In the course of the seventeenth century the manors lost their social and economic functions and became solely legal instruments, a way for landowners to handle the legal and administrative business connected with their tenants and a protection for tenants' rights.

---

122 SHC, DD\CC/B/110233, Biddisham court papers.

123 *Ibid.* The manor had 16 tenants in 1650: SHC, DD/CC/B/110001, vol. 1; DD/CC/B/110225, f. 79.

124 Williams, *Draining of the Somerset Levels*, pp. 82, 86. The early records of the Commission unfortunately are lost, but the court of the Commission was probably held at least once a year; there are references to courts held in July 1612, May 1620, Oct. 1622 and June 1623, in TNA, E 134/5Chas1/East8.

The switch to leasehold for lives

The tenurial role of the manor courts was also maintained when copyhold for lives was changed to leasehold for lives. The change from copyhold to leasehold is a contentious issue in the great debate about the removal of customary rights and the introduction of capitalist farming, but leasehold covers a wide spectrum of tenures that show very different histories, many of which were not commercial leases at rack rent, but rather types of beneficial leases with substantial entry fines and low ancient rents. So, for example, in the village of Highley in Shropshire the landlord decided to sell 2,000-year leases to the tenants, to whom the freehold was also later sold, turning their copyholds into freehold.[125] On the Durham Cathedral estate the customary tenant right was challenged by the Durham Chapter and eventually the tenants had to settle for 21-year leases, renewable after seven years, with right of inheritance, controlled fines and rents – a secure tenure, but financially less beneficial.[126] In the western half of England, in areas where copyhold for lives was prevalent, conversion to leasehold for lives was the most usual progression in the sixteenth and seventeenth centuries.[127] This form of leasehold, sometimes for two or three lives but eventually most usually found as 99 years determinable on three named lives, was fairly common by the sixteenth century as the tenure by which demesne land was farmed out on ecclesiastical manors, but copyholds also in some manors were switched to what is generally known as life leasehold. In the lay-owned manor of Edingworth copyholds had become life leaseholds by the early seventeenth century and in the manor of Cheddar Episcopi, also lay owned, most copyholdings were leasehold by 1700.[128] However, in other lay-owned manors, such as Cheddar Berkeley,[129] as well as in the majority of manors belonging to the Church, customary or old auster tenements were still copyhold in the later seventeenth century, but most manors also included several life leaseholds as well, for farms of demesne and other property in the lord's hands.[130] Although occasionally the manor house and most demesne land might be farmed out together, as at Allerton, which had only two other leases of meadow or pasture,[131] in most manors for which adequate surveys survive the demesne and overland were leased out in several relatively small parcels of land, making such leases quite common. The form of the lease was fairly uniform throughout the manors here, and was fairly similar to those found elsewhere in the south-west:[132] the lessee was often

125 G. Nair, *Highley: The Development of a Community, 1550–1880* (Oxford, 1988), pp. 79–80.

126 J. Morrin, 'The Transfer to Leasehold on Durham Cathedral Estate, 1541–1626', in Whittle (ed.), *Landlords and Tenants*, pp. 117–32.

127 C. Clay, 'Lifeleasehold in the Western Counties of England 1650–1750', *Agricultural History Review*, 29 (1981), pp. 83–96.

128 SHC, DD\WY/70; TNA, C 108/182, survey book, manor of Cheddar [c.1727].

129 SHC, DD\PO/1.

130 e.g. SB Huish 1567: 18 leases for 92yrs/two or three lives: Straton, *Survey*, II, pp. 471–86; Cheddar Vicars Choral, seven inds for three lives: DD\CC/L/116013.

131 Coleman, 'Manor of Allerton', pp. 72–82.

132 Clay, 'Lifeleasehold', pp. 91–3.

the first life named, though frequently the lives were three children of the lessee, both because hopefully the lease would then run longer and because the lessee was often providing for those children. The annual rent was the same as the ancient rent under copyhold tenure, a heriot was payable on the death of each life – sometimes still best beast or good but increasingly a fixed cash sum – and, generally, suit of court and rhyne works were required as under customary tenure; common rights such as pasture, turbary or timber for repairs were also included, usually encompassed by the expression 'all accustomed appurtenances'.

The reason for the change from copyhold to leasehold is not immediately obvious, as the incidents of the two tenures were so similar. The lord probably gained by the lifting of the control of custom over fines, but, apart from the relatively high fines in Edingworth, there is no evidence of large rises as a result: they were still governed, presumably, by demand. The removal of widows' right was also of benefit to the lord, as its existence added an element of uncertainty for them over the length of time a copyhold for lives might run, and therefore their calculations over possible income, when the widow of one or all of the lives might also hold the property.[133] However, the tenants also must have seen some advantage to themselves, as the change required their agreement to extinguish customary tenure and though, in some instances, pressure might be applied this is unlikely to have been widespread given the relatively high social status of many copyholders. Active agreement by the tenants is evident. In 1683, for example, Thomas Owen alias Griffiths, a gentleman of North Curry (near Taunton), bought a lease from the Dean and Chapter of Wells for the lives of himself and his two children of two messuages and 37 acres in Biddisham, which he was already holding by copy, surrendering the copy and paying a further fine.[134] There are two main advantages of the switch for the tenants. One is that the leaseholds were demisable by will and could be held by anyone, regardless of the lives named, which gave the holders more freedom in disposing of their property. The other is the extinguishing of the custom of widow's right in the holding, which seems to be the only customary right or obligation that was not carried over from the copyhold tenure. A study of the cases concerning copyholds for lives in Somerset brought to the Court of Requests in the sixteenth century shows the difficulties that widows' right was creating, especially where the copies were for three lives, both in widows not receiving their entitlement and in opposition to their doing so; the conclusion was that although the system did not always operate smoothly, it was 'a formidable entitlement' for widows, and, although the cases in Requests were exceptional, the level of opposition was evidence of its significance, and of the unhappiness felt by many tenants about a custom which placed so much land in the hands of widows to the disadvantage of the next tenant.[135]

The position of tenants does not appear to have deteriorated in the short term by becoming life leaseholders rather than copyholders: the holdings remained in the family of the lessee by replacing lives or taking a new lease for three lives. These life

133 *Ibid.*, p. 93.

134 SHC, DD\CC/B/110300.

135 T. Stretton, *Women Waging Law in Elizabethan England* (Cambridge, 1998), pp. 166–72. Below Chap. 5, Roles of women in rural society: Responsibility given to women.

leases were not chattel leases like commercial leases for years only, but conveyed a form of lifehold estate. As regards security and status, leaseholders for lives were in the same category as copyholders, and much of the discussion that follows on aspects of copyhold applies equally to these life leaseholders.

Free and copyhold land in the provision for children

The security and flexibility of copyhold for lives also influenced the ways in which landholders could provide for their children through land, and this differed substantially from the way they disposed of freehold land, which was controlled and conveyed by set formulae under common law.

Freehold land

The number of freeholders found in the Brent Marsh manors at the beginning of the sixteenth century is small, and in some surveys they are mentioned but not listed separately; where they are given, they usually amounted to five to six holdings, of which two to three formed sub-manors, and the remainder were generally small in size, such as a half virgate, or five acres.[136] However, in the course of the sixteenth and seventeenth centuries the number of freeholdings held by local residents increased, firstly through the sale of chantry lands, much of which ended up in local hands, and then through the break-up of manors and sales of the freehold in parcels, as in South Brent, Wedmore, Burnham and Huntspill. Freehold in Brent Marsh not held as a manor increasingly occurs in *inquisitiones post mortem* and in licences to alienate enrolled on the Patent Rolls, and also crops up quite often in the provisions made by local residents for their heirs.

Though freehold land could be devised by will under the Statute of Wills of 1540,[137] the majority of holders in the Levels followed the common law rules of descent that were established by the end of Henry III's reign:[138] the eldest son of the holder, or his own son, would inherit; if the eldest son died without male heirs then the land passed to the second son of the holder and so on; if the holder had no sons or they died without children then the daughters of the holder would inherit as co-heirs. Only if the land was entailed on *male* heirs would it pass, on the failure of sons, to the nearest male relative by the rules of male primogeniture, to the exclusion of the holder's daughters.

Deviations from this descent could be made by settlements in trust, by pre-mortem transfers or by will. Not many references occur in wills in the Levels to lands in fee, 'lands of inheritance' in local usage: only about 30 out of some 900 wills have such references, despite the fact that most of the 900 were proved in the PCC,

---

136 BL, Egerton MS 3034, ff. 149d–168d; Straton, *Survey*, II, pp. 471–86; TNA, E 315/385, ff. 90–95d; LR v, ff. 29–31; LR 2/225, ff. 53–114.

137 32 Henry VIII c. 1. All land held by socage and two-thirds of land held by military tenures could be devised by will.

138 F. Pollock and F.W. Maitland, *The History of English Law before the Time of Edward I*, vol. 2 (2nd edn, Cambridge, 1911), p. 260.

where freeholders' wills would be more likely to be found. The conclusion must be that most freeholders, large and small, were content to follow common law where they had a son to inherit, or they had made a settlement of the land before death. It was usually when they had no sons that they devised their freehold land in wills, either to a daughter or to a kinsman where the heir was not obvious. John Hide of Biddisham left his freehold land in the manor of Tarnock to Florence, his only child, and her heirs or, in the event of her death, to her mother for life and then to Hide's sister's son.[139] Leonard Younge of Compton Bishop left his land in West Pennard to John, the son of Harry Younge (relationship not specified), 'in the same manner as I had them in dissention from my auncestor'.[140] William Prowse, gentleman, also of Compton, had both a brother and sister with children, but chose to leave his manors of Compton Magna and Badgworth and lands in 25 parishes to the eldest son of his cousin John Prowse of Hemyock in Devon, naming him 'my next heir at law'.[141] These lands were almost certainly purchased by Prowse, who came from Devonshire,[142] and not inherited from his parents, so that he had no moral or legal obligations to consider his brother's claim.

Some men used their wills to mitigate the effects of common law inheritance. Thomas Kenn, gentleman, of Compton Bishop, a member of an armigerous family, was heir apparent to his uncle Christopher Kenn of Kenn in north Somerset. He referred in his will to his eldest son George as his heir, who would possibly inherit the uncle's lands, but if he did so George was to pay his brother Thomas £100.[143] This kind of arrangement for the younger sons is similar, if on a lesser scale, to arrangements made among peers and great landowners.[144] Thomas Kinge of South Brent left £300 to his unborn child, but if twins were born the heir was to receive £100 and the other child £200, in recognition of the greater benefits the heir would receive from his landholdings.[145]

Where freehold was purchased rather than inherited, testators were more likely to divide it up. John Draper of Huntspill made his will in 1608 benefiting the children of his only son, who had just died leaving two sons, a daughter and an unborn child. Draper left 17½ acres freehold, 'which is my own purchased land', including a house, windmill and land in Shapwick and Huntspill, to his younger grandson and his heirs, and in default of such heirs to the unborn child if it was a boy, and if not to the elder grandson. The phrasing suggests that Draper had other, possibly inherited, freehold that would descend to the elder boy, as in his will he left him only £10 and the reversion of a lease of six acres.[146]

---

139 TNA, PROB 11/98/190.

140 TNA, PROB 11/77/69. By 'dissention' he meant descent, but it makes a superb pun considering the amount of litigation land attracted.

141 TNA, PROB 11/335/258.

142 Monument inscription in Axbridge parish church.

143 TNA, PROB 11/104/206.

144 J.P. Cooper, 'Patterns of Inheritance and Settlement by Great Landowners from the Fifteenth to the Eighteenth centuries', in Goody *et al.*, *Family and Inheritance*, pp. 313–27.

145 TNA, PROB 11/97/237.

146 TNA, PROB 11/114/351.

Occasionally daughters also received freeholds: William Counsell of Mark divided up his land in 1712 between all his children, and this included lands in fee to a son and a daughter.[147] Usually, however, the first choice to receive freehold was a son, and only in default of the son's heirs was the land given to a daughter and her heirs. Daughters usually received leaseholds for life as their share: John Draper, mentioned above, while giving freehold to his grandsons, gave his two daughters leases and cash.[148]

An alternative to dividing up land was to give a younger son an estate in the property for a term of years. In 1625 John Lythyate of Mudgley in Wedmore left his tenements in Sand to his second son for 70 years, with a reserved rent to be paid to the heir, his eldest son John.[149] The tenement was probably one of the copyholds purchased in fee by Lythyate *c.*1609 and listed in the Court of Wards survey in 1625 as a messuage and 16 acres in Sand. His other free lands were a messuage and 23 acres and a four-acre close of pasture,[150] so his younger son had a fairly equal share in the land for his lifetime, even if it did not establish the younger line as freeholders. Such grants, particularly grants for the life of the beneficiary, were a fairly common method of providing for dependants such as a wife or daughter without destroying the patrimony of the heir.

Copyhold land

Copyhold for lives was the most prevalent secure tenure in the Levels, but, like freehold, it was rarely mentioned in wills as it descended automatically through the manor court to the next life in the copy or in reversion, and wills could not override this descent. The holders established their children in the succession to the land by taking new copies during their lifetime, and the way copyhold land was transferred and used to provide for children may be examined in manorial documents such as court rolls and surveys.

Though in many cases copyholds were inhabited and worked by the holder, this was not always nor necessarily the case, and copyholdings need to be examined and assessed more for their legal and tenurial role than for their agricultural one. Such landholdings were used for the same purposes as freehold land and the increased sophistication in the use of copyhold, discussed in this chapter, may be the result of the desire to use such land to provide for dependants. While it often worked out that the customary land ended up in the hands of one obvious heir, such as the eldest son, and was passed on to his children, this was not necessarily arranged from the start; rather, a holding devolved onto a single heir when other siblings had been provided for.

The copies taken in the manors examined here do not show any particular discrimination against daughters: the extant court rolls for the manor of Biddisham

147 SHC, DD\PLE/40.

148 TNA, PROB 11/114/351.

149 TNA, PROB 11/150/94.

150 Hervey, *Wedmore Chronicle*, II, pp. 46–7; Hawkins, *Sales of Wards*, p. 37.

between 1535 and 1676, for instance, record 89 copies taken for 20 holdings, 34 of the copies for the sons and daughters of the current holders in a roughly equal division between the sexes.[151] However, in no case is a daughter named in a copy ahead of her brother in those examples, and when this does occur in other manors it is because the son already has some other copy in his name. Usually copies were taken as the children were born, or even before birth, in the order of birth regardless of gender, and then later as family circumstances changed the father altered the names in the copy or surrendered it and took a new one, depending on the usage of that particular manor. For example, Richard Wall took a new copy of his messuage and 14 acres *c.*1635 for himself, his wife and their first child, as yet unborn, and about the same time George Popham took one of his messuage and nine acres for his next child, who was a daughter. John Boulting took a new copy in 1662 for his son William, then about 11 years old, and William's future wife; John's wife and his other children had all died.[152]

The process by which the customary holdings devolved onto one heir over two or three generations can be illustrated by the Hide family in the manor of Biddisham. John Hide I held three tenements there of 14 acres each, one including 11 acres of overland, by copies dated 1499.[153] In 1533 his son John II was named in a copy for the third holding; in 1546 John I bought a reversion of the first holding for John II, the latter's first wife Agnes and their daughter Julian; and in 1551 he bought a new copy for the second holding for himself, John II and the latter's son Thomas. John I died in 1553, his widow Edith was admitted to the three holdings for her widowhood and John II was admitted to the overland. By 1562 John II was in possession of all the property, and he took a new copy for the second holding for himself and his son John III, after his son Thomas had surrendered his interest.[154] In 1565 John II (d. 1579) bought a reversion of the third tenement for his children, John III, Joan and Julian, and in 1573 surrendered the copy of the first tenement in order to put in the name of John III after himself and his wife in place of Julian; she married at about this time and had probably been given some other part of her father's goods or land.[155] After his father's death John III was admitted at once to the overland, and to the three tenements when his father's second wife, Joan, remarried.[156] When he made his will in 1601 he had only one child, Florence, and, as he had not bought further copies, he bequeathed to his daughter £100 for the purchase of the reversion of his living in Biddisham. John III also had some freehold in the manor of Tarnock, which he left to his daughter,[157]

151 SHC, DD\CC, Biddisham court rolls, *passim*.

152 SHC, DD\SE/65/1–2, surveys 1657, 1663.

153 The Hide transactions are taken from: SHC, DD\CC/B/131922/1, 131923/2 & 4, 131907/6 & 15, 131924/4, 131925/7, 131909/15.

154 Thomas thereafter drops out of sight and is mentioned neither in his father's will nor in his brother's.

155 TNA, PROB 11/61/523.

156 See above, Customary tenure, for account of Joan's remarriage.

157 TNA, PROB 11/98/190; LR 2/191, ff. 29–31. Judging by rents for other freeholds in the survey whose acreages are given, Hide's holding was *c.*20 acres.

and a house in Compton Bishop where he lived, having a licence to live outside the Biddisham tenements; his widow Grace was living in Bristol at her death in 1609.[158]

Although a sister's interest would generally be removed by the father or bought out later, occasionally her stake in the property continued, especially if the father died before he could make any further provision, and a subsequent holder might have to wait until the daughter also died before he could change the copy. John Cole held a message and 33 acres for his life in 1657, to be succeeded by his sister, Alice. After she died in 1660 he was able to take a new copy for himself and his second and third children, a son and daughter.[159]

Where a copyholder had more than one tenement and additional children, he would often take the copies for himself and a different child each time. Richard Wall held three copies: the first was taken for himself, his wife and his first child; the second for a messuage and 21 acres was taken for himself and his second and sixth surviving children (both sons); and the third for a messuage and nine acres for himself and his fourth and third children (both sons).[160] Stephen Champion held two copies, one for a messuage and 18 acres he took for himself and his two elder children, a son and daughter, and the other for two messuages and 23 acres for himself, his second wife and his third surviving child, a son.[161]

Despite the fact that custom usually gave the widow of a copyholder the tenement after his death, wives are frequently named as the second life in the copy in some manors, partly because the custom could be challenged and widow's estate voided under certain conditions,[162] and partly because the widow could hold only while unmarried and chaste: if she held the land as one of those named in the copy she had an estate regardless of any future marriage, an important aspect if the holding or the money to purchase it had come from her family. For this reason putting the wife's name in the copy was a form of marriage settlement which ensured the woman's support regardless of marital changes. As discussed below in Chapter 5, in the section on pre-mortem transfers, such arrangements were generally made at the time of the marriage, but occasionally had not been made by the time the woman's father made his will, which he then used to put pressure on his son-in-law with a bequest conditional on some settlement being made. John Hide II, mentioned above, made a bequest of £20 towards the fine of the tenement of Thomas Deane, whose son John had married Hide's daughter Joan, if it was bought for Joan for her life – that is, if she was named in the copy; if they died before the purchase was made, the £20 was to go to Deane's two daughters.[163]

Naming children in copies did give them a stake in the holding or an estate of some kind even when fourth or fifth in reversion, and this interest could be redeemed later for cash, such as the £40 William Colston paid to Joan Deane (née Hide) for her

158 TNA, PROB 11/117/608.

159 SHC, DD\SE/65/1–2, surveys 1657, 1663.

160 *Ibid.* His 5th child (daughter) and 7th (son) were not mentioned in copies in this manor.

161 SHC, DD\SE 65/1–2, surveys 1657, 1663.

162 Above, Customary tenure: Forfeiture.

163 TNA, PROB 11/61/523.

right in one of the Hide tenements in Biddisham.[164] The stake in the property could also form the basis of a reshuffle of property among family members, giving the second and third lives in a copy another holding in possession or cash in lieu of their interest. The Hayward family holdings in Biddisham illustrate the kind of arrangement that was made. In 1576 a reversion was bought by Richard Hayward for his daughters Joan, Dorothy and Anne, to hold successively in that order a tenement and 14 acres being held by his mother with remainder to himself, and another reversion for himself, Anne and Joan of a messuage and 20 acres held by his mother to be followed by his wife.[165] Joan married Christopher Day and was holding the tenement and 14 acres by 1601 when her sisters surrendered their interests and Joan took a new copy for herself and her sons, George and Thomas Day. At the same time Joan surrendered her interest in the messuage and 20 acres to which Anne had been admitted in 1598, and Anne's husband John Neighbour, who held it in right of his wife, took a new copy for himself and their sons, John and William. The second sister Dorothy had no further interest in her father's holdings, but one may deduce that a *quid pro quo*, possibly in the form of cash, had been provided to make her share of her father's estate equal to that of her sisters': her husband, Henry Taunton, held a messuage and 14 acres inherited from his father in 1585, and he bought a new copy at this time for himself and his son and daughter by Dorothy.

Usually, therefore, the children of one generation shared an interest in the holding only until the next generation was born. If the child who held the tenement had no children of his or her own, a brother or sister would inherit and take a new copy for their own dependants. Shares by siblings, however, were only a retention of legal interest in the property to be realised at some distant date, and rarely took the form of profit-sharing. Only occasionally are copies bought for three *jointly* rather than successively, an arrangement which can be a form of partible inheritance used in preference to a physical division of the holding.[166]

Copyhold for lives, therefore, gave the means by which children could be provided for easily, and supplemented provision by will. The general pattern was as follows: when the copies were bought the children were usually very young, but by the time the copyholder came to make his will his eldest children at least would be grown up with children of their own, so that the customary land would pass to the eldest of the children and his or her offspring. The copyholder, therefore, would use his will to provide in some other way for the second or third lives in his children's copy. If, however, the copyholder died while his children were still young, at least they had

---

164 SHC, DD\CC/B/131907/6.

165 Hayward and Taunton transactions taken from following court rolls: SHC, DD\CC/B/131925a/7, 131907/19, 131924/1.

166 E.P. Thompson, 'The Grid of Inheritance: A Comment', in Goody *et al.*, *Family and Inheritance*, p. 342 and n. 32. Among examples of land disposed of in these wills are a few of parcels of land, leases or other holdings being left jointly to children, and even these are often left to one child first and jointly to the remaining children if the first died without heirs. They were mainly intended to provide an income from rents rather than to divide the land or the profits from direct farming. Below, Chap. 5, Payment of legacies and the economic effects.

some inheritance secured to them which they could resettle among themselves when they reached adulthood.

The use and attraction of copyhold for lives

The value of copyhold for lives becomes apparent in the number and range of cases – whether claims were legally justified or not – brought to the equity courts in London, which could deal with aspects of claims that did not fit the accepted grounds necessary for the common law courts. The increasing litigation concerning copyhold property reflects the importance of this tenure: even one John Hawkins, 'so poor that [he] now at this present liveth on the charity of good people', felt impelled to the expense of a Chancery suit in 1565 in order to be reinstated in a copyhold.[167] The Brent Marsh area produced an increasing number of suits in the equity courts,[168] especially Chancery, between the mid sixteenth and late seventeenth centuries.[169] Cases concerning land and rents always outnumbered other subjects, but became even more dominant by the middle of the seventeenth century. A breakdown of the Brent Marsh cases in one class of Chancery proceedings for the period 1558 to 1660, examined in detail in Table 5, shows that 28 of the 105 suits involved copyhold land, forming the largest category. Life leaseholds were involved in 19 suits, disputes over legacies, some of which also involved land, accounted for 18, and disputes over manors or large freehold estates, mainly concerning non-resident parties, accounted for 14.

The point at which a manor changed from an economic institution managing agrarian matters to one principally concerned with tenure is made most apparent with the influx of non-farming outsiders who bought copies or reversions, but this change may be more apparent than real: the early sixteenth-century court rolls are blandly uninformative about the residence or status of tenants, but this need not mean they were all local husbandmen, nor that they worked the land themselves. However, by Elizabeth I's reign personal information is more common and the purchase of tenancies by outsiders and non-farmers can be charted; these purchases go to show that copyholds by this date were far from being regarded as a servile and insecure tenure, but could be used in ways similar to freeholds. However, most studies of copyhold tenure have dealt with copyhold of inheritance and express reservations

167 TNA, C 3/81/18.

168 Common law courts, Common Pleas and Kings Bench were probably equally important and well used, as Garrett-Goodyear ('Common Law and Manor Courts') indicates, but the records were not indexed by place when this research was carried out, so could not be surveyed in the same way. References often occur in Chancery proceedings to related suits in another court, and pursuit of a case through several courts was common. T.G. Barnes found over half the Star Chamber cases he surveyed involved cases in other courts: J.H. Baker (ed.), *Legal Records and the Historian* (London, 1978), 12.

169 Croot, 'Agrarian Society', p. 484, Table 9, has breakdown of 536 local cases in eight classes of Chancery procs, 1529–1700.

Table 5
Breakdown of Brent Marsh Chancery suits, 1558–1660

Cases between local residents	Over copyhold	15
	Over life leasehold	7
	Over freehold	1
Cases between non-residents	Over copyhold	6
	Over life leasehold	9
	Over freehold	2
Tenant v. landlord	Copyholders	5
	Leaseholder	1
Landlord v. tenant	Copyholders	2
	Leaseholders	2
Payment of legacies		18
Between lords or estate owners, usually non-resident		14
Farms of manors and other leases		6
Advowsons, parsonages, tithes		6
Other		11
Total suits		105

Source: TNA, C 3, Chancery Suits, Series II, 1558 to 1660.

about copyhold for lives.[170] It is true that, financially, lives was less attractive than inheritance, as entry fines were more substantial than the fines for inheritance, but the 'finite' nature of lives is more implied than real, since in reality the lives were constantly being renewed.[171] No examples of lords refusing to renew have come to light in Brent Marsh, and custom apparently supported the right of renewal; in the case of life leasehold, too, it has been pointed out that in practice they established hereditary tenancies as landlords customarily allowed automatic renewals.[172] The idea that the lord could sell the reversion to anyone he wanted, auctioning it off to the highest bidder against the wishes of the sitting tenant, is not borne out by the Brent Marsh manors. The body of customs covering copyhold land, acknowledged and upheld in the central courts, created a secure and worthwhile form of land tenure that could be used to provide for dependants via various legal instruments,[173] and copyhold for lives proved just as attractive to outside investors as copyhold of inheritance.

170 Whittle, *Landlords and Tenants*, pp. 14–15; French and Hoyle, *Character of English Rural Society*, p. 8.

171 Constant purchase of reversions has also been found in some Hants manors: J. Gayton,'Tenants, Tenures and Transfers: The Landholding Experience of Rural Customary Tenants in some Hampshire Downland Manors, 1645–1750', PhD thesis (University of Exeter, 2013), pp. 5–6.

172 Clay,'Lifeleasehold', p. 84.

173 French and Hoyle, *Character of English Rural Society*, pp. 184–207; C. Brooks, 'The Agrarian Problem in Revolutionary England', in Whittle (ed.), *Landlords and Tenants*, pp. 193–4, 198–9. Below, Chap. 5 for provision and inheritance generally.

Many men outside the local farming community – lawyers, churchmen, gentlemen and merchants – showed great interest in acquiring copyholds for lives in the Levels, in the same way that has been recognised for copyhold of inheritance.[174] The manors belonging to the dean and chapter seem to have been particularly prone to sales of copyholds to outsiders, especially to relatives of the canons or to officials of the chapter. In Biddisham, 13 of the 18 copyhold tenements passed into the hands of outsiders through the purchase of reversions between about 1580 and 1635. Six of these tenements went to children and other connections of the canons, five to gentlemen or merchants from London, Bristol and elsewhere in Somerset and two to lawyers who acted for the chapter.[175] Similar purchases occurred in Allerton, where eight of the 18 copyhold tenements went to outsiders, mainly gentry from Wells. The lands of the dean and chapter form an extreme example, and a certain element of corruption seems to have slipped into the canons' estate practices: a note of each grant was supposed to be signed in the proposals book by the dean and several canons, which many of the grants to clerical relatives were not, and reversions were granted to Canon Bower's children for fines of only 5s instead of the £10 or more that others had to pay.[176] However, a few purchases by non-farming outsiders appear in most manors: in Edingworth, which had 12 holdings, one was held by the steward for two generations, and three others passed to another steward, a gentleman from Axbridge, and merchants by the late seventeenth century.[177]

The desire to obtain these copyholds led men to pay sums to the copyholders that were greatly in excess of the fines paid to the lord in order to buy out the interests of those named in the copy and in any reversions. Since court rolls were intended only to record dealings between tenants and lord, it is unusual to find a record of the amount of the consideration paid by the incoming tenant to the outgoing holder. A rare example is the recorded £262 that Stephen Browne paid in 1631 to William and Robert Celey for their holding of two messuages, 28 acres of customary land and nine acres of overland in Biddisham, and he paid another £40 to the reversioners of 23 acres of this holding; this far exceeded the fine of £24 10s that the lord of the manor received.[178] Seven years later Browne surrendered the holding to Tristram Towse, a notary and deputy to the chapter-clerk, for £200. Towse paid a fine of only £5 to the chapter, presumably either because of his office or because of his relationship with Canon Bower.[179]

The deals made by Browne and Towse also indicate that copyholds were acquired not just to make a living from farming or even from rents. The copies bought were

174 Whittle, *Landlords and Tenants*, pp. 15, 216–19; Whittle, *Development of Agrarian Capitalism*, pp. 200–03; this trend became even more marked nearer Bristol in the north Somerset Levels: Rippon, *Landscape, Community and Colonisation*, pp. 153–4.

175 SHC, DD\CC, court rolls of manors of dean & chapter, *passim*.

176 The reversions might have been made in lieu of some stipend, though there is no indication that this was the case.

177 SHC, DD\WY/70, Edingworth court papers.

178 SHC, DD\CC/B/131911a/7, Biddisham, 7 Oct. 7 Car. I.

179 SHC, DD\CC/B/131926/7, Biddisham, 7 July 14 Car. I. Towse was also married to granddaughter of Walter Bower, canon of Wells (below).

almost all reversions and must have been regarded principally as investments unless the holders were also bought out, as the purchasers could have no idea when they would be able to take possession of the land and derive any benefit from their copies; the only return in the meantime would be from selling the reversion at a profit. Many of the reversions granted by the lord never came into possession at all, and appear to be just this form of speculation in land. For example, in 1571 William Billingsley, citizen and haberdasher of London, bought the reversions of two tenements and 28 acres for his three sons,[180] who five years later surrendered their rights in the holdings to William Mills, the husband of the tenant in possession.[181]

This later conveyance of reversions to the sitting tenants might seem to counter the argument that the sitting tenants had first refusal, but possibly they were unable or unwilling to take up the reversion at that time, and purchased it later. It is more likely, however, that rather than being just random speculation, this kind of temporary purchase by outsiders may have been a form of mortgage arranged by the sitting tenant, who took advantage of the ability to change the names in the copy to give security for a loan by putting in the name of the lender or his nominee as one of the lives; this would explain the instances where the third life in the copy is the child of a man known to have been wealthy but who had no known connection with the purchaser of the copy. So, for example, Margaret Hatch, widow, took a reversion in 1613 for her two children plus Sara, the daughter of Adrian Bower (below), and Thomas Welsh, son of the holder, took a reversion for himself and two older men, Thomas Wrentmore senior of Axbridge, member of a prominent merchant family, and Richard Vayle of Glastonbury.[182] This also suggests a reason for the short-term connection with a property and the area of outsiders, such as Colston of Bristol or Billingsley of London. This use of lives was certainly the case with life leaseholds in south-west Lancashire, where the third life in the lease was to secure the loan for the entry fine, an arrangement made explicit in the estate's contract books,[183] although it does not seem to have been employed for creating mortgages in two Hampshire manors, where customary tenants holding for lives used surrenders and sub-letting instead.[184]

Some of the outsiders who bought copyholds did establish a more permanent tenancy by residing in the area and engaging in farming. The most outstanding example of these was the Bower family of Wells and Allerton. Walter Bower, whose father had been mayor of Shaftesbury, was a canon of Wells who died in 1580, and his eldest son, Edmund, died without heirs, leaving all his lands in Somerset and Dorset to his brother Adrian. At his death in 1630 Adrian had freehold in South Brent Huish (21 acres), Allerton (five acres) and Alston Sutton (14 acres), and in Butleigh, Wootton, Elm, Chesterblade and Wells elsewhere in Somerset, and Shaftesbury and Buckhorn Weston in Dorset, as well as copyhold in Allerton (32 acres) and Biddisham

180 SHC, DD\CC/B/131907/21, Biddisham, 29 Aug. 13 Eliz.

181 SHC, DD\CC/B/131925a/7, Biddisham, 27 June 18 Eliz.

182 SHC, DD\CC/B/114067, Allerton, 11 Jas. I; DD\CC/B/110225, Biddisham, 15 Car. I.

183 A.J. Gritt, 'The Operation of Lifeleasehold in South-West Lancashire, 1649–97', *Agricultural History Review*, 53 (2005), pp. 1–23, esp. 20.

184 Gayton,'Tenants, Tenures and Transfers', pp. 213–16.

(seven acres) and the lease of East Brent vicarage. His youngest son John went to Oxford and received the degree of MA in 1638, and two of his four daughters married churchmen or diocesan officials.[185] His eldest son, Edmund, inherited his freehold and much of the rest, living principally in Allerton, where he held the farm of the vicarage and the 132-acre demesne of the manor by lease for lives from the dean and chapter. He was one of the few men in the area to fight for the king in the civil war, as a captain, and his lands in Bempstone hundred, sequestered in 1645, consisted of 190 acres in Allerton, 64 acres in Wedmore and 28 acres in Tarnock, valued at a total of £160 a year, some of which he was farming himself, and rents totalling £19 10s. His brother John, also a royalist soldier, held 70 acres in Allerton, Burnham, Biddisham, Mark and Weare valued at £23 a year. At his death in 1660 Edmund also had land in Northgrove, Brent, Wells, Wookey, Mells and in Dorset. His son Adrian kept a household at Allerton, but died in 1685 at his principal house, Seymours Court in Wraxall, holding most of the land of his grandfather Adrian. Another of Edmund's sons, John, was vicar of Burnham from 1681 until his death in 1727.[186] The family's connection with the area was therefore close and long-lasting, but it was confined to the traditional paths of Church and State. Edmund's support for Charles I cannot have made him popular in a predominantly Parliamentarian area, and a degree of animosity between him and his neighbours emerges in the complaints made against him at the quarter sessions in 1657, that he was in the habit of leaving a few sheaves of corn in the fields for several weeks after the harvest, so that he could impound any cattle turned into another part of the field.[187]

The advent of the 'new' copyholders of the seventeenth century of gentle status, such as Edmund Bower or Eleanor Barker, daughter of the chancellor of Wells, marks the transition from the medieval manors of large- and small-scale husbandmen to the growth of the eighteenth-century rural and professional middle class, and, indeed, many of the families in this group were descended from those gentlemen who bought land in the area in the seventeenth century. However, they did not disturb a pattern of equality in wealth or holding size among existing landholders, as from among the earlier copyholders also emerged minor landed gentry and professional men who purchased along the way some freehold land, the *sine qua non* of gentle status. Even in the early sixteenth century differences are apparent between the customary tenants, as the acreages they held varied considerably. In East Brent in 1516 85 customary tenants held anything from 62 acres to less than five, and in 1607 from 108 acres to less than five, as Table 6 shows.

---

185 Alice married John Smith, clerk; Mary married Tristram Towse, notary.

186 Information on the Bower family taken from J.M. Horn and D.S. Bailey (eds), *Fasti Ecclesiae Anglicanae 1541–1857*, vol. V, Bath & Wells Diocese (London, 1979), p. 67; Colby, *Visitation 1623*, p. 12; TNA, C 142/688/23; C 142/760/59; SP 28/214, Seq. Accts Bempstone Hundred; F. Brown (ed.), *Abstracts of Somersetshire Wills*, 6 vols (privately printed for F.A. Crisp, 1887–90), pp. 54–5; T.J. Hunt and P.N. Dawe (eds), *Notes and Queries for Somerset and Dorset*, 26 (1955), pp. 232–6; F.W. Weaver, *Somerset Incumbents* (Bristol, 1889), p. 39; J. Foster, *Alumni Oxonienses: 1500–1714* [1892], I.

187 SHC, Q/SR/95/40–41.

Table 6
Size and number of customary holdings in East Brent

Total acres held by each tenant	No. of tenants in 1516	No. of tenants in 1607
Houses, shops, curtilage under 2 a.	5	11
Under 5 a.	3	2
5–10 a.	5	9
11–20 a.	20	16
21–30 a.	23	28
31–40 a.	11	12
41–50 a.	13	7
51–62 a.	6	6
Over 90 a.[(a)]	0	2
Total of customary tenants	86	93

Notes: (a) Holdings of 91 a. and 108 a. each consisting of two copyholds. Two other tenants each held by two copies (31 a. and 20 a.; 21 a. and 27 a.).
Sources: 1516: BL, Eg. MS. 3034, ff. 105–30; 1607: TNA, LR 2/225, ff. 53–114.

The subsidy-payers in 1525 who can be identified as copyholders also varied considerably in the value of their assessed goods, and testators in the 1540s definitely identified as copyholders had inventories valued between £3 and £38. By the late sixteenth century certain individuals and families became prominent in building up holdings of land in the area, and illustrate the continual undulation and change in rural society.

John Lyning of Tarnock was a member of such a copyholding family in the area. He, or a namesake, held two messuages and 29 acres in East Brent in 1516, and with his mother Joan he definitely held two tenements, 20 acres of customary land and 23 acres of overland in Tarnock by copy from 1525. He also took a 99-year lease of a windmill in the manor of Lympsham and held a freehold messuage and 12½ acres,[188] and another 3½ acres in Tarnock, possibly property he had bought *c.*1558.[189] Lyning died in 1564 followed by his only son, also John, about two years later, leaving the latter's sister Edith heir to his property. Soon after her father's death Edith had married Thomas Sayard of Lympsham, son of a copyholder who had also died in 1564 holding land in Lympsham, Berrow and Brent. In 1565 and 1566 Thomas was involved in a number of Chancery cases, mainly involving his wife's inheritance. He brought a case against Edith's stepmother for her marriage portion of £20, and paid £20 to settle another claim on the windmill, which was also part of Edith's portion. The most important case, however, was that brought against him by Edward Seymour, earl of Hertford, in 1566. Hertford stated he had previously

188 Another source gives 13½ acres: SHC, DD\FD/2.

189 BL, Egerton MS 3034, ff. 121d, 127; SHC, T\PH\vch/38; TNA, C 3/39/59; Hawkins, *Sales of Wards*, p. 41.

brought a case against Lyning, who had claimed to have bought a quarter part of Seymour's manor of Tarnock, but who was later said to have admitted he had only bought a quarter of the rents. Lyning had died before signing an agreement to this effect with Hertford, and the Sayards now claimed the quarter part, 'presuming on the wealth they had inherited from their fathers to get the earl's lands'. In 1572 an agreement was reached whereby Thomas and Edith sold to the earl their share in Tarnock and the earl assigned to them and to Edith's heirs the freehold of various closes, oxenleases and rents totalling 60 acres in the manor of Lympsham Parva.[190] Though Hertford was suffering political eclipse when the case began, he was still a great nobleman and landed magnate with considerable property and influence in Somerset, yet first Lyning and then Sayard, both just local husbandmen, were able to resist his claims against them and obtain a successful settlement. Sayard was living in Axbridge and styled gentleman at the end of his life: he was godfather to one of the Wrentmore children, and Jasper Wrentmore and Thomas Hall, two of Axbridge's leading citizens, were among the overseers of his will.[191]

Another family who established themselves in local society were the Boultings of Wedmore, who held copyhold in Mudgley and Godney, but took advantage of the break-up of manors to acquire freehold as well. William Boulting of Wedmore, husbandman, was one of five men who bought parts of the freehold of the manor of Mudgley when it was sold off from 1610; Boulting bought two messuages and 50 acres and the ten-acre Park Close. By the time he died in 1654, styled gentleman, he had also purchased part of the parsonage of Blackford, formerly a chapelry, land in Weare and Blackford and leaseholds in Burnham and Langport. He married three times, his second wife bringing him leasehold property in Blackford. Two of his daughters married local gentlemen and both his sons were designated 'Mr' in the parish registers. The elder son, William, received his father's freehold and in 1670 built or rebuilt his house at Theale, known as Theale Great House.[192] His eldest son, also William, who died in 1705, bore arms, and the year after his death the latter's son and heir, yet another William, was admitted to Corpus Christi College, Oxford, and later to Lincoln's Inn.[193]

The most interesting of these well-to-do copyholding families is perhaps the Westovers, who provided two members who combined farming with medicine. The family had two principal branches, one in Wedmore and the other in Allerton, both with land in both parishes. From the Wedmore branch, John Westover senior (d. 1679) had a freehold near the borough as well as copy and leasehold land. His eldest son John (d. 1706) made further purchases of freehold, including the freehold of two parcels the family had rented for some decades. Both John senior and John junior were barber-surgeons, but both were also fully engaged in farming as well; John junior's particular

---

190 TNA, PROB 11/49/259; C 3/115/61; C 3/25/8; C 3/159/27; C 3/160/21; C 3/174/91; C 3/161/30; SHC, DD\AB/22: the fine said the Earl paid 170 marks (£113 6s 8d).

191 SHC, D\D/cd/36, 11 Sep. 1604, dep. of Thomas Sayard; TNA, PROB 11/118/90.

192 Above, Chap. 2.

193 SHC, DD\SAS/C795/PR/462; BL, Egerton MS 3034, ff. 64d, 66, 68d; TNA, PROB 11/253/492; Hervey, *Wedmore Chronicle*, II, pp. 47–8, 291, 317; Foster, *Alumni Oxonienses: 1500–1714*.

claim to fame rests on being the first doctor known to have provided residential care for mental patients.[194]

Conclusion

Local farming families did not disappear from the copyholders' ranks, but economic and social changes meant that many of their descendants ceased to be farmers, and the demand for copyholds and the consequent high fines and purchase prices meant that few ordinary husbandmen who were not already secured tenants could find the capital to buy a copyhold, however small the parcels of land. Copyholds became more and more just pieces of landed investment which enabled their holders to live on an income from rents and pursue other occupations.

Viewed from the position of the nobility and gentry – the view taken by many agrarian historians, and one that blurs the distinctions within local society – the manorial tenant is the bottom rung of an economic and social hierarchy of landholders. Viewed from within that society, however, the copyholder – however small his holding – ceases to be some kind of servile peasant at the bottom of the pile: the existence of the manor and the security of customary tenure gave the copyholder a financial position among the richest inhabitants of the area, with an income derived more and more from rents than from direct farming. Much of their independence was a result of the manorial structure, and the security and value of copyhold set the tenants apart financially from the rest of the agrarian population. The fact that copyhold land in the Levels was held only for life was not perhaps as much of a disadvantage as it might seem today. Many freehold estates were held only for life: from the late Middle Ages it was common for the owner of a freehold to settle it by conveying it to trustees to hold for the benefit of the owner and his wife for their lives, and then some further life – possibly a bride or groom as part of a marriage settlement, for example. These arrangements were common in all levels of society, quite apart from the strict life settlements that became commonplace among large aristocratic landowners, and copyholds and life leaseholds performed a similar function. Though they did not confer the gentle status that freehold could, the holders were certainly considered to be yeomen.

Customary law in the early sixteenth century should not be regarded as a quaint survival soon to be swept away, but rather as just another level of property law that had been left to local control by the Crown three centuries earlier when freeholders received the protection of the central common law courts. By the late fifteenth century the situation was changing: serfdom had largely disappeared[195] and customary

194 See Ch. 4 for John junior's farming activities; farm work was done by agents, employees and patients (in lieu of fees): SHC, DD\X\HKN. Sources for Westover family: DD\X\HKN, ff. 152d, 211; Hervey, *Wedmore Chronicle*, II, pp. 82–168.

195 A few manumissions occurred up to 1540s in Cheddar, Mark and Wedmore: Historical Manuscripts Commission, *Calendar of the Manuscripts of the Dean and Chapter of Wells*, 2 vols (1907–14), II, pp. 208, 217–18, 259. In 1568 a bondman of manor of Mark was reported to hold in villeinage and had no goods except by licence of the lord: SHC, D\D/cd/12 (Pricker v. White, 18 Jan. 1568/9).

tenants sought the same central and royal protection for their property rights as freeholders enjoyed.[196] At the same time, copyhold and copyholders were fast losing their agricultural connection in the same way that the manor was changing from an economic to a solely tenurial institution. As the subject of litigation, copyhold shows its similarities with freehold and, like freeholds, copyholds were no longer land in the sense of an area of soil, but had become articles to be shuffled around in legal processes, or counters in investment and speculation. Just as the relationship of the copyholder to agriculture had become more tenuous, so had the relationship of secure tenure to the land: the price of freehold or copyhold land was as much the result of financial and market factors as of the value of its produce.

Nevertheless, the value placed on land in the Brent Marsh area must always to some extent depend on the quality of that land and its agricultural produce, and at certain periods this meant that very small proprietors and husbandmen without a secure tenancy could also enjoy some prosperity, an aspect which is discussed in the following chapter.

196 Simpson, *History of the Land Law*, pp. 152–5; Garrett-Goodyear, 'Common Law and Manor Courts', pp. 35–51.

Chapter 4

Making a living from the land

Any study of Somerset's agriculture in this period is hampered by the lack of a most important source, probate inventories, the bulk of which were destroyed in the Second World War. This loss has made it impossible to make a detailed analysis of a large sample of farmers, such as those carried out for other parts of England, but in many ways this is no bad thing, since an inventory, recording the situation at one moment in time, can conceal some of the most important aspects of animal husbandry. Plenty of other evidence does exist from which to draw a general picture of the field systems of the area, the types of husbandry followed and the choices made by individual farmers in deciding their farm production. It is also possible to assess the sorts of income that could be made from farming or from renting out land.

Land use in the Levels

This part of the Somerset Levels included three types of terrain: the inland, low-lying parishes among the moors; the coastal parishes with large enclosed pastures and access to moors; and the Mendip edge parishes with both rough hillside grazing above and low-lying meadow and moor below.

The edges of the moors shaded off into cultivated areas of enclosed meadow and pasture,[1] which, like the moors, benefited from winter flooding by the rivers, while the arable lay on higher and dryer ground. Meadow and pasture held in severalty lay in parcels or closes within enclosures. The formation of enclosures was essential if the land was to be used productively, as enclosures in the levels were made by digging rhynes whose most important function was to drain the land. They made useful boundaries, as major rhynes were about eight feet wide at the top, narrowing slightly towards the base, and were five feet deep; they were much cheaper to construct than any other form of enclosure and in summer could be stopped up for watering the stock.[2] The fields thus formed were comparatively large, from about 20 acres to as much as 60 in the old rich grazing lands described by Locke.[3] They were rarely in the hands of one tenant but were shared by several, and in some the use varied between arable, meadow and pasture, sometimes in open strips, sometimes in closes within the fields, which also occurred in arable fields.

As was generally the case throughout England, good meadow was by far the most valuable land in an economy which included large numbers of livestock that needed to be fed through the winter: in 1525 meadow in Huntspill was valued at 3s

---

1 Often called meadow-and-pasture, and differentiated from pasture or meads. Possibly a local usage referring to its dual use; Prof. John Broad suggested it might refer to rotational mowing.

2 Williams, *Draining of the Somerset Levels*, p. 187 and n.

3 Locke, 'Historical Account of the Marsh-Lands', p. 259.

4d an acre, twice as much as arable or enclosed pasture,[4] and in Burnham in 1694, while some land described as meadow or pasture fetched 11s or 12s an acre, the best meadows were said to be worth 30s an acre.[5] This, together with conversion to pasture in the coastal parishes – described below – confirms the importance of animal husbandry over arable. Rental rates for arable consistently fell below those obtained for meadow and pasture: in 1645 land in the hundred of Brent fetched an average of 7s 3d an acre for arable, 9s 9d for pasture and 13s for meadow, while in the hundred of Bempstone an average of 13s 6d was obtained for meadow-and-pasture and 11s 10d for pasture.[6] In the 1650s pasture in the coastal parishes of East Brent and Huntspill used for grazing was let at 20s an acre.[7]

Direct evidence of field patterns in the form of maps and plans, with or without field books, does not survive for any of the 16 parishes before the mid eighteenth century, when a few pre-enclosure estate maps can be found. Surveys are more numerous, but are tenurial rather than field surveys, and the details of each holding tended to become 'fossilised' and ceased to refer accurately to the land and its use: most were apparently drawn up from the copies of court rolls or from previous surveys rather than from a view of the land and holdings. Surveys of manors of the dean and chapter of Wells in this area were particularly prone to repeating former descriptions of tenements giving only the barest details, such as a 'tenement and 14 acres of land, meadow, and pasture', or 'tenement and 15 acres 3 yards (roods) of land and 4 acres 1 yard of meadow': these descriptions are repeated in every grant, surrender or survey of the property throughout the period.[8]

Though surveys are not a reliable guide to actual cultivation, they do indicate what many eighteenth-century surveys labelled as the 'quality' of the land – fitness for a certain use – and, though the land use may have changed, the surveys indicate the original use and origin, whether part of the original settlement or taken out of the moors later on. Much additional information can also be gleaned from manorial court records, deeds and legal records to give a picture of field systems which differed between the inland, coastal and Mendip parishes.

Inland parishes

Despite the growing economic importance of animal husbandry in the area, arable remained a significant part of the local farming economy, especially in the inland parishes. Where detailed surveys exist they show that the percentage of arable in inland manors could be quite high: in the two manors in Wedmore that have surviving surveys, arable formed about 60 per cent of each manor (excluding moor and common meadow) in the late sixteenth and early seventeenth centuries,[9] considerably more

4 TNA, E 315/385, ff. 90–95d.

5 TNA, E 134/5WandM/Mich23.

6 TNA, SP 28/214, sequestrators' accounts.

7 TNA, E 126/6, f. 252d; SHC, D\P\hun/3/2/3.

8 SHC, DD\CC, court documents of manors of Allerton and Biddisham.

9 Croot, 'Agrarian Society', p. 485, Table 11.

than in those coastal manors for which surveys exist. Most arable lay in open arable fields in the seventeenth century. A map drawn up in 1787 of the manor of Allerton showed the outlines of three large arable fields lying north, south and east of the main settlement, with much of the arable still in open strips, although by the eighteenth century many strips had been enclosed and the fields had been subdivided and renamed. The village of Allerton lay on the western slope of Wedmore island, with the arable on the higher ground of the parish; to the west of the village lay meadow in large closes, and further west again were Allerton and Binham moors, lying at the lowest point in the parish. The droveways and the common pasture of Binham moor were still open common in 1787.[10]

Other manors seem to have been based on a two-field arable system, which may have been common to all the manors in the parish of Wedmore, using different combinations of the parish's several fields. In the manor of Churchland in Wedmore, for example, the two-field system had not yet broken up when it was surveyed in about 1610.[11] Over half the land in the manor was open-field arable, which lay chiefly in the east and west fields: tenants holding arable had parcels more or less evenly divided between two of the many open fields in Wedmore, with 28 tenants holding land in the east and west fields, three in the south and west fields, two in Cocklake and Crickham fields, two in east and south fields, and three in other combinations involving Wedmore field. Though no contemporary plan of the parish exists, a plan of 1805 shows remnants of the open fields, which apparently covered most of the land over 50–75 feet above sea level. Piecemeal enclosures had eroded a great deal of the open-field area by then, but enough remained to indicate where the fields lay. Blackford's south field was so named on the plan, and there were about six or seven other fields, unnamed, most of which contained strips belonging to several manors in the seventeenth century, which accounts for the great discrepancy in the total acreage of each field in any one manorial survey.[12] In 1610 Churchland manor had a few closes of arable and two enclosures totalling 2½ acres had been made in the west field, one converted to pasture, but otherwise the open-field arable system was intact. However, there are no court rolls nor any other firm evidence to show that a common rotation was followed, and incidental evidence, discussed below, seems to indicate that it was not. One-fifth of the land in the manor was meadow, 137 acres in closes and 64½ acres in open parcels; some meadows, such as Southmead, contained both.

Although the open arable fields were maintained in these inland parishes, strict regulation of rotation and common management was seldom found here by the sixteenth century because of the large quantity of common grazing on the moors. Orders and bylaws concerning the arable fields are few among the extant court rolls and are mainly concerned with keeping stock from straying onto the sown fields from the paths and ways where many were grazed, or with excluding stock from the corn fields at the appropriate times. However, as in the case of the moors, attempts were occasionally made to reduce the number of sheep grazed, as most arable fields were

---

10 SHC, DD\CC/T/10860 (map); DD\CC/B/110563 (reference book for map).

11 SHC, DD\GS/20. Date and identity of manor from internal and other evidence.

12 SHC, DD\X\MRD, plan of Wedmore 1805.

still subject to common rights of pasture for the customary tenants in the sixteenth and seventeenth centuries. Those with grazing rights in the fields could turn their animals out onto the stubble after harvest, but ran the risk of having them impounded if any grain was still left in the field.[13]

Though tenants made use of grazing in the arable fields, they probably did so more to manure the fields than because they needed somewhere to graze their stock.[14] Since grazing the stubble was not as beneficial to the stock as grazing the moors and pastures, some farmers preferred to buy loads of manure for their fields, and distinguished between the qualities of the various types.[15] Manuring is not referred to very often, but was clearly a commonplace of farming practice here: a common expression for someone who actually inhabited a holding and worked the land was 'manuring' the farm rather than just 'occupying' it, which could refer simply to tenure of the property and not necessarily to the physical presence there of a person or his stock.[16]

The lack of necessity of grazing rights on the arable is reflected in the lack of concern over the enclosure of parcels in the fields. Though the enclosure of parcels was apparently not yet widespread in the inland parishes,[17] where it did occur only half-hearted steps were taken by the tenants to prevent it: the main objection seems to have been the failure to pay a fine for the licence to enclose, rather than any disruption to farming that resulted. In 1520 seven named tenants 'and many others' of the manor of Allerton were presented for enclosing land on which all tenants should have common between midsummer and the beginning of February, but no further steps against them are recorded.[18] In 1566 the homage of Biddisham was ordered to enquire whether the enclosure by John Cooke and others of a common field called 'souther parte' of Biddisham field was injurious to the tenants, but again no further action was taken.[19] In 1615 a lease of demesne land of the manor of Blackford included a close of seven acres one yard of arable called New Close, 'lately inclosed and taken in out of the north common field of Blackford', but most of the demesne arable was still in open strips. Even cottages were built on parcels of open arable in Blackford, such as 'as little cottage newly erected on the north-east end of one acre of arable in the Southfield'.[20] Clearly a great deal of enclosing went on without remark. The Levels was not generally an area where large-scale and widespread enclosures were made by gentry or outsiders, but was typical of areas where much

---

13 SHC, Q/SR/95/40–41.

14 TNA, E 134/4WandM/East8.

15 SHC, DD\X\HKN, f. 154d.

16 TNA, E 134/4WandM/East8; E 134/5WandM/Mich23.

17 However, this assumption is made from surveys, and they cannot be relied upon to reveal recent enclosure and other changes.

18 SHC, DD\CC/B/131920/10, Allerton 24 Oct. 12 Hen. VIII.

19 SHC, DD\CC/B/131907/17, Biddisham 2 Apr. 8 Eliz. See Chap. 3, Customary tenure: Forfeiture.

20 SHC, DD\SE/26/2–16, leases Sexey to Harris, 20 Aug. 13 Jas I, and others, Sexey to Smith alias Martin, 16 Apr. 10 Jas I.

more enclosure was carried out piecemeal by the inhabitants themselves.[21] One of Charles I's enclosure commissioners in 1635, a Mr Powell, was a Somerset man who remarked on the enclosure movement as 'increasing and transcending from mean tenants to great landlords' and from small quantities of land to whole townships.[22]

Lack of control over enclosure was matched by lack of control over rotation and conversion: the sources give the impression that land use was left to individual choice. Occasional references are made to ploughing up and converting to tillage, which was prevented by covenants in leases,[23] probably because arable was worth less than meadow and pasture and the wrong treatment could damage good grassland.[24]

With the freedom to enclose and convert land went freedom in the choice of crops, despite the continuation of common grazing over the arable fields. John Westover, in a note of plough-work to be done in 1695, wanted three yards at Blackford Causeway furlong ploughed for wheat if it could be done in time, but if not then it was to be used for beans. Another time he paid a man who carted, at the same time, both a load of peas and two loads of wheat for him from the east field.[25] In 1638 a furlong of 3½ acres in Wedmore called Short Rodford divided by a path was in the same season ploughed on one side for wheat and on the other for beans.[26] Where there is information for a few years in succession, individuals do appear to have followed a three-course rotation for their own parcels, with a period of fallow before spring ploughing.[27]

Overall, although the extent of enclosure and changes in land use cannot be ascertained, the layout of the types of land shown in the plan of Allerton was typical of most villages in the inland parishes, confined as they were by the uncompromising topography of the moors.

Coastal parishes

Villages on the coastal belt had a different layout, and for the manors there more useful surveys survive, many giving the location of each parcel of land in the holdings,

---

21 Tate, *Somerset Enclosure Acts*, pp. 13–14. S. Brent is cited as one of the places without open-field arable in 1567, based probably on the survey of that date of the manor of S. Brent Huish. However, looking at this survey I can find no reason to suppose that land described, for example, as'1 acre in otegrotten' was not in open strips, as closes are described as such, and the descriptions are similar to those in the E. Brent Survey of 1607, which H.L. Gray used to demonstrate a manor with some open-field arable remaining.

22 Quoted in Tate, *Somerset Enclosure Acts*, 21.

23 A leaseholder with 60 acres in Moore would agree to pay his rent only if the steward would give him a discharge for having ploughed up the meadow contrary to the terms of his lease: TNA, REQ 2/44/59.

24 J. Broad,'Alternate Husbandry and Permanent Pasture in the Midlands, 1650–1800', *Agricultural History Review*, 28 (1980), pp. 83–4.

25 SHC, DD\X\HKN, f. 173.

26 SHC, D\D/cd/51, Hodges & others v. Gailerd, Hodges v. Tincknell, 19 July 1638.

27 e.g. the will of Ric. Jennett of Allerton in Weare, 1626, specified that fallow was to be broken the following spring: TNA, PROB 11/151/550.

so that, while the actual use may have changed, the field pattern is clearer.[28] Little common moor lay within the parish boundaries of most of the six coastal parishes (Berrow, East Brent, South Brent, Burnham, Huntspill, Lympsham) and only small parcels of waste, the tenants having common rights in the inland moors, principally Thurlmore; the entire area within the parish boundaries was divided up into irregularly shaped fields by the drainage rhynes. Some of the fields were predominantly arable, composed mainly of open strips, but certain parcels in those fields were also enclosed, and from an early date. In East Brent in 1516, for example, William Ballet, a customary tenant, had 2½ acres of arable in the west field in a close and another three acres in three strips in the same field.[29]

This system made conversion of land use fairly easy, so that some fields in the manor of South Brent contained arable, meadow and pasture, and common meadow,[30] and in Burnham the predominantly arable Worston field had some strips described as meadow in 1525.[31] As in the inland parishes, the arable fields were subject to common grazing. In Huntspill mares were grazed on the stubble in 1656,[32] and some of the common field of Worston still had open arable strips with common of pasture in 1674.[33] The percentage of arable in the coastal manors of Brent Marsh was generally less than in the inland manors, ranging from 20 to 44 per cent, and, where surveys for the early sixteenth century can be compared with those for the late sixteenth or early seventeenth, they all show a decline in the percentage of arable.[34] Incidental evidence supports the impression that there was more conversion to pasture from arable than *vice versa* there. In a case concerning the rent of tithes in Berrow, some witnesses commented in 1625 that only a quarter as much land had been 'ripped up' and converted to tillage than had been laid to pasture and meadow in the previous 12 years.[35]

In these manors the division of the individual holdings' open-field arable between the various common fields was not even, so clearly any common field rotation must have broken down long before; the survey of East Brent of 1607 was used by H.L. Gray to show the uneven breakdown typical of the coastal manors for which detailed surveys exist, with the bulk of the land held in enclosed parcels.[36] The arable land in 1607 can be compared with the survey of 1516, where 21 acres (about 3 per cent of the total arable land) was in closes, while in 1607 178 acres (about 28 per cent) was in closes.[37]

---

28 Though more detailed, the descriptions may also have descended from an earlier period, as the way they are described, including some idiosyncratic spellings, also occurs in descriptions of land in S. Brent in 1312: Dom A. Watkin (ed.), *The Great Chartulary of Glastonbury*, 2 vols (Somerset Record Society 63, 1952), II, pp. 541–3.

29 BL, Egerton MS 3034, f. 110d.

30 *Ibid.*, ff. 149–170d.

31 TNA, E 315/385, ff. 90–95d.

32 SHC, Q/SR/93/58.

33 SHC, DD\ALN/6, lease, Pittard to Wall.

34 Croot,'Agrarian Society', p. 485, Table 11.

35 TNA, E 178/4467.

36 H.L. Gray, *English Field Systems* (Cambridge, MA, 1915), p. 525.

37 Not all the arable land was used for crops, however; some was under grass.

The unevenness of the division of arable between the various fields was as apparent at the beginning of the sixteenth century as in the seventeenth. In 1516 a full holding in one of the four Glastonbury manors (Berrow, East Brent, South Brent, Lympsham) typically consisted of a messuage with curtilage and garden, an adjoining croft of an acre or so of pasture, a certain number of acres of land, meadow and pasture, all enclosed and held in severalty, together with a number of acres of open arable subject to common grazing.[38] It was not unusual for the holdings in these manors to have arable divided between two, four or even eight different places: overall, the arable parcels in East Brent manor were located in 31 fields or areas, but the largest acreages were in five fields: Westfield, 64½ acres; Snyghhampton field, 63½ acres; Hardland, 60¾ acres; Northyeofield, 54½ acres; and Eastfield, 52½ acres. Clearly, some time before the sixteenth century any strict two- or three-field system (if it had ever existed) had given way to a far more irregular pattern of cultivation. The names of many of the fields suggest that they were assarts probably originating during the period of medieval reclamation under successive abbots of Glastonbury between the twelfth and fourteenth centuries.[39]

Mendip parishes

Fields on the Mendip slope followed the disparate field pattern of the coastal parishes but were grouped rather like the inland parishes because of the limitations of the terrain. In 1674 the rectory manor of Compton Bishop consisted of parcels of arable totalling 31½ acres spread among seven fields, in addition to seven acres of arable in closes. Fourteen acres lay in closes of pasture, ten acres in closes of meadow or pasture and 23½ acres in closes of meadow, with another 4½ acres in two common meadows.[40] Though the settlements and fields were confined by the terrain, the inhabitants had the advantage of two types of extensive common grazing. On the upper slopes of the Mendip range was rough grazing suitable for sheep, while below the settlements were the rich moors watered by the river Axe. The meadows were formed near this river and the arable fields lay above them on the lower slopes around the settlements and roads. Only one manor, in the parish of Cheddar, has a surviving survey with details of the type of land held, which shows that only a quarter of its land was arable.[41]

Farming in the Levels

The wide range of field systems in the Levels, all under constant and gradual change, and the piecemeal nature of the field patterns, the strips and the closes, was reflected in the farm husbandry practised there, which was characterised by

---

38 BL, Egerton MS 3034.

39 P.J. Helm, 'The Somerset Levels in the Middle Ages (1086–1539)', *Journal of the British Archaeological Association*, 3rd ser. 12 (1949), pp. 42–4.

40 SHC, D\D/rg/74, terrier 1674.

41 Cheddar Vicars Choral, 1650: SHC, DD\CC/L/116013.

diversity and flexibility. The three types of land – arable, meadow, pasture – could be managed separately to a great extent and, as illustrated in connection with the arable fields, individuals had a good deal of freedom in deciding their farming practice. The Levels maintained dairy herds, steers and oxen, ewes and wethers, mares, horses and pigs, while ducks and geese were also kept on the moors. The region produced butter and cheese, wool and mutton, beef and hides, bacon, wheat, barley, beans, oats, apples and pears, honey, reeds, peat and timber. On the edge of the Mendips rabbits were farmed, and turnips, teasels, garlic and onions were added to the arable production. From this plenty, however, three strands emerge as the principal sources of income and the main commercial production of the Levels: dairying; the rearing and grazing of sheep, cattle and horses; and arable farming. However, while the grazing of animals, especially fattening, often involved people living outside the area, dairying and arable farming were rarely carried on by non-residents, since both were labour-intensive and, in the case of dairying, required close daily attention. Only one non-resident had arable in Huntspill in 1693, and Edward Strode of Downside (Shepton Mallet), with his few acres of arable in Badgworth, was exceptional, and gave rise to a discussion in the Exchequer Court in the 1690s about whether he counted as an inhabitant of the parish or an outliver, since he kept a house, servant and plough in the parish.[42]

Dairying

Dairying was the most widespread husbandry throughout the period for residents of the area: all but two of the 25 surviving inland inventories had dairy cattle, in herds of two to 16. Almost everyone kept pigs in conjunction with dairying, since they could be fed on the whey from cheese-making, and only three inventories did not also list calves or year-old stock to maintain the herd; in many cases they were obviously buying in to rear either for milk or beef. Wills also give an indication of the importance of dairy cattle here: out of the 414 lowland wills, 187 mention bequests totalling 562 dairy cattle alone, while sheep, which tended to be a common token bequest, are found in only 89 wills, and the total number of *all* adult sheep involved, ewes and wethers, is 552.[43]

Dairying was also the most widespread husbandry in the coastal parish of Huntspill in 1693, when 44 out of the 58 resident tithe-payers had herds in milk which ranged from one to 16, with a median of six, and only 10 per cent of the calves born during the year were sold within the year, the rest being kept either for the herd or for beef. The number of dairy cows kept was closely related to the amount of meadow mown by each individual, and on average between one and two acres of meadow were mown for every cow owned, with only three farmers keeping more cows than they had acres of meadow.[44]

---

42 SHC, D\P\hun/3/2/1; TNA, E 126/16, f. 45d.

43 In a few cases numbers were not given.

44 SHC, D\P\hun/3/2/1. Surprisingly, though pigs were tithable they are not listed in the book, though other evidence shows they were kept in the parish.

In the Mendip parishes, too, out of 17 inventories showing involvement in farming all but one had dairy herds ranging from one to 31. In three cases the cows kept were obviously for household supply only, but in 13 cases there were calves or young stock, indicating a well-balanced dairy interest; 15 inventories also had pigs. The overall farming picture differs from the lowlands though, and the wills illustrate the emphasis placed on sheep: while only 85 dairy cows were bequeathed in 49 of 164 Mendip wills, 601 adult sheep were bequeathed in 67 wills.

Dairying was an obvious and ideal husbandry for small family farms: it required intensive and constant labour, but in this period milking and cheese- and butter-making were carried out by the female members of the family or maidservants, leaving the men free for other husbandry tasks.[45] A good-sized herd could be managed by one or two women: in a big Suffolk dairy in the early sixteenth century there were around 15 cows for each woman employed, and it was claimed that in Suffolk one woman could manage 20 cows, presumably working full-time in the dairy, while in Hampshire the number was put at eight to nine, a more reasonable number if the dairywoman was also the housewife or a maidservant with other house or farm duties to perform. Twenty was also claimed for Norfolk and Somerset in the eighteenth century, but the average overall was probably around ten. A good rate of milking was considered to be six cows an hour, milked twice a day generally, and butter or cheese would have to be made daily or every couple of days, depending on the size of the herd.[46] Production and therefore income were spread over six to nine months of the year. Calving was usually timed for February to March, so that the cow's highest yield at the beginning of the lactation cycle would coincide with the new spring grass, thus boosting the yield still higher.[47]

Pigs were fed on whey plus anything else that was available, and beans were used here as elsewhere for fattening before slaughter for bacon: an Axbridge yeoman who left a bacon hog to his wife also left her six bushels of beans to fatten it with.[48] Much of the pig-meat produced was probably kept for home consumption, and 19 inventories record the presence of bacon. However, not all households reared their own pigs and some pig-dealing and selling to butchers was also carried on, particularly by small-scale husbandmen. John Gane of Wedmore, a husbandman or labourer, gave evidence regarding a few small purchases and sales he made in a period of about six

45 e.g. wives going to milk their cows in the moors: SHC, D\D/cd/51, 'detection' v. Hen. Lange, deps. of Eliz. Petheram and Katharine Napper, 3 Apr. 1623.

46 J. Whittle, 'Housewives and Servants in Rural England, 1440–1650: Evidence of Women's Work from Probate Documents', *Transactions of the Royal Historical Society*, 15 (2005), pp. 70–71; G.E. Fussell, *The English Dairy Farmer, 1500–1900* (London, 1966), pp. 160–63; R. Trow-Smith, *A History of British Livestock Husbandry, 1700–1900* (London, 1959), pp. 31, 179.

47 Material for dairying generally is from R. Trow-Smith, *A History of British Livestock Husbandry to 1700* (London, 1957), pp. 237–8; Fussell, *English Dairy Farmer*, *passim*; and for eighteenth-century Somerset, Billingsley, *General View*, pp. 144, 247–52.

48 Robert Loder of Berkshire used between four and six and a half bushels of dried pulses to fatten baconers in 1612 and 1613: Trow-Smith, *British Livestock Husbandry to 1700*, p. 251; TNA, PROB 11/143/45.

weeks. He bought two pigs, killed one and sold the other to a butcher; he then bought another pig, which he killed a week later, giving half to his lodger, and sold another pig he had to a Wedmore woman.[49]

Rearing and grazing of livestock

The grazing and fattening of animals in the Levels involved non-residents to a far greater degree than other farming. Grazing had low labour requirements which could be fulfilled by local men retained to keep an eye on the stock or employed as part-time herdsmen. Hugh Day, a butcher from Bishop's Lydeard near Taunton, hired a man who lived half a mile from a pasture in South Brent where he was grazing 60 to 80 sheep,[50] and a South Brent yeoman had been a herdsman in his youth to an Axbridge butcher and victualler, as had a Badgworth husbandman for another non-resident.[51] The interest of non-residents in taking land in parishes which included much rich pasture, especially in the coastal parishes with large enclosed pastures, is apparent in the sixteenth and seventeenth centuries,[52] and there is evidence to show that they were not just interested in investment in land, but used it to graze their own stock. They included butchers from local towns as well as graziers, but some of those keeping grazing animals along the coast lived quite far away, such as the Wiltshire man who kept sheep in Huntspill around 1632.[53] A grazier from Bath, William Master, took a new lease of a close of pasture of 48 acres in Biddisham plus two closes of meadow totalling 19 acres from the lord of the manor in 1617, surrendering a previous lease he held.[54] Ralph Synock (Senox), a butcher from Wells, held customary land in East Mark and Tarnock as well as Blackford.[55] In 1657 some 15 non-residents gave evidence concerning land they held in East Brent: a victualler from Ston Easton in the Mendips rented 30 acres, and another from Wells rented 120 acres, both using their land to graze cattle; a butcher, also from Wells, rented 40 acres in two closes, again for cattle. The information given indicates that these non-residents had been leasing land from at least the early seventeenth century.[56] In Huntspill in the same period several non-residents leased land to graze animals, and in 1693 about 28 non-residents owed tithes for agistment to the rector of Huntspill.[57] Edward Strode used most of the land he held in Badgworth for stock, fattening about a dozen oxen and 12 to 14 heifers in the 1680s.[58] In the same decade, and for several years previously, non-residents had

49 SHC, Q/SR/23/99–100.

50 SHC, Q/SR/40/15.

51 TNA, E 134/1657/E.15.

52 Above, Chap. 3, The use and attraction of copyhold for lives.

53 SHC, Q/SR/64/10.

54 SHC, DD\CC/B/110358.

55 TNA, E 134/20Jas1/Hil8; SHC, DD\S\WH/209; DD\SE/65/1–2, Survey 1657.

56 TNA, E 134/1657/ East15.

57 SHC, D\P\hun/3/2/1, /3.

58 TNA, E 134/4WandM/East8.

grazed cattle and sheep on Burnham's pastures, and one man grazed 100 sheep in a period of three months.[59]

Judging the involvement of residents in grazing and fattening can be problematic. Inventories do not show when the animals were bought nor when they would be sold, and many farmers with common grazing rights might buy in steers for the summer or just rent out keep to others, though the largest profit was to be found in wintering animals and selling in the spring. The accounts of a local grazier give a good indication of the kinds of transaction available to farmers large and small. Thomas Lovell was based in Axbridge and, in addition to actively buying and selling throughout the year, owned grazing in Burnham and elsewhere and also grazed sheep in Mark moor. His purchases varied in type from year to year: for example, in 1677 he bought 93 beasts (44 from Worcester fairs[60] and 20 at Stow) and 130 sheep in three transactions from Shroton (Iwerne Courtney, Dorset, near Blandford), and only 14 dairy cattle, but the following year, in addition to 40 beasts and 185 sheep, he bought 89 cows and heifers, mainly in single transactions and from named sellers in the Levels and parishes elsewhere in Somerset, sometimes at local fairs or markets.[61] The range and number of his purchases indicates both a ready market for farmers with one or two animals to sell and the importance of the local markets and fairs in enabling small farmers to prosper by tapping into the growing livestock trade.

Cattle

How far residents, particularly husbandmen, were involved in grazing and fattening cattle is unclear. The sample of inventories is too small to do more than indicate involvement in beef farming. Steers and two-year-olds are mentioned in 11 lowland inventories, both inland and coastal, in numbers from two to 23, always in conjunction with dairying. Oxen occur in 12 inventories in numbers of one to six: their presence may be primarily for labour rather than for fattening, though one inventory appraised fat oxen and plough oxen separately. Steers, bullocks and two-year-olds occur in only 35 wills and in small numbers, only once exceeding eight, when John Sheres of Burnham left 18 or more in 1559.[62] Of the 18 Mendip inventories, ten listed steers, generally in addition to dairy herds, in numbers from one to 12, plus one of 19 including calves, and ten had between two and six oxen, plus the 16 of George Rodney, of which 12 were working oxen.[63]

Evidence from Huntspill at the end of the seventeenth century shows that beef farming was pursued on an erratic scale. Some men just reared their own calves for market; others made odd purchases and sales of cattle during the year. However, the short-term fattening of sizeable herds, similar to the sheep fattening discussed below, is not apparent as far as residents are concerned, and was probably not very

59 TNA, E 134/5WandM/East10.

60 Worcester had four annual livestock fairs, important for droving trade from Wales: Wrightson, *Earthly Necessities*, p. 96.

61 Wilts & Swindon RO, 161/57 (bdl. 3).

62 TNA, PROB 11/43/75.

63 TNA, E 178/1992.

common here.[64] Since the main markets for beef were the urban centres, principally London and Bristol, this area of England was not so useful for the final fattening before slaughter, and was better placed for rearing over a longer period. On the other hand, since steers did not beef-up until four or five years – three years for heifers[65] – rearing home-bred stock was not recommended, since it would make a strain on the small farmer's grazing and winter keep unless he had access to moorland grazing. For those with grazing on the moors or good pasture the situation was easier, as the animals required only light winter keep until near slaughter. The dual purpose of oxen and steers – a yoke of steers, for example – also obscures the prevalence of fattening, and even cows of most of the breeds common in the period were useful beef animals when their milking life was over. Eleven men out of the 58 farmers in Huntspill in 1693 were grazing cattle comprising ten steers, 23 yearlings and six cows (two barren). The balance here seems to be in favour of rearing and selling off quite young, allowing others to do the final fattening. However, the sales made that year are fairly evenly balanced between young and mature stock: four steers, six yearlings, one heifer and two oxen, fattened, plus 28 of the calves born that year.[66] It seems likely that most of the farming residents of the Levels would use their pasture to fatten a few animals, in addition to some other source of farming income such as dairying, and could participate profitably in the growing fatstock trade of the area. John Westover of Wedmore is a good illustration of this. During the years covered by his journal he made a number of transactions concerning beef cattle. He grazed yearlings from the end of April for 21 weeks, renting grazing for them in addition to using the moors, and sold them in the autumn; he bought steers which he sold in the spring, and bought oxen in April, which he sold the following February.[67]

Sheep

Sheep were kept both for wool and for meat, but the evidence is too disparate to say which was more prevalent, nor the number of sheep involved; certainly there is plenty of evidence for breeding and wool production, as well as fattening. In Huntspill in 1693 38 out of 58 farming residents kept sheep long enough to obtain wool and lambs from them, notwithstanding the emphasis on fattening in the area, and wool still played a large part in the economy of the small farmers here. Some 923 sheep were shorn in 1693, nearly twice the number kept for fattening only, but only 323 lambs were born, which, even allowing for low lambing rates, probably means the majority of the sheep were wethers. The median flock size in Huntspill was about 20.[68] Wool was in any case a by-product of all sheep farming, as any flocks kept through the summer would have to be sheared if the sheep were more than a year old.[69] The breeds of sheep kept are also something of a mystery, but the white horned Dorset was present in the

---

64 SHC, D\P\hun/3/2/1.

65 Trow-Smith, *British Livestock Husbandry to 1700*, p. 239.

66 SHC, D\P\hun/3/2/1.

67 SHC, DD\X\HKN, ff. 97, 169d, 171, 182d.

68 SHC, D\P\hun/3/2/1.

69 SHC, DD\SH/33, Wedmore parsonage accounts.

area in 1680, as were Irish sheep, and a white 'Tittling or Suckwell' ram was reared by a Compton Bishop labourer in 1649.[70] Sheep were more important in the Mendip parishes, with the rough grazing available there, than in the lowland, and were more often mentioned in wills.[71] Of the 18 Mendip inventories only eight list sheep, but these are in sizeable numbers: one a 'flock', the others 20, 33, 40 ('fat sheep'), 75, 133, 249 (including 59 lambs) and 251. In the lowland inventories sheep are mentioned in 13 inventories (including a man with a single wether), but in the seven which give numbers the totals of all kinds of sheep and lambs reach double figures only twice, with 15 and 50, and in wills the numbers of adult sheep are rarely in double figures: about 30 was the largest, apart from a flock of '100 rams' in 1528, which, though owned by a lowland resident, were kept on land he held on Mendip.[72]

The larger flock sizes of the Mendips were also reflected in the wills, where half the sheep bequeathed were in groups of ten or more: two groups totalled 100 and 160 and another seven were over 50, and these, of course, represent minimum flock sizes, not totals. Flocks of 40 to 150 were probably common: it was not an area suitable for vast numbers, but moderate flocks could make good use of the large area of rather poor common grazing on the Mendips to provide an income from wool and lambs. In the lowlands, however, inhabitants would not squander all their grazing resources on sheep, but might keep some for wool or meat on the moors: numbers ranging from 10 to 100 are mentioned in various disputes, but most men probably had only a few. Sheep appear to have been a great nuisance and crop up in records such as quarter sessions rolls with a frequency out of all proportion to their importance, and certainly more often than all other stock together. They were always straying or being stolen or dying under mysterious circumstances, and their presence obviously provoked acute temptation in some of the inhabitants who needed the odd fleece or joint of mutton, since men and women were constantly being forced to think up ingenious explanations for quarters of mutton found in their pots, heads hidden in their gardens, skins in their lofts and bags of tallow hanging in trees.

Grazing sheep for short periods is even less likely to show up in inventories in a representative way not only because of its short-term nature but because it required active bargaining and selling, and was less likely, therefore, to be undertaken by ailing or aged farmers. Evidence from the Huntspill tithe book is therefore particularly welcome. In Huntspill the late seventeenth-century tithe customal laid down a rate for 'sheep bought in and sold out at divers times in the year by the parishioners and inhabitants ... which are kept and depastured on the enclosed lands for every score 4d by the month'[73] with a similar rate for grazing on the commons and moors, where tithe wool was not paid. To compute the tithe, the flock size and time kept were noted in the tithe book. In 1693 16 of the 58 farming residents grazed sheep in flocks numbering between five and 50 for periods ranging from one month to eight months,

70 SHC, Q/SR/146/20; 81/93–5.

71 See above, Dairying.

72 F.W. Weaver (ed.), *Somerset Medieval Wills, 1501–30* (Somerset Record Society 19, 1903), pp. 270–71.

73 SHC, D\P\hun/3/2/2.

with six months being the most common. Three of the 16 farmers grazed more than one flock during the year, and the total number of sheep grazed in this way was 540.[74] The fact that the tithe customal makes provision for short-term grazing suggests that this had been carried on for some time past, since customals tended to become fixed and took time to change.

Short-term grazing was also carried on in Wedmore in the early seventeenth century. The numbers were the subject of a tithe dispute so cannot be relied upon and the evidence, concerning stock grazed by Robert Hole in 1624, is slightly conflicting, but the timing of the purchases and sales seems to have been agreed by both parties: Hole bought between 60 and 100 sheep in late summer and grazed them through the winter, buying more in the spring, and then selling some before shearing while keeping the rest to shear himself. The buying and selling could thus be easily varied as dictated by the prices for sheep or wool, the amount of feed available or the need for cash.[75]

Horses

Horses were used for personal travel and hauling to markets and for farm work, though oxen were still also commonly used for the latter. The make-up of plough teams varied a good deal between individuals: in 1690 John Westover's accounts for plough work done for him record several individuals and their teams, which varied between two oxen, four oxen, four oxen and one horse, and four oxen and two horses,[76] while Edward Strode kept a team of four oxen and one horse for his arable in Badgworth.[77] Most of the extant inventories mention horses or mares, and some list 'horse beasts', suggesting working horses. Riding horses are often specified as such. Though only four of those inventories giving numbers have more than five horses listed excluding young, the value for unenumerated horse beasts suggests herd sizes around three, four, seven and 12. One Cheddar inventory lists 15 horse beasts in addition to six oxen, while another listed three pairs of horses and their harness. In a Wedmore inventory there were six mares and four colts. Only rarely are more than a couple of horses mentioned in wills.

Horses were fairly widely kept, therefore, and most owners bred from their mares if they were not required for heavy work on a full-time basis, but, as has been pointed out, horse-breeding and rearing as a staple occupation required more capital and meant waiting longer for returns than any other type of husbandry.[78] However, like the grazing of cattle and sheep, it fitted in well in a mixed farming economy that included large grazing resources. This part of the Levels was noted for horse-breeding by the end of the seventeenth century, when Defoe commented on the numbers of very large

74 SHC, D\P\hun/3/2/1.

75 TNA, SP 16/165, no. 56.

76 SHC, DD\X\HKN, f. 107.

77 TNA, E 134/4WandM/East8.

78 *AHEW4*, p. 673.

colts bred there for the last hundred years at least;[79] indeed, a tradition of breeding dates back to the activities of the abbey of Glastonbury in the fourteenth century.[80] Evidence from specialist horse fairs indicates that many residents of the Brent Marsh parishes regularly sold horses at fairs such as Winchester in July, where they were sold to buyers from elsewhere in Somerset and other southern counties, as well as Devon and Cornwall. In the years 1620–25 breeders from the Levels provided about 60 per cent of the horses in the Winchester toll books, and of the horses described in detail nearly 80 per cent were colts.[81] The sellers included 53 men from ten of the Brent Marsh parishes (the six coastal parishes plus Cheddar, Wedmore, Mark and Badgworth), who paid tolls on sales of 79 colts, eight horses, two nags, one gelding and six unspecified. Six of the men appeared in more than one of the four years examined for the 1620s: John Lion of Lympsham was one of the regular attenders, selling a horse and a colt in 1620, two colts in 1621, three colts in 1623 and two colts in 1625. Although the number participating had dropped in the 1640s, four men from East Brent, Huntspill and Mark in 1647 and seven from Allerton, East Brent and Mark in 1648 paid tolls on a total of 12 colts, five horses and one gelding. These local men were rarely recorded as buyers, though, interestingly, several of the buyers of the Brent Marsh horses came from nearby parishes in Somerset, such as Ditcheat and Castle Cary, and those buyers in turn sold horses on at fairs as far afield as Shrewsbury, Kidderminster and Derby.[82]

Incidental references bear out the interest in breeding and selling. The two wills with the largest totals of horses mentioned were those of Isabel Councell of Wedmore in 1580, with eight mares, and of John Hooper of East Brent in 1587, with seven young horses.[83] Hooper had formed a partnership with another local man, John Boulting, in some horse-dealing enterprises, selling 11 colts for a profit of 40s in 1583, and was owed 3s 4d for the profit on a colt bought from a Burnham man and 36s 8d for a colt sold on his behalf by Boulting.[84] George Carde of Draycott in Cheddar had 18 unspecified horses in 1689: although he had a good deal of arable, he also had four oxen, so it is likely that some of the horses were largely for breeding and selling.[85] In Huntspill 40 out of the 58 farmers in 1693 had colts born during the year; one man had seven born and another had five, while two or three were common. About six of the residents had mares, colts and young horses in excess of reasonable requirements for draught and carriage. The largest herd belonged to George Winter, who had six mares, one colt, one stallion, five yearlings and three other horses, but no arable to work. Sales were made by residents during the year of seven colts, three

79 Defoe, *Tour Thro' Great Britain*, I, p. 271; P. Edwards, *The Horse Trade of Tudor and Stuart England* (Cambridge, 1988), p. 32.

80 I.J.E. Keil, 'The Estates of the Abbey of Glastonbury in the Later Middle Ages', PhD thesis (University of Bristol, 1964), p. 81.

81 Edwards, *Horse Trade*, pp. 34–5.

82 Information taken from Prof. Peter Edwards's transcripts of the Magdalen Hill Fair toll books.

83 TNA, PROB 11/63/485; PROB 11/71/68.

84 TNA, PROB 11/71/68.

85 Hervey, *Wedmore Chronicle*, II, p. 160; SHC, DD/BRC/27.

young horses and three other horses: two colts sold at Matthews fair (Huntspill) to another parishioner fetched £2 each, but another colt bought for £2 was sold for £6, suggesting that the colts were bred for different uses or quality.[86]

Other livestock

While most people kept some poultry, whether hens, ducks or geese, near their dwellings or on the moors, a few farmers kept geese in numbers that suggest a commercial enterprise. In Huntspill in the 1570s one resident had six brood geese and some 40 young,[87] while particularly large numbers were found near Wedmore and on its common moors. One resident kept about 140 geese at a time for several years around 1678, while his uncle had 200, and he reckoned there were nearly 3,000 in the parish as a whole at that time.[88] These large numbers seem to be concentrated on Panborough moor, which lay to the north of Wedmore and was crossed by the river Axe, rather than the moors to the south, which were drier and more useful for cattle. Geese were valuable enough to be worth stealing on a large scale: in 1680 a Wedmore man drove about 30 out of Burtle moor just before Christmas, putting six in a hog's sty to fatten.[89] Though some birds were no doubt eaten, the large flocks were mainly kept to supply goose down and feathers, which were live plucked.[90] Rabbits were also farmed, using warrens on Mendip and Brean Down. Sir Edward Rodney had a rabbit warren at Stoke Gifford on his sequestered property in 1645, which was let to a tenant who complained at having to sell some 200 couple of rabbits to the County Commissioners at 14d to 16d a couple, as this was lower than the price he could expect at Bristol, even taking his costs into account.[91]

Arable crops

Inventory evidence concerning arable crops is disappointingly thin: of the 36 inland and coastal farmers' inventories only nine give acreages under crop, ranging from one to 16 acres, of which six specify wheat, one six acres of beans and peas in addition to five of wheat, and another ten acres of wheat, six acres of barley and 9½ acres of beans and peas. While the date of the inventory does not appear to have any bearing on whether crops are included at all, it may account for the absence of spring-sown crops with the wheat, since the six with wheat only were all taken in November or February. However, although acreages were rarely specified, many inventories list growing corn or corn in the barn, sometimes indicating quite large acreages: Edward Urch of Mudgley had growing wheat valued at £65, possibly representing around 26 acres. The wills give some additional information, but, apart from one case of 9½

86 SHC, D\P\hun/3/2/1.

87 SHC, D\D/cd/15, ff. 8d–9.

88 TNA, E 134/29Chas2/Mich2.

89 SHC, Q/SR/149/20.

90 Williams, *Draining of the Somerset Levels*, p. 173.

91 TNA, SP 28/242, part 1, f. 136.

acres of wheat, bequests were generally of very small parcels of two or three acres. Only a few instances of pulses occur and even fewer of barley, and, though bushels of oats appear in probate records, there are only three instances of it actually growing.

Other sources show that the picture given by the few probate records is misleading in this regard, however, for while wheat was clearly important as a cash crop, beans and barley were produced in greater quantities. The balance of crops also depended on the quality of the arable in each parish. In the coastal parish of Berrow total crop production for 1622 was about 4781 bushels, of which 39 per cent was beans, 28 per cent barley, 18 per cent wheat, 13 per cent oats, and just under 1 per cent rye, a small quantity of the last also being grown in their orchards and gardens by three parishioners.[92] The acreages devoted to each crop by 30 of the inhabitants are available for 1620, totalling 39½ acres of beans, 35 of barley, 35 of wheat, 12¼ of oats, and three of rye.[93] Though some arable was devoted to a cash crop, wheat, far more was given over to higher-yielding crops for which the land was better suited: tillage land in Berrow was described as poor and the wheat yield per acre was two-thirds that of neighbouring parishes in 1801.[94] The other crops were not necessarily all consumed on the farms, of course, as they too were easily sold locally and the area had long been known for its production of beans in particular: in 1531 a licence was granted for the purchase of beans in Brent Marsh for export via Bridgwater.[95]

Corn-growing had a different emphasis in the neighbouring coastal parish of Burnham, where 12 of the parishioners in the mid seventeenth century concentrated their rather small arable acreages on wheat as far as possible. Nine individuals held acreages ranging from one to 33 acres, and there were also three joint enterprises involving around three acres or less. Excluding the shared crops and the man with one acre (wheat), eight farmers had between four and 33 acres. All grew wheat: on the smaller acreages it represented about three-quarters of the total; for the four larger farmers with 21 to 33 acres it was about half. All also grew both barley and beans, except the two with the smallest acreages, who grew only one or the other, and the two farmers with the largest acreages also grew about an acre each of oats and included peas with the beans. In all, 37 acres of barley were grown against 25 acres of beans, but 81 acres were devoted to wheat, so clearly a decision had been made to use the better arable land of Burnham for the most valuable cash crop and grow rather less of the others.[96]

In Huntspill at the end of the century the same emphasis on wheat is evident. Of the 58 inhabitants 32 produced crops, though a third of these cropped less than five acres. Wheat covered the largest area, 147 acres; except for five men who had

92 Figures obtained by multiplying by ten the quantities of tithing corn sold, listed in TNA, E 135/5/45. There is no indication of any unsold grain remaining for these years.

93 TNA, E 178/4467.

94 TNA, HO 67/2/29.

95 *Letters and Papers, foreign and domestic, of the reign of Henry VIII*, 23 vols in 38 (London, 1862–1932), Addenda vol. 1, part 1, p. 245.

96 TNA, E 134/1654-55/Hil8.

only one acre of arable each, everyone with arable grew some wheat and it generally formed the largest proportion of the acreage. Nearly everyone with arable also grew some peas, beans or the two mixed, which altogether covered 101 acres. Barley, however, covered only 25 acres and was grown only in addition to wheat. There were also a few acres of mixed crops: 22 acres of pulses and barley, three acres of French beans, peas and wheat, and nine acres of wheat and barley.[97]

In the Mendip parishes the evidence for arable is slight. Very few grains are mentioned: most inventories do not give acreages and the wills very few, the largest being two acres of wheat plus two acres of barley. Oats are never mentioned even loose and beans only four times, while eight references to cut crops refer just to 'corn' and price it in with the hay. Before the late seventeenth century the only inhabitant for whom crop acreages are available is Sir George Rodney, who had an exceptionally large area of demesne arable: in July 1601 he had 39 acres under crop, over half of which was wheat and a quarter oats.[98] Two or three inventories for more prosperous residents of Cheddar and Compton Bishop are available for the late seventeenth century. John Prowse, esq., who was possibly holding the manor of Compton Bishop at his death in 1688 as well as land in Cheddar, had 15 acres of wheat and 30 acres of spring-sown crops.[99] John Thomas, husbandman of Compton Bishop, had 15 acres of wheat, two acres of teasels and 18 acres of beans, peas and barley.[100]

The poorer prospects for grain in Mendip parishes was probably the reason for growing teasels, which were being grown in and around Cheddar by the late sixteenth century. Ten inventories (all but two from Cheddar) of out the 19 surviving for the Brent Marsh parishes on the Mendips listed teasels and, in addition to John Thomas mentioned above, another also listed one acre of growing teasels as well.[101] Teasels could tolerate poorer and wetter soil, and one man mentioned teasels 'growing in the marsh' in his will.[102] The value of teasels was about on a par with that of wheat, at £1 an acre in 1595,[103] or sometimes better,[104] and Thomas's teasels were priced in with his wheat. The farmers clearly felt it was worthwhile to switch from wheat to teasels: a rector in the Mendip parish of Winscombe, the northern neighbour of Axbridge and Cheddar, tried to establish in the Court of the Exchequer that teasels were grown on land previously sown with wheat following the spring-sown crop, greatly reducing the amount of grain grown in the parish and therefore his tithes, and so ought to be tithable like wheat,[105] though it was argued in another tithe case that, as teasels were often grown on newly broken pasture that was later sown with wheat or other grain,

97 SHC, D\P\hun/3/2/1.

98 TNA, E 178/1992. Below, The production of individual farmers.

99 TNA, PROB 4/8771.

100 TNA, PROB 4/12846.

101 SHC, D\D/ct, inventory of John Croker, Cheddar, 1589.

102 *Ibid.*, will of John Ducket, Cheddar, 1576.

103 *Ibid.*, inventory of Joan Howlet, Meare, 1595.

104 J.H. Bettey, 'Cultivation of Teazles in North Somerset', *Notes and Queries for Somerset and Dorset*, 34/348 (1998), pp. 235–6, from TNA, E 134/11Wm3/East4.

105 TNA, E 134/13Wm3/Trin19.

the arable acreage was increased to the benefit of the holders of great tithes.[106] The rectors of the great tithes in Cheddar were certainly aware of its value: in the 1590s pasture paid 2d an acre agistment tithe, but if sown with any grain *or* set with teasels or garlic the tithe of the crop was to be paid.[107] A cleric in the Mendip parish of Compton Bishop had £8-worth at his death in 1604, possibly tithes.[108]

Some wills, all from Cheddar, also throw light on teasel-growing. Besides teasels in the marsh, one woman grew a crop of barley and teasels together,[109] and a man had teasels growing in three different furlongs in 1629.[110] The references to teasel-growing are concentrated in a fairly short space of time for these particular Mendip parishes, from the 1570s until 1635, when a close of teasels belonging to a Compton Bishop husbandman was mentioned.[111] In part this is probably the result of poor survival of sources, but the petering out of information does coincide with a recession in the Somerset cloth industry, where teasels were used in finishing cloth. However, sales were also made much further afield, in Wiltshire, Gloucestershire and Reading in the 1590s.[112] Fullers were recorded in Axbridge, Cheddar and Huntspill until at least the 1650s, and demand probably picked up again later in the century,[113] when teasels continued to be a notable crop in the Mendips area, especially in parishes on the northern side, where in one parish the crop was said to have been introduced with seeds brought from Cheddar in the 1650s.[114] Richard Durban of Cheddar had two or three different kinds of teasels in 1681, valued in all at £53 10s, while Joel Gardiner, also of Cheddar, had £42-worth of dry teasels in 1683.[115]

The Mendip parishes' more limited and poorer arable land produced other crop innovations. Garlic, mentioned above, and onions occur a few times, especially in the Cheddar area, but the most interesting reference to a garden crop being put to a wider use occurs in Rodney Stoke, where turnips were being grown in the field before 1609, having been very common as a garden crop for some time in the parish.[116] Though details of other crops grown by this farmer are not given, it is almost certain that the turnips were grown to supplement the winter feed of cattle or sheep. Turnips are strangely absent from any other evidence, though the existence of more inventories might have produced more examples, but they may have been omitted by inventory appraisers, being considered as a form of pasture because they were often grazed by stock in the field.

---

106 Bettey, 'Cultivation of Teazles'.

107 SHC, D\D/cd/129, Croke & Boucher v. Lane, dep. of Thos Brooke (*c*.1590).

108 SHC, D\D/ct, inventory of James Welsh, Compton Bishop, 1604.

109 *Ibid.*, will of Joan Webbe, Cheddar, 1579.

110 TNA, PROB 11/222/132.

111 SHC, Q/SR/72/53.

112 TNA, PROB 11/89/273.

113 There were 1½ acres of teasels growing in Huntspill in 1693: SHC, D\P\hun/3/2/1.

114 *AHEW5*, I, p. 375.

115 TNA, PROB 4/10651; PROB 4/10369.

116 SHC, D\D/cd/45, Hill v. Cade, 27 Apr. 1613.

The production of individual farmers

Clearly, then, the Levels supported a wide range of produce, but it is possible to some extent to see which crops individual farmers produced and how they made their choices. In Huntspill information is available for all the farmers in the parish in 1693, enabling a comparison between the larger and the smaller regarding the choices they made among the main types of husbandry: dairying, permanent sheep flock, fattening/ grazing and arable.[117] The size of the farms has been reckoned from the acreage given in the tithe book, which includes meadow, arable and enclosed pasture but does not include gardens, orchards, crofts and curtilages, fallow arable or common grazing. Though the farm size need not necessarily equate to size of output, an order based on acreage, particularly the holdings of meadow and arable, must bear a close relation to the financial rank of the farmer.

Seven farmers had over 50 acres, with 85 acres the largest holding, and they each had between 19 and 22 acres of meadow. The only other common factor was their diversity: five of the seven had all four elements of dairying, sheep, grazing and arable, but the emphasis on each varied a good deal: their arable, for example, varied from six acres to nearly 40. Of the remaining two, John Jeffreys junior had no permanent sheep flock, while George Winter is an unusual case: he had the largest acreage and kept a herd of 12 dairy cows and a flock of 25 sheep, but he had no arable and used his large amount of enclosed pasture (63 acres) for horses rather than fattening. Either his holding simply did not include arable, or he had converted it to pasture.

Despite the individual variations, the larger farmers in the parish obviously aimed at a wide range of production. Mr William Maundrell, a local gentleman with 60 acres, made 20 acres of hay, kept 12 cows and nine sheep and, though he had no enclosed pasture listed, grazed 151 sheep for short periods, on either the moors, the fallows or unrecorded pastures. He also had an exceptionally large amount of arable, nearly 40 acres under crop, of which 23 acres was wheat, and his diversity was rounded off with three orchards, some geese and a withy bed. Another large mixed farm belonged to James Stole, with 62 acres. In contrast with Maundrell he had only six acres of crops – three acres of wheat, two of pulses, one of barley – but the same number of cows and the same acreage of hay. He kept a far larger sheep flock though – 60, which produced 21 lambs – and on his 35 acres of pasture plus the moors he grazed two steers and four yearlings in addition to his yoke of oxen and a couple of horses and mares.

The median acreage for the Huntspill farmers was quite low, at 14–15 acres. Robert Mogg had 15 acres, which were all used for hay. He had eight cows and a flock of 25 sheep, and grazed ten other sheep for one month. He also had a few horses and sold one colt. Robert Andrews had 14 acres, of which one acre was used for hay and 13 acres for crops: 4½ acres of wheat, 2½ of barley and six of pulses. He had no dairy cattle nor a sheep flock, but grazed 47 sheep for various periods and collected 11 lambs from them, and sold two yearling cattle that year for £4. Again, there is a variety of production, though on a slightly lesser scale than that of the larger farmers, but the

117 Following paragraphs on Huntspill farmers based on SHC, D\P\hun/3/2/1.

disparity in production was not as great as the disparity in acreage might suggest because of the common grazing that holders of customary land could enjoy.

At the bottom of the scale were nine men with less than five acres and two others with no land. Of the latter, Andrew Batts ran the mill and presumably grazed his horse and few sheep on the moors; Richard Trows grazed 20 sheep for six months, either on the moors or on rented grazing. Two of the men with small acreages attempted mixed farming: one or two cows, one or two acres of hay, a handful of sheep and two or three acres of wheat and peas, with the odd mare or two. Generally, though, those who appear to be small farmers farmed in only one or two categories: they either kept a permanent sheep flock or grazed sheep short-term (two men with 16 and 50 sheep). Three of them also had quite a few horses as well: John Varman, for example, had six mares, three colts and two horses. Only three of them kept dairy cattle, the obvious occupation for a small farmer, which suggests that most of these men were obtaining their income principally from other sources, perhaps by working for other farmers.

Evidence from earlier dates and other places in the Levels bears out the picture of mixed farming given for Huntspill in the 1690s. The richer farmers at all periods seem to have kept up a mixed farm economy. Thomas Wychefield of Allerton, whose goods were listed in March 1557, was a copyholder whose personal wealth (£45 11s 8d) was the eighth highest among the totals surviving for the sixteenth century in this area, and whose will was one of the few to be proved in the PCC in the mid sixteenth century. No crops or produce were listed, but he kept two plough-oxen, a wain and wheels and other equipment, suggesting some arable farming; he also had 16 cows and heifers, two steers, two yearlings, three mares with colts and four pigs.[118]

In 1604 Thomas Crypes of Berrow, yeoman, died possessed of £114 5s in goods.[119] His inventory, taken in March, listed 16 acres of 'corn' and he had the use of the herbage of 42 acres of pasture. His stock included nine cows and heifers, five calves and 11 steers or two-year-olds. He also had four pigs and unspecified numbers of sheep, horses and poultry. Produce on his farm included quantities of hay and corn, and he possessed plough gear and other equipment, including a pack saddle. Here again his inventory shows a very wide spread of interests: dairying and the grazing of cattle were pre-eminent, with sheep kept either for wool or for meat, and arable which probably included some wheat. In addition to his rented herbage he probably had other meadow and pasture held on customary or life tenancies and therefore not valued in the inventory.

Edmund Bower was a gentleman who, in addition to legal and other interests, farmed land in and around Allerton. In 1645 his goods were sequestrated as he had served in the royalist army.[120] He held land valued at £160 a year in Allerton, Wedmore and Tarnock, totalling 190 acres of meadow and pasture and 92 acres of arable, which included the demesne farm of Allerton,[121] but some was leased out to others. His stock included six oxen with plough harness, six cows, two heifers, six calves, four

---

118 TNA, PROB 2/291.

119 SHC, D\D/ct, inventory of Thomas Crypes, 1605.

120 TNA, SP 28/214, sequestrators' accts, Bempstone hundred.

121 Coleman, 'Manor of Allerton', p. 73.

steers, 14 yearlings and a colt. Undoubtedly he had once had other horses, which had either gone to war with him or been commandeered by passing armies. The inventory was taken in October and no standing crops were specified, only round totals given of £30 in wheat, barley and beans and £15 in hay. However, the sequestrators' accounts include payments for harvesting 31 acres of wheat, 30 acres of beans and 14 acres of barley and oats, reflecting the greater extent of arable available in the Wedmore area.

Farming in the Mendip parishes is illustrated by the wealthiest and socially most pre-eminent inhabitant of the area, Sir George Rodney, who farmed the demesne of his manor of Rodney Stoke. His goods and property were listed by a commission following his suicide in 1601 and, although his wealth far outstrips the resources of anyone else in the area, the farming he carried on shows the same wide range of interests.[122] The inventory taken in July specified the growing crops: 22 acres of wheat, three acres of rye and wheat, 20 acres of oats and four acres of beans; some corn and beans also remained in the barn, as well as the newly mown hay. He had 12 working oxen, two wains and ploughs and other equipment. His stock included 13 cows plus a cow and calf obtained as a heriot as lord of the manor, three heifers and their calves and two bulls, together with 14 pigs of all kinds and five young. He had four fat oxen, four yearlings and ten two-year-old beasts, and he was also fattening 20 sheep. The bulk of his farm inventory, however, was taken up with specifying individually his great number of horses. He had 12 'trotting' nags, geldings, mares and colts: these were not pack animals, but horses bred chiefly for military purposes, or where speed was required.[123] He also had 11 other mares, 11 colts, two stallions and five geldings, and was evidently breeding horses with some enthusiasm. Apart from the horses, Rodney's stock is very comparable to the large farms in Huntspill at the end of the century, but he was probably more fortunate than most farmers in the Mendips in having a large amount of arable. His relatively large herd of pigs may have been kept not only because of the dairy herd but also to make use of the woods, of which manorial demesnes on the slopes of the Mendips had large areas.

These larger farmers, whose resources would presumably have allowed them to specialise in fattening or sheep-farming should they have wished, chose instead to maintain a mixed farm economy, which made the best use of the very mixed qualities of land that most residents in the area had in their holdings. Those who were fattening cattle and sheep all had other sources of income, either from other kinds of husbandry, chiefly dairying, or outside farming altogether, and those with the latter tended to own or rent only pasture; butchers and victuallers were particularly numerous amongst those graziers, for obvious reasons.

Thomas Hawkins alias Tarr was both a grazier and a butcher with land in Berrow in the 1650s, which he had held from at least 1620.[124] In the years 1657 to 1659 Hawkins held Weeks Farm in Berrow, which consisted of about 80 acres, and he rented another 13 acres of pasture. Only 3½ acres of the farm were arable; the rest

---

122 TNA, E 178/1992.

123 My thanks to Prof. Peter Edwards for this information.

124 TNA, E 134/13and14Chas2/Hil3; E 178/4467. Material is taken from dispute over tithe of wool, but numbers of animals were not in dispute.

was meadow or pasture, and he mowed between four and 16 acres for hay in those years. He kept no dairy cattle but he grazed between 40 and 50 fattening beasts from May to Michaelmas each year and 30 from Michaelmas to Christmas. Each year he also kept about 100 sheep, mainly wethers, from Michaelmas until the following summer, when he sheared from 50 to 80 and sold the rest in their wool. Hawkins kept 'one sort of cattle or another, or sheep, as he thought convenient being both a grazier and a butcher'. He was clearly a man of substance, and one of his descendants, Richard Tarr alias Hawkins, was described as a gentleman in 1712.[125]

The evidence available for the Levels is too sparse to indicate whether the balance between arable and animal husbandry altered in the course of the two centuries of this study, nor whether the balance between different crops changed: the large wheat production of Huntspill in the 1690s, for example, may have been a change from an earlier emphasis on barley. Dairying was always an important element in the husbandry and the mainstay of the smaller farmers, but it is reasonable to suppose that the interest in grazing for meat was growing amongst resident farmers as markets expanded and prices rose, illustrated by the active trading in livestock shown in Lovell's accounts in the late seventeenth century.[126] Arable continued to hold its own in the Levels: those farmers who grew wheat probably did well out of it, but the profits, given the difficulties of much of the land, did not warrant a concentration on arable, especially with the financial advantages of other produce, and inhabitants did not feel impelled to bring marginal land under crop. In the Mendip area, however, where arable land was more limited and the soil thin, cash crops such as garlic and teasels could be grown rather than grains.

The husbandry revolved around the moors, which enabled flexibility in farming systems and field use and allowed farmers to retain a wide mixed production. The vital contribution of the moors to the local farming economy is illustrated by the experience of the commoners of Alder moor near Street, the one moor in the Somerset Levels to be enclosed in the early modern period; after enclosure and drainage the allotment received by the commoners meant that they could pasture far fewer animals, possibly only a quarter of their previous stock, and had to convert their arable into pasture to accommodate the rest.[127]

Mixed farming benefited farmers both large and small. They were not trapped in the production of one crop regardless of changes in prices and other market conditions, and were not so much at the mercy of harvest failures as, for example, small sheep–corn farmers elsewhere.[128] Though the majority of holdings were quite small by the standards of arable farms in some parts of England, this did not preclude an income well above subsistence, whether from rents or produce, nor the participation of small farmers in commercial, market-orientated farming.

125 SHC, DD\DN/2/19/4.

126 Wilts & Swindon RO, 161/57 (bdl. 3).

127 Williams, *Draining of the Somerset Levels*, p. 104.

128 *AHEW4*, p. 653.

The income of small farmers and landholders

Income from land in Brent Marsh was derived from direct farming or by renting it out, and even small farmers seem to have obtained a reasonable living in these ways. As mentioned in Chapter 2, little trace has been found of the industrial by-employments among farmers that occur in many other pastoral areas[129] and, indeed, many craftsmen looked to farming for additional income; this suggests that the local husbandry was profitable enough to support most small farmers without the need for additional sources of income.

Farm incomes

Except for a very few people who left accounts, the sources and amounts of individual incomes in this period are virtually impossible to discover. The 'richer farmers' discussed above are defined by their tithable acreage or the total of their farm capital, not from any knowledge of their actual income or even, in most cases, the extent and nature of all their landholdings. However, the gross income that local husbandry, particularly dairying, might produce can be calculated, and this in turn can be used to establish the acreage necessary to support the stock that would support a family and give a surplus. There is a dearth of actual dairy accounts for Somerset (and few for anywhere else) for the seventeenth century. However, calculations can be made of the profits for dairy farmers whose produce was sold as cheese, using a conservative average yield per cow of 300 gallons[130] and a price for cheese at three-quarters of the decennial average listed by Rogers,[131] to allow for costs of a middleman or transport, giving a gross income per cow in the mid seventeenth century of £3 2s 6d in addition to its calf. High-yielding cows on rich pasture could produce 50 per cent more.[132] The potential value of dairy cattle for farmers is underlined by their value for labourers: in the late eighteenth century it was calculated that the produce of one cow in milk or butter with its calf would amount to around half the average labourer's annual wage; net profit obviously varied according to costs, but could range from £3 to £8 a year at that time.[133]

Even harder to estimate is the profit on grazing cattle and sheep, which depends on the price of the animal and the length of time kept. John Westover made a gross profit of £8 8s on two oxen bought in May 1695 and sold nine months later for an

---

129 J. Thirsk, *Economic Policy and Projects: The Development of a Consumer Society in Early Modern England* (Oxford, 1978), pp. 167–8.

130 For details of the factors and sources used see Croot, 'Agrarian Society', pp. 205–8; Trow-Smith, *British Livestock Husbandry to 1700*, p. 121; idem, *British Livestock Husbandry, 1700–1900*, pp. 20, 185; Page, *VCH Som.* II, p. 539.

131 J.E.T. Rogers, *A History of Agriculture and Prices in England*, 7 vols (Oxford 1866–92), V, p. 378. Cheese taken to the marketing centre of Weyhill, as some local produce was, fetched the prices listed by Rogers.

132 For more details of the calculations and sources used, see Croot, 'Agrarian Society', pp. 205–8.

133 J. Humphries, 'Enclosures, Common Rights, and Women: The Proletarianization of Families in the late Eighteenth and Early Nineteenth Centuries', *Journal of Economic History*, 50 (1990), pp. 24, 26.

exceptionally high price of £11 each, his costs amounting to approximately £3.[134] Fatstock and oxen were valued in various local sources at £3 6s 8d to £4 5s between 1685 and 1695, and Westover's other sales at the end of the seventeenth century were £3 for a bull, £10 5s for two cows, £23 for three steers and £9 for two three-year-old heifers. In the same period, the grazier Thomas Lovell generally paid between £2 and £4 a head for steers, cows and oxen, and regularly made a profit of £100–200 a year in the second half of the seventeenth century on an outlay of around £400 a year buying cattle and sheep, although occasionally he did fail to make a profit in a particular year.[135]

Despite the attractive nature of the prices to be obtained for beef cattle, John Billingsley still considered in 1795 that the profit per acre from dairying was nearly twice that from grazing, at 50s and 28s per acre respectively.[136] Furthermore, prices for cheese were often higher than for beef, because of the extra labour involved in production.[137] Prices for dairy produce, though less spectacular, were substantial when added up over the time it took to fatten a steer, and the area was possibly just too far from the nearest large urban market, Bristol, to be really important for large-scale fattening before slaughter. However, where grazing was available for little or no rent, as was the case for farmers with customary holdings, a couple of beef animals sold each year would give a sizeable boost to the income of a small farmer, even though to concentrate on fattening alone might be impractical and risky for him.

Obviously, given the diverse combinations in mixed farming, it is impossible to calculate an average income for a mixed farmer. Even Westover's accounts are too erratic and incomplete to allow an accurate balance sheet to be drawn up, though in 1696, a year with a large number of transactions, his farm income was £75 5s 10d, all from sales of cattle apart from seven bushels of beans (£1 6s 10d) and rents (£1 9s). Farm expenditure amounted to £52 12s: £47 1s on purchases of various cattle and one colt, 10s in commission and expenses, 10s on rhynework, £2 13s on ploughing, 15s for haulage of crops and turf, 17s 6d for rents and (approximately) 5s 6d for tithes.[138] This does not include all his expenditure – he was purchasing building materials to enlarge his house – nor his medical income. On the farm accounts he had a balance of £23 in his favour, and this does not include his own crops and home consumption, which were not mentioned.

Actual farm sizes

Farm sizes for the early modern period are usually calculated from inventories or from surveys. Inventories for Leicestershire, for example, usually give acreages

134 SHC, DD\X\HKN, f. 182d.

135 Wilts. & Swindon RO, 161/57 (bdl. 3).

136 Billingsley, *General View*, p. 252. However, cheese prices at this time were very high: TNA, HO 67/2/141.

137 C. Muldrew, *Food, Energy and the Creation of Industriousness: Work and Material Culture in Agrarian England 1550–1780* (Cambridge, 2011), p. 104.

138 SHC, DD\X\HKN, ff. 169d–183d.

of crops grown, allowing reasonable estimates of overall farm sizes.[139] For areas where arable was not so important or inventories not so detailed manorial surveys have been used, but they have little value in assessing farm sizes for the Levels not only because they record tenurial rather than farm units but also because sub-letting was so prevalent here. This is likely to be true in other parts of England, and occasionally evidence shows how important sub-letting was: in Cannock Chase a field book giving the actual occupants of the strips in the fields as well as the manorial tenants showed that much of the land was held in subtenancies, and a customary tenant with just a few acres in the survey turned out to be one of the largest farmers; in all, some two-thirds of the land was sub-let.[140] Whether these findings in Cannock Chase affect the average farm size or not,[141] the fact that there can be such a difference between the numbers and personnel of owners and occupiers in an area suggests that a high degree of sub-letting may be possible everywhere else; it has certainly been found in some other areas with suitable sources,[142] and most recent local studies comment on its existence, even when comprehensive evidence is lacking.[143] Where the size of farm is considered to be the main factor in the 'disappearance' of its holder, it is the total amount of land that a cultivator held that matters, and not the size of an individual holding as listed in a survey. If the holder has land elsewhere then he obviously has greater economic resources than suggested by the one holding he has in a particular manor. Furthermore, where farm sizes are an important factor in the emergence of agrarian capitalism, it is obviously desirable to have accurate farm size figures, and where these are wanting to acknowledge the fact.

When looking at the viability of farms, another approach has been to make calculations for arable farms in the early modern period to find the minimum acreage necessary if the farmer was to make a profit,[144] and show where small arable farmers were in danger of disappearing because their farms were no longer viable. However, in many ways these examples of the minimum farm size necessary are pointless because they concentrate on a specialised form of agriculture, the sheep–corn farm, and, as all the critics of small farms in the early modern period point out, part of the small farmers' backwardness lay in their lack of specialisation, while other forms of farming, such as dairying, have shown that agricultural history based on grain prices and production over-simplifies and ignores the benefits of diversification.[145] In animal

139 W.G. Hoskins, *Essays in Leicestershire History* (Liverpool, 1950), p. 145. The 'normal' sixteenth-century farm there had 30–35 acres of arable, which formed between two-thirds and three-quarters of the total holding.

140 C.J. Harrison, 'The Social and Political History of Cannock and Rugeley 1546–97', PhD thesis (University of Keele, 1974), pp. 84–6.

141 Allen, *Enclosure and the Yeoman*, p. 75 and n.

142 Shaw-Taylor, 'The Rise of Agrarian Capitalism', pp. 45–7.

143 e.g. French and Hoyle, *Character of English Rural Society*; Whittle, *Development of Agrarian Capitalism*.

144 *AHEW4*, p. 653.

145 Broad, 'Regional Perspectives and Variations in English Dairying', p. 94.

husbandry, particularly dairying, the criterion for survival is the number of animals necessary to make a profit, and, where there was a large amount of common grazing available all year, the farm's acreage is no longer the most crucial factor. For dairy and livestock farms, then, it is perhaps more worthwhile to examine the sizes of farms in terms of their principal stock.

The figures in the section above for the profit per dairy cow are gross, and do not take into account the amount of milk consumed at home, and an allowance also has to be included for the purchase of grain or bread for the household if grain is not grown or not consumed at home. The annual breadcorn consumption for a household of six in the Levels would cost £4 16s at 1645 prices,[146] and the value of the produce of a cow in the decade 1643–52 would be £2 18s 4d.[147] One cow might be adequate for a widow living alone, while three cows would produce a gross income of £8 15s plus £2 6s 8d for their calves,[148] a total of £11 1s 8d, which would be adequate for food as long as the farmer's land was held by customary tenure and not rack-rented. A herd of five cows (£14 11s 8d plus their calves) was a viable concern, particularly as part of a mixed farm. The costs to set against this are harder to compute. Cows required around two acres of hay each for the winter, and two acres each of summer pasture; though those acreages could overlap to some extent, the greater the amount of grass per head the better the yield was likely to be. If the farmer had to pay an economic rent for his meadow of 15s an acre and 10s an acre for his pasture then his profit per cow would be halved, but if he had customary land and common pasture in the moors then he was much better placed, with only a few pennies for rent and a few shillings for haymaking labour to set against the income.

Turning to the examples of known farm stock, 60 per cent of the 43 inventoried farmers and 70 per cent of the 58 Huntspill farmers of 1693 had three or more cows in milk.[149] Though they are for only one parish, the Huntspill figures are probably a truer sample than the inventories, and show that well over half the farmers there had enough cows to show a profit, the median herd size being six cows. In order to support a stock of cows or any other animals, however, a farmer needed some land of his own in addition to common grazing, especially meadow for hay. In this respect the farm's acreage and the type of land *was* an important factor in getting the best out of the dairy herd. The tenure of this land was also important, since a high rent could reduce a nice profit into an inadequate income. However, the sizes of holdings, the tenures and the rents paid of the actual husbandmen, as opposed to the manorial landholders, are mostly very obscure, and the only concrete evidence lies in sources such as the Huntspill tithe book.[150]

---

146 TNA, SP 28/214, sequestrators' accts, hundreds of Bempstone and Brent. For Bowden's household of six, three bushels of wheat and three bushels of barley per person.

147 Gross income per cow was £3 2s 6d in the 1650s: Croot, 'Agrarian Society', p, 208.

148 Three calves from S. Brent fetched £2 6s 8d in 1645: TNA, SP 28/214.

149 SHC, D\P\hun/3/2/1.

150 And even then the inhabitants may have held and worked land in another parish as well.

Rental income

The presence of sub-letting in the Levels obscures actual farm sizes and, although there are no direct and comprehensive sources to show the extent of sub-letting, various sources do indicate that the practice made parcels of land of all kinds available to farmers large and small. The demand for such parcels meant that holders of life tenures had another source of income besides farming their land, and the rental market contributed a great deal to the viability of both small landholdings and small farms in the Levels. The copyholder with a holding too small to make a viable farm unit, far from being on the point of disappearing into the mass of wage-labourers, was near the top of the economic scale because of the value placed on customary tenure by inhabitants and outsiders alike,[151] and much copyhold land was actually farmed by others who rented it on a commercial basis. More comprehensive evidence on the actual occupation of holdings is available for the eighteenth century and the extent of sub-letting has been assessed for Earls Colne in Essex, showing that not only all the demesne and former demesne but also at least 40 per cent of the copyhold acreage was leased out by the first half of the eighteenth century.[152]

A viable income

To assess whether individuals were making a living from their farms, whether in produce or rents, it is necessary to ascertain the minimum income that a household required to provide it with bread and other food with some surplus. The figures for the expenditure of a hypothetical 30-acre sheep–corn farmer assumed, based on eighteenth-century figures, that the family of two adults and four children would consume in breadcorn 18 bushels of wheat and 18 of barley in a year,[153] which, as calculated above, for a family in Brent Marsh in 1645 would have cost £4 16s, and a similar amount could be added to cover expenditure on other foodstuffs, making a total of *c.*£10 for the family, with the largest part being consumed by the man. However, while bushels of breadcorn are helpful in considering farm incomes, they do not really help assess how much money people required for a sufficient diet to allow them to work. It has been generally assumed that poorer people, such as labourers, and doubtless some struggling husbandmen, in the sixteenth and seventeenth centuries would subsist on cereals with only a little meat, mainly bacon, or cheese.[154] However, recent research into labourers' diets, and diets generally, has shown that meat, particularly beef, played a surprisingly large role in the diets supplied to the indigent, even in workhouses.[155] In this period both meat and beer were considered good for a working diet,[156] a belief confirmed to some degree by modern knowledge of nutrition, because although bread provides some protein it is a rather poor source.

---

151 Above, Chap. 3, The use and attraction of copyhold for lives.

152 French and Hoyle, *Character of English Rural Society*, pp, 251–4.

153 *AHEW4*, p. 657.

154 *Ibid.*, p. 451.

155 Muldrew, *Food, Energy*, pp. 122–5.

156 *Ibid.*, p. 11.

In order for men and women to do a full day of physical work they required both adequate calories and sources which provided more of the indispensable amino acids making up protein to give them sufficient energy while maintaining the body and preventing muscle wastage, and the best and most accessible sources of protein for humans are animal products.[157] Thus in the diets examined for the sixteenth and seventeenth centuries bread is the staple food, but meat runs it a close second, while the high consumption of barley (malt) was ingested in the form of beer or ale, which also provided a high proportion of calories.[158] In the London Bridewell in 1600 the daily allowance to women and men who worked was 2 lb of bread, 1.5 lb of meat and one pint of porridge, with four pints of beer for men and two pints for women; cheese and butter replaced meat on fast-days[159] and, as the Bridewell was the most under-financed of the London hospitals, such a diet must be what the governors thought necessary for a poor person to work hard.[160] This amount of food is fairly comparable to that provided by Robert Loder for himself, his wife and five servants (three men, three women, one boy) in 1614: their daily average was 2.1 lb bread, 1.8 lb meat, 1.5 lb malt brewed into beer, 2.2 oz fish, 4 oz cheese, and 1 oz butter a head. The men's portions would be larger and the women's smaller, and men would have had a gallon of beer using 2 lb of malt, plus hops, each day.[161] Loder's accounts seem to be the only ones available for the seventeenth century that give quantities, number of people fed and costs, so enabling a reasonable assessment of the diet for a farmer and his labourers. Loder himself worked out the average cost per head: in 1614–15 it was £9 16s 6d and in 1615–16 it was about £11 18s 6d, costs that include the value of items the farm produced, such as some of the pigs and the beans used to fatten them, some of the cheese and the cost of fuel (wood), straw and bushes used in the processing of beer and in cooking.[162] This suggests a cost of around £10 a head on average for a working adult, so the £10 for food for a family must be an absolute minimum, but £15 to £20 a year would probably cover food and some other essentials.

A local day-labourer in the harvest in Charles I's reign received 10d a day without provisions,[163] and his maximum income would be about £13 a year, though almost certainly few day-labourers would work anything approaching a full year, and an income of about £8–9 a year would be more likely. The few figures for boarding found

---

157 Department of Health, *Manual of Nutrition* (12th edn, London, 2012), p. 22. Wholemeal bread gives 9.4 g of protein per 100 g of bread, compared with 29.2 g from beef, 23.8 g from bacon, 25.4 g from Cheddar cheese: p. 26, Table 6. Energy values per 100 g are: wholemeal bread 217 kcal, beef 203 kcal, bacon 337 kcal, Cheddar 416 kcal: Table 3.1, pp. 172, 174.

158 In Loder's household in 1614 beer was the leading provider of calories on Muldrew's calculations, at 2,478 kcal per person, against bread at 1,922 kcal and meat at 1,800 kcal: Muldrew, *Food, Energy*, p. 128.

159 Muldrew, *Food, Energy*, p. 125, Table 3.4.

160 *Ibid.*, p. 127.

161 *Ibid.*, pp. 128–9; figures extracted from Loder's accts.

162 G.E. Fussell (ed.), *Robert Loder's Farm Accounts 1610–1620* (Camden Society 3rd ser. 53, 1936), pp. 86–7, 106–7.

163 SHC, Q/AWa [date illegible].

in local sources suggest that a family of two adults and one child could be fed on good husbandman's fare for about £11 a year in the 1620s.[164] Calculations regarding small tenant sheep–corn farmers whose gross income was £40–50 have concluded that they could hardly be better off than a labourer after their expenses, with a net income of £10–15, but the net figure for farmers depends a great deal on the level of their expenses. If a tenant farmer paid a rack rent and was heavily dependent on one type of farming regardless of market or harvest conditions, then he undoubtedly might often have little beyond a subsistence income in some years, as the figures for the 30-acre arable farmer show,[165] but when the mixed farming of the Levels is being considered the picture becomes much better.

If they were to live from the rent of their holdings rather than farming, a family would need slightly more than a bare minimum as in theory they would have to buy all their food. From the rents obtained locally in 1645 and other years an average rent has been calculated of about 7s an acre for arable, 10s an acre for pasture and 15s for the best meadow ground. Therefore, a typical half-virgate tenement in Lympsham, for example, would bring a total rental of £27 7s 9d, with a net profit of *c.*£26 after the manorial rent was paid. Two typical ferdel holdings would net around £10 and £7 respectively.[166] Clearly, not all the customary holdings would provide an income adequate for the needs of a family for a year, and but they did provide a good return, considering that it was unearned income and the recipient was still free to work another farm or earn a living some other way. Those rental incomes are on the conservative side, since the rates used were about four-fifths or less of the pre-Civil War rates. They do not take account of any common rights, such as grazing, that might also be included.

Table 7 gives the actual rentals for some tenements in South Brent, Berrow, East Brent and Lympsham in 1645, with their pre-war values, and shows that the averages used in the calculations for the right-hand column are fairly accurate, as in only two of the examples does the calculated rental exceed the pre-war rental value. Clearly, then, many customary tenants in the area had holdings that would provide an adequate income from rents. The sums calculated are on the conservative side and were perhaps three-quarters of the amount a judicious lessor would achieve.

Whether it actually paid such copyholders to let their land rather than to farm it themselves is another matter. Figures for Burnham in the 1650s give the value of growing wheat at between 48s and 93s 9d an acre.[167] Even when the tithes are subtracted this still represents a far higher gross profit on the arable than its rental income, and even allowing for one-third fallow and one-third spring crops would give a gross profit of about £22 for the first holding in Lympsham described above; labour costs for arable were high, though, if hired labour had to be employed. The meadow and pasture of the Lympsham holding would support eight cows, allowing a minimum

164 SHC, D\D/cd/76, dep. of Nic. Teeke, 18 Dec. 1633.

165 *AHEW4*, pp. 657–8.

166 BL, Egerton MS 3034, ff. 134, 139d, 141.

167 TNA, E 134/1654-55/Hil8.

Table 7
Customary holdings let in 1645

	Rental achieved 1645	*Rental value pre-war*	*Rental value per my average calculations*
T 33 a. A, 4 a. M, 23 a. P	£28 0s	£32 0s	£28 7s
T 2 a. A, 3 a. P	£2 10s	£ 3 0s	£ 2 10s
T 6a. A, 13 a. P, 3 a. M	£8 0s	£10 0s	£12 3s
House, 4 a. A, 20 a. P	£15 0s	£17 0s	£13 8s
T 5 a. A, 29 a. P	£14 0s	£16 0s	£19 3s
T 2 a. A, 1 a. P	£2 0s	£ 2 10s	£ 1 6s
T 60 a. P	£30 0s	£40 0s	£36 0s
T 58 a. P	£35 0s	£45 0s	£34 16s

Notes: T = tenement; A = arable; P = pasture; M = meadow
Sources: for cols 1 and 2: TNA, SP 28/214, sequestrators' accounts, hundred of Brent.

of four acres per cow,[168] giving a gross profit of £25 plus calves. Since the customary rent paid for this holding was only *c*.27s, and the dairying was carried out chiefly by family or female labour, expenses to set against the gross are not high, particularly taking into account the unlimited common of pasture on the moors that went with the holding and would support oxen and other stock. Evidently, a great deal would depend on personal circumstances in determining whether to let the holding rather than to work it directly.

Commercial leasing in the Levels

An important theme in early modern agrarian history and the development of capitalist farming is the emergence of substantial tenant farmers in the sixteenth and seventeenth centuries. They formed a tier between landowners on the one hand and landless labourers on the other, leasing large blocks of land, often engrossed and enclosed, from the landowners on fairly long leases for years at a commercial rent and working the land with the help of labourers. The high level of rent is thought to have forced them, with their landlords' encouragement and often financial help, to improve their land and increase production in order to pay their rent. This picture, though somewhat simplified, may undoubtedly be true for some areas of England with large demesne farms and strong landowner control, but in this part of the Somerset Levels developments were different, involving something more like a four-tier system. As far as large units were concerned, the nature of the topography and the type of husbandry that resulted did not lend themselves to large-scale management in the way that arable and sheep farms did, and the Levels had few demesne farms in the lord's hands: where they existed the land was scattered, preventing the development of large consolidated farms.

168 TNA, E 134/5WandM/East7.

Leases of manorial demesne, where they exist in this area, were generally for 99 years determinable on (usually) three lives, which was not a commercial tenure. Some leases for terms of years made by lords of the manor did exist, but they were rare; in Cheddar only the lands forming the demesne woods were let in this way, with leases for 21 years.[169] In Blackford there were also a handful of leases for 21 years, all for demesne land.[170] The development of the landowner–tenant farmer dichotomy occurred below the manorial level here, with the customary or life leasehold tenants taking the 'landowner' role.

Leases other than those issuing from the lord of the manor are much harder to find, however. There are many references to lands being let for a term, but no evidence that these were actually engrossed in legal form, and, however arranged, they have left little trace in document collections. Information about the terms and rents are even scarcer. The references made in wills, inventories and other sources to rented land might mention the term, or the rent, or the acreage, but rarely all three for one transaction.[171] There are only a few studies of the kind of sub-letting in the sixteenth and seventeenth centuries found by Harrison: a study of Nutley in Surrey showed that 80 per cent of the land was sub-let in 1613, and in Keevil (Wilts.) 29 out of 35 copyholds each had one subtenant in 1623, while the other six had two or more, and undertenants also held 17 newly created cottages.[172]

The information about renting most usually obtained is that a person had held a piece of land for so many years: this may have been a term lease, but equally possibly may have been on a year-to-year basis, known as an annual tenancy. This form of rental had no long-term security, in that the tenancy could be terminated by either party at the end of the year, allowing the tenant to harvest any crops; nevertheless, it is probably true to say that this was by far the most common tenure existing in England in terms of numbers of people involved, if not number of acres as well. In his study of Cannock Chase Dr Harrison concluded that, though there was in theory no protection for subtenants either in the manor court or anywhere else, the large amount of sub-letting there suggests that there must have been some kind of security of tenure.[173] The only security that can be deduced for Brent Marsh is the influence of society and tradition. A sense of honour and responsibility towards neighbours and the pressure neighbours could put on dissenters were possibly enough to keep the majority from throwing out their subtenants at a whim. A more cynical interpretation might be that landlords did not want to risk being without tenants. Though there was much demand for purchasing freehold and copyhold land, causing prices of these to rise, it does not necessarily follow that there was an equal demand for land to cultivate,

169 TNA, C 108/182, copy of survey of Lord Weymouth's manors, pp. 1–38.

170 SHC, DD\SE/65/1–2, Blackford surveys, 1657, 1663, 1679.

171 e.g. TNA, E 134/20Jas1/Hil8.

172 J. Whittle, 'Leasehold Tenure in England c1300–c1600', in Bos van Bavel and Phillipp Schofield (eds), *The Development of Leasehold in Northwestern Europe, c.1200–1600* (Turnhout, 2009), p. 146.

173 Harrison, 'Cannock and Rugeley', p. 86. He thought that the large number of debt pleas entered but not prosecuted in the manor courts might have been a way of securing these subtenancies. Such pleas are not found in Brent Marsh courts, which were courts baron only.

since free, copyhold and long leasehold land fulfilled different functions in providing secure investment and a landed income. In the Levels there may well have been enough land to go around to form the small family farms. Engrossing of land to make large units of cultivation does not seem to have occurred here in this period; men who had large acreages were content to let out part, and where manorial tenements were rack-rented for a short period the holding was often parcelled out among several tenants.[174] Therefore, the limitation that engrossing would put on the supply of land to the numerous small husbandmen did not occur. By and large there was no reason or advantage in terminating a yearly tenancy where there was no great demand for land which would bring the owner a better return than the rent from his present tenant.

Some annual tenancies might last only a year, while others were renewed indefinitely. Their basic characteristic was that the land was let without an entry fine for an annual rent that equalled its value. Some manorial examples of annual letting occur, as holdings that had just fallen in hand might be let annually at a rack rent until a new long-term tenant could be found. In 1601 two vacant holdings in Cheddar were let for one or two years at rates that obtained total annual rents of £8 6s 8d and £6 18s 0d respectively, and similar arrangements were made in the early eighteenth century.[175] Two tenements in the manor of Edingworth were let by the bailiff in 1682 at a rack rent,[176] and in Lympsham the bailiff had been letting parcels of land to two or three men for several years by 1680 on what seem to have been annual tenancies: Nathaniel Deane held 16 acres of land at a rent of £26 a year for one or two years, Jeremiah Banwell held 22–23 acres at £22 a year for about five years and John Toomer had rented an unspecified amount for £43 a year for 18 years until part had been let to another man and his rent reduced to £36.[177] Generally, though, annual tenancies from manorial lords were rare here. The lords were mainly non-resident and had to administer the land and guard against waste and dishonesty from a distance; they probably preferred to have in a tenant for a foreseeable period with a lease which gave them legally enforceable rights of re-entry if the terms were violated. Possibly they also preferred to receive a lump sum in the form of a fine rather than a rack rent spread over the term.

The manorial examples are useful, however, because the written records involved mean they form most of the existing examples of yearly tenancies. Examples do occur of farmers whose land was obviously held by those sort of tenancies, though such precise details are lacking. John Stirt (Steart), who was born in 1645, had lived in Tarnock since childhood and was a householder there from 1669 to 1693, during which time he had worked several farms valued at over £20 a year, including for several years an estate of a Mr Hasell of Chew Magna (north Somerset). In 1693 he was renting an estate worth £20 a year from Edward Strode of Downside in addition to land worth about £10 a year from others. The land from Strode consisted of Pease tenement with nine acres, Seacroft containing seven acres, and one acre three

174 See below, following para.

175 SHC, DD\SE/17/4; TNA, C 108/182, survey book.

176 SHC, DD\WY/70, lease Wyndham to Brookehouse, 4 May 1682. Possibly the lease was arranged by the previous lessee rather than the bailiff.

177 TNA, E 134/31Chas2/East12.

yards in an open field. Other men gave similar information about themselves: Robert Dean, of Lower Allerton in Weare, had rented 3½ acres of meadow and pasture in Badgworth for 30 years, and three acres one yard more for ten years. John Cutler of Biddisham rented several parcels over 11 years, with 21 acres of meadow and pasture the smallest amount at any one time. George Counsell of Badgworth, yeoman, had been a farmer or renter of lands there for 18 or 19 years.[178] Some of these men rented land in addition to land they held by secure tenure, while others had only the rented land, and, though some holdings remained in the same hands for many years, other parcels might change several times, often at short intervals.[179]

Apart from the enclosed pastures of the coastal belt, land was rarely let in large parcels, a considerable advantage to small farmers. The small parcels were probably the result of the piecemeal nature of most holdings, with scattered strips of arable and small scattered closes. Presumably, though, it would have been more convenient for the lessor to let all the parcels of a holding to one tenant, and, as the available examples suggest that this was not often done, possibly the demand was for small quantities only. Edward Strode, who held 113 acres in Badgworth, farmed some himself and let what he did not want. In 1690 the parcels he let, to eight tenants, consisted of two acres; 1½ acres; a 4½-acre close or paddock; 11½ acres of pasture; the backside and orchard to the new house; one acre; 1½ acres of pasture, a pasture called Millclose and three acres; and the nine acres, seven acres and one acre three yards mentioned above as let to Stirt.[180]

A further reason for these small parcels being let to different tenants is suggested by the circumstances surrounding the letting of the two tenements in Cheddar in 1601 mentioned above. Those tenements were parcelled out for a short term at improved rents. Comer's tenement of 18 acres was let to 11 tenants in 14 parcels ranging from a half acre to six acres, with the house and backside let separately to a twelfth tenant. Bole's tenement of 28 acres was let to ten tenants in 15 parcels, and the house and garden let separately for two years. A few rents were quite high, at 12s or 16s an acre, but most parcels fell in the range of 6s to 8s an acre. However, although the same tenant rarely took more than one parcel in each holding, several of the tenants rented parcels in both holdings and in three cases the parcels were in the same furlong or named place in the manor. A deed giving abutments in Cheddar in 1571 shows that several of these tenants may already have been holding land in the places named for these tenements,[181] suggesting that sub-letting was perhaps the easiest way for husbandmen to overcome the difficulties of the scattered parcels which made up most manorial holdings. Tenants in the Lincolnshire fens consolidated their holdings in much the same way, by leasing strips to one another,[182] but this form of rationalisation is not often visible because so little information on subtenancies is available.

178 TNA, E 134/4WandM/East8.

179 e.g. TNA, E 134/5WandM/East10.

180 TNA, E 134/4WandM/East8; E 134/5WandM/East7.

181 SHC, DD\SE/17/4; Harbin, *Somerset Enrolled Deeds*, pp. 95–100.

182 J. Thirsk, *English Peasant Farming: The Agrarian History of Lincolnshire from Tudor to Recent Times* (London, 1957), p. 14.

Convenience may also lie behind John Westover's land rentals, as he held customary parcels in Allerton which he let to others, while renting similar parcels in Wedmore, where he lived. In 1686 he let his five yards of ground in Allerton to Thomas Whiting for 14s for the year. The following year he let it to Andrew Hewishe at the same rent, and Hewishe rented it until the end of 1693, at which time Westover, having received three years' back rent from Hewishe, let it to Isaac Petherham in 1694 and 1695. In 1696 it was let to Edward Day, who rented it for the next three years. Westover also let an acre of meadow in Wedmore for a year, nine acres of meadow and pasture in Brent from time to time, and one or two other small parcels in Wedmore and Allerton at various times, always on a year-to-year basis and usually to farmers living near the parcels. At the same time, Westover himself rented one acre in Clemence furlong in Wedmore in most years at 14s, using it for a different crop each time. The period that the land was held was actually usually less than a year, the arable being held for the crop, and pasture and meadow entered in February or April until the following Christmas.[183]

No evidence suggests land lying idle for want of tenants, but equally there is no indication of a shortage of land to rent in the area. Non-resident copyholders and freeholders were one source. Many references to customary tenants living outside their tenements without licence, and grants of such licences, occur in the court rolls: in Biddisham, for example, 17 tenants in the 20 holdings of the manor were mentioned in this connection between 1543 and 1610, and by the latter date copies were being granted regularly with licence to let for life included in the copy and fine. The amount of land available increased as more copies in the chapter's manors were taken by clerical and legal families who were both non-resident and non-farming; for those copyholders whose background is unknown, the heriots taken at their death indicate whether they were farmers. Most heriots were stipulated as the best beast, and household goods were taken only if there was no livestock: a featherbed and coverlet were taken on the death of Agnes Griffen of Biddisham in 1639, while a pair of virginals, a featherbed and a brass vessel were claimed for three heriots on the death of Grace Hide in 1609.[184] Land held by the parish churches was another source. The church of Wedmore, for example, held 20 acres of meadow and 28 acres of pasture for 99 years from the manor of Mudgley in 1558, and sub-let it to local tenants. The meadow lay in six closes, five of them let individually to single tenants and the sixth let jointly to four tenants. The pasture lay in three closes of 18, five and five acres respectively, each let to a different tenant.[185] The pastures of the coastal parishes, on the other hand, may not have been quite so readily available, as they were in demand for their rich grazing. They were also in larger blocks, which would make it difficult for a small family farmer to afford or to make full use of the land. A large number of non-residents took land in the coastal parishes, and some specifically used it themselves for grazing, while others may have sub-let it.[186]

---

183 SHC, DD\X\HKN, *passim*.

184 SHC, DD\CC/B/110233, court 9 Aug. 1639; DD\CC/B/131925/7, court 10 July 7 Jas. I.

185 SHC, DD\SAS/C795/PR/462.

186 Above, Rearing and grazing of livestock.

Despite the many difficulties of accurately assessing the sizes and incomes of farms, the fact is that small mixed farms, particularly those based on dairying, survived in the Levels into the twentieth century. Evidently farmers could make a good living from the land here, including a marketable surplus, and the supply of small parcels of land that made their farming flexible and profitable continued to be available to them beyond the early modern period.

Chapter 5

Family and inheritance in Brent Marsh

The aspects of land tenure peculiar to this area and the flexible nature of its agriculture also had important social effects on relations between parents and children and between husbands and wives. They allowed flexible portions for children; pre-mortem transfer of portions and early independence for children; and an equal spread of assets among siblings, avoiding a heavy concentration on one heir. The way that land, particularly customary holdings, was passed on to the next generation was examined in Chapter 3, but this chapter looks generally at how and to whom landholders and farmers passed on their real and personal property, and some of the ensuing effects on both the local economy and the sustainability of small-scale farming. Women also benefited from the tenurial customs, which gave them full right of inheritance as widows in customary holdings, and the wider implications for their role in local society are looked at here.

Handing on assets to children

The ways in which property is transmitted from one generation to the next, and its timing, can have a deep significance for individual families and for the wider society of which they are part, influencing demographic change, family relationships and the survival of the economic – and therefore the social – status of the individual family or of the class or occupational group, and all this in turn influences the economic development of the country as a whole. It is not too far-fetched to see inheritance in its broadest scope as the driving force behind much of our social, economic and political history: E.P. Thompson has pointed out that inheritance should be seen not just in terms of the physical property being inherited but in its context of the rights, usages and networks of opportunity open to different groups in society. The political activities of certain groups were largely concerned with preserving opportunities for their children: for example, the efforts of the aristocracy and gentry in the eighteenth century were directed towards securing 'the Church and State as a kind of Trust for their own class' with regard to offices and financial organisation, by maintaining their influence with those who could grant such offices. Parents' desire to transmit their own standard of living to their children could also tax the resources of individuals and social groups to the limit, and is thought to have contributed to the disappearance of the yeomen as a large and recognisable social class during the eighteenth century.[1]

An emphasis on the wider implications of inheritance is a reminder that the subject includes more than just physical blocks of land. Nevertheless, as the transmission of

1 Thompson,'Grid of Inheritance', pp. 337, 346, 358.

land influenced agricultural development in England – where much of the argument centres on the disappearance of the small landowner, the rise of large farms and the economic consequences – and as land was the basis of status and generally the safest form of investment, the study of inheritance has often concentrated on land. The nature of the inheritance customs that controlled a great many of the traditional customary manorial holdings has been seen as crucial in this respect, and was particularly important in agrarian societies where access to land might be limited. Where partible inheritance was the rule holdings might be fragmented into small acreages that were not economically viable, which not only prevented the introduction of many new methods that would have increased production but also kept a large part of the population tied to the land without giving them an adequate surplus from it. Impartible inheritance, with the whole holding, stock and equipment going to one child, meant a better chance of economic survival, of improving resources and of increasing profit and production, to the point where a labour force without connection with agriculture could be supported and made available for industry. It also meant that the status associated with land passed to only one child. However, little evidence has emerged in studies in England to show that variations in inheritance custom were so significant, principally because other means, chiefly the will, were used to ameliorate the effects of custom and ensure a fairly equitable share of resources among all children.[2] Where a father had more than one child, therefore, his property was almost always divided up in some way, and where a landholder had no children he might well divide his land among several relatives. Thus wills allow a study of the attitude of testators towards their children and of differences, if any, in the way in which sons and daughters were considered, while the increasing number of studies of these topics is also showing up local differences as well as changes over time.[3]

Male primogeniture was the norm for inheritance under common law, covering all freehold land, and was therefore the norm among the aristocracy and gentry, who sought to maintain the power and standing of their family by passing all landed property to one male heir, who, in the Middle Ages, could fight for the monarch when required. It has been suggested, however, that there was a 'presumption' of male primogeniture in English society generally, so that the eldest son would generally receive the household's main source of living, whether land or workshop.[4] However, this 'norm' of primogeniture seems to be more the assumption of historians, who then express surprise at the efforts made to provide for the younger children. A desire to divide the testator's wealth equitably among all children seems far more normal than favouring just one, and there is little evidence of primogeniture in any actual examples concerning copyhold land outside the areas – mainly limited to the east of England – where the custom was for copyhold to pass to the eldest son. Even there, however, the ability to transfer or sell customary land, or to dispose of it by will, meant that in

2 W. Coster, *Family and Kinship in England, 1450–1800* (London, 2001), p. 34.

3 J. Whittle, 'Inheritance, Marriage, Widowhood and Remarriage: A Comparative Perspective on Women and Landholding in North-East Norfolk, 1440–1580', *Continuity and Change*, 13/1 (1998), pp. 33–72; A.L. Erickson, *Women and Property in Early Modern England* (London, 1993), chap. 4.

4 Wrightson, *Earthly Necessities*, p. 62.

Table 8
Number and source of wills used

Decade written	*From PCC*	*Diocesan & others(a)*	*Total*
Early 16th cent.	6	-	6
1539–46	-	116	116
1550–59	7	38	45
1560–69	13	-	13
1570–79	23	12	35
1580–89	38	24	62
1590–99	49	5	54
1600–09	33	1	34
1610–19	48	7	55
1620–29	66	9	75
1630–39	86	8	94
1640–49	59	6	65
1650–59[(b)]	162	1	163
1660–69	26	3	29
1670–79	19	3	22
1680–89	14	5	19
1690–99	8	1	9
Totals	657	239	896
	73.30%	26.70%	

Notes: (a) the majority of these were proved in diocesan courts, but a few are in solicitors' collections and other private deposits, and may not have received probate. Where probate took place in the PCC they are included under PCC only; (b) from 1653 to 1660 the only probate court was the Court of Civil Commission, whose records are with the PCC.

practice only a small percentage of such land was transferred by inheritance custom.[5] Elsewhere custom allowed a variety of inheritance, especially when the tenure was copyhold for lives, and here it is hard to find any presumption or 'norm' of male primogeniture. Men who held land in free socage generally, but not always, followed common-law practice and left it to their eldest son, particularly if it had been inherited, but this never extended to the other tenures they held, and certainly not to chattels, nor to the position of 'head of the family', as wives were preferred as executors.[6]

The discussion below looks at the ways that inhabitants of Brent Marsh provided for their children, but there are a few difficulties in creating an overview of inheritance for the Somerset Levels. The first is that so many locally proven wills and inventories

5 e.g. only 4–12% of customary acreage in Hevingham Bishops was transferred under inheritance custom in the first half of the sixteenth century: Whittle, *Development of Agrarian Capitalism*, p. 121, Table 3.5.

6 Below, Roles of women in rural society: Responsibility given to women.

have been destroyed, and while a surprising number of wills were proved in the PCC[7] this has tended to slant the sample towards the better-off; the absence of most of the inventories also prevents an assessment of the relationship of bequests to the total stock. The number and source of the wills used in this study are given in Table 8. Secondly, as discussed in Chapter 3, the transfer of freehold and copyhold land did not have to be done by will, and consequently freehold land was only rarely disposed of by will, and copyhold almost never, in Brent Marsh. Thirdly, the availability in the Levels of many small parcels of land, and the flexibility of farming here, meant that much pre-mortem transfer of assets and provision for children occurred during their parents' lifetime, and these transactions are only sparsely documented.

Pre-mortem transfer

The transfer of all or part of their portions to offspring during their father's lifetime provides the greatest obstacle to a full understanding of inheritance in the rural community. Pre-mortem transfers usually generated fewer documents: they were often not recorded at all, or their details must be pieced together from many sources, principally manorial records and wills.[8] Probably the majority of farmers' children in the Levels were provided for by the father during his lifetime, since the good supply of small landholdings meant that fathers could enable their sons to become economically independent while they were themselves still economically active, and this factor may also have contributed to the small proportion of wills made by inhabitants.[9]

The wills of men without dependent children form about 30 per cent of the surviving wills for Brent Marsh, and they show that many men here had established their children during their lifetime and still continued working for themselves: sojourners and early retirement, with transfer of the parental home and holding to the eldest son, were apparently not as common here as in, for example, Cambridgeshire and the Midlands.[10] In the Somerset Levels, as in other areas of mainly pastoral farming,[11] references abound to married sons farming on their own account during their father's lifetime. John Masters of Wedmore, for example, bequeathed to his married eldest son a yoke of oxen already in the son's custody.[12] William Boulting of Theale left to his married son John half the ground at Southams, of which John already held the other half.[13] Setting up sons during the father's lifetime was aided, in this region, by the availability of small leaseholds,

7 Below, Sources and bibliography: Note on probate sources for Brent Marsh.

8 The level of detail of landholding and inheritance strategies that can be achieved using a range of sources is shown in Whittle, *Development of Agrarian Capitalism*, pp. 119–67.

9 Below, Disposal of personal estates by will.

10 J. Goody, J. Thirsk and E.P. Thompson (eds), *Family and Inheritance: Rural Society in Western Europe, 1200–1800* (Cambridge, 1976), p. 6. No such arrangements were found in material for Brent Marsh.

11 e.g. K. Wrightson and D. Levine, *Poverty and Piety in an English Village: Terling, 1525–1700* (London, 1979), p. 96.

12 TNA, PROB 11/178/639.

13 TNA, PROB 11/253/492.

tenements and other parcels, and many husbandmen and yeomen had several such parcels by one form of tenure or another. Robert Crosman, a yeoman of East Brent, bequeathed to his son James all the furniture in the house where James lived, and Crosman had at least two other houses attached to various tenements.[14] Thomas Looke of Wedmore, who had several leases of small acreages dotted over the area, left to his son Robert some land belonging to the house where Robert was living.[15]

Occasionally a son predeceased his father and the son's independence is then apparent in his own will. John Reeve junior of Cheddar died in 1621, leaving a wife and two young daughters; his father John and brother William were appointed as overseers.[16] In his will he disposed of a lease for years in Weare and listed a great number of sums owing to him, totalling about £60, for stock and crops sold, on bonds and for rents of land. He owed his father £40 and a widow of Cheddar £60 at the following Michaelmas: possibly rent or loans. He was, therefore, an active farmer, buying and selling stock and renting out land. His father died ten years later and bequeathed a number of leases to his grandchildren: both his other sons, William and Thomas, were married with children and he apparently had two married daughters with children as well.[17] Despite the fact that the sons were already established to some degree, he gave Thomas his plough gear and some farm stock and William the residue, so John senior had evidently carried on farming after setting up his children. That sons were sometimes handed a lump sum on their marriage is suggested by the £200 that John Marshall of Cheddar promised his son John on his marriage, though John received it only after his father's death, by which time he had three children of his own.[18] There were also many other ways in which sons were set up during their father's lifetime, such as in apprenticeship and trade, which leave less trace than land and farming.

Some share in the father's holding might also be made over to a daughter and son-in-law on their marriage, usually where the father had no son. According to John Huchyns junior, William Hayne and Ellen, his wife, promised that if Huchyns married Ellen's daughter Christian they would assure to Huchyns their three tenements in Cheddar and half of all their lands there during the lives of William and Ellen, and would buy the reversion of the property for John and Christian. He had occupied the premises for three years after this marriage, in common with William and Ellen, but was complaining that the latter had refused to make the necessary legal security. However, William and Ellen answered that Huchyns was a very poor man with only some stock to bring to the marriage and it had required the mediation of friends before they had agreed to it and made over to him a dwelling with the backside, half the barn and 6½ acres with the fruit on it, and 5½ acres of other land.[19]

For married daughters it was even more important that the portion was such that the woman and her husband could take and use it freely. A lump sum was obviously very

14 TNA, PROB 11/296/293.
15 TNA, PROB 11/312/127.
16 TNA, PROB 11/138/81.
17 TNA, PROB 11/160/387.
18 TNA, PROB 11/170/445.
19 TNA, C 1/829/44–5.

suitable where the father could afford a large sum all at once, but in some ways cash was too flexible to fulfil the father's requirements, which were not just to promote his daughter's marriage but also to make sure she had adequate support for the future. A lump sum in the hands of a son-in-law did not ensure the daughter's support should he die or mismanage his affairs, and no doubt prudent fathers handed over the money only when the husband had made some security for the daughter in a similar way to the security demanded for sums given in a father's will. Edward Urch alias Fry left £20 to his daughter Elizabeth provided her husband buy her a life estate to that annual value, and £200 to another daughter Jane provided her husband buy an estate for her life in his property in a specific manor, or the equivalent annual value elsewhere.[20] In 1619 John Griffin left £50 to Elizabeth, the wife of Thomas Burnell, to remain in a stock for her until her husband secured her in a living, either his own or one as good as his.[21] Marriage portions of land were easier to secure and some daughters were named in copies or given leases for their lifetime to provide support for them independent of anything their husbands might provide, and while the husband lived he, of course, received the benefit of the property. This was a simpler alternative to a formal settlement of land made by either the father or the husband.

Pre-mortem transfers to children and the forms of land tenure also make it difficult to assess the equality of inheritance between siblings when studying wills. This region is worse than many because its customary land was not often mentioned in wills, but surely cannot be unique, and whenever a will apparently dismisses a child with only a token it can be assumed that the child had already been established. A few examples will illustrate the kind of situations encountered. Thomas Wall senior, yeoman, of Compton Bishop mentioned his wife, six sons and three daughters in his will of 1639, which he used to ratify and confirm a conveyance of lands he had made earlier in trust for certain uses (not specified in the will), and gave his eldest son Jasper all his lands in South Brent. Apart from that, his six sons, including Jasper, were to receive '20*s*. each and no more in respect they are otherwise provided for by me heretofore', and his married daughter Joan was to receive '10*s*. and no more in respect she hath her marriage portion already given by me unto her'. The other daughters, Orian and Jane, were to receive £150 each when 21 or married and were each given a bed and bedding, pewter and other goods. One of the younger sons, Thomas, was given all the wainscots, wooden furniture, locks and keys in Wall's dwelling house, which Martha, his wife and executrix, was to have while a widow, and the overseers were to see that the four youngest sons were 'bred at school' till 21 from the profits of the lands that Wall had already conveyed to them for their maintenance.[22]

The only land mentioned in the will of Richard Bowltinge, yeoman, of Theale is a 99-year lease of some 20 acres of overland in the nearby manor of Wookey, which he left to his youngest child, a son. His second son was left the executorship of the will, but his wife, his eldest son and his three daughters received only 20s each, and no mention is made in the will of his property in Theale.[23] Clearly other arrangements had been made

20 TNA, PROB 11/366/191.

21 TNA, PROB 11/135/479.

22 TNA, PROB, 11/182/88.

23 TNA, PROB 11/242/244.

or the children had either already received their portions or would inherit land. Similarly, Thomas Hodges, gentleman, of Wedmore made detailed bequests of leases and goods, mainly for his grandchildren, but made no mention of the freehold land he held, which descended automatically by common law to the eldest son of his deceased son.[24]

A similar situation, but relating to copyhold, lay behind the will of Stephen Champney, husbandman, of Blackford in Wedmore.[25] Champney held by copies two tenements and 23 acres and one tenement and 18 acres, all in the manor of Blackford, to which his brother Richard (who in the event died at the same time as himself) was next heir, with remainder to Stephen's son, also Stephen, as the third life in the copies.[26] In Champney's will the son Stephen received only furniture, and the bulk of the personal estate went to the testator's other two children, John and Grace, his wife having predeceased him. John received a lease of seven acres of meadow in the neighbouring parish of Mark, which the testator had inherited from his mother's brother,[27] and Grace was given two leases totalling three acres three yards of arable and three acres of meadow, plus a further 1½ acres held 'by bond' (presumably a mortgage) for the lives of the testator's three sisters, but Stephen was to have this if he paid Grace £12. John and Grace were also to receive £13 6s 8d a year 'out of Stephen's means' towards their upbringing until Stephen was 14,[28] and they also received the residue of the estate between them. As the only other bequests were the clothes of the testator and his mother, this would consist of all his stock, implements, crops, household goods apart from the furniture left to Stephen, and debts due to the testator, after debts owing and funeral expenses had been paid. Obviously there was considerable disparity between the land holdings that Stephen and the other two would have in adult life, but Champeny did attempt in his will to redress to some extent the inheritance of copyhold by one son and ensure that all his children had some means of support.[29] Examples similar to these are very common, and in many cases it is only an indirect reference in the will that shows that the testators had other lands, particularly where few surveys or supporting records survive.

In the Levels then, the number of sons farming on their own account during their father's lifetime suggests that many men transferred part of their property before death to sons, as well as to daughters on marriage, often by investing in land which they could hand over early. These pre-mortem transfers make studies of the division between siblings and the economic effects very unreliable for this area. They also show a more relaxed, less paternalistic family structure, where fathers

---

24 TNA, PROB 11/97/80.

25 TNA, PROB 11/183/91.

26 SHC, DD\SE/65/1–2.

27 TNA, PROB 11/151/385.

28 He was around six years when the will was written.

29 It seems a little hard that Stephen should inherit only a little furniture and would have to restock the holding if he were farming it himself. However, since no custom has been found whereby certain stock or implements went with a customary holding here, one must assume that the holding did just mean the land and buildings. Woods belonged to the holding, but crops to the executor. Possibly in cases like this the child inheriting the holding would buy the stock and equipment from his siblings.

were willing to relinquish some of their control over the next generation, compared with areas where the sons were dependants in their father's household until his death or retirement.[30]

Disposal of personal estates by will

Though inheritance is largely associated with making provision for dependants through a will, this was a comparatively recent development in the early modern period, and the will became important when it began to be used as a legal instrument to defeat both inheritance custom and common law, giving the testator greater freedom in disposing of his property. Under the general inheritance custom of medieval England, a man leaving wife and children could dispose freely of only one-third of his chattels; his wife received another third and his children shared the remaining third.[31] Glanville recorded that, where only the heir survived, a half was set aside for him and the other half could then be freely disposed of by the testator. As the portions for wife and children were determined by custom they were often omitted from medieval wills, and a testator might just make some small bequest to a child out of his own remaining third, the 'dead's part' as it was called. In general, however, this third was reserved in the Middle Ages for the soul of the deceased: that is, for masses or pious and community uses. Besides the general custom, there were local customs that could often override the usual division and which might also reserve certain chattels for the heir, such as equipment for the house, plough gear or the tools of a trade. Finally, a man without spouse, issue or dependants was free to dispose of all his goods.

These restrictions on testamentary powers were being disputed or had fallen out of use in the later Middle Ages, and had disappeared altogether in southern England before the reign of Elizabeth I, though the reasons are not clear: the changed legal status of married women or the influence of the common law, which avoided tying up property in this way, have been suggested.[32] In the course of the sixteenth and seventeenth centuries the influence of common law increased, partly for political reasons, in matters where other legal systems had formerly been pre-eminent, taking the place, for example, of ecclesiastical law, which included probate matters, and customary law (concerning land tenure and use).[33] Whatever the reason, the custom of thirds ceased to be upheld in the ecclesiastical courts, but it may still have influenced the way some men divided their property between wife, children and other uses, even though little indication of this occurs after the

---

30 e.g. C. Howell, 'Peasant Inheritance Customs in the Midlands, 1280–1700', in Goody *et al.*, *Family and Inheritance*, p. 145.

31 Erickson, *Women and Property*, p. 28. Remainder of paragraph based on Pollock and Maitland, *History of English Law*, II, pp. 348, 350.

32 Pollock and Maitland, *History of English Law*, II, pp. 351, 353n; A.G. Guest, 'Family Provision and the Legitima Portio', *Law Quarterly Review*, 73 (1957), p. 81; W.S. Holdsworth, *A History of English Law* (3rd edn, 1923), III, p. 554.

33 Erickson, *Women and Property*, pp. 28–30.

mid sixteenth century. John Day of Badgworth willed in June 1541 that 'my chylder shall have the third part of my god [sic] to be delivered to them when that my wife doth marry agayne', and his wife received the residue.[34] When bequests were made to several children it was common throughout the early modern period for the testator to specify that if any child died under age his or her portion was to be left to the survivors, treating children's portions as belonging to all the children rather than to the executor or to the residue of the estate. However, although some testators continued to give part of their goods to pious uses in the sixteenth and seventeenth centuries, with bequests to parish church, the poor and community uses, the amounts given, particularly to the parish church and the diocesan cathedral, dwindled into a rather arid token gesture, and where larger sums were given they went to the poor.

A feeling of obligation to make a will also stemmed from medieval ideas, quite apart from any need to make provision for dependants,[35] and by the seventeenth century it is apparent that many men and women regarded the making of a will not so much as a moral obligation laid on them by others but as a responsibility that they wished to perform for their own peace of mind. One man who fell ill set out with his son to go to the house of a neighbour who could write the will, so anxious was he to get it done, and eventually the will was written sitting under a hedge in the lane.[36] Mary Churchouse of Wedmore had to send three or four times for a busy neighbour to come to write her will for her, and when it was finished she gave thanks to God 'because she was troubled in her mind until it was done'.[37] It brought criticism if a man died with his property unsettled, as when Thomas Wride of Burnham died in 1661 leaving his estate 'in an unsettled condition', having no obvious heirs such as a wife or children. The man with whom Wride shared a house told a neighbour that when *he* died he would leave his estate 'in a better condition'.[38] Unsettled property led to quarrels, bad feeling and litigation, so it was considered irresponsible not to make suitable provision and one's wishes known.

Despite these pressures to make a will, however, relatively few exist considering the number of deaths, and the making of wills seems to have been relatively uncommon among the population in general.[39] In the small rural town of Banbury in Oxfordshire only a quarter of the men and one tenth of the women who could have left a will did so across the period 1558–1723,[40] while for two Norfolk parishes in the period 1560–80 27 and 12 per cent, respectively, of adult males left wills.[41] In Brent Marsh figures for the large parish of Wedmore show that for the period 1653–60, when

---

34 SHC, DD\SAS/SE/30.

35 M. Sheehan, *The Will in Medieval England* (Toronto, 1963), p. 232.

36 SHC, D\D/cd/51, Thurston v. Vowles, dep. of William Pitt, 12 Mar. 1617.

37 *Ibid.*, Llewellin als. Morris v. Churchouse, dep. of William Martin, 22 Dec. 1623.

38 SHC, D\D/cd/135, Wall v. Wride & others, dep. of John Lane, 6 Nov. 1661.

39 J.S.W. Gibson, *Wills and Where to Find Them* (Chichester, 1974), p. xv.

40 R.T. Vann, 'Wills and the Family in an English Town: Banbury, 1550–1800', *Journal of Family History*, 4/4 (1979), p. 352.

41 Whittle, *Development of Agrarian Capitalism*, pp. 129–30.

the Court of Civil Commission in London was the only probate court, out of 113 adult male residents buried only 16 (14 per cent) left proven wills, with a further seven wills proved for men not in the Wedmore burial register for that period, a total of 19 per cent of 120 men. Of 49 adult females buried not designated as wife or daughter, only two (4 per cent) left wills, with one further will of a woman designated as a daughter.[42] It is likely, too, that many wills were never proven where they were not required to convey ownership of property, and occasionally a will was proven a long time after the death of the testator to establish title.[43] However, it should not be assumed that the wills that do exist belong to the better-off. While it may be generally true that the better-off were more likely to leave wills, detailed studies show that there were other influences to consider. In towns such as Banbury, where labourers were under-represented among the will-leavers, the wealthier were more likely to leave a will, but in rural areas this was not always the case. In some areas, such as Brent Marsh, landholding and the possession of livestock and other capital stock were spread across the spectrum of wealth, even though landholders did not necessarily mention land in their wills,[44] and different local economies may have influenced will-making. In the fen village of Willingham in Cambridgeshire, for example, nearly two-thirds of the will-makers between 1575 and 1603 were smallholders or landless, and only a quarter of them were larger landholders; further consideration of the family circumstances there suggested that it was the necessity to provide for children, rather than the level of wealth, that determined whether a will was made.[45]

Enough wills do exist, fortunately, to make a worthwhile study, even in Brent Marsh, where most locally proven wills have been destroyed. Many men were still active heads of households with one or more dependent children when they died: they often married more than once and had families with widely spread age ranges. Overall, of the 756 wills by men in this study, 34 per cent had dependent or unmarried children.[46] Even though most of the wills used here were proven in the PCC, however, the wealthy do not stand out as the predominant group of testators. Between 1503 and 1699 there were 459 wills in Brent Marsh by men who had an occupational or status designation, and out of these the largest category, at 45 per cent, was that of husbandmen. Yeomen accounted for 29 per cent, 16 per cent were craftsmen, tradesmen or merchants and 9 per cent gentry or clergy.[47] However, as in Willingham, some leading landholders in the Levels do not appear among the surviving wills nor in the calendars of destroyed wills, so not all the wealthiest inhabitants made wills, and the tradition of will-making in a family also seems to have influenced whether a will was made or not.

---

42 Burial figures taken from Hervey, *Wedmore Parish Registers*. The number of male adult burials may, like the female adults, also be underestimated, as a few 'sons of' may be adults.

43 e.g. will of William Strowde of Rodney Stoke written 1593, and will of his son Thomas written 1629, both proven 1652 to establish title: TNA, PROB 11/222/132; /133.

44 Whittle, *Development of Agrarian Capitalism*, pp. 130–31.

45 M. Spufford, 'Peasant inheritance customs and land distribution in Cambridgeshire from the sixteenth to the eighteenth centuries', in Goody *et al.*, *Family and Inheritance*, pp. 169–72.

46 Figures from Croot, 'Agrarian Society', p. 488, Table 16.

47 *Ibid.*, p. 487, Table 15.

The use of wills and the dispositions made

Wills made primarily to dispose of the goods, cash and land which the testator had in hand, where he had no dependants to provide for, reveal a wide range of aims and attitudes. Men and women whose children were married are frequently found giving the bulk of their estate to their grandchildren, often with preference given to females over males. Richard Counsell of Mudgley, yeoman, left the bulk of his personal estate to his son's two daughters, including silver spoons, chests and crocks, a half interest in a tenement and £100 each.[48] Richard Adams of Wedmore, husbandman, left only token bequests to his son and the latter's children, and to his youngest daughter and her children, but gave the two daughters of his eldest daughter a close of meadow and a lease for years, while their brother received only £6 in cash.[49] Though testators may well have chosen those in greatest need, or the grandchildren who would receive the least from their parents, it is possible also that personal preference played a greater part in this type of bequest. However, while need is sometimes mentioned in wills as a determinant of the bequests,[50] the personal likes or dislikes of a testator towards his children or grandchildren were never mentioned in the wills examined:[51] equity is the pervading attitude that emerges regarding the testator's role, particularly where he is the head of a household and family. In the wills of testators who had dependants, the predominant theme was the provision of some kind of living to every child, or at least maintenance until he or she was of an age to provide for themselves. As indicated above, if a child was not mentioned in the father's will, or received only a small bequest, it is fairly safe to assume that this was because he or she had been provided for in another way.

Provision for dependants in wills falls into two categories: to provide maintenance while the children were under age or to provide a living in adult life. Some wills that make provision for a large number of children provide maintenance for some and a living for others. William Phippen of Wedmore, husbandman, had seven sons to provide for, ranging in age from 19 years to 1 year, his wife having died shortly before the will was written.[52] The eldest son (19) was left a house and land with its lease, and the second son (17) was to have four acres of meadow and three yards of arable with the lease, plus the corn and implements at a house in Lympsham and the herbage of meadow and pasture of another tenement at Lympsham; the next holders of the tenements are unknown. The next three sons, aged 14, 9 and 6 respectively, were to receive the profits of all the lands given to the two eldest, except an orchard, for six years, during which time they presumably would make some provision for their future, while the two youngest (3 and 1) received a lease of land and the residue of the estate. The desire to ensure that all dependent children had adequate support is strongly implied in most

48 TNA, PROB 11/104/18.

49 TNA, PROB 11/228/130.

50 e.g. 'the portions of children dying to go to those most in need': TNA, PROB 11/140/44.

51 The only personal reasons found were a few explaining bequests to non-relatives.

52 TNA, PROB 11/144/68.

Table 9
Number and percentage of portions in goods, cash and land

Decade	Goods only		Cash & goods		Cash only		Land only		Land & cash		Land & goods	
	No.	%	No.	%	No.	%	No.	%	No.	%	No.	%
1503–28	1	10.0	1	10.0	8	80.0	-		-		-	
1539–46	95	78.5	6	5.0	17	14.1	-		-		3	2.5
1550–9	16	57.1	8	28.6	1	3.6	2	7.1	-		1	3.6
1560–9	-		4	44.4	4	44.4	1	11.1	-		-	
1570–9	6	19.4	9	29.0	16	51.6	-		-		-	
1580–9	18	23.7	8	10.5	38	48.7	3	4.0	6	7.9	4	5.3
1590–9	16	23.2	4	5.8	41	59.4	5	7.3	3	4.4	-	
1600–9	10	23.8	-		22	52.4	4	9.5	6	14.3	-	
1610–9	4	5.3	3	4.0	48	63.2	11	14.5	7	9.2	3	4.0
1620–9	5	3.9	3	2.3	75	58.1	26	20.2	15	11.6	5	3.9
1630–9	8	7.3	7	6.4	69	63.3	9	8.3	10	9.2	6	5.5
1640–9	5	5.4	2	2.2	64	69.6	6	6.5	12	13.0	3	3.3
1650–9	12	6.4	10	5.3	111	59.0	32	17.0	12	6.4	11	5.9
1660–9	10	19.2	2	3.9	16	30.8	13	25.0	7	13.5	4	7.7
1670–9	2	12.5	2	12.5	2	12.5	3	18.8	7	43.8	-	
1680–9	-		-		2	20.0	3	30.0	2	20.0	3	30.0
1690–9	1	3.2	-		20	64.5	10	32.3	-		-	

Notes: Taken from the wills of men with children. The numbers given above are for individual *portions*, not the number of wills. The portions exclude the residue given as a portion, and tokens under £1 and small bequests to married children are also excluded. Wills are grouped in decades according to date written, not of probate. For sources of wills in each decade, see Table 8.

wills, and is occasionally made explicit. Thomas Evans of Weare, yeoman, made some provision for his son out of land but, 'because this legacy is not sufficient maintenance', gave him additional rents.[53]

Portions for children in wills consisted of six permutations of three main categories – goods, cash and land – and are set out in Table 9. The two principal constituents of the portions were goods only and cash only: the other combinations rarely exceeded 10 per cent, especially in decades with the greatest numbers of portions. Goods only was highest in the early decades, but by the 1570s was overtaken by cash-only portions, which thereafter generally formed around 50 to 60 per cent of all portions, and sometimes more. This was not the only change over the 150 years studied here; in addition to changes in the content of children's portions, the length and content of the wills themselves altered considerably, as the comparison below of two separate decades shows.

53 TNA, PROB 11/264/248.

Wills of the 1540s

The earliest group of wills large enough for comparison are the 116 wills proven in the years 1539–46 in the local diocesan court of the archdeacon of Wells, which cover nine of the parishes;[54] no wills from this area are found in the PCC in this period. In a few cases occupations are given, including husbandman, cheesemonger and butcher, and in most cases the inventory value was entered against each copy will, showing a wide range from 19s to £55.[55] The striking point about the wills is their simplicity and, in most cases, their brevity, compared with later wills. Practically all contain some bequests to the cathedral at Wells, as well as to the local parish church or its services, lights or altars, and for about two-fifths of the wills this accounts for all the bequests, the only additions being the disposal of the residue and executorship. About the same proportion of wills also contain one or two additional bequests, usually to children. The wills for estates with an inventory value over £20 tend to have more bequests, but there is not much difference in the structure of the will.

Of testators who mention children, those including cash in the children's portions were not necessarily those with the highest inventory values. Twelve wills contain cash portions for children, ranging from £2 to £40, but not necessarily in correlation with inventory size: the cash portions in the estate worth £55 were £5 to each of an unspecified number of children, while a will with an inventory worth £14 10s left a portion of £9.[56] The most important constituent of children's portions in this decade was livestock, and for many children their only legacy by will was animals: Thomas Burrow of Berrow left each of his five sons and daughters a cow and a ewe; John Kyng of South Brent left to his son and two daughters jointly his four best beasts grazing in his mother's lease and, should one be taken for a heriot, one of his best plough oxen instead, and to each child also a cow, a calf and three colts; while from one of the lower-value estates, at *c.*£3, John Allen of Huntspill left to his son two bullocks of four years and two years, and to his two daughters six sheep.[57] The division of stock between several children, which meant that the capital assets of the farm were being divided up, can give the impression of sparse resources shared round as far as possible, but the wills in this period are notable for their lack of information about the testator's total assets. John Kyng, mentioned above, obviously held a customary tenement because he mentions a heriot, and had enough arable land to warrant a plough team. Andrew Donett of Overweare, husbandman, whose inventory was valued at only £3 6s 8d, nevertheless had plough gear, wain wheels and other farm equipment to bequeath, indicating enough arable to justify the possession of valuable equipment; these items were mentioned only because he apparently had no children and wanted the gear

54 The wills survive in three registers and part of a fourth, and give no indication of the court, but the parishes represented fall within the jurisdiction of this archdeacon: Axbridge, Badgworth, Berrow, Burnham, East Brent, Huntspill, Lympsham, South Brent, Weare.

55 Shilton and Holworthy, *Medieval Wills*, p. 163; SHC, DD\SAS/SE/30. Inventories apparently no longer exist.

56 SHC, DD\SAS/SE/30.

57 Shilton and Holworthy, *Medieval Wills*, pp. 3, 5–6, 39.

to go to a particular person after the death of his wife.[58] Very few wills mention land of any kind, but the few that do, together with other sources, show that the testator's resources were probably far greater than their bequests suggest. The will of Richard Evans (Yevans) of Lympsham makes the usual religious bequests and leaves four kine to the four children of his son John; John received the residue because Richard's wife, Joan, had agreed to surrender her widow's right in the tenement to John in return for £4, a silver mazer and Richard's chamber with its contents. Of these, she had received £2 and the mazer when the will was written and a clause to this effect was added so that it could be witnessed conveniently with the signing and witnessing of the will. Customary tenements were not valued in inventories as they were considered to be freeholds, so Evans' inventory total of £8 7s 2d is far from revealing the true state of his economic position.[59]

Another chance indication of land occurs in the will of John Burton of Burnham, who left £9 in money to his eldest son John, unless the testator's wife 'buys the bargain for him', in which case he was to have only 40s.[60] In most cases, however, the holding would already have been settled and the copies purchased during the testator's lifetime: the widow held the tenement while single and was generally left the residue and made executor, either alone or with her children,[61] and those children with reversions had to wait to succeed. Many testators appear in surveys or court rolls for manors in the area, and most of those who cannot be identified with certainty to a particular holding had family names that constantly occur as customary tenants. Many of the testators or their widows appear in the subsidies of 1524 and 1545 and the Relief of 1548, assessed at several pounds' worth of goods.[62]

These wills present difficulties when used to examine provision for children. In this period they had not yet become the established medium for providing for children that they later were, which accounts for the greater simplicity in the bequests made. Many testators left the residue for pious uses: Philip Deane of East Brent left the residue to his wife Agnes, the executrix, to dispose of for the 'wealth of my soul', and similar instructions were left to the wife and son of William Donne of East Brent,[63] so clearly other provision had been made for the wife and children in these cases. However, where provisions of resources for a living were made in a will, they still appear very small in scope, probably because this period lay before the main increase in prices: not only were farm incomes on a lower scale, making a father's resources smaller, but also a little would go a long way to support an individual.

Bequests of land or of cash that could be used for buying a means of livelihood, either in land or in trade, can easily be seen as providing a living, but bequests of goods are more complicated and divide into those of limited use and those which

58 *Ibid.*, p. 114.

59 SHC, DD\SAS/SE/30.

60 *Ibid.* In 1524 he was assessed on £6 in goods, a fairly high amount for the area: TNA, E 179/169/171.

61 Below, Roles of women in rural society: Responsibility given to women.

62 Below, Chap. 6, Wealth in the Levels, and Table 11.

63 Shilton and Holworthy, *Medieval Wills*, p. 3; SHC, DD\SAS/SE/30.

would provide an income. Bequests of goods in this first group included household goods, plate and clothes, such as silver spoons (in about 11 wills), crocks (12 wills), pans (11) and pewter (4); other items frequently found include articles of furniture such as cupboards, coffers and bedding, and the testator's clothes. Some of these items were valuable, but almost certainly they were not intended for sale but as useful or valuable keepsakes or heirlooms. Daughters frequently received large crocks or pans, valuable items they could take with them to their marriage. However, though such goods were sometimes pawned, they did not provide an income or a capital sum.

The other group of goods was intended to provide some degree of income, or as capital assets, and a few wills make this clear, using expressions commonplace by the early seventeenth century indicating that goods should be put out to increase for the profit of the legatee. In 1540 William Kyng of East Brent left to his daughter Joan four kine, a heifer and a calf. Her brother was to have the first year's profit but after that the profit was to remain to her. Two overseers were appointed in trust to see that the cattle were used for her profit and to deliver them to her when she was of lawful age.[64] She also received a crock, pan, bedding and a coffer, but these goods were listed after the clauses concerning the cattle, so presumably were not expected to be put out for profit. Since the renting out of stock was common in this period, it is easy to see how the bequest of one or two animals, though perhaps not enough to stock a holding, could be used to obtain an income. In many cases, too, the animals would be kept by a member of the family, perhaps the one who took over the holding, usually the executor. In a will made in a later decade, for example, John Keene left to his brother five nobles (approx. 33s 4d) for the cow that had died and, to his sister, her cow and two sheep, obviously their own stock that he was keeping for them.[65] Hence the appointment of overseers to make sure the individual received the profits of their legacies. It has been suggested that bequests of beasts or implements without any land indicate that the children 'expected access to land somehow, such as unacknowledged but practised grazing rights'.[66] It may be that such illegal grazing (grazing rights being attached to a customary holding in the Levels) existed here, and was later suppressed, but one cannot assume from such bequests that access to grazing was expected, as there were other ways that these legacies could be used.

In the context of the rural economy of the 1540s, for legatees without other resources bequests of animals were of more use than bequests of cash, unless the latter was enough to buy a customary holding or set up in a trade. There were few opportunities for secure cash investment that would get a certain return and the extent of rural borrowing is unknown for this period, but may well have been less extensive than later on. Animals were therefore easier to make use of, though they did have the disadvantage of being mortal. The expressions concerning the investment of the children's portions are also found in wills with cash bequests, such as the £3 that John Lyan left to each of his four younger children: when each child was 14 years old the

64 SHC, DD\SAS/SE/30.

65 TNA, PROB 11/68/153 (written 1585).

66 Thompson, 'Grid of Inheritance', p. 342.

overseers were to see their goods were 'put out to increase', and presumably until then the executrix, Lyan's wife, had the use of the legacies and would bring up the children.[67] Though there are one or two other wills with similar clauses, such exact dispositions are rare at this time: in many cases the beneficiaries would be of age in any case and no instructions to protect their legacies and invest them were necessary.

As the inventories for these wills have not survived it is not possible to discover what proportion of the farm stock the bequests of cows and other beasts represented, and thus the economic effect on the remaining holding of the form of legacies made in this period. The effect of bequests of livestock can be approximately estimated by taking the average prices for cows, sheep and oxen in this period and pricing the bequests: at best this is an extremely rough guide, and inventory pricing is almost bound to be lower than the market prices found in various price series and used to provide annual average prices in the *Agrarian History of England and Wales*,[68] but, using this as a guide, the value of bequests in this group of 1540s wills generally amounts to no more than half or two-thirds of the inventory total given. The lack of PCC wills to compare with for this decade is a problem, since for the rest of the period studied PCC wills form the majority of the available wills. For the period from 1503 to 1580, when PCC wills are still rare for Brent Marsh, 55 portions were left to children by men in 21 wills, with goods only accounting for 24 per cent, cash and goods 36 per cent and cash only 29 per cent; land in any combination accounted for only 11 per cent. So, though goods alone are rarer in the PCC wills, in this period they still made up nearly a quarter of portions, even though cash is certainly more significant.

Wills of the 1630s

A hundred years later the complexity, content and purpose of wills had greatly altered.[69] As Table 9 shows, portions that included goods now formed a very small part, while those including some land made up nearly a quarter, but bequests of cash on its own formed by far the greatest proportion, at nearly two-thirds. Most of the 95 wills examined for the 1630s were proven in the PCC, and the wills of men with children include 109 children's portions, excluding the grant of the residue as a portion.[70] Only eight wills proven locally have survived, and the three giving bequests to children are varied but reflect the predominance of cash and are similar to those proved in the PCC: one bequeathed only one portion, in cash and goods; another left leases to three children, cash to one child and token goods to a fifth; another left cash, furniture and land (leases) to one child and cash and goods, including furniture, crops and horses, to two others.[71]

The complexity of these 1630s wills is linked to their purpose. Wills now employed far more legal phrasing and the purpose seems to have been to ensure that the

---

67 Shilton and Holworthy, *Medieval Wills*, pp. 4–5.

68 *AHEW4*, tables on pp. 815–38, based on price series listed on pp. 865–8.

69 Section based on 1630–39, since the 1640s present a disturbed picture.

70 TNA, PROB 11/157–184, *passim*.

71 SHC, D\D/ct, will of William Langcastell: no date on will or probate, but inventory dated 9 Mar. 1634; *ibid.*, Edw. Parker, 1630; DD\BD/99, will of Geo. Davie of Berrow, 1633.

correct property was secured to the appropriate beneficiary. For example, most land was specified as a lease or chattel and bequeathed with 'all my estate and term of years', or as freehold: 'I bequeath and devise ... to him and his heirs and assigns ... for ever'.[72] Wills had increased fivefold or more in length to incorporate the legal forms, and short wills with only one or two bequests are rare. The absence of most wills proved in local courts probably includes many very short wills, but content and the intention of testators is similar in both groups, as far as surviving examples show: the 1650s, with its single probate court, also has few short wills. Goods were still bequeathed in most wills, but their place as part of a child's portion had diminished or disappeared. Household goods rarely formed the only legacy a child received, and where a child, usually a daughter, did receive only house goods, such as pans or furniture, this was because she had already received her main portion. Household goods were very often left as bequests to other relatives, grandchildren, servants or friends, rather than forming part of a child's inheritance. Beds and bedding were commonly left to children, though, and silver was often shared around as heirlooms, with crocks or pans bequeathed as keepsakes, especially to married daughters. A wife who did not receive the residue was often given specified goods which she had brought with her on her marriage,[73] or goods suitable for her comfort.

Farm stock and equipment were still useful ways of increasing a child's income, but on a far lesser scale than a hundred years previously. In the intervening decades the standard of living of many agricultural producers had risen steadily and a single cow or ewe hardly reflected the status most copyholders, for example, would aspire to, nor that which their children would hope to enjoy. Animals are mentioned in detail in only one or two of the wills, and in general they were bequeathed individually as a token to kin such as brothers and sisters or their children. Plough gear is mentioned only twice: in the will of John Reeve of Cheddar, yeoman, which is also one of the few that makes substantial bequests of stock to his children, and in the will of John Rogers of Mark, where the reference is obscure because a line has apparently been omitted from the register copy, but seems to refer to a debt or credit, not a legacy.[74] In another will wains and wheels are left to two sons, one of whom was married and the other of whom also received £5, and are more in the nature of token bequests than portions.[75] The will of John Reeve, which gives both stock and gear, is perhaps typical of wills where the testator is disposing of all the goods still in his possession, rather than making provision for his children with goods. All his children were married and the goods, stock, produce and chattel leases in Cheddar and Oldmixon (near Weston-super-Mare) were divided among his surviving children and their offspring.[76]

Much variation is found in the size of bequests, even in the same will, and this can usually be ascribed to pre-mortem provision, which is sometimes mentioned in the will, as when John Marshall left his son John the £200 which was promised to

72 TNA, PROB 11/165/1; PROB 11/167/489.

73 TNA, PROB 11/164/204.

74 TNA, PROB 11/160/387; PROB 11/170/161.

75 TNA, PROB 11/165/476.

76 TNA , PROB 11/160/387.

him at his marriage, while his two daughters, both also married, received only £20 each.[77] Cash now played the largest part in the legacies to children, and, as might be expected, showed a sizeable increase in the amount compared with wills of the 1540s: 78 cash bequests over £3, 49 of them between £10 and £30, were made to children both married and single for their own use. While some cash portions were made in addition to goods or land, in many cases cash was plainly given instead of a holding. As in the 1540s, one testator left £20 to his son towards the fine for the tenement where the testator dwelt and a similar legacy of £20 to one of his daughters for a further life in a lease the testator held.[78]

In summary, wills, the most easily studied form of transfer of property, had two purposes: to dispose of the testator's assets and to provide for his dependants. Wills purely disposing of assets were more likely to include a number of goods and leases to be shared among many, and grandchildren, servants and friends were more likely to be mentioned. In wills providing for dependants the legatees were generally limited to the wife and children of the testator: this appears as a narrowing of the circle of kin and friends, but may simply be a result of the change in the use of wills in this period, to secure provision for dependants. A change also occurred between the mid sixteenth and mid seventeenth centuries in the content of the portions left to children. In the 1540s the most important element in children's portions was farm stock, which could be used by the recipient or rented out if the legatee had no land. However, wills were not used as much in that period as they were later for providing for children, who were generally mentioned only as residuary legatees after small bequests to the Church. Wills for the 1630s present a striking contrast. Far longer on average than those of a hundred years previously, they incorporated legal forms to secure the legacies; land, in the form of leases, is mentioned more frequently, while cash bequests have now become the most common, forming more than two-thirds of children's portions by will in that decade.

The increase in the use of cash portions from about the late sixteenth century probably occurred throughout England, but changes can show a different pattern in other areas: in one Leicestershire parish, for example, though portions in cash increased they did not exceed those in goods until the late seventeenth century.[79] The Brent Marsh figures are not strictly comparable to other areas, as locally proven wills are not available, but even in the 1650s there is no sign of any return to portions in kind such as that found in Leicestershire, and the contents of children's portions may reflect more the readiness with which they could be used in the local economic community than the testator's level of prosperity. In the Levels, where cash could be invested in a number of ways, where there was a demand for loans and where small parcels of land could be readily bought for a term, cash might appear the best form of legacy apart from land itself. Payments in cash for younger children, leaving the stock with the farm for the heir, is seen in Leicestershire as leading to the growth of large

77 TNA, PROB 11/170/445.

78 TNA, PROB 11/181/463.

79 Howell, 'Peasant Inheritance Customs', pp. 150, 152.

commercial farms;[80] in the very different economic structure of Brent Marsh, where the farming economy was more flexible, the concentration on one heir was not so necessary for economic growth and, indeed, earlier wills here rarely diminished the stock too far or left the farm gear away from the tenement. In any case, all the portions had to come out of the testator's land and goods one way or another.

Payment of legacies and the economic effects

The tendency of fathers to divide up their land and goods to provide for all their children is regarded in economic terms as rather culpable, though from a human point of view nothing could be more natural. Indeed, it is doubtful whether many fathers sacrificed the younger children for the benefit of the eldest son, and both common law and local customs suggest that among most families all the children received some provision from their father's property, even though its content may have changed from period to period and place to place. In the case of landholders, therefore, a 'burden' of some kind was always put on the father's total assets after his death.

The legacies were paid by the executor of the will and, in almost all the wills examined for this area, the executor also received the residue of the estate, out of which she or he had to pay for probate, bury the testator and pay all debts. The executor, rather than the common law heir, was regarded in law as the successor of the testator, even though the heir was successor to freehold land, and by this period the executor had come to assume a greater importance than the heir in relation to an estate.[81] Among married men with children in the Levels, the wife was appointed executor in over half the cases and jointly with a son in another 12 per cent.[82] However, the practice of appointing overseers also allowed some testators, particularly widowers, to give the residue and executorship to the youngest child – even if an infant – as his or her portion, relying on the overseers to discharge the duties of the executor.

The content of the legacies made a difference to the way in which and the ease with which the executor could pay them. Bequests of goods, animals or leases were not so burdensome to the executor in the sense that such bequests were generally goods in the possession of the testator, whereas cash usually was not. As long as bequests of goods did not present a major part of the productive capacity of the holding, or were chattel leases held in addition to a viable farm, their absence from the holding would not be a serious blow to its economic strength. The effect on the holding is difficult to evaluate, however, unless an inventory survives, and even then the acreage and value of the main holding will probably not be included. In cases where inventories and wills both survive the legacies do not appear to reduce the residue of the estate to a level that would no longer support a household, even though in some cases the testator's goods were divided in half. In most cases no more than a quarter of the stock was bequeathed away from the executor, and where cash

80 *Ibid.*, p. 153.

81 R.J.R. Goffin, *The Testamentary Executor in England and Elsewhere* (London, 1901), pp. 56–7.

82 Below, Roles of women in rural society: Responsibility given to women.

bequests were made the produce left and money owing to the testator either covered the cash required or came close to doing so.

The switch from goods to cash as legacies during the sixteenth and seventeenth centuries coincides with a rise in prices for agricultural produce, a greater cash flow and a consequent rise in the prosperity of testators. Loans to pay legacies were easier to raise as a mortgage or on bond at a time when surplus cash was available in the community. However, large sums of money were still hard to find for most executors. Money did not lie idly around the house: cash surpluses were ploughed back into the farm or business in some form, spent on building, plate or furnishings, or lent out on bond, and many men also spent part of their working years buying copies or leases for their children. Few inventories reveal large sums in the house, and few men were in the position of William Boulting of Wedmore, who left to his two daughters and two daughters-in-law 'all my gold which I have now sealed up in a box'.[83]

In some areas of England the custom was for legacies to be paid from the future profits of the tenement, rather than the testator's savings.[84] In Brent Marsh the evidence does not reveal any particular custom regarding payment, and there is no way of knowing whether some men did put money aside to pay the legacies, by, for instance, lending it out on bond; bonds do form part of some legacies. Indications are that some testators, at least, expected the legacies to be paid from the future profits of their tenements and made arrangements to lessen the strain of those payments. Many wills specify payment in instalments spread over several years, or one child's legacy to be paid in the first year after the testator's death, the second child's in the second year and so on. In one will the wife was left the testator's tenement for eight years to enable her to find the £100 for two daughters.[85]

Annuities and rent-charges levied on the testator's land were another way of providing for dependants without reducing the capital of the estate and first appear in the surviving wills for this area in 1590, when Thomas Davis of Axbridge provided £7 a year for his wife from lands he had purchased in East Brent, to be paid quarterly by his son. His wife and son also shared the residue of the estate after other bequests.[86] In 1612 Edward Letheatt of Wedmore willed that his married sister should receive 5s a year for 20 years from the rent of his windmill, and in 1630 Edward Parker of Huntspill bequeathed five marks a year to his stepmother for life out of his ground of five acres near Edithmead, to be paid by his executor twice a year.[87]

By the 1650s this device was being used by some men to provide portions for several children, often in combination with outright payments of legacies. In 1651 John Warman of Mark bequeathed to his son John a ground called Great Lease on condition he allowed his mother to have the first five years' profits, paid £10 to a legatee in the sixth year and thereafter paid £10 a year to his sister Joan.[88] A much

83 TNA, PROB 11/253/492.

84 Spufford, *Contrasting Communities*, p. 106; Howell, 'Peasant Inheritance Customs', p. 146.

85 TNA, PROB 11/268/474.

86 TNA, PROB 11/77/8.

87 TNA, PROB 11/121/562; SHC, D\D/ct, will of Edw. Parker, 1630.

88 TNA, PROB 11/217/446.

more complicated arrangement was made by a widower, Thomas Evans of Weare, yeoman, in 1652 to provide for his six sons, of whom Valentine was the eldest.[89] A house and messuage in Overweare in possession of Evans's sister for her life was left to sons Thomas and William after her death, and meanwhile, for their maintenance, Thomas was given an annuity of 40s, to be paid by Valentine out of the chattel lease of the testator's dwelling house, and William 40s from 20 acres of freehold left to son Robert and his male heirs. When they took possession of the house Thomas and William were to pay 10s annual quitrent to Valentine and £5 a year to another son Richard, who had right of entry to one-third of the profits if the sum was not paid. Since this was not enough for Richard's maintenance, his father also gave him an annual rent of £5 from the 20 acres given to Robert, to continue until either William or Thomas died, whereupon Richard was to have the portion of the first to die. Son Nicholas was also to receive a rent of £10 a year from the dwelling and tenement in Weare, plus 9½ acres in Weare after the end of the term of lives then in being, paying the reserved rent to Valentine. Robert, in addition to the 20 acres, was given a chattel lease of 18 acres for the remainder of the term. Valentine received all the freehold land, acreage unknown, lying in Overweare, except the 20 acres, with remainder to his male heirs, plus the lease of the dwelling house for the remainder of its term. If nothing else, this example illustrates the amount of effort and thought some men went to in considering their children's portions and support.

Other wills provided for legacies to be paid out of specified lands in much the same way as annuities. Anne Allen, widow, of Mark left her tenement and 16 acres of land in Burnham, which she held on a lease for 99 years or the lives of her sons, to one of those sons, Henry, on condition that he paid her daughter £5 in the first year, her son-in-law £5 in the second year, and £5 during the third year and 40s during the fourth year to the use of the children of another son-in-law. After the four years he was to pay her son Thomas Allen 40s a year for life.[90] William Boulting the elder, of Theale in Wedmore, one of the substantial yeomen of the area, also made similar arrangements for his children and grandchildren out of lands and leases still in his possession at his death. Some legacies were annuities, such as £5 a year to a grandson out of ground in Wedmore and £4 a year to another grandson from ground in Weare. A granddaughter was to receive £40 to be paid as £5 a year from rents of a parcel of land, and her sister a similar amount out of another parcel.[91]

Annuities for life were not very common, but several wills made short-term charges on the lands bequeathed in order to pay portions, sometimes as in the complex examples given above or in more simple wills such as that of Gabriel Wall of Wedmore, who left cash legacies of £40 each to his two eldest daughters, £30 and two acres of arable to a third daughter and the first three years' profits of a tenement in the neighbouring manor of Moore to a fourth, with the following two years' profits going

89 TNA, PROB 11/264/248. No inventory survives, and the will contains no other bequests nor indication of source of Evans' income.

90 TNA, PROB 11/268/518.

91 TNA, PROB 11/253/492.

to the fifth daughter.[92] His son received only a colt in the will, and his wife received the residue: the son, aged 11 when the will was written, was probably the next life in the tenement in Moore, as the daughters who inherited the profits there were to allow him his maintenance until he was 16 if the wife died. In effect, these arrangements set down in specific detail the way that most cash legacies would be found from testators' estates for the general run of bequests.

The investment of portions

While the payment of legacies might be a strain for many families, the growing sophistication in provision for minors benefited the community by making available the cash legacies for investment. From the beginning of the period studied some testators expressed the desire that the goods they bequeathed should be employed for the use and profit of the legatee. Among the earlier wills admittedly only a small number make these provisions,[93] but from the 1590s the proportion of wills specifying investment grows steadily. Not all the legacies for investment are on behalf of minors (whether the testator's children or not); they also include bequests for the poor, community uses, the maintenance of schoolmasters and the widows and parents of testators. From the 1590s also, these legacies are generally cash: only about half a dozen are of stock, two are of the residue of the estate and another is of a house.

The result of this trend was to make available quite substantial sums of money. Where legacies were left to minors testators were generally careful to appoint overseers, usually at least two, and often different men for each child, to whom the legacy was to be paid on bond and who were to put it to use for the child. In many cases the legacy was used by the overseer himself, who then had to pay the principal and interest to the child at the age stipulated, generally 21 years. Those connected with the Axbridge Corporation sometimes gave money to the Borough in trust for their legatees, as did William Keene, who gave £200 to the magistrates of Axbridge, who were to pay the interest of £16 a year to Keene's wife for her life and then hand over the £200 to his brother's son.[94] As usual, there is little evidence for the cases where these duties were performed satisfactorily; only when overseers or guardians failed in their trust does information about the arrangements come to light. Occasionally wills give the rates testators expected for the investments: one gave his daughters £25 each 'to be put forth to use according to the Statute'[95] – that is, the statutes of the sixteenth century that permitted a rate of interest of up to 10 per cent on loans.[96] Rates mentioned in instructions varied from 1s to 2s in the pound (5 to 10 per cent).[97] Between 1580 and 1700 about £7,430 was bequeathed in extant wills in the Levels for investment for the use of minors and other uses – a considerable sum in this small

92 SHC, D\D/pd/21, will of Gabriel Wall, 1647/8.

93 Shilton and Holworthy, *Medieval Wills*, pp. 138–9; TNA, PROB 11/63/33; PROB 11/67/274.

94 TNA, PROB 11/104/499.

95 TNA, PROB 11/114/230.

96 P. Ramsey, *Tudor Economic Problems* (London, 1968), pp. 152–3.

97 Rates mentioned are 2s in the pound, and 8%.

rural area – most of which was concentrated in the sources available between 1610 and 1660.[98] The bulk of those cash investments were to be made on behalf of minors and would therefore be fairly short-term, depending on the age of the child, as in most cases the loan would come to an end and the money be returned to the child when of age. The figure given for cash available for investment represents the minimum amount from this source, however, as many wills have not survived, and one can assume that many other legacies were invested even when not so specified in the will.

Conclusion

Overall, looking at both the disposal of land, discussed in Chapter 3, and the portions given by will, the division of land and other property among children was governed less by any custom than by the father's natural desire to ensure a living to each child. The inheritance of land in Brent Marsh was impartible in the sense that customary holdings were not divided up; only rarely were profits shared and then usually for a limited term, to provide cash or maintenance. However, testators did share out land among their children where they held more than one customary holding or parcels of land on different leases: there was no attempt to keep all the land in one pair of hands. Leaseholds for lives or years appear with increasing frequency in the seventeenth-century wills for the Levels, particularly for small acreages of pasture, and the husbandry and landholding pattern in Brent Marsh lent itself to the provision by a father of small leaseholds to all his children, male and female. Thus, where their father's resources permitted, daughters were not discriminated against but received land as their portion equally with their brothers, though that land was generally in the form of leaseholds. If the father's supply of land was limited, however, the sons usually received the land and the daughters some other provision, generally cash, but attempts were still made to give all the children portions of equal value. This tendency to divide up land among all the children was thought noteworthy in the nineteenth century by the Revd Dr John Allen Giles, scholar and author, born in Mark in 1848, who thought it was responsible for maintaining the large number of small proprietors in Somerset, though he also thought that it led to a lot of the family property going into the hands of lawyers.[99]

As cash became the most common form of provision, leading to fairly heavy cash demands on testators' estates, it increased the availability of quite large sums of money for investment. The change to cash portions was probably not intended to enable greater physical mobility for their children – goods could just as easily be sold, after all – and probably did not result from the greater prosperity of farmers; rather, it presumably came about because cash became a more useful bequest with wider opportunities to use it, while it also became easier to raise cash to pay the legacies. Wills grew longer and more complex as testators' instructions grew more involved, reflecting the desire for greater personal control, and show an inclination to make use of various legal and financial devices to ensure their children's future. Local society

98 Croot, 'Agrarian Society', p. 491, Table 20.

99 D. Bromwich (ed.), *The Diary and Memoirs of John Allen Giles* (Somerset Record Society 86, 2000), p. 1.

had developed a more sophisticated and legalistic outlook and a desire for greater legal security: wills were frequently drawn up by attorneys to incorporate the correct legal wording and were used for securing legacies and regular incomes from land, and for ratifying conveyances and settlements.

The transmission of property in the Levels did not follow definable inheritance customs but differed according to family circumstance. However, the ways in which property was secured to the next generation by a more sophisticated use of wills is one of the indications of a change in local society – the emergence of a rural middle-class, far removed from the dependent villein – and the particular ways in which property was transmitted in the Levels seem to be the result of the flexible economic and tenurial structure there.

Roles of women in rural society

The type of agriculture and tenure in the Levels, and the economic opportunities that resulted, also had their effect on the economic and social position of women. Manorial custom was important in determining the position that women held in the family and in the local community: it could differ considerably from that among the nobility and gentry, while the differences in custom between areas of England meant that the experience of women in comparable social groups could differ also. The type of agriculture, too, could give women economic opportunities that might not be available elsewhere.

Until recently, the lack of detailed and local studies of women's lives and activities meant that the roles of women in the household and in society were generalised from legal theory and literary evidence, such as contemporary discourses and sermons on the duties of family members. There were, however, other dimensions to women's existence besides those of common law, which mainly concerned property, and contemporary literature, which often represented an ideal rather than reality. Theories of the perfect household were doubtless far from the actuality, and one could argue that the only reason for some of those discourses was the writer's perception that real life was totally different from what he (usually a he) thought of as ideal.[100] Studies of women's experiences have now given a far better picture of the actual lives of women at all levels and in all types of society, both from restricted localities and wider areas. Though the lack of much probate material prevents a comparable study in depth for Brent Marsh, the actual roles and opportunities in the lives of women in the Levels can be assessed in relation to two aspects: landholding; and economic and social life.

The legal position of women

The position of women in law in regard to real and personal property was two-fold. If they were single adults or widowed they could inherit, hold and administer land and goods in the same way as men. Though the rules of inheritance in common law put sons before daughters in succession to their father's freehold land, daughters always

100 The literature, and tension between ideal and real, is discussed in S.D. Amussen, *An Ordered Society: Gender and Class in Early Modern England* (New York, 1988), chap. 2.

inherited before any other male kin, while in respect of chattels the law favoured equal shares among kin of the same degree, rather than primogeniture.

Once married, however, a woman became a *femme couverte* and virtually a non-person in law, '*nil valet quia nupta est*', as female witnesses in the ecclesiastical courts were described.[101] A married women could not own any personal property; goods she owned before marriage became her husband's unless a pre-nuptial settlement arranged otherwise, and this legal position also meant that a husband could not 'give' his wife any goods during marriage.[102] Nor could a wife buy or sell on her own account, because without property she could not make contracts on her own behalf, only as her husband's agent.[103]

The real (land) property of a married woman went the way of chattels, though with a limitation. A husband had complete control over his wife's freehold property during their marriage, or for his life if the wife's heir was his child, but he could not alienate any part of it unless the conveyance was made by a fine to which the wife agreed on being examined separately; without this agreement the wife could recover the property after her husband's death. Property termed real chattels, which covered leases for years or wardships, fell between land and goods: they were similar to goods in that they became the property of the husband, who could dispose of them as he wished, but if he had not alienated them they remained to his wife on his death as did her land, and did not pass under his will with other chattels. Common law also affected the wife's position after her husband's death. The only concession it made to a married woman was to recognise her right to dower, so that the widow could hold one-third of her husband's land for her life. The dower was inalienable and could not be seized for her husband's debts, but could only be forfeited by voluntary surrender by the widow, or her desertion or adultery during the marriage. This body of common law concerning women had evolved early on from a few fixed principles regarding property, and the law rejected all idea of a community of property between husband and wife, leaving women at a great disadvantage.

Women's position in law was not entirely static, however. Married women in the early medieval period seem to have been able to make wills freely, a right which was strongly resisted, until, by the sixteenth century, they generally could make a will only with their husband's permission. Towards the end of the seventeenth century their position and rights to the property of their husbands in cases of intestacy deteriorated when a statute led to the reduction of the proportion they were allotted by the ecclesiastical courts to one-third, rather than the more flexible proportions of earlier, which might be as much

---

101 SHC, D\D/cd, *passim*, depositions of married women in the church courts: 'worth nothing because married'.

102 The passages on the legal position of women are based on Holdsworth, *History of English Law*, III, pp. 526–7. For a more detailed discussion see Erickson, *Women and Property*, esp. pp. 23–6.

103 Clearly, though, married women did buy and sell and it was tacitly assumed that their husbands were aware and agreed to the bargain. Fitzherbert thought that farmers' wives should do the marketing and handle their husbands' financial matters: A. Clark, *Working Life of Women in the Seventeenth Century* (London, 1919), pp. 46–7.

as the whole estate.[104] Some reflection of this change in attitude towards the economic role of women also occurs in the Somerset Levels in the later seventeenth century in connection with the executorship of wills and in land tenure.[105]

Those changes by statute were presumably ones which suited the men from the governing class which brought them into being, but this class frequently circumnavigated the disabilities visited by the law upon women when their own daughters were the women concerned. From the sixteenth century dislike of the rigid common-law rules became apparent, particularly among the wealthy, whose daughters took with them considerable property. Pre-nuptial contracts and trusts were increasingly used to bypass common-law rules, to make sure the wife's property remained within her or her family's control. Lesser folk followed suit, with pre-nuptial arrangements increasingly being enshrined in deeds or secured by bonds. The rival legal system of equity, in direct conflict with common law, was used to limit the husband's control by giving effect to such settlements, as equity accepted the possibility of the ownership of land being separated from the enjoyment of it, thus allowing the creation of trusts which could circumvent the rules of common law. Equity courts became the place where all manner of family arrangements were challenged or upheld,[106] and were in particular an attractive alternative to common law for married women, who were particularly disadvantaged in common law: equity did not demand the documentary proofs required by common law, which might often be difficult for married women to obtain.[107]

The equity courts also became involved in the support of customary law. The tenure of many rural inhabitants was governed, rather than by common law, by custom, often peculiar to a certain manor and administered by manorial courts. Some of those customs have been discussed in Chapter 3 in relation to land tenure and to inheritance, but tenurial custom also specifically affected wives and widows. The position of a married woman was not altered by custom: her customary land was enjoyed by her husband in her right in the same way as freehold. However, custom did give a woman a greater share in her husband's estate when he died. While in common law a widow received only one-third of her husband's land, under customary tenure she might have anything from a half to the whole of the property for her life, taking precedence over any male heirs.[108] In the Brent Marsh manors the custom was for the widow to hold the whole of her husband's customary land as long as she was single and chaste,[109] and this fact could greatly influence the position of women in their society. Though not all husbands held customary land for their wives to take over, the presence in the community of such a custom both reflects the way countrymen saw their wives' role and continued to influence the ways in which they regarded their wives and disposed of other tenures.

---

104 Erickson, *Women and Property*, pp. 139–40, 178–80.

105 Below, Roles of women in rural society: Responsibility given to women.

106 Erickson, *Women and Property*, chaps 6–8.

107 Stretton, *Women Waging Law*, pp. 25–9.

108 R.H. Hilton, *The English Peasantry in the Later Middle Ages* (Oxford, 1975), pp. 98–9.

109 SHC, DD\SG/22.

Table 10
Disposition of residue and executorship

Decade	*To wife only*		*To son(s) only*		*To wife & son(s)*		*Total wills*
	No.	*%*	*No.*	*%*	*No.*	*%*	
1540–49	30	63.8	2	4.3	9	19.2	47
1550–59	5	38.5	1	7.7	7	53.9	13
1560–69	-		-		4	66.7	6
1570–79	5	33.3	2	13.3	2	13.3	15
1580–89	16	55.2	6	20.7	4	13.8	29
1590–99	11	55.0	6	30.0	2	10.0	20
1600–09	5	45.5	2	18.2	3	27.3	11
1610–19	11	45.8	6	25.0	1	4.2	24
1620–29	23	74.2	7	22.6	1	3.2	31
1630–39	25	75.8	5	15.2	-		33
1640–49	12	52.2	5	21.7	1	4.4	23
1650–59	33	62.3	11	20.8	3	5.7	53
1660–69	2	33.3	3	50.0	-		6
1670–79	3	75.0	1	25.0	-		4
1680–89	-		3	50.0	-		6
1690–99	-		2	40.0	3	60.0	5
	181	55.5	62	19.0	40	12.3	326

Notes: Figures are taken from the wills of men who have both a wife and children. The last column includes wills where executorship was left to someone other than the wife and/or sons.
Source: See Table 8 for source of wills by decade.

Responsibility given to women

As the wife typically received the holding it was common for the husband to make her, rather than, say, the eldest son, his executor. The eldest son seems to have been less important here than in some other parts of England or among other social groups; similarly, the wives of testators in the Levels seem to have held a rather more important position than in many other places. Table 10 gives an analysis of wills in the Levels made by men with both wives and children, and shows that men who left a wife and sons appointed the wife alone as executor in a half or more of the wills examined, especially in the decades with most examples. In a sample of 80 reconstituted families, mainly from Wedmore, there were 44 wills for testators who left a wife and sons: of these, the wife was sole executor in 28 and a joint executor in five more. This was not solely because the children were under age either: of the 28 testators who appointed their wife alone, 11 had sons over 21, or married where their age is unknown, and six more had sons over 16. Of the 11 cases where the wife had nothing to do with the executorship, only in three was the eldest (or only) son appointed, and in one case the testator's brother. In the other cases the executorship was given to one of the younger children or grandchildren as a portion. The wife was the mother of the testator's children in five of those 11 cases, and was not the mother in four, the remainder being unknown. Despite the exceptions, however, it is unusual to find the executorship and residue left away from the wife, whatever the family circumstances: between 1539 and 1639 84 per cent of the 376 wills of men mentioning a wife appointed her as executrix. This reflects the experience of most other areas studied, where in the sixteenth and seventeenth centuries it was common for the wife to receive the executorship and the residue of her husband's estate; in cases of intestacy, moreover, the wife was legally entitled to administer her dead husband's personal estate if she wished. The proportion of wives appointed as sole executor did vary a good deal, but this seems to be linked to a given locality rather than any general change in attitude.[110] It is not clear, however, whether the variation is linked to custom, to agrarian typology or to local economic factors, as few studies of wills also look at all those aspects. There were marked differences between localities depending on the family circumstances as well: in Leicestershire, for example, although the wife was generally (*c.*80 per cent) sole or joint executor when the children were minors, the proportion fell to *c.*60 per cent when some or all children were over 21.[111] In Brent Marsh, however, the proportion remained at a higher level for both groups.

Two reasons stand out for the choice of the wife as executor. She can be seen as the obvious choice to head the family and carry on the source of livelihood, having been a partner with her husband. Additionally, in many cases the force of customary tenure made this sensible, as was the case in the Levels: by custom the wife would inherit the tenement for her widowhood, so might as well receive the bulk of goods and settle the children's inheritances, and, even if she did not receive the holding by custom, she was very often the next life in the copy. However, though the appointment of women as executors may not be surprising in view of the tenurial custom, it still indicates that men saw their wives as partners who were perfectly capable of administering their property and business, as other arrangements could have been made, including a lease of the holding to a son, if the testator had wanted a male successor.

While appointing the wife as executor was fairly widespread in England, studies for other areas show that the provisions made for wives, as well as the responsibility given to them, differed considerably from place to place.[112] In one Leicestershire parish if there was a son over 21 he usually inherited the holding and was responsible for maintaining the widow.[113] In six Norfolk parishes between 1540 and 1579 over half the bequests (51 per cent) by men to their widows included land, while 15 per cent gave them a dwelling and maintenance without land, and widows were more likely to receive land than sons.[114] In Cambridgeshire three different parishes reveal three different forms of provision. In Orwell a widow was normally left the holding if

110 Erickson, *Women and Property*, pp. 156–60, 174. Figs summarised by Erickson are almost entirely for the eastern half of England.

111 Howell, 'Peasant Inheritance Customs', pp. 141–3.

112 Erickson, *Women and Property*, chap. 9; Whittle, 'Inheritance, Marriage, Widowhood', pp. 49–55.

113 Howell, 'Peasant Inheritance Customs', p. 142.

114 Whittle, 'Inheritance, Marriage, Widowhood', pp. 51–2 and Table 7.

her children were under age, but only until the eldest son was 21, when she received specified house room and maintenance in her son's house for life, which ceased if she remarried. In Chippenham three-quarters of the testators left the widow a life interest in the house and land, a pattern followed even by the less wealthy; wives were given considerable rights in customary holdings through admission in the manorial court after marriage. In Willingham the norm was for the widow of a landholder with young children to receive his holdings for a specific term of years, again until the eldest son came of age. Frequently no further provision was specified, but, when it was, it was often in the form of a separate dwelling, and overall there was a greater variety of types of provision for widows.[115] In both Brent Marsh and the Cambridgeshire examples the reason for the differing forms of provision does not seem to be tied in with the type of agriculture as such, but rather is related to the tenurial customs of individual manors and presumably stems from arrangements found suitable in the Middle Ages.

In Brent Marsh, when wives were not given the executorship and residue of the estate the kind of provision made for them still seems to indicate that they would have a landholding or house, even though wills do not mention this. Twelve of the married testators whose families have been reconstituted did not leave their wives the residue and executorship, but bequeathed to them specific goods, which often included the best bed, produce and farm stock. No house room is ever mentioned among these reconstituted families, and land only peripherally: for instance, John Rowley confirmed to his wife the ground left to her by the will of her former husband.[116] The widow was often left corn to maintain her for a very limited period, which suggests that she held, or would inherit, a tenement, and other evidence sometimes confirms that the wife would hold a tenement not mentioned in the will.[117] Since provision for housing widows is rarely made in the wills examined here it is presumed that most widows had tenements coming to them from the husband or in their own right.

The return to the wife of goods that were hers before the marriage seems to reflect the same attitude that lay behind the development of family law in equity and a community of property in marriage. This attitude can also be seen in bills in the Chancery court, where next of kin are claiming a share in a dead man's property with his widow: they are careful to make it clear that they were not claiming a share in property that the wife had brought to the marriage. John Horsington of Compton Bishop died without leaving any children, and the six children of his sister, Anne Baylie, claimed through their father that Horsington had intended to settle his estate on his widow with remainder to his sister's children. Horsington's widow, Joan, had since remarried and obviously the Baylies feared they would lose their inheritance. Before detailing the estate and the dead man's riches, the plaintiffs took care to mention Horsington's marriage, about ten years previously, to Joan Needes, who they claimed had brought only £80 to the marriage. Horsington had intended to leave his leases and mortgages to his eldest nephew and £50 among the rest and he had died

115 Spufford, *Contrasting Communities*, pp. 88–9, 113–14, 162–4.

116 TNA, PROB 11/213/300.

117 e.g. SHC, D\D/ct, will of Ric. Alger, 1640; DD\SE/63/2, Blackford court roll 15 Oct. 20 Car.I; presentments, 17 Oct. 1656; TNA, PROB 11/251/405.

before arranging this, but had left a 'fair' house and lands worth £20 a year and goods worth £300, in addition to several chattel leases. Their meaning is plain: that Joan had contributed but little to Horsington's wealth and his kin were therefore entitled to claim a share in practically all his estate. Joan's answer to the bill was to emphasise how little Horsington had had before he married her, and that the fair house and lands were not all that the bill had implied.[118]

The indications are that the provision made for widows was changing in the seventeenth century, though the time span of this study is not long enough to gauge this thoroughly. Widows' rights were being affected by the switch from copyhold for three lives to leases for three lives: though the latter included many customary rights, the change did remove the automatic inheritance by the widow.[119] Since it is hard to see what advantage the tenant obtained by the change from copy to long lease, which the lords could not legally force on their tenants, it is possible that tenants welcomed the opportunity to remove the widow's succession and allow the landholder freedom to dispose of his land as he wished. Leases for lives continued to be taken for the life of the lessee, his wife and his eldest child, to cite a common example, much as copies had been, but the property did not automatically pass to the next name in the lease, as the wording of copies would usually direct.[120] The inference is that the landholder might prefer to pass his land direct to a son, for example, rather than to his wife. Reasons of status or a changing attitude to the roles of women, discussed below, may be involved, but another reason may be the greater alternatives available to provide for widows by the late seventeenth century, such as an annuity from invested funds or rents. There is also some indication that the position regarding the executorship in the Levels may have been slowly changing as well. In the two decades from 1640 to 1659 121 wills mentioned wives and in 74 per cent the wife was appointed executor, but between 1660 and 1699 only 55 per cent appointed the wife. This latter group is a very small sample of only 31 wills, mainly for higher-status families of merchants and gentlemen, so is not directly comparable with the earlier period. However, in a similar group of merchants and gentlemen in the period 1600 to 1640 with both wives and sons, half appointed their wife alone, whereas in this later period only just over a third of men with both wives and sons appointed their wife alone or with a son.

Such a change in the provision for widows may be connected with the changing economic position of landholders, who with rising social status were moving closer to the gentry in their attitudes as well as in their wealth. The emergence of copyholders as a landed class of minor country gentlemen, discussed in Chapter 3, meant that many copyholders ceased to be working farmers, and thus the position of their wives in the family economy changed too. Doris Stenton has suggested that 'the nearer the household was to the land, the more nearly they were on equal terms',[121] whereas among the landed classes, and among those whose education took them away from

118 TNA, C 2/JasI/B31/71.

119 Above Chap. 3, Customary tenure: The role and value of the manor courts.

120 Above Chap. 3, The switch to leasehold for lives.

121 D.M. Stenton, *The English Woman in History* (London, 1957), p. 98.

the land into professions, a division was created between husbands and wives by different education for men, different activities, participation in local administration and politics, and commercial activities away from home,[122] which the vast majority of women in those social groups could not share, but which could be shared by their sons as they reached adulthood.

The divide was not so great among agricultural families, but was beginning to emerge. In the medieval Midlands women can be found sharing or assisting in most agricultural tasks, such as ploughing and harrowing, with men.[123] In the sixteenth and seventeenth centuries there is no evidence that that kind of heavy farm work was done by women, although Fitzherbert, in listing all the occupations of a sixteenth-century farmer's wife, included winnowing corn, making hay, shearing corn and, 'in time of need', helping her husband to fill the dung cart, drive the plough and load hay and corn.[124] While women from poorer farming and labouring families continued to carry out a wide range of agricultural work,[125] some wives of wealthier producers moved into a more supervisory and managerial role in their households,[126] and it was clearly reasons of status as well as of lack of financial necessity that moved women more and more into household roles that were not directly productive – these being, of course, an indication of financial well-being and higher status. That status was an important consideration is underlined by the number of wills both in Somerset and in other counties, which make provision for the widow 'appropriate to her degree'. For example, William Maundrell, a local gentleman of Huntspill, left his widow £10 and diet, washing and chamber 'fit for her degree', or, if she did not agree to that, then £20 a quarter.[127]

Most married women in village society here, as elsewhere, were still involved in a range of economic activities, however, such as keeping accounts, marketing and running farms: some carried out such duties only when their husbands were away, but others took them over altogether to free their husbands for other activities, particularly in gentry and professional/literary families, where account-keeping by women was relatively common.[128] The wide range of work and responsibilities actually undertaken by the wives of working farmers, particularly in dairying, has been examined for the eighteenth century.[129] In the seventeenth century sources

122 W. Notestein, 'The English Woman, 1580 to 1625', in J.H. Plumb (ed.), *Studies in Social History, presented to G.M. Trevelyan* (London, 1955), pp. 81–3; Clark, *Working Life of Women*, *passim*.

123 Hilton, *English Peasantry*, pp. 101–2. Based on little evidence and not found elsewhere, but evidence for medieval peasants' activities is always slight except when working on demesnes.

124 Quoted by Clark, *Working Life of Women*, p. 49.

125 Below, Role of women in rural society: Women in economic life.

126 Clark, *Working Life of Women*, p. 50.

127 TNA, PROB 11/195/41.

128 e.g. Clark, *Working Life of Women*, pp. 44–6, 50–51; J. Whittle and E. Griffiths, *Consumption and Gender in the Early Seventeenth-Century Household: The World of Alice Le Strange* (Oxford, 2012), pp. 30–32.

129 N. Verdon, '"… Subjects Deserving of the Highest Praise": Farmers' Wives and the Farm Economy in England, *c.*1700–1850', *Agricultural History Review*, 51/1 (2003), pp. 23–39.

are not as rich, but women were obviously expected to farm for themselves and men who did not leave the executorship and residue to their wives still frequently left them goods for active farming. In 1649 John Taylor alias Griffin, husbandman, of Wedmore left his wife enough wheat and beans to sow her ground, so she obviously would have had a farm holding after his death. She also received the two oldest cows and enough beans to fatten the pigs.[130] In 1640 Thomas Wall, husbandman, of Weare left his wife the plough harness, the house that was hers before their marriage, the lease he held and goods to the value of £50.[131] Richard Trubb, husbandman, of Mark left his wife the plough harness for life, two cows and corn to sow her ground for six months after his death.[132] One of the most comprehensive bequests of this kind was made by Richard Latham senior of Wedmore in 1677, who, though he gave her no land in his will, was obviously stocking a house and smallholding for his widow: in the house the best bed and bedding, the pewter and brass, timber vessels, all the provisions in the house, a chest, box, coffer and all the linen, while for the holding she received the best wheat in the yard and two hayricks, a red heifer calf, two pigs and growing crops of 2½ acres of beans, one acre of wheat and some barley.[133]

Though many widows were given standing crops or produce, those were not capital stock and on their own were probably for support or sale. Bequests of cows and other livestock may also have been for sale, but were more probably intended to be kept for long-term support, while a bequest of land alone was probably for the widow to lease out rather than to work herself. However, bequests of the plough harness surely indicate that the widow would be involved in farming and, out of the ten or so wills in each decade that made a specific provision for the widow, there were usually one or two that bequeathed to her the plough. In other parts of England, where probate inventories survive in greater numbers, it is apparent how often widows continued farming. In a study where inventories for both the husband and his widow exist, taken from seven differing areas across England, 31 widows out of 45 farming couples continued farming in some form during widowhood.[134]

The effects of widow's right

The tendency to leave the bulk of the estate to the widow was, perhaps, less damaging to the financial stability of the estate than giving her an annuity or other provision. In the former case the whole unit, be it farm(s) or business interests, passed to the widow. If there were minor children she would bring them up and provide for them, and in due course pay them their portions, which were usually bequeathed to them by their father at his death. Children who were given stock, land or tenements would take them out of the estate when they could or wished to do so. In the majority of cases it is probable

130 TNA, PROB 11/211/433.

131 TNA, PROB 11/186/49.

132 TNA, PROB 11/199/662.

133 SHC, DD\FS/12/1/3.

134 J. Whittle, 'Enterprising Widows and Active Wives: Women's Unpaid Work in the Household Economy of Early Modern England', *The History of the Family*, 19/3 (2014), pp. 291 (Table 5), 294–5.

that the next heir to the tenement or principal farm of the estate would remain with the widow, or at least help her work the farm: Robert Oakley of Panborough, Wedmore, for example, managed his mother's tenement for 25 years, from the age of 20.[135] The next heir very often was the youngest son, his elder brothers having been provided for as they reached maturity, so that the effect was very similar to land governed by Borough English custom, where the youngest inherited.

Even if this were not the case, the fact that the son was still waiting to inherit did not necessarily stop him marrying before the widow died. Robert Oakley, in the case cited above, was married.[136] In another case John Paen of Weare, with a wife, five children and a sixth expected, was in financial difficulties, while his mother still held a living of 30 acres valued at £16 a year.[137] However, it could make it difficult for children to marry as they chose if they were economically dependent and their parents objected to a match. Richard Fry, who worked on his father's farm, was asked by John Wilsheire, father of the girl he was courting and a friend of his, whether he intended to marry Elizabeth, and he said he certainly did. Wilsheire said he would do his utmost for her (financially) and went with a friend to negotiate the marriage, but found that, though Fry's father seemed pleased, his mother seemed 'much discontented'. A year or so later Elizabeth had to ask the son of her employer to ask Fry why he had not yet kept his word regarding her, and Fry replied that 'she was his wife, but that she must stay his leisure, for he could not do as he would'.[138] Either he was unable to go through with the marriage for financial reasons, or his mother's dislike of the match had made difficulties.

The effects of widow's right on the next generation could be good or bad depending on family circumstances and the age of the next heir, but the effect on the position of women was quite marked. In a society where the possession of land meant political and social power at national level, it will come as no surprise to find that the possession of land, even just for widowhood, gave women a strong position in their family. It was as true then as it is now that financial independence gave an influence and authority only otherwise given by a rare amount of personality, and it was women's economic position rather than any social attitude towards them that carried more weight.

Marriage

Though widows could be expected to manage their own farms there was a strong chance that they would marry again if they were left with substantial property in land or goods, especially where the property was theirs for life rather than for widowhood only. The number of female heads of households among the better-off landholders was not large at any one time, and figures derived from various taxation records from 1523 to 1670 show that among the richer inhabitants women headed only about 10–12 per cent of households, though this rose to about 25 per cent when poorer households

135 SHC, D\D/cd/51, Godd v. Gorway, dep. of Robert Oakley, 29 Mar. 1617.

136 *Ibid.*, Oakley v. Gorway, 24 Oct. 1616.

137 SHC, Q/SR/16/99.

138 SHC, D\D/cd/70, Wilsheire v. Fry, depositions of William Cullock and John Storie, 8 Mar. 1630.

are included, using, for example, the Poll and Hearth taxes. It was not necessary for widows to remarry to get their farms worked, however. With farm incomes rising in the sixteenth century, holders of customary tenements could afford to hire labour, and examples of hired men working for single women appear regularly in various records. Overall, wealthy widows as a group were less likely to remarry than those of middling or little wealth; poorer widows, however, had to try to remarry if they could because they would find it difficult to survive financially on their own, especially if they had a young family.[139]

The material, businesslike quality of marriage in the early modern period, when parental arrangements and the involvement of wider kin were common, can be over-emphasised, although many of the examples given below will tend to substantiate this aspect; plenty of examples can also be found of marriages contracted for emotional or sexual reasons.[140] Whatever the basis for the choice of partner, a judicious marriage still had important economic results for the individual; it was desirable for men as well as women to marry well financially. Apart from inheritance, marriage was about the only honest way of substantially and quickly increasing a person's capital stock, as opposed to building up capital out of profits, while for a woman it was in a sense an investment, where she placed herself and her goods in the hands of a man whom she hoped would husband her stock and leave her well provided for if she survived him. The economic resources left to widows made marriage with them attractive, and even led to suits for breach of promise being brought by men against well-to-do women. In 1612 Richard Moore brought a suit against Agnes Dawkes, widow of Berrow, described as a 'young woman'. Richard, who had been a servant to Agnes and her husband for 20 years, had been seen in bed with Agnes, and it was stated that Richard had wasted most of his money on her, only to find that she refused to have anything to do with him. Other witnesses stated, however, that Agnes had refused to accept gifts from Richard and that there had been no talk of marriage between them, and denied that Richard had behaved in a familiar fashion which Agnes had accepted.[141] Another such case was brought by Thomas Abbai against Joan Harvard in 1570. The only evidence is that given by Abbai's relatives: they claimed that Joan had admitted to being Thomas's wife, but wanted to keep it quiet for fear of losing her copyhold tenement. She held about 30 acres in or near South Brent, while Thomas had only four.[142]

A judicious marriage could bring a man a large acreage by the standards of this part of Somerset. When John Gilling married Julian, the daughter of Nicholas Bibble, *c.*1557, he acquired 33 acres of copyhold and nearly ten acres on a life lease.[143] As discussed in Chapter 3, daughters frequently received copies or leases for their

---

139 Erickson, *Women and Property*, pp. 196–8.

140 The complexity of influences on marriage arrangements, particularly the necessity for financial resources for both partners, have been studied in depth for Kent: D. O'Hara, *Courtship and Constraint: Rethinking the Making of Marriage in Tudor England* (Manchester, 2000).

141 SHC, D\D/cd/45. Moore v. Dawkes, depositions of Sam. Moore and others, 16 ?June 1612.

142 SHC, D\D/cd/12, Abbai v. Harvard, depositions of Roger Hardwich and others, 24 May 1570.

143 CCC Oxford, Fn 14, rental 1568; Straton, *Survey*, II.

'preferment' in order to make a good marriage and even though these were not freeholds the difference is really very slight in economic terms: John Gilling acquired *c.*43 acres in secure tenure to add to his property and augment his income. Just what his property was before marriage is hard to ascertain, however: the Gilling family were long-established landholders with many branches in the area, and a good half of the members of each generation were named John.

Women also benefited from marriage. Their husbands were expected to endow them in some way, to provide for them in the event of the husband's death. Maurice Llewellin, a husbandman of Mark, agreed to the marriage of John Batt to Marian Llewellin if Batt could obtain her consent and provide some living to bring her to. When Marian was asked if she could find it in her heart to love John, she replied she could if he was able to provide some living for her. Llewellin promised Batt £10 if he would buy her a living, meaning a lifehold copy or lease.[144] At the other extreme in legal involvement, a land settlement was made when Richard Blake married Elizabeth Bale in which Blake conveyed to trustees his lease of the rectory of Overstowey in West Somerset to his use and to that of his wife after his death, and his freehold messuages and 80 acres in Burnham to himself and his heirs by Elizabeth, while the bride's father Peter Bale was to give his daughter £100 and to convey his tenement and 40 acres of freehold land in Stogumber (West Somerset) to the use of Elizabeth and her heirs after himself and his wife.[145]

If a woman did not receive an adequate endowment when her husband died she felt entitled to complain. Margaret Aldridge, widow, of Burnham claimed she had held a tenement in Street valued at £20 a year and goods valued at £300 when she married Richard Aldridge, yeoman, about 22 years previously. He had persuaded her to agree to the sale of her tenement and promised instead to leave her a good estate in land and goods when he died. However, his will gave her only £45, a featherbed, some corn and other small legacies, 'being but slender recompense for so good an estate as he had received by marrying her', and she sought a fairer share from Aldridge's executor, who, she claimed, had embezzled her husband's goods.[146]

Even on a lesser scale, marriages brought valuable stock to the new household or to the man's family farm, to judge by the number that left their wives all the household stuff and goods that were hers before marriage; many more left her a few items suggesting they were part of a larger stock. Jeremy Browning left his wife her father's silver,[147] while William Fry of Berrow left his wife all the household goods at East Brent and the cattle that were hers before their marriage.[148]

Most of the evidence concerning marriage arrangements was produced when the bargain was not fulfilled, and the equity courts were constantly used by rural inhabitants seeking to enforce agreements. Generally it was the husband, with his

---

144 SHC, D\D/cd/28, (Batt and Llewellin), dep. of Maurice Llewellin, 1598.

145 TNA, C 2/Eliz/B24/36.

146 TNA, REQ 2/391/37.

147 TNA, PROB 11/190/123.

148 TNA, PROB 11/153/253.

wife, who was trying to force his wife's father or family to hand over the agreed portion. For example, John Dean of Wedmore brought a bill in Chancery *c.*1550 against his wife's father, Thomas Tincknell, of Theale in Wedmore, claiming that when the marriage was being considered some 11 years before Tincknell had agreed to give with his daughter 40s, a bed and bedding, pewter and four cattle. Only two animals and some bedding had been delivered, however, despite several requests.[149] These goods seem quite a slight matter to bring to Chancery, but are by no means unusual. More commonly, however, cases concerned land. A common occurrence was where occupation of certain land was given to the man and woman, but without secure tenure, and cases were brought to try to persuade the court that secure tenure had been part of the agreement. This was the basis of the case in the 1530s in which John Huchyns and his wife, Christian, complained that William Hayne and his wife, Ellen, had refused to secure three tenements to them as agreed.[150] In another case the groom, Richard Hodges, claimed that the bride's father, Robert Comer, had agreed to pay him £13 6s 8d within a year of the marriage 20 years earlier, and to assure to him Comer's tenement in Compton Bishop for his life, but had refused to do so. Comer's sons answered the bill, claiming that the agreement had been that Hodges should possess the tenement on payment of 10s a year, and had held it on those terms ever since his marriage.[151]

Marriages could bring large endowments, but also great legal tussles. Thomas Sayard married Edith, the daughter of John Lyning of Tarnock, who had promised to leave them the remainder of his 99-year lease of a mill in Lympsham as part of the marriage agreement. Edith also inherited two tenements and 40 acres of copyhold in Tarnock, and was left £20 by her father in his will. Her brother John died shortly after their father and Edith was therefore heir to her father's freehold land as well, which was, the Sayards later claimed, a fourth part of the manor of Tarnock, the rest being held by Edward Seymour, earl of Hertford. John senior had also purchased some other freehold land in Tarnock from John Castle in 1558. For two or three years after their marriage (*c.*1565) Thomas and Edith were involved in six Chancery suits, three as plaintiffs against Edith's stepmother and a cousin to try to get possession of parts of Edith's inheritance, and three as defendants, including a case brought by Lord Hertford, who disputed their right to the fourth part of Tarnock.[152]

By the same token, the lack of a suitable portion damaged a woman's chances of marrying within her own socio-economic group and gave grounds for complaint. When two brothers and their sister were claiming rights in an estate, the sister Julian, 'being now of years lawful to take some honest and convenient husband according to her estate and degree', was likely to remain unmarried because she had not received her legacy.[153]

149 TNA, C 1/1214/19.

150 TNA, C 1/829/44–5.

151 TNA, C 1/1360/36–8.

152 TNA, C 3/25/8; 39/59;159/27; 161/30; 174/91.

153 TNA, C 3/39/59.

Women in economic life

The economic role of women in the community is often obscure, but was not simply that of pensioner or annuitant; nor were married women simply dependants of their husbands. Until comparatively recently the economic role of women in rural communities was hardly ever noticed, despite the ground-breaking work of Alice Clark, first published nearly a hundred years ago.[154] Reference might be made to estate accounts where women were employed as day-labourers in agriculture,[155] without acknowledging the implications for rural and household economies, and, where a household had evidence of dual occupations, via probate inventories for example, the occupations were usually attributed to the male head of the household. It was not only the law that considered wives as *femmes couvertes*; historians have also covered up their roles in the local economy, tacitly accepting the premise that emphasised the domesticity of married women and confined their activities to the home or supplying the home through domestic farm activity, and simply taking female servants for granted.

More recently, though, general and local studies have begun building up a much more detailed picture of economic activity by women, to the point where it has been recognised that 'women's economic contribution was indispensable'.[156] Evidence for women's roles in the economy has been teased out by revisiting sources such as the probate inventories of men, formerly taken as evidence just for male occupations, but which include the tools used solely by their wives, for activities such as spinning, brewing and dairying; probate documents also show the amount of income-generating activity undertaken by married women independently of the husband's activities and the success of widows in continuing their husband's business or generating other income in widowhood.[157] Estate accounts, too, though more plentiful in the eighteenth century, show how much work was available for female servants and day-labourers, the range of work usually allotted to female servants, such as dairy work and cheese-making, washing and much of the brewing and malting,[158] and the range and value of the work of labourers' wives.[159]

The work of wives, daughters and female servants was particularly important in an area such as the Somerset Levels, with its growing emphasis on dairying, almost entirely the province of women.[160] Dairying, in particular, has always been seen as a domestic activity – the cow for the house – perhaps just because milking was carried out by women, but an activity that was becoming the mainstay of the income of small farm households in much of Somerset cannot be equated with the modern 'housewife role' that has traditionally been attributed to it. In a manner similar to the assumption

154 Clark, *Working Life of Women*.

155 e.g. *AHEW4*, pp. 430, 432.

156 Wrightson, *Earthly Necessities*, p. 44.

157 Whittle,'Housewives and Servants', pp. 51–74; *idem*,'Enterprising Widows and Active Wives', pp. 282–300; Erickson, *Women and Property*, pp. 193–4.

158 Whittle,'Housewives and Servants', Table 2, and pp. 61–3.

159 Muldrew, *Food, Energy*, *passim*; see below, this section.

160 Broad, 'Regional Perspectives and Variations in English Dairying', pp. 94, 106; Verdon, '"… Subjects Deserving of the Highest Praise"', pp. 23–39.

that subsistence peasants consumed what they produced rather than selling it, it is assumed that activities in the home such as dairying, brewing, baking and spinning were for domestic consumption only, but, as not all households carried out all these activities, some, at least, must have been selling to others. It is reasonable to suppose that in many dual-occupation households with evidence of by-employments the wife managed one or more sources of income independently, such as dairying, spinning and brewing, while her husband was engaged in another, rather than the man himself having several occupations.[161] A tucker's wife and a blacksmith's wife who milked their cows on the moor in Brent Marsh,[162] rather than just tending the cow for the house, may well have been running small dairying concerns on their own, while their husbands followed their respective crafts. Because only men's occupations are usually given in sources, and because married women could not trade in their own right, the wife's role in the general and household economy is obscured. Other wives in the Levels are, of course, found assisting in their husband's business: the wife of a farmer was one of those selling wool to Welthian Browne, described below, while the wife of a linen-draper sold cloth in her husband's shop in Axbridge.[163]

Women then, whether married or single, were not cut off from economic life, nor did wives operate solely in the shadow of a husband, but could and did participate successfully and in a fairly independent way. In Huntspill in 1632, for example, when Robert Browne, a husbandman/labourer, was suspected of having stolen some fleece wool from a barn where he had been threshing, he and his wife Welthian had to account for wool found in their house by the constable, some of which was afterwards sold before further action had been taken in the matter.[164] Welthian Browne claimed that she had made all the purchases of the fleece wool and lambtoe found in their house from four Huntspill residents and at Bridgwater market, in quantities from 1 to 17 lbs. Though the constable had warned her not to sell any of it until the case was cleared up, she said she had been forced to do so because she needed some money, and had sent word to that effect; when nobody came to see the wool again, she had sold 6 lbs at Bridgwater and a little more that she had spun. Her husband, she said, knew nothing about the buying of the wool. Robert Browne confirmed that he had little to do with his wife's wool activities. When she had told him that a farmer had offered her 20 lbs, to be paid for at Michaelmas, he had advised her not to buy so much, as it would be hard for him to spare so much money at one time. Otherwise, he had no idea where his wife had bought the wool 'because he never used to meddle nor question her dealing but doth usually deliver her all the money which he earns to be employed and bestowed by her as she thinks fit'.[165]

---

161 Whittle, 'Housewives and Servants', pp. 68–73.

162 SHC, D\D/cd/51, 'detection' v. Henry Lange, depositions of Eliz. Petheram and Kath. Napper, 3 Apr. 1623.

163 SHC, Q/SR/33/134.

164 SHC, Q/SR/64/10–11.

165 Lack of knowledge of where his wife bought the wool was stressed because when the constable had first approached Browne he had given the impression she had bought wool from the farmer mentioned, whose brother denied any dealings; that naturally made the Brownes' position look suspicious.

Women at the lower end of the economic scale were more likely to pursue their own economic activities than those higher up, out of necessity. They were forced to work to bring the family's income to a viable level or to keep going if their husband died or deserted them. As elsewhere in England, female alehouse-keepers, both licensed and unlicensed, were fairly common in Brent Marsh, but other examples can be found of women engaged in supporting themselves, such as Edith Smith of South Brent, the widow of a sieve-maker. She had been born and married in Wiltshire, and after ten years of marriage she and her husband had come to live in East Brent, where they had hired a house for three years, living there for one and travelling the country making sieves for the rest of the time. After her husband died, leaving her with three children, she and the children had worked at the harvest at Burnham, staying with Widow Board, who lodged poor people, and after the harvest she and her 14-year-old son had walked about the county making sieves.[166]

Another example is the wife of a Dorset tailor, Arthur Snowe of Shapesbury (?Shaftesbury). Snowe was arrested for having sold a piece of flannel believed stolen. He said he had been at Edithmead fair, on his way to Exeter, and had by chance met up with his wife, Jane Snowe, whom he had not seen for a week as she was travelling up and down the country with a pack of 'small wares' on her back, and he had got the flannel from her. Because of the circumstances his explanation may be suspect, but his wife's employment must have been at least credible to the magistrates.[167]

For labouring families the evidence is less visible, but a recent study has shown how significant was the contribution from wives, and also children, in making up the household income. Estimated figures for the income of labourers and their wives suggests that the income of the wives in spinning and agricultural work could add another 40 to 60 per cent of their husbands' income to the household total in the period from the mid sixteenth to the late seventeenth century.[168] Both married and unmarried women were required for milking and dairy work, and women were also employed as day-labourers on arable land for weeding and hay-making, for example, for working on roads, doing washing, and spinning wool and later flax; spinning increased in importance for labouring income from the late seventeenth century as demand for yarn grew. In the later seventeenth century evidence for a West Somerset farm shows that women worked for only 6 per cent of the labouring days per year, with peak employment during the eight weeks of May and June, but carried out a wide range of jobs, which, in addition to the usual harvest work and clearing of weeds and stones, included driving horses, carrying corn and vegetables and spreading dung. More figures are available for the number of women employed in agriculture in the eighteenth century, and vary considerably by region and season, but examples show that where women were employed they might account for from 20 per cent of the days worked to as much as 50 per cent

---

166 SHC, Q/SR/34/20.

167 SHC, Q/SR/51/17.

168 Calculated from Muldrew, *Food, Energy*, figures on pp. 217 and 257.

in harvest. Wages for women were generally only about half of those for men, but this may be partly because married women worked fewer hours owing to their necessary domestic work and child care.[169]

Towards the top of the economic scale, however, evidence of independent economic activity is hard to find: the economic role of a yeoman's or gentleman's wife does seem to be confined to traditional country housekeeping. Their widows' participation in economic life, however, was much wider. Of the wills for reconstituted families, 11 were for women, all widows except one who was unmarried. Four of the wills show that the women were active farmers, the remainder having little to show what they did for a living. These latter included Eleanor Hodges, widow of George Hodges, esquire, of Wedmore, who made the conventional sort of will for a lady of her social position, with bequests of clothes, linen and money, giving the residue to her five daughters rather than to either of her sons,[170] and most of the widows' wills are of this kind. The wills of the farming widows are similar to those made by male farmers. Isabel Popham of Wedmore, the widow of John Popham, who died in 1591, left four children aged 22, 21, 19 and 7 when she died in 1593, the second child, a daughter, being married. At her death, Isabel possessed crops growing on land at Clewer, Crickham and elsewhere in Wedmore, and wheat, pease, a cow and 4 lbs of wool were among the bequests she made, which otherwise consisted of house goods, pewter, brass and furniture. The residue was left to her eldest son, who had to bring up the youngest.[171]

Alice Blake, another Wedmore farmer, had been widowed twice. Her first husband, Alexander Tutton, died in 1587, and some six months later she had married Thomas Blake of Blackford. He died in 1613, but Alice lived on until 1632 and was described as 'senex' (old) in the burial register.[172] In his will Tutton had left all his goods, apart from a few small token and charitable bequests, to Alice and their two sons, John and Edward, equally between the three.[173] By the time Alice wrote her will, her son Edward had married and had five children, and her two daughters by Blake were also married with children; the other son is not mentioned. Alice had a house for her life and left some furniture to remain in it for the next possessor, and she had parcels of land in Wedmore out of which annuities totalling £32 were to be paid. She had a wain and wheels, a putt, several colts and cows among the goods she disposed of, and had several covenant servants assisting her.[174]

Since Tutton's sons were 9 and 4 when he died, it is not surprising that Alice was left in charge of the family. Anne Tutton, however, is an example of a widow made head of a household that included adult sons. Anne, or Agnes, was the

---

169 H.V. Speechley, 'Female and Child Agricultural Day Labourers in Somerset, *c.*1685–1870', PhD thesis (University of Exeter, 1999), pp. 60–65; Muldrew, *Food, Energy*, pp. 235–8, 241–5; Wrightson, *Earthly Necessities*, pp. 48–9.

170 TNA, PROB 11/210/259.

171 TNA, PROB 11/81/420.

172 Hervey, *Wedmore Parish Registers*, Burials.

173 TNA, PROB 11/70/355.

174 TNA, PROB 11/163/190.

widow of John Tutton of Theale, who died in 1647. He left £50 to each of his four sons: John, aged 23; William, age unknown; Joseph, 12; and Robert, 7.[175] John also received his father's lease for years of six acres of arable, and Robert the leases for years of a tenement and 11 acres of meadow or pasture, all in Burnham.[176] The residue was left to Anne, who was the sole executrix and was responsible for finding and paying the £50 legacies. In 1652 Anne made her will and disposed of a quantity of farm stock: a yoke of oxen called Browne and Pretty, a yoke of steers, plough harness, a mare, five yearlings, corn growing on another's ground[177] and the crop of apples in the orchard. She left the bed that her son John lodged on to William, and the bed that William and Joseph shared to Robert. The legacies left by her husband to the three elder sons had evidently been paid, but Robert's had not, because he was left additional bequests, including £18 due in rent from a tenant and £20 borrowed by John, specifically in full satisfaction of his father's legacy. John was left the residue and appointed executor and William was the overseer. John's bed, mentioned above, suggests that he may have lived in the house, but possibly he used it only when he stayed there: his mother's control of the bulk of his father's property had not prevented him from marrying, which he did in 1649, and by 1652 he had a son. His relationship with his mother as far as finance went was on a business footing, since the £20 he borrowed was secured by a bond.[178]

Social participation

'The only public appearance of women and children, almost their only expedition outside the circle of the family, was at service in church. Wives and maidservants might take and sell their poultry ... to market, ... but otherwise they stayed at home.'[179] This has for a long time been the common assumption regarding early modern women in the village community, but it is a gross exaggeration to suggest that women's social life, as well as their economic life, was confined to the home and the family circle, and in the last few decades much new research on various aspects of women's lives has been published to demonstrate this. Evidence for the Somerset Levels also contradicts this assumption in several ways. Married women and single often differed in their activities, but all women went out and about a good deal and interacted with both men and women in the community, quite apart from the economic activities described above.

---

175 Ages calculated from date of baptism. The known children were baptised in 1624, 1630, 1632, 1633, 1635, 1640 and 1642. If John listed his surviving children in age order, William was baptised between 1624 and 1635, probably before 1630. John and Agnes were married in 1622 in Wedmore, but lived in E. Brent for several years. Bapt Reg for EB 1623–52 does not survive.

176 TNA, PROB 11/204/427.

177 Probably a short-term rented acreage.

178 TNA, PROB 11/221/593.

179 P. Laslett, *The World We Have Lost – further explored* (London, 1983 edn), p. 73. But the remainder of the references to women in his book concern activities outside the home, so it is unclear what Laslett was thinking of.

A surprising degree of interaction and independence is revealed in the case concerning Mrs Eleanor Hodges and her poultry. Mrs Hodges sent a warning by Marie Warman to a neighbour, Nicholas Barker, that he was not to come on her ground nor meddle with her turkeys, ducks and geese again,[180] a message that led to three defamation cases in the ecclesiastical courts and the examination by the justices of Barker and others for theft. While it would not be surprising to find a married woman complaining to another woman, it seems more unusual to find the wife of a gentleman delivering a complaint to a man, and one not so far below her in social position, rather than letting her husband handle the matter. Furthermore, the woman Mrs Hodges sent with her message was not a household servant, but the wife of a Wedmore tailor, and was either a friend or a neighbour who was glad to oblige Mrs Hodges. She seems to have had no qualms about getting involved in this local row, though she did ask Cicilia Fraunces alias Kempe to accompany her, probably for moral support. Cicilia is the third woman in this case who does not fit a conventional role. She was a 30-year-old singlewoman who had lived in Wedmore for 15 years, and she had been at the house of Robert Hole, brother-in-law to Nicholas Barker, that day, a Sunday, before morning prayer, 'to do some churing woorke about the said Mr Hole's house'.[181] She was not a living-in servant and was returning to her own home when she met Marie Warman on her errand for Mrs Hodges and returned to Hole's house with her. Cicilia had had two illegitimate children, one still living aged 7, but witnesses to her character testified that she had mended her way of life after being whipped for the second child, and by all reports had since behaved herself honestly. Presumably she worked as a day-labourer and probably did casual work for many households.

Women of respectable character also visited local inns and drank there. Ann Roynon, who was connected to an armigerous family living in and around Compton Bishop, visited an inn called the Roebuck at Crosse, in Compton Bishop. As she was a neighbour, the innholder, Samuel Andrews, called to her to come into the kitchen, where he was playing at 'tables' with Joseph Tripp. Ann Roynon and Tripp seem to have had a long-standing quarrel which continued until Andrews told them to be quiet. After the game was finished Andrews brought a jug of beer 'to make them friends', but unfortunately the quarrel flared up again: Tripp made some offensive remarks and Ann left, but when she slipped in the doorway Tripp had said '[it is] Mrs Roynon who is drunk now'.[182] The outcome was a defamation case from which this evidence is taken, and it illustrates that a neighbourly drink at an inn was not impossible for unaccompanied women; presumably not all such activities ended in the courts. These and many other incidental examples illustrate the range of activities of women, in addition to the more frequent ones of visiting neighbours both male and female and attending markets and fairs, and counters the stereotype of the woman confined to domestic and social activities in her own home.

Women's roles in public life, as opposed to economic and social life in the community, were indeed more circumscribed. No evidence has been found for

180 SHC, D\D/cd/51, Hodges v. Barker, 23 Mar. 1625.

181 'Churing' could mean churning or charring.

182 SHC, D\D/cd/81, Roynon v. Tripp, dep. of Sam. Andrews, 10 Nov. 1635.

parliamentary elections in the area, but in any case a general study of elections has concluded that even where women were legally entitled to vote the social attitudes of the day were against it, and candidates, sheriffs and recorders of votes can be found refusing to admit the votes of women.[183] Few records survive for early modern parish officers in Brent Marsh, or how the offices were filled; in general, where offices went by property female holders would pay a substitute to carry out their duties, but a surviving Wedmore church rate of the late seventeenth century lists Mrs Alice Stocke as one of the four overseers,[184] suggesting a more active role. Women were not sworn as members of the homage at manorial courts here, but occasionally court papers record their presence: at Blackford in 1644 four widows were present in court in addition to the homage of 11 men,[185] and women regularly appeared in court to surrender or be admitted to property, either singly or with their husbands, and if single were also sworn in as tenants or essoined,[186] so it is not always true that only men attended the manorial courts.[187]

The evidence for women's activities is always sparse, but the fact that documentary evidence overlooked their roles in the economy and in community life does not mean that the roles were negligible. In fact, it is impossible to assess the economy accurately if the economic activities of half the population are ignored. The legal and social status of women was not a fixed one, but subject to change, not necessarily because of an ideological change in attitudes towards women or how they should behave but perhaps more as a reflection of change in society generally in the later seventeenth century. Attention has been drawn to the greater deference that appeared in local society after 1660: local notables were able to enforce their authority and settle differences, avoiding the need for court procedures in local rows, and opposition to the social hierarchy had become muted or was channelled in new ways after the Restoration. Two reasons have been put forward to explain the paradox that civil war and revolution, which should have led to increased familiarity with doctrines of social equality, were instead followed by acceptance of social inequality: one, that population pressure eased and the land market slowed down, leading to more stability in local society; and, two, that the elites strove to ensure social stability by strengthening informal social control.[188] More than that, though, it is likely that the trauma of the Civil Wars and interregnum, the doctrines of social equality and the threat that some of the political and religious ideologies posed to many people of all ranks in society brought about a shocked reaction not just in the ruling elite but also among local villagers and townspeople, who saw the dangers to their own religious

183 D. Hirst, *Representative of the People? Voters and Voting in England under the Early Stuarts* (Cambridge, 1975), pp. 18–19.

184 SHC, DD\SAS/C795/PR/201.

185 SHC, DD\SE/63/2, Blackford court roll 17 Apr. 20 Car. I (1644).

186 e.g. in manor of Moore, 1592–4, 1612–28: SHC, DD\S\WH/209.

187 Laslett, *World We Have Lost*, p. 73.

188 Amussen, *An Ordered Society*, pp. 177–8.

beliefs and to their social and economic position from sectarian and levelling ideas.[189] The concern to impose order and repress political and religious thought and activity in Restoration society may therefore have been paralleled by efforts to reduce and control the activities and economic independence of women.

189 Below, Chap. 6, Reactions to the Commonwealth and Interregnum: Conservative opinion in the Interregnum.

Chapter 6

Wealth, society and national politics

Uncovering the social and political attitudes of people who do not record their opinions or motives in writing has always been an intransigent problem in English history. It is easy to dismiss an indistinguishable mass of small landholders and farmers as being concerned only with their cattle and crops, and it is often hard to escape the conclusion that anyone with any ideas or a wider vision would have left the countryside for the more literate and articulate society of the town. When villagers emerge in history by their involvement in political action, whether as individuals or as a group, their activity was usually recorded by more literate, but often uninvolved, contemporaries, who dismissed it as the work of either subversive malefactors or ignorant misled fools, and historians in the past have tended to take a similarly dismissive attitude towards people outside the ranks of the gentry. Some serious effort has, however, been made to throw light on popular political opinion during the Civil War and its aftermath, when the opinions of a far wider range of people were recorded, to produce reasons for overt support, such as deference, localism, class or agrarian typology, and also to question the distinctions previously made between 'elite' and 'popular' politics.[1] Social historians, too, are now looking at the interrelationships of social and political history and viewing the political activities of all ranks of society in terms of social history.[2]

In Brent Marsh the manorial structure, together with a type of husbandry that benefited farmers in this period, produced conditions which allowed a degree of political involvement in the events of the mid seventeenth century, freedom from the influence of royalist gentry, the development of radical ideas in politics and religion among a number of committed adherents and a politicisation of local society that was revealed again in the 1680s. The strength of manorial custom here left the landowners without any really effective tenurial weapons to use against their tenants for the purpose of social control. Moreover, the lack of resident lords, or even of substantial gentlemen tenants, meant that most parishes of Brent Marsh had no clear social leaders, leaving the social and political organisation of the village without a link to the governing class. Most of this area had no resident justices or other county governors in the sixteenth and seventeenth centuries to maintain a gentry-led social hierarchy.[3] The effect of this was apparent during the Civil War, when the Somerset

1 In particular, D. Underdown, *Revel, Riot, and Rebellion: Popular Politics and Culture in England 1603–1660* (Oxford, 1985), has explored this theme in a study of three counties in the South West. I am indebted to the late Prof. Underdown for his comments on an earlier draft of this chapter.

2 Wood, *Riot, Rebellion and Popular Politics*, pp. 5–17.

3 The only gentry family resident was Rodney, of Rodney Stoke, and the last of that line, Sir Edward Rodney (d. 1657) was JP 1616–40: Barnes, *Somerset*, p. 315. Axbridge also had its own justices and its own social hierarchy and is not included in the general theme of this chapter.

Table 11

Subsidy 1524: number and percentage of taxpayers

Parish	Total Taxpayers	Wages 20s		Goods £2–£5		Goods £6–£10		Goods £11–20		Goods £21–40		Goods £50–60		Land	
		Number and percentage of inhabitants assessed on													
		no.	%	no.	%	no.	%	no.	%	no.	%	no.	%	no.	%
Berrow	51	7	13.7	30	58.8	10	19.6	4	7.8	-		-		-	
S. Brent	82	7	8.5	43	52.4	16	19.5	11	13.4	4	4.9	1	1.2	-	
E. Brent	109	19	17.4	56	51.4	22	20.2	11	10.1	1	0.9	-		-	
Lympsham	52	5	9.6	22	42.3	11	21.2	12	23.1	1	1.9	1	1.9	-	
Burnham	68	18	26.5	35	51.5	13	19.1	2	2.9	-		-		-	
Huntspill	105	22	21.0	57	54.3	23	21.9	3	2.9	-		-		-	
Biddisham	33	9	27.3	12	36.4	6	18.2	3	9.1	3	9.1	-		-	
Mark	88	17	19.3	39	44.3	17	19.3	14	15.9	1	1.1	-		-	
Weare	20	1	5.0	12	60.0	4	20.0	3	15.0	-		-		-	
Allerton	17	-		8	47.1	8	47.1	-		1	5.9	-		-	
Wedmore	162	52	32.1	64	39.5	22	13.6	21	13.0	1	0.6			2 (£4; £1)	1.2
Badgworth	21	3	14.3	9	42.9	8	38.1	1	4.8	-		-		-	
Axbridge	62	11*	17.7	30	48.4	10	16.1	5	8.1	2	3.2	-		4 (£4; £3; £2; £1)	6.4
Cheddar	102	13	12.8	52	51.0	27	26.5	8	7.8	1	1.0	1	1.0	-	
Compton Bishop	29	-		19	65.5	4	13.8	2	6.9	1	3.5	-		3 (£40; £20; £1)	10.3
Rodney Stoke	28	7	25.0	13	46.4	5	17.9	2	7.1	-		-		1 (£140)	3.6
Total	**1029**	**191**	**18.6**	**501**	**48.8**	**206**	**20.0**	**102**	**9.9**	**16**	**1.6**	**3**	**0.3**	**10**	**1.0**

Notes: * Assessed on wages of 23s 4d to 33s 4d. Total assessed on: Wages 191 (18.6%) Goods 828 (80.5%) Land 10 (1.0%).

Sources: TNA, E 179/169/171; 169/182; 169/169; 169/175.

Levels showed far less support for royalism than areas with resident royalist gentry.[4] However, this is not to say that local society was homogeneous, without differences in class, status and wealth: as indicated in earlier chapters, residents here, whether landholders or farmers, merchants or craftsmen, had a wide range of income and status, a divergence which was by no means new in the sixteenth century.

Wealth in the Levels

Outside the local market towns the predominant source of wealth was agriculture, in which the bulk of the population was directly involved, so nearly all the inhabitants rated for tax apparently obtained the greater part of their income from rents or farming. Where the taxation returns can be matched up with manorial surveys and rentals, most of the taxpayers have been found to be copyholders.[5] In 1524, out of 52 subsidy-payers in the two tithings of Lympsham, only 19, of whom five were those assessed on wages, could not be matched up with customary tenants in the manors of Lympsham and Lympsham Parva.[6] Only nine of the 42 tenants in the Lympsham surveys do not appear in the Lympsham tax list. In view of the fact that some Lympsham residents are known to have held land outside the parish, and that some tenants did not live in the parish where they held land, the match between the two sets of names is a good one.

Similarly, when the 1597 subsidy return for East Brent is compared with surveys for the three manors in that parish, out of the 52 taxpayers only six of those assessed on goods and five on land cannot be identified in one or more of the three manors.[7] Two of the identified tenants were freeholders, two were life leaseholders and the remainder were holding by copies for three lives. Wherever taxpayers have been identified for landholdings or for occupations, nearly all have been found to be either copyholders or yeomen and husbandmen. This contrasts with the parish and borough of Axbridge, where the majority had other occupations: in 1597 ten out of the 18 taxpayers are known to have had occupations in commerce and trade; six were drapers, two were tanners and one an innkeeper, even though two of these – William Braddie, woollen draper, and David Jones, innkeeper – were assessed on land rather than goods.[8]

Analysis of the subsidy of 1524 in Table 11 shows that the division of wealth between landholders was already very unequal by the early sixteenth century. This tax was to be levied on everyone over 16 with land, movable goods or wages of £1 or more, taxing them on whichever source would produce the most tax. However,

---

4 Below, Grass roots politics in the Civil War.

5 Of the 16 freeholdings in the four Brent manors (E Brent, S. Brent, Berrow, Lympsham), only five holders were residents: vicar of E. Brent, John Dinghurst, John Hodges, John Sayard and Thomas Somerset. They are not especially highly placed among the taxpayers.

6 TNA, E 179/169/171; BL, Egerton MS 3034, ff. 132–47 (Lympsham 1516); SHC, T\PH\vch/38 (Lympsham Parva 1540). Though the latter is rather later in date than the subsidy, the copies listed in it date from Henry VII's reign.

7 TNA, E 179/171/324, Brent hundred; LR 2/225, ff. 53–114; CCC Oxford, Fn 13, survey 1609; SHC, DD\WY/70, survey of Edingworth 1600.

8 TNA, E 179/171/324, Winterstoke hundred. The occupations of the rest are unknown.

though the subsidy assessments are useful to show the relative wealth among the population, they are unlikely to be accurate guides to the absolute wealth of individuals, nor to the resources of the area as a whole.[9] Besides the perennial problem of under-assessment, only freehold land was apparently taken into account, and not customary land, the most common tenure among taxable residents here. Some customary tenants held as much as 100 acres, at ancient valuations of about 1s an acre, but its potential value in produce or rents was not taken into account. Compared with some other areas in England,[10] Brent Marsh parishes had a lower level of wealth at the top of the scale, but also had far fewer, at less than a fifth, taxed on wages, which was appreciably lower than some areas.[11] The percentage of taxpayers assessed on goods of £20 or more also compares very favourably to those other areas, but, despite this, the wealthiest taxpayers in the Levels, apart from Sir John Rodney, assessed on lands worth £140 a year, had far less than the substance enjoyed in parts of Lincolnshire, for example. The absence of resident manorial lords apart from Rodney was one reason for the lack of very wealthy taxpayers, together with the absence of large demesne holdings.[12] The customary tenants did not hold the acreage that would result in several hundred pounds' worth of goods, and the wealth of townsmen was notoriously hard to assess, which is probably why several men here from Axbridge and Compton Bishop, where many Axbridge merchants lived, were assessed on their small quantity of freehold land. The wealthiest taxpayer assessed on goods was Isabel Wall of Lympsham at £60: she was the widow of John Wall, who had held *c.*66 acres of customary land in Lympsham manor in 1516, and she and John were named together in a copy in the manor of Lympsham Parva for 17½ acres and part of 18 acres, making a known holding of about 90 acres in all.[13] However, while the farming and landholding residents of the area by no means enjoyed the same amount of wealth, the area produced few great extremes of wealth and few individuals living in the area who could dominate the community financially.

For the later seventeenth century two taxation returns give information about nearly all the inhabitants of the parishes with extant returns: the Poll Tax of 1660 and the Hearth Tax of 1664–5. Both lack complete coverage of all the parishes in this study, but several parishes, particularly those in Bempstone hundred, have both returns. The hearth tax returns are widely used for the analysis of wealth in England in the later seventeenth century because there seems to be a reliable correlation between the number of hearths and status and occupation categories over a parish.[14] Looking at Brent Marsh, however, where 11 parishes (in the hundreds of Bempstone, Winterstoke

---

9 Whittle, *Development of Agrarian Capitalism*, pp. 205–7.

10 Hoskins, *Essays in Leicestershire History*, pp. 129–30; Spufford, *Contrasting Communities*, p. 30; Thirsk, *English Peasant Farming*, pp. 46–7.

11 e.g. Spufford quotes 36% for Devon: *Contrasting Communities*, p. 31; Whittle found 58.6% in South Erpingham Hundred in Norfolk, and the rest of East Anglia and Sussex were between 39% and 43%: Whittle, *Development of Agrarian Capitalism*, pp. 209–11, Table 4.6.

12 Above, Chap. 3, The manors.

13 BL, Egerton MS 3034, f. 133d; SHC, TH\vch\38.

14 Spufford, *Contrasting Communities*, pp. 36–41.

Table 12

Hearth Tax 1665: breakdown by number of hearths

Parish	*No. of entries*	*% with 1 hearth*	*1*	*2*	*3*	*4*	*5*	*6*	*7*	*8*	*9*	*12*	*No. void**	*No. exempt**	*1670 exempt by cert.*
Huntspill	151	60	90	29	10	2	2	1	0	0	0	0	12	5	14
Burnham	80	60	48	19	1	0	0	1	0	0	0	0	8	3	23
Biddisham & Tarnock	41	38	13	15	4	0	0	0	0	0	0	0	5	4	
Mark	139	58	81	30	4	1	1	2	0	0	0	0	9	11	48
Weare & Badgworth	53	28	15	19	9	1	1	1	1	1	0	0	0	5	2
Allerton	47	38	18	15	2	4	0	0	1	0	1	0	4	2	16
Wedmore	235	41	97	82	19	7	3	3	0	0	0	0	7	17	129
Axbridge	99	10	10	29	30	14	2	4	4	0	0	0	1	5	
Compton Bishop	100	27	27	31	13	4	3	0	0	0	1	0	2	19	
Cheddar	90	52	47	14	9	4	2	0	0	1	0	0	1	12	
Rodney Stoke	72	61	44	20	5	0	0	0	0	0	0	1	0	2	

Notes: Tax collected by tithings and hundreds, not on a parish basis, so Biddisham, Badgworth and Weare cannot be separated out; Tarnock is a hamlet on the boundary of Biddisham and East Brent. Compton Bishop includes the tithing of West Street, Axbridge.

* Exempt: Payment not taken as too poor to pay parish rates, but included in no. of hearths.

* Void: Houses empty, decayed or put to other uses, but included in the breakdown of no. of hearths.

Huntspill: 1670 certs. only for Alston Maris tithing.

Sources: TNA, E 179/256/16 (covering hundreds of Bempstone, Winterstoke and Huntspill); exemption certs. from E 179/172/434, printed in Dwelly (ed.), *Dwelly's Nat. Recs*, vol. 2, pp. 44–9 (Allerton, Burnham, Alston Maris, Mark, Weare, Wedmore and the four parishes in Brent H.). No hearth tax returns found for Brent H.

and Huntspill) have fully legible returns, it is clear that on occasion a taxpayer with, say, three hearths was actually paying on three cottages each with one hearth, and since the criteria used by the collectors in different parishes may not be the same, conclusions drawn from the Hearth Tax on both population size and wealth may be rather unreliable.[15] Table 12 gives a breakdown of the number of hearths for each parish. Interestingly, in three cases there are more houses with two hearths than with one. Two of these cover three small parishes just south of Axbridge, and the third is Axbridge itself, which not unnaturally shows a very different profile from the rural areas, with the largest category being houses with three hearths. The information given in the returns is interesting: the number of empty houses, or those marked as being put to other uses, for example, while for some entries with several hearths nothing is known about the taxpayer to account for this. The difficulty with the hearth tax, however, is that it was levied during only one short period, and without similar returns for the sixteenth century, say, it is hard to know what is significant or changing regarding housing, wealth or population over time.

For Brent Marsh a more useful source than the hearth tax for population, and to some extent for assessing wealth, is the Poll Tax of 1660, levied for the disbanding of the army. Complete and legible returns are available in Brent Marsh for ten parishes (in the hundreds of Bempstone and Brent), but they are again not without pitfalls when seeking reliable figures. The tax was set at a fixed amount on peers, certain office-holders and members of craft and trade guilds, with a rate of 2 per cent on the net disposable income of everyone else with land, goods or wages which produced an income of £5 a year or more. Below that, unmarried people over 16 paid 1s each and married people paid 6d a head, but anyone receiving alms was exempted.[16] In theory, therefore, the returns should indicate the farming and rentier income of most commoners and the division of wealth within the parishes, but in practice the actual figures are generally far from reliable, as individuals more or less valued their own incomes, with obvious results.[17] Furthermore, while the 6d-payers are often distinguished either singly or as man and wife, the higher taxpayers sometimes paid a lump sum which included the 6d-a-head for their wife, their children over 16 and their servants; as far as the effect on the wealth figures is concerned (as opposed to population), this is probably not very serious, assuming a level of under-assessment in any case. An additional problem, though not likely to affect Brent Marsh very much, is that those paying the fixed amount as a member of a guild are not differentiated in the returns, so everyone has to be treated as though the tax they paid reflected their income.[18] In Brent Marsh there is also great inconsistency between parishes in the way that taxpayers are recorded and, though the tax over the basic rate of 1s is supposed to be based on income, it is apparent that the rating is probably based on the local church rate lists, and in many parishes is a land tax, rather than a poll tax:

15 Above, Chap. 2, Table 1, for population from Hearth Tax.

16 Statute 12 Car. II, c. 9, Act for Levying an Income or Poll Tax for Disbanding the Army and Navy.

17 S. Dowell, *A History of Taxation and Taxes in England* (London, 1888), II, p. 29, who cites Samuel Pepys's experience of under-assessment.

18 The amount varied from £6 to 5s. for different groups of guilds.

Table 13
Poll Tax 1660: number of taxpayers by amount paid

Tithing	*1s single payers*	*1s married couples*	*6d payers mainly F often wives*	*Total no. of minimum payers as % of pop.* No.	%	*Income represented by the tax* *<1s>4s* (c. £5>£10 pa)	*4s>10s* (£10>25 pa)	*10s>20s* (£2>£50 pa)	*20s–28s* (£50–£70 pa)	*Other*	*Total taxed pop inc. wives*
Berrow	55	33	23	144	74.6	21	21	6	1	-	193
South Brent	54	44	-	142	57.7	40	52	10	2		246
East Brent	79	36	-	151	62.7	12	57	20	-	1x £3 10s	241
Lympsham	49	19	14	101	67.8	15	22	9	1	1x 35s 2d	149
Huish	11	7	3	28	59.6	10	9	-	-	-	47
Burnham & Burnham Moor	64	34	17	149	65.6	37	33	5	3	-	227
Alston & Worston	25	25	1	76	69.7	16	14	3	-	-	109
Biddisham & Tarnock	24	16	-	56	50.5	17	23	11	3	-	111
East Mark	47	23	-	93	64.1	25	20	6	1	-	145
Moore	63	47	19	176	69.8	32	39	5	-	-	252
Weare	36	9	7	61	57.0	30	8	6	1	1x £2 5s	107
Allerton	34	22	-	78	63.4	22	19	3	-	1x 30s 5d	123
Wedmore	146	70	-	286	76.1	44	34	4	7	1x £3	376
Wedmore borough	14	24	-	62	96.9	2	-	-	-	-	64
Churchland	26	21	1	69	67.6	19	14	-	-	-	102
Blackford	44	23	23	113	66.1	33	20	4	1	-	171

Source: TNA, E 179/172/416 (Bempstone H. with tithings of Wedmore, first part of East Mark, last part of Burnham, Alston & Worston; Brent H. tithings of South Brent, Berrow, Lympsham and East Brent). 5 mm missing from this roll, but form E 179/171/336, pt 30 (misidentified and dated to 1667×78, but clearly the missing mm as tear in m.2 marries up perfectly). Covers missing part of East Mark, Biddisham & Tarnock, Moore, Blackford, Weare, Allerton, Wedmore borough, Churchland, first half of Burnham and Burnham Moor. Huish is a sub-manor mainly in Burnham parish but lies in Winterstoke H. (TNA, E 179/256/7).

entries occur for the tenants of someone, the bishop's old rents or the vicarage, and in some cases landowners paid in more than one parish on the land they held in each, so clearly a parish return may include a number of non-residents.

Table 13 gives a breakdown of the number of taxpayers in the minimum categories and in various bands of income, and also the percentage of the total taxpaying population who paid the minimum tax. It immediately becomes clear that there is very little precision in the actual recording of wealth from this source. In the large tithing of Wedmore, for example, there were 304 entries (excluding two entries for tax on the parsonage) covering 376 people: 158 households or couples, and 146 single persons.[19] In this tithing the 286 married and single men and women paying the minimum 6d or 1s comprised 76 per cent of the total taxed population, while 89 households were assessed on net annual incomes from £5 up to £70, with one more on an income of £150. The poll tax probably covers a wider range of the population than the subsidy 140 years earlier, and though 60 people in Wedmore tithing were exempted from paying the hearth tax in 1670,[20] many of those can be identified on the poll tax return among the 1s and 6d payers. Their income may have diminished in the intervening decade, but perhaps, though poor, they were not receiving alms, the criterion for exemption from the poll tax. In all the parishes in the table the number of minimum payers is around two-thirds of the total taxed population, indicating incomes of less than £5 a year net. However, as the examination of diets in Chapter 4 shows, even £5 a year would hardly provide a labouring man with adequate food, never mind his family, so this would mean that the majority of the population were at starvation level, which is certainly not indicated in other sources. Clearly no effort was actually made to establish anyone's income; only those with a recognisable landholding, such as free or lifehold tenure, and a certain standard of living were being considered for the higher rates of tax, while the majority of farmers without life tenures, as well as most crafts and tradesmen, simply paid the minimum. Of the 45 higher-rate taxpayers in Allerton, for example, 16 appear as life leaseholders or copyholders in the 1650 parliamentary survey of the manor[21] and all but one of the tenants can be accounted for in the tax list, while another two were the vicar and the dean and chapter of Wells. In Blackford, a manor with many more holdings, some of them very small, the tenants of 58 of the 79 copyholdings in the surveys of 1657 and 1663[22] could be identified in the tax list: 49 were higher-rate payers and nine paid the minimum 1s and were holders of a cottage or three acres, for example. Some of the remaining higher-rate payers may also have had leases for one life, but are harder to identify. In both Allerton and Blackford there is a close correlation between the annual value of the property held and the amount of tax paid for many of the holdings identified. The returns can

19 TNA, E 179/172/416. Forty-eight of these, by their name and position in the list, were probably living in the household of a married couple or another single person, i.e. with parents, widowed parent, or other kin; this affects number of households, but since the tax assumes they had their own income they are considered as separate units.

20 E. Dwelly (ed.), *Dwelly's National Records*, vol. 2, *Directory of Somerset* (Fleet, 1929), pp. 46–7.

21 Coleman,'Manor of Allerton', pp. 72–82.

22 SHC, DD\SE/65/1–2.

give a picture of the distribution of wealth in the area, then, but mainly in a broad and statistical way: in most of the parishes only around a quarter to a third of residents appear in the higher-rate categories, and the great majority of those were in the range of £5–£25 a year.

Increase in the gentry

While, overall, Brent Marsh still supported a middle range of wealth, it was a society in which the gulf between the top and bottom of the economic scale had apparently widened by the late seventeenth century, with a large proportion in the lowest tax categories, although most parishes had one or more individuals who stood out among their neighbours, either in the highest band of taxation or with more hearths than most. The early modern period saw a noticeable increase generally in the number of Somerset parishes with resident armigerous gentry, from one-fifth of the parishes in 1502 to half in 1623, though the gentry still tended to avoid the parishes of the Levels and the moors.[23] Although Brent Marsh did not have any of the top rank of county gentry after the death of the last male Rodney in 1657, several of the area's residents did have gentle status of varying degree, ranging from new armigerous families to those locally accounted as gentlemen. Some were newcomers, but others were from local families, generally copyholders, who bought freehold land on the break-up of manors such as Wedmore and South Brent or on the sale of chantry lands.[24]

Recent arrivals included the Bower family and Tristram Towse, who were connected with the clerical and legal communities in Wells and obtained property from the Church.[25] The Stone family, on the other hand, had been established in Wedmore before the sixteenth century, when Thomas Stone bought 130 acres of the manor of Wedmore and some chantry land from Sir Thomas Gresham, which he left to his brother Edward, footman to Queen Elizabeth. Edward's son Edward, who bore arms at the visitation of 1623, apparently lived in Westminster and let the property, eventually selling it to an almshouse charity in Wells in 1630.[26] Some, such as Henry Wogan, the leading taxpayer in Wedmore tithing in 1660, had married into families of gentry rank who had bought lands in the area.[27] Others, however, emerged from the local copyholders, such as the Boultings, a copyholding family in the sixteenth century who had bought the freehold of part of the manor of Wedmore in the early seventeenth, after which they were styled gentlemen.[28]

Possibly the most socially pre-eminent family after the Rodneys were the Hodges of Wedmore, who built up a large, though scattered, estate in Somerset and made

---

23 M. Havinden, 'The Increase and Distribution of the Resident Gentry of Somerset, 1500–1623', *Southern History*, 20/21 (1999), pp. 68–107.

24 Five men, from Mark, Wedmore and Allerton, were disclaimed at the visitation, 1623: Colby, *Visitation 1623*, pp. 137–8.

25 Above, Chap. 3, The use and attraction of copyhold for lives.

26 Colby, *Visitation 1623*, p. 105; SHC, D\P\w.st.c/17/1/1–2.

27 He married one of the heiresses of George Hodges (below).

28 Above, Chap. 3, The use and attraction of copyhold for lives.

connections with county families through judicious marriages. Mr Thomas Hodges (d. 1601) married the heiress of a Wedmore freeholder[29] and bought the freehold of the manor house and 64 acres of the manor of Wedmore. His son Captain Thomas Hodges, who had married a Rodney, died at the siege of Antwerp c.1585; the latter's son George (d. 1634) succeeded to the family property in 1601 and bore arms at the visitation of 1623.[30] George had married Eleanor, daughter of John Rosse, esquire, JP, through whom he received lands in east Somerset, and also possessed the manor of Overweare and other land in Weare and South Brent.[31] He held a manor court for his lands and therefore had the status accruing to a manorial lord, but he had only about a dozen tenants in the neighbourhood of Wedmore, so wielded little tenurial power there.[32]

Moreover, though Hodges was one of the wealthiest inhabitants of Brent Marsh – his subsidy payment was exceeded only by the Rodneys and was half as much again as the next highest in Wedmore[33] – he and his family were linked with their neighbours and had to take care to avoid offending them. This was evident in the series of defamation cases that arose in 1626 between Mrs Eleanor Hodges and Robert Hole, his wife Temperance and the latter's brother Nicholas Barker.[34] Eleanor Hodges accused Barker of stealing some poultry from her; Barker made various insulting remarks about her and said she was unworthy to be Mr Hodges's wife; Temperance Hole also made defamatory remarks about Mrs Hodges when the constables came to serve a warrant for good behaviour on Barker, and said that Barker was as good a gentleman as Eleanor was a gentlewoman. When asked why she and her brother abused Eleanor Hodges so, Temperance said it was because Mrs Hodges had not come to see her while she was sick, and she obviously felt slighted by this neglect. At the same time, Robert Hole was brought to the ecclesiastical court for defaming Agnes, the wife of David Russe or Rosse and probably Eleanor's cousin Ann, who had formerly been staying at Mrs Hole's house.[35] The various comments made show considerable resentments, and the social position of the Hodges family was evidently not enough to gain outward respect from the Holes and Barker. At the same time as these cases came to court Hole was withholding tithes from Hodges, lessee of the parsonage, but whether this was the cause of the conflict or another symptom is not clear.[36]

The Hodges, like many other minor gentry families, took advantage of opportunities presented by the Civil War and parliamentarian government to become politically

29 TNA, PROB 11/52/123.

30 Memorial in Wedmore parish church; Colby, *Visitation 1623*, p. 53.

31 SHC, DD\SH/23.

32 Above, Chap. 3, The manors: The formation of sub-manors.

33 TNA, E 179/171/324.

34 SHC, D\D/cd/51, 23 Mar. 1625/6, Elinor Hodges v. Nicholas Barker, Agnes Russe v. Robert Hole, 29 Mar. 1626, Elinor Hodges v. Temperance Hole. Also Q/SR/57/76, examination of Robert Hole, 17 Apr. 1626.

35 He was not her brother according to visitation pedigree: Colby, *Visitation 1623*, p. 95.

36 TNA, SP 16/165, no. 56; SP 16/169, no. 76.

active. George's eldest son Thomas (d. 1649) ran for election with William Strode, a moderate Presbyterian, against the radical candidates supported by the county committee and the army for the parliamentary seats of the borough of Ilchester in 1646, a bitterly contested election which Strode and Hodges were eventually held to have won.[37] The family also had several links through its daughters with parliamentarian gentry active in Somerset affairs during the Interregnum. Presumably they shared Strode's moderate and anti-army views, but they achieved no further distinctions and the name in fact died out with the death of Thomas's younger brother George in 1654. Any influence they had over Wedmore inhabitants before the Civil War was personal rather institutional: for instance, they had no control over the pulpit, as the dean of Wells had held the advowson.[38]

So, though some gentry newcomers held quite substantial freehold estates, they apparently wielded little power in their parish of residence, partly because their property was widely scattered, but possibly also because they were not long established. Many local inhabitants seem to have been strongly 'non-deferential', as they showed resentment of any assumption of status. This became more apparent during the Interregnum, when the local justices were of a slightly lower status than before the Civil War. One of those justices, Colonel John Gorges, who was involved in a couple of cases in Cheddar, also found the political and social opinions of some of his fellow parishioners unacceptable, particularly when they did not accord him the respect he felt they should. He was the second son of Henry Gorges, esquire, of Batcombe in Cheddar, members of a junior branch of the Gorges of Wraxall, a leading gentry family in the county, though of lesser standing,[39] and he had become important in county government, owing his position as a sequestration commissioner to John Pyne.[40] When the excise collector, John Rogers, also of Cheddar, was brought by the Cheddar parish constable before the justices and was called a rogue by Gorges, Rogers answered that he had not been a rogue 'when he lived with him in London, nor when he came with him out of the West [from the parliamentary army] nor when they were schoolefellowes together',[41] a retort that lacked any element of social deference. Though Gorges's father had borne arms at the visitation in 1623, clearly not all his Cheddar neighbours regarded him as above them in status and deserving of deference. Another Cheddar man, Thomas Hawkins, brought before Gorges in connection with a different case, likewise did not stand in awe of Gorges or think it necessary to be deferential, refusing to be brow-beaten when Gorges treated him in a high-handed manner. Hawkins was a tailor from Cheddar, aged around 30, formerly a soldier for the Commonwealth who had been imprisoned at Bristol for 25 weeks while it was a royalist garrison. He no doubt aggravated Gorges greatly by his attitude: he 'carried himself uncivilly' in front of Gorges, not giving him due respect and using

---

37 D. Underdown, 'The Ilchester Election, February 1646', *Proceedings of the Somerset Archaeological Society*, 110 (1966), pp. 40–51.

38 Weaver, *Somerset Incumbents*, p. 206.

39 Colby, *Visitation 1623*, p. 41.

40 D. Underdown, *Somerset in the Civil War and Interregnum* (Newton Abbot, 1973), pp. 167–8, 176.

41 TNA, SP 23/66, p. 69.

slighting expressions such as 'good neighbour Gorges'.[42] Gorges was clearly in a difficult position trying to obtain deference from neighbours who did not see his position as all that different from theirs, and who were quick to resent an assumption of superiority on his part, particularly when they had strong politico-religious beliefs to support them.

Growth of religious divisions

The lack of gentry leaders with power to influence local society, coupled with an independent attitude produced by tenurial and economic freedom, may well have contributed to the development of the deep religious and political commitments that emerged in the area in the mid seventeenth century: studies elsewhere have shown that dissent tended to flourish where social control was weak because the parish had more than one manor or lacked a resident lord.[43] More information about the number of Brent Marsh residents serving in the parliamentarian army and their regiments would have been welcomed in this regard, because service in the army exposed villagers to new and radical religious ideas, or at least directed and vitalised dimly held beliefs, and this might have been significant for Brent Marsh, where, prior to the Commonwealth, there is little trace of an evangelical tradition.

While there is evidence, in wills, of strong protestant feeling among a few inhabitants in the late sixteenth century, particularly Axbridge burgesses, parishes here had on the whole little exposure to early puritanism within the established Church. The religious outlook of Somerset in general in this period has been summarised as predominantly puritan, but only to the extent of a loathing of Roman Catholicism and an acceptance of the tenets of Calvinism; the clergy were on the whole undistinguished, good preachers were rare and there was generally a lack of respect for the clergy.[44] The parishes of Brent Marsh typify this. The only minister noted for puritan preaching was William Sclater (d. 1627), vicar of Pitminster (south-west of Taunton), who was presented to the rectory of Lympsham in 1619 by his patrons, John, Lord Poulett, and his wife Elizabeth. However, he retained Pitminster and left Lympsham to the care of a curate, so is unlikely to have had much influence on the latter. The only work of his to be published during his incumbency was entitled *The question of tithes revised: arguments for the morality of tithing* (1623),[45] so he would in any case be unlikely to have won an enthusiastic following in an area where non-payment of tithes was quite widespread. Most livings in Brent Marsh were in the hands of various diocesan bodies: only three were in private patronage, so the opportunities for puritan influence from this source, such as that exercised by

42 TNA, SP 23/171, pp. 361, 447, 449, 451.

43 A. Everitt, 'Nonconformity in Country Parishes', in Thirsk (ed.), *Land, Church and People*, pp. 178–99; Spufford, *Contrasting Communities*, pp. 307–13.

44 T.G. Barnes, 'County Politics and a Puritan Cause Celebre: Somerset Churchales, 1633', *Transactions of the Royal Historical Society*, 5th ser. 9 (1959), pp. 105–6.

45 *ODNB* sv. William Sclater (bp. 1575–d. 1627).

the earl of Huntingdon and his brother Francis in some south Somerset parishes,[46] were limited.

At the same time the established Church made equally little impression on the neighbourhood through ardent Arminian vicars, or by the enforcement of church and royal policies that would provoke strong resistance, as happened in parishes involved in the dispute over churchales. Up to the 1620s the Church of England, its leading clergy and many of the more educated laity were Calvinist in outlook, holding that God had arbitrarily predestinated people as the elect or the reprobate; the former would go to heaven and the latter to hell, and there was nothing that man could do to change this outcome. Under William Laud, archbishop of Canterbury from 1633 to 1645, and with the support of Charles I, Calvinism became outlawed and Arminian views came to dominate the Church, rejecting predestinarianism and holding a belief in God's universal grace, whereby man had the free will to obtain salvation, while stressing the importance of the clergy to assist this by intercession in the sacraments. At a local level the rearrangement of the altar and other theological changes in the parish churches, and the encouragement of Sunday sports and traditional feasts such as churchales by the king, which offended many puritan-minded parishioners, made this one of the strands which fed into the outbreak of the Civil War.[47] In parishes where the attack on Calvinism was strong, with the presence of an Arminian incumbent, the result was often the formation of a zealous puritan elite,[48] but in the Brent Marsh parishes no such incumbents, nor indeed puritan elites, have been identified. No evidence, either, has come to light of earlier radical religious ideas from which a continuity with the 1640s might be traced:[49] no fifteenth- and sixteenth-century lollardy, early separatism or other radical opinions are obvious, though the quiet existence of such opinions under the noses of somnolent church officials cannot be ruled out.[50] Occasional expressions of anti-clerical feeling do emerge, and the widespread and unusual proving of wills in the PCC between the mid 1500s and 1660 may possibly have been caused by a deep dislike of the Wells clergy, who were also local landowners. This may not be so much anticlerical feeling, therefore, as anti-landlord, and a continuation of the dislike of Glastonbury Abbey, the former landowners: at South Brent (Brent Knoll) the medieval bench-ends in the parish church satirised the abbot of Glastonbury as a rapacious fox

46 C. Cross, *The Puritan Earl: The Life of Henry Hastings Third Earl of Huntingdon, 1536–1595* (London, 1966), pp. 42–3.

47 N. Tyacke, 'Puritanism, Arminianism and Counter-Revolution', in C. Russell (ed.), *The Origins of the English Civil War* (London, 1973), pp. 119–21; Barnes, 'County Politics', pp. 103–22.

48 e.g. Wrightson and Levine, *Poverty and Piety*, pp. 159–61.

49 e.g. C. Hill, 'From Lollards to Levellers', in M. Cornforth (ed.), *Rebels and their Causes: Essays in Honour of A.L. Morton* (London, 1978), pp. 49–67; P. Collinson, 'Cranbrook and the Fletchers: Popular and Unpopular Religion in the Kentish Weald', in P.N. Brooks (ed.), *Reformation Principles and Practice, Essays in Honour of A.G. Dickens* (London, 1980), pp. 173–202.

50 Unfortunately only a few of the relevant ecclesiastical records were fit for production when this research was carried out, so this important source for religious activity has not been examined comprehensively. However, see Spufford, *Contrasting Communities*, pp. 255, 257–8, for lack of information in this source for religious dissent.

who is finally hung, probably a protest by the local priest as well as the parishioners at the demands of Glastonbury Abbey, who held the manor and tithes.[51]

In the 1640s changes in the official Church in the area were slight, despite the activities in parliament towards a radical overhaul which included the abolition of the episcopacy, removing the bishops and other diocesan clergy, and the ejection during the 1640s and 1650s of parish incumbents found unsuitable because of their Arminian or royalist views: presumably just as no eager Arminian vicar can be found at work in the 1630s, so there was little need for sweeping ejections of incumbents from Brent Marsh parish churches. Matthew Law, a pluralist, was ejected from Wedmore but retained Allerton; another pluralist had both his livings, one of them East Brent, sequestered.[52] The majority of incumbents remained where they were, reflecting the situation in England as a whole, as it has been calculated that only about 30 per cent at most, and possibly only 25 per cent, of livings were affected by sequestrations.[53] Three or four of the local ministers were cited by the Somerset Quakers as examples of those who became 'ardent presbyters', only to turn coat again at the Restoration and become equally ardent Anglicans.[54]

The lack in Brent Marsh of puritan zeal within the Church and the absence of puritan parish elites left this area with little means for moral and spiritual regeneration under the Commonwealth, even with the Presbyterian reorganisation which parliament decided on in 1646 to replace episcopal church government.[55] This involved forming a group of parishes into a classis to perform the functions of the former diocese and deaneries: in 1647 the Somerset county committee wanted to divide Somerset into nine classes, but had to settle for four owing to the shortage of suitable ministers and elders to carry out the functions.[56] The parishes in Brent Marsh showed signs of this shortage. Axbridge, Compton Bishop and Cheddar came within the Bath classis and the nearest suitable ministers were on the northern side of the Mendips.[57] Three of the elders did live in those parishes though: James Wrentmore of Axbridge, Hercules Comer of Cheddar and Henry Gorges of Batcombe in Cheddar. The remaining 13 parishes in Brent Marsh had no elders within their bounds and only one suitable minister, Thomas Walrond at Huntspill, described by Calamy as a man of eminent

51 Orbach and Pevsner, *Somerset: South and West*, p. 131; leaflet from St Michael's, Brent Knoll.

52 Weaver, *Somerset Incumbents*: the lists of incumbents are not complete, especially for the Interregnum; A.G. Matthews, *Calamy Revised* (Oxford, 1934); A.G. Matthews, *Walker Revised* (Oxford, 1948).

53 C. Cross, 'The Church in England, 1646–1660', in Aylmer (ed.), *The Interregnum*, pp. 110, 225 n.16. In Somerset as a whole only a fifth of parishes were affected by ejections: Underdown, *Somerset in the Civil War*, p. 145.

54 SHC, DD\SFR/8/1.

55 C. Cross, 'The Church in England', pp. 101, 108–9.

56 The certificate of division is undated but was published in March 1647/8, and is printed in W.A. Shaw, *The History of the English Church 1640–60*, 2 vols (1900), vol. II, pp. 413–21.

57 That is, suitable *Presbyterian* ministers; Cheddar's pre-war vicar, Thomas Wickham, still lived in the parish and presumably officiated at services.

piety and learning, 'of great use in recommending Religion among the Gentry',[58] a faculty which was not really relevant to a local society with few gentry within it.[59]

Outside the Church, secular authority also had few representatives in these parishes. The list of elders includes most of the parliamentarian gentry and lesser gentry in the county, and, apart from these, the only residents of the area that can be identified as playing any significant part in politics or county government were Thomas Hodges, MP for Ilchester, and John and Thomas Gorges, the sons of Henry of Batcombe. The situation in fact resembled the pre-war arrangements when almost all the diocesan authorities and justices lived outside the area, and in this respect presbyterian government was very similar to its predecessor and put down only shallow roots in the area. This, and the fact that ultimately they moved into alliance politically with the royalists, may account for the small impact presbyterians made here and the disappearance of Presbyterian religion in this area in the period immediately after the Restoration, while other forms of Protestant nonconformity flourished.

This lack of direction from religious and secular authorities left a vacuum into which unofficial groups were happy to step to promote their own views. After the wars radical sectarian ideas flourished among certain villagers, who, though possibly small in number, were extremely vociferous and ardent in their support of the Commonwealth. Several inhabitants of the Levels belonged to, or were influenced by, two new sects in the area, the Baptists and the Quakers, whose radical social and theological attitudes reinforced their own pride and self-respect, while challenging the social order of the parish.[60]

The Baptists were closely linked with the army: they believed in war to further their aims, and a large number were found in the ranks of the New Model Army. The most popular drill books for both cavalry and infantry were written by Baptists, and Baptist officers were also preachers to their troops.[61] Residents of Brent Marsh accused of being 'Independents' were more likely to have been members of a growing Baptist congregation in the area, converted either in the army or by the preaching of Thomas Collier. Collier, a former army preacher living and preaching in the 1650s at Westbury-sub-Mendip, just east of Cheddar, was one of the most influential Baptist preachers in the West Country. Very little is known about his origins, though his detractors described him as an illiterate carter or husbandman and a 'base mechanical fellow',[62] which was interpreted by an historian of the Baptist movement as indicating that Collier was 'one of the great band of lay-preachers which was typical of Baptist energy and practice'.[63] Collier clearly had some education, to judge by the works he wrote, and a sophisticated intelligence capable of intricate theological arguments. He preached in

58 Matthews, *Calamy Revised*, p. 508.

59 Wedmore also had a Presbyterian minister from sometime in 1647, followed by an Independent from 1650: W.M. Acres, *A Brief History of Wedmore* (Wedmore, 1954), p. 38.

60 Underdown, *Revel, Riot and Rebellion*, pp. 247–51.

61 W.T. Whitley, *A History of British Baptists* (2nd edn, 1932), p. 74.

62 *DNB*: the entry for Collier repeats almost exactly the note about him in *Notes and Queries*, 3rd series, VI, 322, but a lack of information makes them both misleading; now superseded by *ODNB*, Collier, Thos (d. 1691) (accessed online 17 Feb. 2014).

63 Whitley, *British Baptists*, p. 71.

many areas in the south and west of England and several works of his were published between 1645 and 1691. He is also thought to have been the author of the Somerset petition calling for the death of Charles I.[64] In March 1651 he held a public debate in Axbridge with John Smith, minister of Badgworth, and Charles Carlile, presumably the minister of Biddisham, after he had been accused by them of blasphemy.[65] The Baptists may have been meeting in the area by the time Collier held the debate; by 1653 the Western Association of Baptist Churches had been formed, largely through the efforts of Collier, who later became its superintendent. Eighteen congregations attended the Association's meeting in Wells in November 1653, including one from Wedmore,[66] ten of whose known members were among parishioners refusing to pay tithes to the vicar of Wedmore in the 1650s. The congregation petitioned Protector Cromwell for the use of the Church House in Wedmore for their meetings[67] and the congregation continued to meet after the Restoration, with Collier as their teacher.[68]

The early history of the Quakers was closely linked with that of the Baptists, from whose ranks many came. Cheddar and Axbridge had about half a dozen known Quaker families by 1670,[69] most of whom attended a meeting on Mendip, but their early history is not well documented: they may have originally been connected with the meeting at Burnham, a few miles to the west, which included members from nine parishes in the Brent Marsh area and others beyond. This meeting came into existence *c.*1656 through the efforts of Henry Moore, a Burnham yeoman, described as one of the 'first receivers of the gospel' in the county.[70] His house at Watchven in outer Burnham was used for meetings and from 1659 he kept the register, in which he also wrote a history of the Christian Church down to 1672; he represented the Burnham meeting at the quarterly meetings of the Friends at Ilchester by the end of 1668.[71] About 12 members, including Moore, had been among a group of 46 farmers in Burnham who refused to pay tithes in the 1650s, some from as early as 1648.[72]

---

64 Underdown, *Revel, Riot and Rebellion*, pp. 232, 247.

65 Thomas Collier, *The heads and substance of a discourse... held at Axbridge, co. Somerset ... about the sixth of March 1650* (London, 1651).

66 D. Jackman, *Baptists in the West Country* (Western Baptist Association, 1953), p. 2; G.F. Nuttall, 'The Western Baptist Association 1653–1658', *Journal of Ecclesiastical History*, 11 (1960), pp. 214–15.

67 TNA, SP 18/95, no. 1. Not dated, but included with documents for Mar. 1655. Identified as Baptist from the names associated with Collier's on the licence in 1669, and names of those who signed the Confession.

68 TNA, E 112/330/34; Whitley, *British Baptists*, pp. 72, 95; Thomas Collier, *A Confession of the Faith of Several Churches* (1656).

69 Friends' Ho., London, QM of Bristol and Som., Digest of Births, Marriages, Deaths; SHC, DD/SFR 8/1.

70 SHC, DD\SFR 8/1.

71 Watchven register (kept at Friends' Meeting House, Street, with a copy in Friends' Ho., London); S.C. Morland (ed.), *Somersetshire Quarterly Meeting of the Society of Friends, 1668–1699* (Somerset Record Society 75, 1978), p. 77.

72 TNA, E 134/1654–55/Hil8.

The toleration of the Interregnum allowed this flowering of religious opinions to take permanent root. Even the Quakers, whose radical tactics made them greatly disliked, were not without support in authority: the Somerset Friends regarded the county committeeman John Pyne as sympathetic, whereas John Gorges was known as a persecutor.[73]

Grass roots politics in the Civil War

The number of countrymen from the Levels who took an active part in the Civil War cannot be reliably assessed, any more than their reasons for joining, though it is probably safe to assume that the active were in the minority.[74] General and anecdotal evidence suggests that in the Somerset Levels and Mendip area there was more sympathy for parliament than the king. When the marquis of Hertford came to Wells to raise troops for the king in 1642 few local men apparently joined him, while a very large number gathered in support of parliament. A parliamentarian army also assembled at Chewton Mendip, north of Wells, and included a large number of countrymen, some armed and mounted, others armed only with pitchforks – some indication that the agricultural population was more responsive to the objectives of parliament than to those of the king. They may also have been influenced by the fact that the parliamentarian gentry were less remote figures to them than Hertford, who had large estates in Somerset but lived elsewhere, and this was certainly a consideration with them in 1644, when the earl of Essex was trying to raise troops for parliament.[75] The royalists, on the other hand, received little assistance, even while they controlled the area from June 1642 until July 1645; they had to resort to impressment in 1644, which led to many charges after the war that parish constables and others had aided royalist troops, though surprisingly few accusations that individuals had actually fought for the king. The list of suspected persons made in 1655 – those from whom bonds for good behaviour had been taken as they were known as royalist sympathisers or had once fought for the king – lists only 88 men in the 16 parishes studied here, 22 from the four Mendip parishes, the rest from ten lowland ones.[76] For three of the lowland parishes with full poll tax returns the number of royalists (6, 11, 17 respectively) represents only about 8 per cent of the male taxpayers listed, and about 13 per cent for a fourth parish (11 men).[77] This proportion is, however, quite high compared with the proportions calculated by David Underdown when analysing the 1655–56 lists for the whole county: the parishes in his south and west Mendips region had a return of 354 suspects, or 15.23 per 1,000, while the central region, which included the Levels, had

73 *Calendar of State Papers Domestic*, 1658–9, p. 354; N. Penney (ed.), *Extracts from State Papers relating to Friends* (1913), p. 106.

74 Problem of assessing allegiance is examined in D. Underdown, 'The Problem of Popular Allegiance in the English Civil War', *Transactions of the Royal Historical Society*, 5th ser. 31 (1981), pp. 69–94.

75 Underdown, *Somerset in the Civil War*, pp. 34–5, 37, 74.

76 BL, Add. MS 34012. The other three parishes were not represented.

77 TNA, E 179/172/416.

264, or 10.42 per 1,000. However, his population figures are only rough estimates, based on the Protestation Returns of 1641, parish registers and back-projection from the 1801 census, and none of the Brent Marsh parishes is represented among the surviving Protestation Returns, so the accuracy of the estimate cannot be checked.[78] The social profile of the suspects is fairly wide: three men had held commissions as captains in the royalist army; there were four other gentlemen, including the son of one of the captains and a surgeon, two yeomen, 55 husbandmen, three innholders and 20 trades and craftsmen. Incidental evidence from other sources shows that at least two of these men had been pressed into the king's service and had tried to escape.[79] It is noteworthy, however, that several of the largest parishes are either not represented, or by only one or two names, which suggests that the comprehensiveness of the list depended a great deal on the zeal and objectivity of the local officials who were presumably called on to supply the names.[80] Furthermore, Somerset lacks even the evidence that can be used when assessing royalist allegiance for Dorset or Wiltshire, which had records of pensions awarded to former royalist soldiers or their widows by local justices after 1660. More importantly, it is hard to judge the significance of the percentage of royalists when there is no comparable list of parliamentarian sympathisers: none of the western counties have suitable sources, such as full parliamentarian army muster rolls, from which to make an assessment.[81]

Though the majority of inhabitants took no active part in fighting, a group in South Brent and the adjoining parishes did rise up in April 1645 against the extortions and violence of a troop of cavaliers from outside the county, who stayed in the area for about a fortnight on their way to join Lord Goring at Taunton. When the troops would not leave until more money was paid to them, residents led by John Somerset, a local gentleman who had been a captain in the royalist army, and Thomas Gilling, yeoman, the constable of South Brent, resisted their depredations. The two principals were imprisoned in Bristol for several weeks, despite the inhabitants' certificate that they had not instigated the uprising and that in any case the resisters were acting legally under warrant from the royalist governor of Bristol, Lord Hopton, to arrest plundering soldiers.[82]

Reactions to the Commonwealth and Interregnum

Although the Civil War is generally described as though it was a straightforward adversarial contest between king and parliament, the two sides were not the opposite sides of a similar coin. While royalism was on the whole support for a conservative and conformist set of traditional values within a safe and known social hierarchy,

78 Underdown, *Revel, Riot, and Rebellion*, pp. 202–4, 293, 297.

79 TNA, SP 23/166, pp. 402, 404, 405.

80 They omitted John Somerset, former royalist captain, possibly because he subsequently led local resistance to royalist depredations (below).

81 Underdown, *Revel, Riot, and Rebellion*, pp. 295–6.

82 H. Symonds, 'A By-Path of the Civil War', *Proceedings of the Somerset Archaeological Society*, 65 (1919), pp. 48–75; Underdown, *Somerset in the Civil War*, pp. 90–91.

support for the parliamentary side encompassed many ideas and was an open-ended opportunity for free expression not just of ideas but of practical alternatives to the existing social structure, a freedom that ultimately undermined the revolution as the ruling class perceived the danger of such unlimited freedom. While general theories may explain allegiance to one side or the other in broad terms, they do not help in understanding political relationships within a village, what the different alternatives actually meant to villagers, nor why the quite widespread support for parliament and the Commonwealth in areas such as the Somerset Levels dwindled away to allow the Restoration to occur without much active resistance.

After the wars the radical sectarian ideas that flourished among ideologically committed villagers in the Levels caused deep and serious breaches in local society in the 1650s. The influence of those ideas, both in national politics and in the formation of new religious sects within the parishes, brought fear and bitterness, and occasionally local events in the 1650s showed how divisive national conflicts could be. One focus of opposition to the regime was the imposition of excise, a revenue device introduced in 1643 that taxed some basic essentials as well as imported goods. The tax was paid by manufacturers/importers, but the cost was widely assumed to be passed on to the consumer, and hit the poor hardest. Though most essentials were no longer being taxed by the early 1650s, beer, ale and other beverages were, and the excise was deeply resented in local society, where hitherto generally only a minority had paid any form of national taxation. Furthermore, the excise involved a bureaucracy of officials and collectors who had the right to enter premises, inspect cellars and so on, which was particularly and deeply resented, and the excise was still being denounced in appeals to the labouring classes 200 years later.[83]

Animosity against the excise lay behind an attack on a sub-collector of the excise, John Rogers, and his assistant in Cheddar in 1652, when they went to inspect the beer at a local inn.[84] Rogers, a 35-year-old husbandman, committed sectarian and former parliamentary soldier who had a small landholding in Cheddar, was attacked by a couple of neighbours, and the 53-year-old parish constable, Henry Bankes, who was called in, then took the opportunity to subject Rogers to such harsh treatment that he was subsequently in bed for a week. Even Rogers's assistant, who had been a complete bystander in the fight, was arrested and put under guard overnight, treatment which was probably also a product of the animosity against the excise. Bankes had already been trying to get neighbours to sign a certificate against Rogers in order to bring him before the justices and also attempted to obstruct the excise a couple of months after the fight by returning a warrant from the Excise Commissioners, which summoned all alehouse and inn keepers to appear at their office in Axbridge, with only two names on it, though Rogers stated that he knew there were about 20 selling beer within Bankes's jurisdiction. Bankes harangued Rogers as a excise rogue

83 J. Thirsk and J.P. Cooper (eds), 'Introduction of Excise, 1643', in *Seventeenth-Century Economic Documents* (Oxford, 1972), pp. 631–4; V. Pearl, 'London's Counter-Revolution', in Aylmer (ed.), *The Interregnum*, pp. 29–56, pp. 39–40.

84 Events in Cheddar are taken from depositions in TNA, SP 23/66, pp. 49–61. More details of the case are given in Croot, 'Agrarian Society', pp. 412–21.

and said that as he had means of £30 a year he did not need to follow that roguish occupation, and none but rogues would follow it. Bankes was not alone in his attitude towards the excise officials: when Rogers appeared before the local justice, Colonel John Gorges, the latter, though professing support for the excise, also called Rogers an excise rogue.[85]

Eventually Rogers and the Excise Commissioners brought Bankes before the Navy Committee for obstructing Rogers in the course of his official duties. The deponents called for each side (some were called for both) included Hercules Comer, a Presbyterian elder,[86] and yeomen, husbandmen and trades and craftsmen, and both groups came from similar backgrounds in leading or long-established families in the parish: the people in this case cannot be divided by social or economic categories, nor is there any suggestion that Rogers or anyone else supported 'levelling' ideas or were making similar attacks on property. Rather, all were part of the same class in local society in which political and religious events produced divided opinions.

Conservative opinion in the Interregnum

The animosity that Bankes felt for Rogers was clearly fairly long-standing, but had wider implications than did a mere row between neighbours. He criticised Rogers and some others for not going to church and called them 'Independents' – though they were more likely Baptists – but also added that Rogers was abusive to his neighbours in his tongue and language, and this seems to be the crux of Rogers's unpopularity with Bankes and others. Rogers was said to be not much given to drinking, a civil quiet man in his conversation and diligent in parliament's service, but the evidence does suggest that he held definite religious and political views that he was not reluctant to express.[87] Several of Rogers's deponents also testified that they had never heard him swear, but on the contrary had heard him reprove others for swearing,[88] and this was unlikely to have made him popular with men such as Bankes, described as given to swearing.

However, Bankes was not just angered because a man several years his junior ticked him off for swearing. Rogers was a vocal representative of radical political and religious views that Bankes abhorred.[89] Bankes wanted to see the militia disbanded not only to reduce the taxation but because of its religious aspect.[90] There is no evidence to suggest that Bankes was, or had ever been, a royalist,[91] but he seems to be an example of the way conservatives and Presbyterians were being pushed towards a royalist standpoint by the triumph of more radical views, a movement which ultimately gave support to the restoration of Charles II. The attitude of men such as

85 TNA, SP 23/66, pp. 67, 69, 91.

86 *Ibid.*, pp. 49–61.

87 For another quarrel he was involved in: Symonds,'By-Path of the Civil War', p. 61.

88 TNA, SP 23/66, pp. 47, 59–61, 71, 85.

89 *Ibid.*; Symonds,'By-Path of the Civil War', p. 61.

90 TNA, SP 23/66, pp. 61, 69, 73, 91.

91 He does not appear in list of suspected royalists 1655. Only one Cheddar resident is listed, John Hannam, gent.: BL, Add. MS 34012, f. 24.

Bankes has been described as 'ultimately localist and traditional',[92] but, however traditionalist he may have been in his attitude to the social hierarchy, his opposition to taxes was surely more universal than localist.

These two elements – heavy taxation and radical religious opinions – were significant causes of conflict between neighbours and of diminution of support for the Protectorate. To these can be added a third, with which religious opinions were closely involved: the attack on the old political and social hierarchy, a matter which also affected the attitudes of the gentry authorities with whom the villagers came into contact. Henry Bankes's dislike of a religious toleration which allowed men to stop attending their parish church was obviously not rooted in deep religious belief – he was hardly a model churchgoer himself[93] – and would be inexplicable but for the implications such a withdrawal had for the structure of society. Religion was the support of social order and until the Commonwealth uniformity of religion within the state was an accepted tenet of government. Now, not only did the growth of new Churches, often with an emphasis on lay preaching, weaken control from the pulpit and undermine the position of the official clergy, but those Churches themselves fostered social and political ideas that challenged and threatened the existing social hierarchy and the inability or unwillingness of the Commonwealth, and later the Protectorate, to prevent their growth lost the republic a great deal of support.[94]

The challenge to the social hierarchy also affected men such as Bankes, who, as parish constable, derived his authority from the justices of the peace, drawn from the gentry. In addition to his feelings about Rogers's opinions, Bankes's actions also show his resentment of the new forms of authority, such as the Commission of Excise, which clashed with the traditional enforcement of the law by constable, justice and judge. These new commissions had also created their own bureaucracy of minor officials such as Rogers, who bypassed the traditional line of command in local government.[95] Furthermore, their authority could be used to overrule the actions of the parish officials, as Rogers had attempted to do by bringing Bankes before the Navy Committee in London. Thus, Bankes resented not just any attack on the traditional social hierarchy but the damage it caused to his position in the community, and this dislike was shared by men such as the local justice, John Gorges, to whom Bankes had turned for advice when he was arrested by the messenger from the Excise.[96]

Even with a standing army county politicians needed to take local opinion into account, and as the divisions in central government became marked and the role and standpoint of the army became more unacceptable to conservative opinion, it was more important than ever to summon up support from conservative elements in the countryside. Although Gorges served the regime as a sequestration commissioner, he may have

92 Underdown, *Revel, Riot and Rebellion*, p. 219.

93 Support for this opinion of Bankes' is given by presentments in 1666 when he was accused of having lived suspiciously for many years with a local woman, and of marrying her clandestinely in another parish: SHC, DD\SAS/C795/PR/150.

94 J.S. Morrill, *Cheshire 1630–1660* (Oxford, 1974), pp. 266, 268, 275.

95 *Ibid.*, pp. 225–6.

96 TNA, SP 23/66, p. 81.

shared Bankes's dislike of the new authorities; he was certainly willing to use this dislike, and seems in some way to have encouraged the more moderate opinion to turn to him for support. Certainly, Bankes thought it worthwhile to consult him rather than any other justice, though Gorges was not openly encouraging disaffection: he warned Bankes that if it turned out that Bankes had abused Rogers in the execution of his office he would be the first to see him severely punished, as he had 'submitted to the Act of Excise and should be against anyone who affronted it'.[97] However, when Rogers appeared before Gorges in connection with another case Gorges had abused him again as an excise rogue, saying 'now see what your masters will do for you'.[98] His position was perhaps typical of Somerset gentry active in local government in the Interregnum, who were in general of a lesser social standing than the pre-war justices.[99] His difficulties were compounded by the challenge to local authority of commissions controlled increasingly from London, of which the excise was in general the most disliked.[100]

Political attitudes in the later seventeenth century

To men such as John Rogers of Cheddar, as well as those more important in county government, such as John Pyne, the Commonwealth was not just part of an aberration that interrupted proper monarchical government; it was an ideal, an organisation of human society that inspired devotion of time and money, and was considered worth fighting and dying for. By the same token, it aroused great bitterness and hatred in those such as Henry Bankes because of the attack on the institutions and social structure of the parish by the sectarians, and did a great deal to reconcile moderate opinion to the restoration of the monarchy, with the promise it held of protection for traditional social values, despite the strong support that parliament had had in the early 1640s and the lack of any real support for royalism.

However, the effect on society of those divided opinions is put into perspective when the results of the Restoration are considered. Though the bitterness and divisions ran deep, the toleration shown by the Independents and the army towards most forms of protestant religion – and, indeed, a tacit acceptance of Roman Catholicism[101] – did at least prevent any one group being driven outside society and the law, and ensured that the conflicts of the period took place within the same community. The restoration of the monarchy with the Anglican Church and hierarchy enshrined the bitterness and divisions of the Interregnum, such as those that emerged in Cheddar, and created lasting barriers in local society as the Church and governing class tried, unsuccessfully, to eradicate the self-conscious doctrinal beliefs and political involvement that the Interregnum had fostered at all levels of society. After 1660 the doctrine and policies of the Church were more rigid and limited than even under the archbishops Whitgift or Laud, and far more protestants were left outside

---

97 *Ibid.*, p. 85.

98 *Ibid.*, p. 69. The occasion was specified in the interrogatories, but these are not extant.

99 Underdown, *Somerset in the Civil War*, pp. 124–5, 133.

100 Morrill, *Cheshire*, p. 226.

101 Cross, 'Church in England', pp. 103, 112–15.

the established Church than in the earlier period. The Restoration succeeded only in a superficial sense; in reality the past could not be restored nor the Interregnum wiped out. Radical ideas in politics and religion among countrymen had received far greater expression than ever before under the Commonwealth, which also left an important legacy: for the first time a radical new form of government was actually put into practice and could be seen as a viable alternative, and this offered the promise – or threat, as far as conservative and moderate opinion was concerned – of further development along the lines advocated by the Independents, Levellers and others.

In the Somerset Levels the impact of the Restoration's religious settlement was immediate and obvious. In the large parish of Wedmore, where a conforming vicar was presented by the dean of Wells in 1660,[102] involvement with official church life fell dramatically. On average the number of baptisms dropped by 20 per cent after 1660 compared with the births registered in the 1650s, and was nearly half the average of the 1630s, not because of any fall in the birth rate but because nonconformists withdrew from the parish church. The number of marriages was nearly half that under civil registration, and the figures continued at these lower levels to the end of the century, though there is no reason to suppose that the population of Wedmore was falling at this time.[103] Though some similar withdrawal from the parish church was fairly common wherever there were strong nonconformist communities, in other parishes where the effect of nonconformity has been studied the baptismal registers show evidence of a return to the established Church from the 1670s, with mass baptisms of entire families;[104] the Wedmore registers show no signs of such a return. In Cheddar, too, although only a few transcripts of the registers survive for the period, the number of baptisms fell to about half that of the 1630s,[105] and in 1666 some 19 men were presented, 14 for not attending church and 12 for not baptising their children, including four known Quakers and James Spencer, an 'Independent'. In 1683 four men presented for not baptising their children included two of Hercules Comer's family.[106]

The unrealistic policies of the Settlement did nothing to check or accommodate dissenting beliefs, which became institutionalised in the face of persecution. The Baptists continued to meet in the area, though they left no records and little can therefore be said about their later membership. Meetings were held in 1669 at Mark and Axbridge, where Thomas Collier was a teacher to congregations estimated at 40 and 20 respectively, and at three houses in Wedmore with a congregation of 50.[107] In 1672 John Collier of Cheddar received a licence to hold Baptist meetings at his house.[108] The Baptist church in Wedmore still flourished in 1689, when they

102 Weaver, *Somerset Incumbents*, p. 206.

103 Hervey, *Wedmore Parish Registers*.

104 e.g. Wrightson and Levine, *Poverty and Piety*, p. 165.

105 E. Dwelly (ed.), *Dwelly's Parish Records*, vol. 1, *Bishop's Transcripts at Wells* (Herne Bay, 1913), pp. 237–56.

106 SHC, DD\SAS/C795/PR/150.

107 G. Lyon Turner (ed.), *Original Records of Early Nonconformity*, 3 vols (1911–14), vol. I, p. 11. Most licensees are given as 'Presbyterian', but names indicate that they are Baptists.

108 *Ibid.*, I, p. 546.

sent George Stant, their minister, to attend the London Assembly, and it may have continued to use the church house, which was registered as a place of worship by dissenters in 1689.[109] The Burnham Friends, for whom detailed records do survive, continued to meet into the eighteenth century. The congregation at Henry Moore's house was estimated at 100 in 1669,[110] although the Friends' records suggest that a more accurate figure would be about 50 adults in the 1670s; there is a steady appearance of new names in their records to the end of the century.[111]

Nonconformity had an impact on local society because it involved not just the poor, the politically and socially insignificant, but a wide social range including landholders and prospective parish officers.[112] Available evidence suggests that the nonconformists in Brent Marsh came mainly from middling social groups of husbandmen and yeomen, with a few craftsmen and poorer husbandmen. Of the nine Wedmore Baptists in the 1650s who appear in the poll tax list of 1660, four were from the two-thirds of the parish who paid the minimum, for an income of under £5, while four others were in the top 14 per cent of the parish, though not among the very highest.[113] Several of the Friends living in Burnham were landholders and four of the earliest Friends, Henry Moore, John Wride, John Hilbert and Thomas Wride, held free, copy or life leasehold land; the first three were also higher-rate taxpayers in 1660. Several later Friends – John Blake, William Rogers, Robert Tutton and Thomas Gould – were also landholders with life tenures.[114] Out of 14 first-generation Friends resident in Burnham eight held land by life tenures, and in 1692 twelve Friends appear among the landholders rated in Burnham, seven on acreages of 5 to 20 acres, three on 22 to 50 acres, one on 62½ acres, and one on 104 acres – the last, Henry Clothier, being the second largest landholder in the parish.[115] The majority of the Burnham Friends were in the middling range of farmers and landholders, and only four men from Brent Marsh – John Brice, tailor, and William Petherham, both of Burnham, and William Harris and Thomas Smith alias Martin, both of Mark – mentioned in the Friends' minutes and sufferings books over a 40-year period were directly or implicitly described as poor.[116]

---

109 *Narrative of the proceedings of the General Assembly of divers pastors, and ministring brethren of the Baptized Churches, ... London, from Septemb. 3 to 12, 1689* (London, 1689), p. 24; TNA, RG 31/7, no. 12. A meeting house was still in existence in 1709, when William Sprake was trustee, but this may have been a Quaker one: Hervey, *Wedmore Chronicle*, II, p. 335.

110 Turner, *Original Records*, I, p. 11.

111 Calculated from the Watchven Register (Burnham) and minutes for North Somerset Monthly Meeting, 1667–1712, at Friends' Ho., Euston Rd, London.

112 e.g. Wrightson and Levine, *Poverty and Piety*, tables on pp. 167 and 35; J.J. Hurwich, 'Social Origins of the Early Quakers', *Past and Present*, 48 (1970), pp. 158–9; Spufford, *Contrasting Communities*, pp. 303–4.

113 TNA, E 179/172/416.

114 TNA, C 107/114, pt. 1.

115 SHC, D\P\b.on.s/23/4. Clothier moved to Burnham on marrying a daughter of Henry Moore (d. 1685), and may have inherited some of Moore's property.

116 SHC, DD\SFR/8/1, f. 61; /8/2, p. 228; Morland, *Somersetshire Quarterly Meeting, passim*; SHC, D\P\b.on.s/23/4.

Rich or poor, persecution for their beliefs only strengthened the resolve of the faithful. Besides paying fines for attending conventicles, some suffered long years in prison for not paying tithes. The longest prison term by a Burnham Friend was 13 years, served by John Wride senior, who died in Ilchester gaol in 1688.[117] Many others, of course, sooner or later compromised with authority and paid outward allegiance to the Anglican Church, but though the Friends sadly recorded members who compounded for tithes, took oaths as parish officials or were married in the Anglican Church as lost to the truth, it is likely that the backsliders still retained a deep sympathy for their former faith as well as a rather puritan outlook, and resented all the more a regime that made them choose between adhering to their beliefs or financial ruin, legal penalties and social disadvantages. Thus, although religious affiliation and political outlook were still linked, political disaffection produced by persecution went further than just the members of dissenting sects and was deep enough to create a willing army that a political adventurer such as the duke of Monmouth could use.[118] The Somerset Friends, while mainly (and officially) adopting a pacific stand during the rebellion in 1685, believed that popular support for Monmouth was due to the religious persecution they and other dissenters were suffering in the county,[119] a result, perhaps of the bitterness of Civil War conflicts. Taunton, for example, as a parliamentarian town had held out against royalist forces at a significant stage in the war, tying them down to a brutal and damaging siege before the town was relieved by the parliamentarian army in 1645 and doing much harm to the royalist war effort in the West Country. After 1660 the town, with its large number of dissenters, was regarded as a centre of sedition, and persecution of dissenters there appears to have been harsher and more divisive than in other parts of England.[120] Even among local non-royalists, the bitterness and dislike felt towards dissenters, the army and the Excise, expressed by Henry Bankes and others in Cheddar in the 1650s, was no doubt replicated by many others across the county.

While the importance of such divisions in the local society is disputed – one parish study of nonconformity concluded that the divisions were not deep, even though recognisably separate groups did emerge[121] – the division between Churches and their members diluted the effectiveness of the Church generally in society and, since membership of Anglican and nonconformist churches tended to divide not only by religious belief but on class lines, deepened long-lasting social divisions as well.[122] Given that Somerset joined the last armed rebellion on English soil, perhaps the

---

117 SHC, DD\SFR/8/2, p. 270.

118 Dr Earle's detailed study of the rebels concluded that they fought for Monmouth because he was available as a leader, rather than for himself, and would have fought for anyone who would lead them: P. Earle, *Monmouth's Rebels: The Road to Sedgemoor 1685* (London, 1977), p. xi. Comments by Burnham inhabitants in 1686 that they could raise an army immediately if they had a leader also bear this out: BL, Add. MS 41804, ff. 154, 156.

119 John Whiting, *Persecution Expos'd, in some memoirs relating to the sufferings of J.W.* (1696), p. 140.

120 Underdown, *Somerset in the Civil War*, pp. 82, 93–6; Earle, *Monmouth's Rebels*, pp. 11–12, 14–15.

121 Wrightson and Levine, *Poverty and Piety*, pp. 168–71.

122 J. Thirsk, *The Restoration* (London, 1976), p. xvi.

effects of the division were more serious and far-reaching here. Events in the West Country during the 30 years that followed the Restoration illustrate both the deep roots of dissenting religious beliefs and the Restoration's failure to obtain at least the outward acceptance of the whole nation.

Monmouth's Rebellion

Discontent in the West Country, particularly over the severe persecution of dissenters there, had led to talk of rebellion in 1683, but the accession of a Catholic king, James II, seems to have created fear of worse repression to come and culminated in open rebellion in 1685, when the duke of Monmouth appeared. For many this was an opportunity to refight the civil wars and reinstate the Commonwealth, but though the rebels were drawn from only three counties many others were prevented from joining them by the government's measures, and other uprisings were probably avoided only by the absence of leaders and organisation. A well-connected foreign observer in London feared that it needed only a victory by Monmouth for London to rise up in his support, while many loyalists there were reluctant at first to show support for King James when it seemed that Monmouth might succeed. The rebellion took place after years of plots and counterplots around the country and, such was the atmosphere of disaffection that, when the government ordered all likely rebels be arrested and the London Livery Companies' halls used as additional prisons, the same observer thought that the whole country would have to be turned into one huge prison to carry out the order to the full.[123]

The Protestant James Scott, duke of Monmouth, the eldest but illegitimate son of Charles II, landed at Lyme Regis in June 1685, believing that the Whig gentry of the West Country would flock to his support, to be followed by most of London.[124] In the event only one nobleman joined him, leaving him without a strong cavalry. He marched northwards through Axminster, Chard, Ilminster, Taunton, Bridgwater, Glastonbury and Shepton Mallet, gathering much support from the inhabitants, especially in the more populous centres: his army was calculated by contemporaries at between 3,200 and 7,000.[125] After marching towards Bristol, where he might have found considerable support, he was deterred from attacking the city by a small royalist force on 23 June and fatally turned back, marching past Bath to Frome and then back to Shepton, Glastonbury and Bridgwater, before the final battle at Sedgemoor in Weston Zoyland on 6 July, when he was defeated by the main royalist forces. Monmouth was executed on Tower Hill in London on 15 July, while in the West Country Lord Chief Justice George Jeffreys prosecuted many of the captured rebels and anyone who had given them assistance with a ferocity that led to the trials later being called the Bloody Assizes; even King James later criticised the severity of Jeffreys' actions,

---

123 Earle, *Monmouth's Rebels*, pp. 61–2, 64.

124 *Ibid.*, p. 26; summary of Monmouth's actions also taken from Earle.

125 W. McD. Wigfield, *The Monmouth Rebels 1685* (Gloucester, 1985), p. vii; his list, collated from national and local sources, has nearly 4,000 names.

though he did not object at the time.[126] Nearly 1,600 people were listed in the gaol delivery books to be prosecuted at the four local assizes, and to speed things up at each assize Jeffreys attempted to persuade prisoners to plead guilty, holding out the likelihood that the king would pardon them, but those that did were still mostly either hung, drawn and quartered or transported to the West Indies to be sold as indentured servants for ten years. However, it made the trials go quicker and enabled the judges to get through a vast number of cases: in five days of trials in Dorchester nearly 300 men were sentenced to death, of whom 74 were executed and the rest either transported or later pardoned; at Taunton over 500 men were tried in two days, and at Wells 542 pleaded guilty on the last day of the assizes, 23 September 1685, with another pleading not guilty being executed the same day. A further lucky 140 were bound over to be tried at the next assizes, by which time they had been freed under the general pardon of March 1686. The actual number of rebels executed, especially in Somerset, is unknown, as the executions from the Taunton and Wells assizes were not carried out immediately. Some died in prison, mainly in a smallpox epidemic, or were transported instead, while others escaped; in all about a third may have avoided execution. A calculation has been made that about 250 were executed after the trials, added to about 100 summarily executed after the battle – as a rough estimate, about 7 per cent of the rebel army – while about 850 were sentenced to transportation. What made the impact of the trials so long-lasting, however, was not the execution of rebels, which was only to be expected, but the full sentence for high treason, with drawing and quartering, being carried out on virtually all those executed: it was done in batches in towns and villages throughout the area, so that everyone in the rebellious areas should see the burning of entrails and butchering at first hand. The pickled heads and thousands of quarters were then even more widely distributed, stuck on poles in prominent places by roads and bridges for all to see. They remained until the summer of 1686, when King James came to visit the area, was sickened by the sight and ordered the rotting remains buried.

The men who fought under Monmouth were chiefly aged from their late 20s to their early 40s – married men with families, leaving farms or businesses to fight. Quite a few were older, however, and many had been officers or soldiers under Cromwell: the wearing of the buff coats of the Ironside troopers or the red coats of the New Model infantry testified to the strength of Commonwealth ideals that 25 years of Restoration rule had only strengthened: sectarian differences were set aside as Presbyterian and Baptist, with Republican and Leveller, fought together for their common goal.[127] The seriousness and danger of their challenge to James II's government can be measured by the savage treatment that followed Sedgemoor, both of the rebels and of the West Country areas from which they came, just because the rebels were not the young and heedless, or the poor with nothing to lose.[128] The fact that a large number of the middling classes in West Country society were prepared to risk their lives and their families' livelihoods to get rid of the king and his government illustrates the depth of their commitment.

126 Earle, *Monmouth's Rebels*, pp. 161, 167–8.

127 *Ibid.*, pp. 4, 10–11, 18, 22, and Appendix.

128 *Ibid.*, pp. 196–212, analyses ages and occupations of rebels for several towns and parishes.

Many men came from the Brent Marsh area to join the rebellion, but only a few of them appear in the official sources.[129] Only three of the 16 Brent Marsh parishes appear in the Monmouth Roll – the lists of those absent from home or in arms for Monmouth: East Brent with six men away from home; the tithing of Alston Maris in Huntspill with seven men in arms; and Wedmore with 19 men away from home.[130] Official sources indicate probably 13 convicted rebels from the area, including a surgeon who treated a rebel who came to his house, and incidental sources mention another 43 men who were suspected rebels or said to have taken part; as some of these came from parishes not on the Monmouth Roll at all, this is presumably only a bare minimum.[131] Those in Brent Marsh were nearly all married and the majority held land that they were willing to risk for their cause.

Four of the convicted rebels, Francis Came, John Leaker, Richard Harris and John Harris, all from Huntspill,[132] appear neither in the Treasury Books nor in the inquisition on the rebels' estates, so presumably had little property worth listing. The remaining seven show a range of backgrounds and financial standing, but were all either freeholders, copyholders or life leaseholders. At the bottom of the scale was Edward Councell, a husbandman of Stone Allerton in Weare, who was sentenced to transportation and died at sea. He held a messuage and dwelling house for two lives valued at 13s 4d, probably the ancient manorial valuation.[133] Robert Thatcher, the Wedmore surgeon executed for treating Colonel John Bovett, held by long leases a tenement and 3½ acres of arable valued at 17s 6d a year.[134]

Two men from Burnham, both with quite substantial estates, were also among the convicted rebels. Joseph Wickham, butcher, was sentenced to transportation, died on board the John Friggott outside Bristol, and was buried ashore. His estate at attainder consisted of a messuage and dwelling with several parcels of land in Burnham totalling nine acres and valued at £3 10s a year, a close of 18½ acres held on a lease for 99 years or three lives and valued at £10 a year and 5½ acres freehold valued at 25s a year. His goods were valued at £20 16s and included seven cows and four sheep.[135] The other, Hugh Roper, husbandman, was the most fortunate of those convicted. He

---

129 i.e. the Monmouth Roll, Treasury Books, Exchequer inquisitions and lists of transportees. Other names occur in incidental local sources, and in only one case does one of those names also occur in an official source. The most complete list of rebels and their origin so far compiled is in Wigfield, *The Monmouth Rebels*, using official and local sources. The judges' lists and most lists of transportees do not give the parish of origin, however.

130 BL, Add. MS 30077.

131 BL, Add. MS 30077; *Calendar of Treasury Books*, vol. 8, *1685–9* (1923), *passim*; TNA, E 178/6676; ASSI 23/3; SHC, DD/SFRw 1 (12 Apr. 1686); Q/SR/169/1–12; J.C. Hotten (ed.), *Original Lists of persons of Quality; Emigrants; Religious Exiles; … who went from Great Britain to the American Plantations 1600–1700* (New York, 1931), pp. 332–3; CCC Oxford, Fn 000, Northgrove MSS, letters from steward, 15 Sept., 14 Nov. 1685; *Calendar of State Papers, Domestic, James II*, vol. 2, p. 279.

132 Hotten, *Original Lists*, pp. 332–3.

133 *Ibid.*, pp. 332, 335; *Calendar of Treasury Books*, vol. 8, pp. 419, 2004; TNA, E 178/6676.

134 *Calendar of Treasury Books*, vol. 8, p. 421; TNA, E 178/6676.

135 *Calendar of Treasury Books*, vol. 8, p. 419; Hotten, *Original Lists*, p. 335; TNA, E 178/6676.

was sentenced to death but £80 was paid by Thomas Tucker for a pardon,[136] and he was reprieved 'under the gallows' to live out his remaining 30 years in Burnham, where he owned 'a considerable estate'.[137] His property at conviction consisted of 25½ acres in Burnham and six acres in South Brent, all freehold and valued at £10 5s 6d a year, with goods valued at £38, including five cows, four steers, six loads of hay and four acres of standing crops.[138] The land listed was all granted out by royal warrant, but Roper may have purchased it back from the grantees, because in 1692 he was rated in Burnham on 25½ acres and a mill.[139] Though he does not appear in the Quaker records he was connected by marriage with the Burnham Friends and was probably the son of Hugh Roper, one of the local farmers who had refused to pay tithes in the 1650s.

Though the religious affiliations of most of the local men involved in the rebellion are not known, in other respects they fit well the analysis by Peter Earle of larger groups of rebels, which shows a preponderance of the middle ranks of society in trades, crafts or farming, with hardly any labourers listed; at least half were over 30 years of age and about 80 per cent were over 25. Many of the rebels were much older, with about a fifth born before the end of the first civil war in 1646. A large proportion were dissenters, and towns and villages with large dissenting congregations provided proportionately more rebels.[140] Earle's analysis of 559 rebels from 19 parishes in the Monmouth Roll which give occupations, including the important towns of Taunton, Frome and Lyme Regis, shows that just over half were involved in various cloth-making crafts, a sixth in clothing trades and 11 per cent in building and metalwork, while 11 per cent were husbandman or yeomen. Only two men out of the 559 were termed labourers, only six were gentlemen and ten were professionals, showing a concentration in the middle rank of society.

The aftermath of rebellion

Like the events of the Civil War, the rebellion under Monmouth shows that ordinary villagers could be involved in political events, had a political outlook and nursed deep commitments, aspects for which evidence is usually lacking but which the act of rebellion supplies. However, just as the political ideals of the Commonwealth were not extinguished in men's minds by the Restoration, so even the defeat of Monmouth's army and its aftermath did not destroy the political aspirations of villagers, even though they never again dared to take up arms for their beliefs. This politicisation of countrymen was reflected in smaller local disturbances which had a political colour, not to say cause, rather than the concern with corn shortages or enclosures that typified so many local riots in England before 1640. Such a disturbance took place in

---

136 TNA, E 178/6676.

137 R. Locke, *The Western Rebellion* (Taunton, 1912), pp. 7–8.

138 TNA, E 178/6676; *Calendar of Treasury Books*, vol. 8, pp. 418, 425.

139 SHC, D\P\b.on.s/23/4.

140 However, being drawn from a rural area, they do not reflect the heavy preponderance of craftsmen found in the army overall, drawn as it was from Taunton and other towns.

Brent Marsh in 1687, a bitter aftermath of Monmouth's rebellion, and again it was not a riot of the poor and landless but involved leading parish officials, educated dissenters and substantial middling landholders from Burnham and Huntspill.[141]

The disturbance began at Burnham revel, held on 23 May 1687 – a popular traditional parish celebration usually involving a feast and cudgel-playing, which attracted outsiders as well as local residents. A large group of men was playing at cudgels when one Burnham inhabitant, William Wride, declared himself for Monmouth and drew around him a group of other Burnham men; they then threatened some men from Huntspill who had apparently helped to capture rebels from Burnham after Sedgemoor, denouncing them as 'papist rogues'. The threats were fulfilled at Huntspill fair on 29 June, when some Huntspill inhabitants were beaten up by men from Burnham and elsewhere, said to number about 40, and William Wride threatened 'to serve them with the same sauce' if they came to Edymead fair (at Edithmead in outer Burnham), to be held soon afterwards. The leading participants were presented at the quarter sessions and bound over,[142] and apparently no further action was taken, but copies of the depositions made by those attacked were sent to the office of the secretary of state, Lord Middleton, in London, since the government was understandably touchy about any disturbances involving Monmouth's name.[143]

There was justification for the belief that the Huntspill men were attacked for their part in capturing rebels: the rioters were heard to inquire for some leading Huntspill residents including two king's officers, Thomas Keball and Thomas Hurman, referred to as 'the men catchers' who had captured several of the rebels. Keball was also one of the constables in 1685 who presented the names of those in Huntspill who had taken arms for Monmouth, one of only three parishes in this study to make returns. Furthermore, the six men they listed were all from one tithing in Huntspill, Alston Maris, which was in the same hundred as the adjoining parish of Burnham, and one of those men, Ralph Hoyle or Howell, took part in the attack on the Huntspill residents.[144] The absence of so many parishes from the Monmouth Roll may well be because the constables were sympathetic to the rebels, which made men such as Keball stand out.

However, animosity against loyalists alone was not likely to have been the prime spur to action after an interval of two years. In the absence of any other evidence of provocation by the Huntspill inhabitants at the fair,[145] antagonism may possibly have been aroused by James II's dispensations to Catholics which enabled them to hold commissions in the army and other offices; this and the Catholic missionary work in England from 1686 aroused public fears and invoked the 'papist menace' once again. Though some measure of toleration for Protestant dissenters was given by James's Declaration of Indulgence in April 1687, they were still unable to hold offices as the

141 The following account is taken from SHC, Q/SR/169/1–12.

142 SHC, Q/SO/7, Mich. term 1687, no. 51.

143 Now in BL, Add. MS 41804, ff. 295–310.

144 BL, Add. MS 30077.

145 The only depositions are from those who were attacked.

Catholics could.[146] The papist threat may have been in the minds of the Burnham rioters when they called the Huntspill men 'papist rogues that were for the King',[147] while William Wride stopped one man and asked him why he was wearing a 'lawd hat' and was riding around at such a great rate,[148] comments which had both religious and social overtones. The political awareness of the Burnham men also extended beyond domestic issues and showed that religious affiliations and foreign affairs were intermixed in the minds of villagers. After beating up the Huntspill men a blood-stained handkerchief was tied to a stick as 'Monmouth's colours' and one William Hurford declared that now Holland (the Burnham men) had beaten France.[149]

The instigators of the fight were by no means among the poor and landless. Some 15 men were named, nine of them Burnham residents, the rest from adjoining parishes. They were led by William Wride of Burnham, a middle-aged former Quaker who had fought for Monmouth and received the King's Pardon. Stephen Wride of Burnham, aged 24, was the son of another Quaker and was said to have been a rebel; five others were also said to have fought for Monmouth.[150] Also involved was Thomas Wall of Burnham, the constable of the hundred of Bempstone, probably in his late twenties, a cousin or nephew of William Wride and brother-in-law of Hugh Roper, the reprieved rebel. Wall's father had held quite a substantial freehold estate in Burnham which had descended to Thomas in 1676.[151] Of the nine Burnham residents, six were rated on land in 1692, Thomas Wall as joint owner of 47¾ acres, William Wride for nine acres and the others for 38, 12, 9½ and four acres respectively.[152]

The rioters threatened the Huntspill men that the duke of Monmouth was expected daily among them and there would shortly be 'an alteration of times'.[153] No doubt these statements were primarily made as part of their effort to intimidate their opponents, but there was also an element of wishful thinking: in 1686 inhabitants of Burnham had been heard to say that 'they could raise the marshes upon a drum beating if they had but a leader',[154] an echo of the rumour that reached Monmouth of a great Club-army 1000-strong in the marshes around Axbridge,[155] and a reflection of a deep anger and unrest that could be given an active expression if the men were properly led. The legacy of bitterness against James II and Judge Jeffreys, which is still expressed today by West Country families,[156] is surely a measure of the conviction of right and the commitment to their ideals felt by those who suffered for their beliefs.

---

146 J.R. Jones, *Country and Court: 1658–1714* (London, 1983 edn), pp. 231, 236–7, 240.

147 BL, Add. MS 41804, f. 307.

148 SHC, Q/SR/169/3.

149 SHC, Q/SR/169/2.

150 None appear on the lists of rebels or men absent from home.

151 TNA, PROB 11/350/457.

152 SHC, D\P\b.on.s/23/4.

153 BL. Add. MS 41804, f. 307.

154 *Ibid.*, ff. 154, 156.

155 BL, Harley MS 6845, f. 280d.

156 Earle, *Monmouth's Rebels*, p. 187; Bromwich, *Diary of John Allen Giles*, p. 9; personal communications to author.

Conclusion

While few historians would follow John Aubrey in linking dairying and the consumption of dairy products with melancholia, litigiousness, Puritanism and witchcraft beliefs, he made a good point when he linked the destruction of the petty manors in dairying regions of Wiltshire with 'mean people' living lawlessly with nobody to govern them.[157] In Somerset, too, the county magnates and leading gentry played an important role in local government and social control, and the manorial structure of Brent Marsh, which did not encourage the residence of leading gentry families with economic and institutional power in the area, no doubt contributed to the sense of self-determination that the leading copyholders showed, and had its results in an independent and non-deferential outlook among Brent Marsh's inhabitants. Somerset's yeomanry have been described as numerous, 'fairly prosperous, and decidedly ambitious'; they paid most of the taxes, served the hundredal and parochial offices and were politically conscious, and the gentry needed their assistance in governing the county and carrying out royal policy.[158] This yeomanry was largely made up of copyholders and in Brent Marsh, as elsewhere in Somerset, the landholding structure had led to their increasing security and wealth. Taxation records show that most taxpayers here were copyholders or life leaseholders, and, while there were few of the very richest that can be found in other regions of England by the early sixteenth century, likewise there were fewer of the poorer taxpayers assessed on wages. As discussed in Chapter 4, farmers in the Levels, both small and large, whether customary tenants or not, benefited from rising prices for their products, while the flexible mixed farming they carried out enabled them to adapt and take advantage of the best opportunities, available even to those with small surpluses. The flexibility of landholding, too, with many small parcels available, helped small farmers to put together viable farm incomes and helped parents provide equitably for their children.

The gulf between rich and poor may have widened by the later seventeenth century, with the emergence of new gentry residents and local families who moved up the social scale, but self-awareness and self-belief were displayed not only by the most prosperous of Somerset's farming community but also by lesser husbandmen, freed by the Civil War and Interregnum to express their religious and political preferences. Even before the war Brent Marsh's inhabitants had shown a lack of deference in confrontations with some new gentry residents, and social and religious freedoms were hard to reverse. Protestant nonconformity continued to flourish among a section of the inhabitants after the Restoration, despite harsh punishment, leaving a religious and social divide in parish life thereafter between Church and Chapel. At the same time, the social radicalism that the Civil War released brought about a reassessment and a return to support for monarchical government among some, and resignation among many more.

Changing political and economic conditions led to political realignments among rural inhabitants, and the middling classes in rural society were not tempted into armed

---

157 Cited in Underdown, *Revel, Riot and Rebellion*, pp. 7, 73.

158 Barnes, *Somerset*, pp. 13, 154–5.

rebellion again. The events of the seventeenth century in this small area of Somerset, however, show that country-dwellers were capable of thinking for themselves and of responding to national political events: national politics could and did influence village society and relationships. The tranquil beauty of the English countryside and the slow, steady rhythms of rural life should not be taken to indicate a placid acceptance of their political environment by the inhabitants or an ignorance of wider, even international, political issues.

Chapter 7

Small farmers and early modern agriculture: An obstacle to change or a commercial contribution?

The small farmers of Brent Marsh demonstrate a wide range of economic circumstances and many had very small landholdings compared with those in some other regions of England, but their land offered them some exceptional advantages. The 16 parishes of the area studied here were unified through their topographical features, the great expanse of moors and meadows interspersed with slightly higher and drier arable areas, and the flexibility of their farming systems and production. The area also included the prosperous market town of Axbridge and lay close to Wells, one of the largest and most important towns in Somerset, and the good communications by road and water to Bristol and elsewhere gave the inhabitants ready markets for their products. However, the inhabitants of Brent Marsh, with their relatively small landholdings and mixed farm production, are typical of the type of cultivators who are dismissed in the agrarian histories of this period as backward peasants, despite the fact that, as discussed in Chapter 1, the assumptions which underlie this attitude towards small landholders and cultivators have nothing to do with the evidence.

One of the first studies of early modern agriculture was carried out by W.G. Hoskins on the parish of Wigston Magna, who concluded that his Leicestershire farmers of the sixteenth century were fundamentally engaged in 'peasant subsistence farming'. His reasons for this assessment were that 'money played only a marginal part', with small sales of produce and purchases of land or goods; and that bequests were usually of goods or stock, not money (apart from dowries), indicating that most people 'still though in terms of goods rather than money'. The 'traditional mixed farming' still went on more or less as it had always done, and 'the peasant economy remained unimpaired by the commercial ideas of the outer world'. Hoskins saw Wigston Magna, which produced everything it needed except iron, stone and salt, as a self-sufficient and self-contained society,[1] yet just because the parish produced a wide range of commodities it cannot be argued that they were shared by everyone, nor that the produce was all used within the parish. In particular, this picture of a rural commonalty does not explain the great differences in wealth apparent in most rural communities by the sixteenth century. Hoskins' description – 'the unchanging traditional life of the peasant system flowed on uninterrupted like a deep, underground river'[2] – sums up the assumptions that underlie many modern ideas about rural life in the past, redolent with a seductive vision of the Arcadia of Elizabethan England inhabited by traditional-

1 Hoskins, *Midland Peasant*, pp. 177–8, 190–94.

2 *Ibid.*, pp. 178–9.

minded and uncommercial peasants. His view is interesting, though, because it runs counter to his own findings in Leicestershire as a whole, where the small farmers that predominated had flexible cropping regimes in their open fields, considerably more scope for initiative and enjoyed a rising standard of living in the second half of the sixteenth century.[3] And, however unchanging sixteenth-century Leicestershire might have been, that is certainly not the case for rural societies in Somerset, which were both changing and commercial.

The 'peasant' model, with its connotations of economic backwardness, self-sufficiency, subsistence farming and lack of personal freedom, does not apply to early modern Brent Marsh, and the use of the term is not only imprecise and derogatory in economic terms but more importantly obscures the very 'modern' attitudes that can be found among cultivators and landholders here: the use of secure tenures as investments; the use of wills in securing property; production for the market rather than for household needs; political and religious self-consciousness.

Rather than being peasants, these cultivators fit the model of the English yeoman drawn up by Mildred Campbell many years ago,[4] but whereas she saw the yeomen as a separate class in rural society with those commercial or even capitalist characteristics, the distinction between yeoman, a status term, and husbandman, an occupational description, is very uncertain, and in Brent Marsh there does not appear to be any substantial difference in outlook or activities between the two groups, only rather in the degree of resources and type of tenure they had – yeomen in Brent Marsh nearly always had a lifehold or freehold.[5] The characteristics of yeomen also applied to many men calling themselves husbandmen, and included their active interest in religious matters, a tendency towards puritanism, which led many to join nonconformist sects, and their important role in carrying out local government in the hundred and parish.[6]

No rural sixteenth-century village existed in a vacuum untouched and unconnected with the world outside. The large degree of mobility, visits to London, dealing in a network of fairs and markets over much of southern England – these factors alone make for wide horizons and exposure to all manner of ideas, as shown by some of the political activities and attitudes in the seventeenth century. Marshland areas such as the Somerset Levels need more attention because the agriculture is so different from the stereotype and reflects a flexible attitude towards farming within a traditional framework of open fields.

Land tenure in the Levels, considered less secure than copyhold of inheritance, in fact gave its holders flexibility as well as security. The smallest owner-occupiers did gradually disappear as their farming units became less viable financially, but disappropriation was by the economy, not landowners, and many small landholders

3 Hoskins, *Provincial England*, pp. 152–3.

4 M. Campbell, *The English Yeoman: under Elizabeth and the Early Stuarts* (London, 1967), esp. pp. 23–6, 99, 130–34, 134–6, 170–78, 194–5, 220.

5 'Yeoman' may also have been applied as a mark of respect, based on personal characteristics not apparent to the historian.

6 Campbell, *English Yeoman*, pp. 290, 292–3, 315.

continued to hold their lifehold leases and copies and let the land to others who amassed enough small properties to make a good-sized farm.

Economic attitudes of small farmers in the Levels

The lack of records concerning small family farms makes their role in the economy and in agricultural change a difficult problem, and encourages the view that only larger farms and estates with good records are worth considering. Inventories are almost the only record that contain economic information for most husbandmen, but, as discussed in Chapter 4, they are not really adequate for judging the farming economics, let alone methods, of dairying and mixed farming. Because of the paucity of evidence for small farmers it is easy to dismiss their efforts or regard them as an obstacle to progress, especially if the ideal of progress is taken to be large farms; there will never be heavy volumes of evidence for individual small farmers to contradict this point of view. Robert Allen, however, who challenged the view that the enclosure of open fields and the amalgamation of holdings into large farms were necessary for increased yields, new crops and innovations in farming practices, was able to produce data using a broad study of several Midland counties to show that yeomen, the owner-occupying family farmers, were responsible for much of the productivity growth of the early modern period.[7] On a small scale, too, evidence and indications can be found in Brent Marsh to suggest that it is wrong to overlook the involvement in change and the contribution that thousands of small farmers made to increased agricultural production in England.

Evidence for their interest in the development of crops occurs fortuitously, and suggests that it was more widespread than is apparent in most sources. One crop for which such evidence has come to light is apples. Somerset has always had a measure of fame for apples – and the cider made from them, often drunk in place of ale – and the Levels show plenty of evidence of their existence. In surveys the presence of an orchard is as common as the curtilage or backside, and almost every customary tenement seems to have had at least one, covering about an acre or so. Despite this, substantial evidence of the value of the fruit to the inhabitants, or its role in their farm economy, is strangely lacking. Out of 217 inventories, only three had apples on the premises; only one will mentions apples,[8] and only two testators mention their orchards.[9] One reference to pears occurs in all the local sources looked at: the theft of half a peck out of an orchard in Allerton in 1634.[10] This orchard belonged to Edmund Bower, and though it is unlikely that he had destroyed his orchard in the interim it was not given a value in 1645 when his goods were sequestered, unlike his other crops.[11] Despite this almost total silence about the fruit, which clearly must have been so common as to be hardly worth mentioning, there are indications of a continual

7 Allen, *Enclosure and the Yeoman*.

8 TNA, PROB 11/221/593.

9 TNA, PROB 11/144/68; PROB 11/161/186.

10 SHC, Q/SR/70/36.

11 TNA, SP 28/214.

interest in the raising and development of fruit trees here. In the 1580s John Trevelyan, esquire, of Nettlecombe in west Somerset, obtained grafts of ten named varieties of apple (including ones from Essex, London and Dorset), a fig and the supplier's own variety of pear from a Mr Pace of Brentmarsh (who cannot, unfortunately, be positively identified).[12] A hundred years later John Westover of Wedmore sold about 550 gribles out of the nursery at Sparkmore to his neighbours and other lowland inhabitants; these were either apple seedlings or stocks for grafting.[13] Here, again, Westover makes no mention in his journal of orchards of his own nor of payments for apple picking.[14] These chance references suggest that lowland farmers had a strong interest in the development of certain apple strains and that these were well-known enough in the late sixteenth century to attract outside buyers. Such examples also illustrate the drawbacks of the usual sources of agricultural history, such as inventories, when trying to assess the level of sophistication and development of farming in an area.

The adoption of new crops, or new ways of using them, can also be found in the Levels. The turnips, grown as a field crop in Cheddar by 1609, as well as garlic and teasels, grown by the later sixteenth century,[15] or the 870 lbs of clover seed which John Westover sold to 18 of his neighbours in 1688–9[16] are unlikely to be the only examples of innovation among the farmers of Brent Marsh. Because of the small-scale and erratic nature of the arable in the area turnips were not grown on a very large scale, but the lack of their widespread adoption was not because of conservatism but because the crop was not needed. In 1801 the vicar of East Brent wrote on his crop return against 'Turnips', of which the parish had none, 'We have natural grass enough for our stock without sowing artificial seeds'.[17] Clearly there is no point in adopting a new crop if it is no improvement on existing ones. Even John Billingsley, the late eighteenth-century improver, made a plea for caution against the too-ready adoption of new principles in place of the principles developed by practice. The dairy cattle preferred by Somerset dairymen in the 1790s were good milk producers but poor in body, and their carcasses were worth a lot less than those of other breeds; yet, as Billingsley pointed out, they had a greater profit during their milking life than the loss of the value on the carcass. He goes on:

> I do not mean by what I have said to detract from the merit of Mr. BAKEWELL, or other great breeders of the North. I only wish to recommend a discriminating principle, and to deter the credulous farmer from *too hasty* a dereliction of the

---

12 SHC, DD\WO/49/7. I am grateful to Dr R.W. Dunning for drawing my attention to this.

13 SHC, DD\X\HKN, f. 214. Definitions of 'grible' taken from Joseph Wright, *The English Dialect Dictionary* (Oxford, 1923).

14 SHC, DD\X\HKN, f. 201. In 1697 he did note payments for making 19 bushels of apples into cider, with ten bushels the following year.

15 See Chap. 4, Farming in the levels: Arable crops; SHC, D\D\cd/45, Hill v. Cade, dep. John Butt, 27 Apr. 1613.

16 SHC, DD\X\HKN, f. 81.

17 TNA, HO 67/2/38. Somerset Returns are analysed in M. Williams, 'The 1801 Crop Returns for Somerset', *Proceedings of the Somerset Archaeological Society*, 113 (1969), pp. 69–85.

> principles and practices founded in experience, and to which he has been long accustomed.[18]

This is quite a reversal from the usual plaint of improving literature, reiterated by historians, that despite the profitable examples of a progressive neighbour farmers persisted in turning their face against new crops and methods. In fact, of course, the words of propagandists are not reliable evidence for the spread of, or resistance to, new farming methods, and it was as true for the early seventeenth as for the late eighteenth century that farmers would be ill advised to change proven methods just because a new method was said to work well elsewhere.

It is surely no coincidence that it was a small farmer who is found growing turnips, as it is more logical to suppose that, rather than the large farmer with plenty of hay, the man with little meadow or pasture and not much arable to produce hay or stock-feed would need to improvise, to adopt new crops, in order to keep his essential dairy herd alive and well during the winter and start off the lactation as high as possible. In the same way, it is hard to believe that farmers who were growing turnips in their gardens needed a book to tell them they might try feeding their stock on them when they could see the plants flourishing in the middle of winter, or that such an idea did not occur spontaneously to many hundreds of farmers once the roots were established in England.

There is no reason why a small farmer has to be a subsistence farmer, if he has markets in the vicinity from which he can buy what he needs. Within the mixed farm economy there are indications that small farmers allowed themselves to be dependent on the market. Grain production is a litmus test of subsistence: it is reasonable to suppose that a farmer with a subsistence attitude would use what arable he had for grain for home consumption and convert pasture to arable wherever possible. This was not what happened in the Levels. Though the inhabitants maintained their arable fields, the crops they grew would have been unusual choices for farmers bent on subsistence first.

Teasels are a prime example of this. It is certain they were grown as a commercial crop: they were not edible and none of the growers were fullers. Even though arable land was limited, farmers chose to grow teasels, a biennial crop, on land that could produce grain, rather than the corn that might have covered their home needs. The same may well be true of small wheat producers, such as those in Huntspill in 1693.[19] Barley had a higher yield per acre than wheat: an average of early seventeenth-century yields puts wheat at three-quarters of the barley yield, while yields in Somerset in 1801 showed wheat to be from two-thirds to three-quarters of barley, depending on the parish,[20] and in most of the lowland areas of England barley was the principal crop, with its multiple uses for bread, ale and stock-feed.[21] Therefore, a farmer seeking to fulfill his family's needs would logically have grown barley. However,

---

18 Billingsley, *General View*, pp. 143–4.

19 SHC, D\P\hun/3/2/1.

20 *AHEW4*, p. 652; TNA, HO 67/2/29, HO 67/2/50.

21 *AHEW4*, pp. 169–70.

commercially wheat was the more attractive: its average value per acre in Burnham in the 1650s was given as £4, while that of barley was £3 10s.[22] Farmers were more likely to grow wheat if the market was their objective, and buy their ale instead of brewing it themselves. Many smaller farmers were far from self-sufficient, even in providing for their stock through the winter. In Huntspill, 13 of the 44 dairy farmers in 1693 had less than the minimum acreage of meadow to provide enough hay;[23] other stock also had to be fed over the winter, and the barley and beans grown would hardly be adequate for all needs. Clearly, they were not trying to be self-sufficient even in stock-feed, and were dependent on buying food both for themselves and their stock.

The one local farmer for whom there is enough evidence to reveal his outlook was John Westover. He made no attempt to farm for his household use first, if at all. He bought cheese and meat, for example, while renting out the cows he had, and reference has continually been made in this study to his wide range of agricultural activities. His profession of barber-surgeon, with an active medical practice, may seem to detract from his value as evidence, but in fact it makes his case more extraordinary in the sense that, presuming he made a living out of his medical practice (as he seems to have done), he could have afforded to farm solely for home use, and did not need to strive after farming profits as he evidently did. He and his father, also a barber-surgeon, came from a long line of farming copyholders and undoubtedly maintained the same attitudes as many of their neighbours.

Perhaps more importantly, though, Westover's accounts also show the range of opportunities for making money in what may seem, compared with large-scale farming, to be very trivial if not subsistence agricultural activities. So, while Hoskins saw the thrift of small farmers in turning every crop and product to use as part of their self-sufficiency, an alternative view is to see it as a drive for profit, for getting the best possible income out of all their available resources. One source that does sometimes make explicit the outlook of a wide range of husbandmen is their wills, and in the Levels these underline their commercial and profit-seeking attitude. The wills existing from the 1540s increasingly specified that legacies left for minors should be invested – be 'put out to increase' or 'to best use' for the profit of the legatee – and this applied not only to sums of money but also to farm stock, even a single cow or sheep. Besides the natural profit in milk or wool, the animals could also be rented out: this was quite common, especially for cows, and was also a way in which children who were given stock but no land could still make money out of their legacy. Livestock, like money and land, fell into the category of capital in rural society, to be used for profit, unlike pots and pans and suchlike, which were not specified for use in that way.[24]

Possibly the most comprehensive evidence that a commercial attitude was widespread and prevalent in Brent Marsh is the multiple marketing network that existed in the Levels, which could only exist if the great majority of its inhabitants were regularly involved in buying and selling. Overton sees the greater density of markets in the sixteenth century, compared with the seventeenth and later, as implying a

22 TNA, E 134/1654–55/Hil8.

23 SHC, D\P\hun/3/2/1.

24 Above, Chap. 5, The use of wills and the dispositions made: Wills of the 1540s.

higher degree of subsistence farming because it suggests a less developed national marketing system.[25] His implication seems to be that the small producers were responsible for the marketing system, but why they should be blamed for the trading networks, it is hard to say: this is surely the 'fault' of the overall economy, with lack of demand, or backwardness among merchants. The existence of so many local markets seems rather to indicate that a large proportion of the local population were dependent on purchasing their food and other necessities, thus sustaining so many outlets. Weekly markets in several towns within a half-day's walk of all the sixteen parishes; a fair held each month somewhere within the area studied, as well as in the surrounding area; middlemen both local and from outside the area; attendance by local producers at the major fairs across southern England: all these point to a strong market economy and a strong commercial outlook existing since at least the late Middle Ages.

Small farmers and economic change

Small farm units survived in the Levels, then, because the land and the tenure there allowed a flexible type of farming with the spread of risk that comes with mixed production. These small mixed farms were more viable than their equivalent in sheep–corn economies and more able to weather economic misfortunes. Specialisation in one product, such as the fattening of sheep or cattle, was carried on only by men with other sources of income, such as local butchers, or men with resources outside the area. Not only the smaller but also the larger-scale resident farmers kept up a mixed farm economy. An increase in farm productivity does not only come from specialisation in one principal product; it may equally well be derived from improved mixed farming, particularly when this includes two or three products for which the market is buoyant. This mixed farming system, with an emphasis on dairying and grazing, remained the most typical husbandry of Brent Marsh into the twentieth century, taking advantage of market demand while at the same time spreading the risk, and this was the most efficient farming system for the area, as it put the land with its various qualities to the uses for which it was best suited. Those farmers whose holdings included land in the arable fields maintained arable production because corn, especially wheat, fetched a good price, and because the arable land was not as rich as the lower-lying meadows and pastures, and where a farmer had access to these he would gain little by converting arable to permanent pasture. On the other hand, he would stand to lose even more should he convert all his land to arable, not least because of its periodic wetness.

The discovery of the economic, social and political characteristics of rural inhabitants relies very much on whether they are searched for, because the evidence for such relatively obscure men and women is fragmented and buried in long series of local and central records. However, such evidence is important for our understanding of rural society, which is too complex to be described by simple economic or political models. Detailed local studies are essential to clarify the way changes took place in

25 Overton, *Agricultural Revolution*, p. 22.

the countryside, and evidence for Brent Marsh shows that small-scale mixed farmers were not necessarily backward in farming methods or economic ideas: they employed new crops and were market-orientated, producing for sale rather than subsistence. Even small farms could generate a profit on the incomes calculated for them, and they contributed to England's economic development both by producing surplus food for the market and by creating demand for goods to purchase.

Agrarian historians have tended to see agricultural change as the result of the activities of outsiders or some special group, presumably because they hold to the belief that the indigenous farmers were all backward. The identity of those outsiders depends on the attitude of the historians or the period in which they are writing: 'kulak' peasants; new bourgeois landowners; the yeoman class; improving gentry; entrepreneurial tenant farmers. Increasingly, however, rural studies are no longer fixated on single models such as an agricultural revolution or the introduction of change by outsiders into the countryside, but rather concentrate on the activities and reactions of the rural inhabitants themselves and their involvement in the process of change. A range of studies looking beneath the surface of broad economic and social changes and examining particular aspects of rural life has produced a greater understanding of the layers of society that existed. The simple dichotomies of lord/tenant, or even capitalist farming/family farming, are being replaced by an awareness of aspects such as the more complex tenurial structures that subtenancies introduced or the way that customary rights such as grazing affected different groups in the same community.[26]

While some change in agriculture and agrarian society is the result of catalysts such as the Black Death or other outside forces – witness the cataclysmic changes to the British dairy industry over the last 70 years as a result of government policies and retailers' control of the market – that is no reason why change cannot also come from within the farming communities themselves as they constantly seek improved profits, enabling a better life for themselves and, especially, for their children, whether in the Middle Ages or the twenty-first century.

26 Whittle, *Landlords and Tenants*, pp. 216–21.

Sources and bibliography

Note on probate sources for Brent Marsh

Owing to war-time bombing in which the bulk of probate records for the diocese of Bath and Wells were destroyed, only a few locally proven wills, inventories and other probate material survive for Brent Marsh. The small local sample has therefore been supplemented by wills proved in the Prerogative Court of Canterbury (PCC). In all, just under 900 wills were examined for this study, nearly three-quarters of them from the PCC; the breakdown of number and source of the wills by decade is given in Chapter 5, Table 8. PCC wills have not been widely used in local studies, apart from those for specific individuals, because they generally concerned only gentry or testators with property in more than one diocese. For Brent Marsh, however, there seems to be an unusually large number of PCC wills, particularly for the period 1580 to 1660. In addition to the wills of gentlemen, Axbridge merchants and many yeomen and widows, there are also many small craftsmen, such as weavers, blacksmiths and joiners, and a large number of husbandmen. Copyholders, identified from manorial records, are well represented, but many of the testators do not appear to be very well-to-do, and for most wills it is not apparent why they were taken to the PCC, as they do not explicitly involve property in more than one diocese.

While a desire to give the weight of the highest probate court to complex trusts or complications such as the death of the named executor may account for a few, there must be something more behind the majority: likely possibilities are a long-standing mistrust of the diocesan clergy and their registrars (since many testators here were tenants of the Church) or a desire to establish a secure title to both land and goods at a time when the proprietorship of land, chattels and even offices was under constant pressure of litigation. After 1660, however, the number of wills proved in the PCC drops suddenly. While the average proved for the period 1580 to 1639 was 5.3 a year, and 16 a year when the Court of Civil Commission was the only probate court (1653–60), after 1660 the average was 1.7. It may have been that economic changes made the business too expensive, or the restored Anglican Church may have been actively preventing use of the PCC where it was not necessary.

Obviously, the predominance of PCC wills affects the nature of the information obtained, but, though this probably means that many poorer will-makers are excluded, the bulk of wills do not differ significantly in content from the diocesan survivals; the PCC wills may contain more leases in the bequests than those proved locally and may slightly distort the testamentary picture by more emphasis on land in children's portions, but this was not felt to be serious enough to preclude the use of the PCC wills.

Manuscript sources

The National Archives

CHANCERY

C 1 Proceedings 1529–58
C 2 Proceedings Series I t. Eliz & James I
C 3 Series II, 1558–1660
C 5–8, 10 Proceedings, Six Clerks series, 1613–1714
C 66, Patent rolls
C 107/114 Chancery Masters Exhibits [Burnham manor, rental and sales *c.*1649]
C 108/182 Chancery Masters Exhibits [Cheddar Ep. manor recs *c.*1720]
C 142 Inquisitions *post mortem*

EXCHEQUER

E 112/330/24 Exchequer bills and answers (tithe suits)
E 126 Entry books of decrees
E 134 Depositions taken by Commission
E 135/5/45 Ecclesiastical documents [Berrow pars. accts]
E 178 Special Commissions of Inquiry
E 179 Subsidies, etc
E 179/169/169, /171, /175, /182 Subsidy 1523–5
E 179/170/241a, /242, /249, /250, /257 Relief of 1548
E 179/171/322, /324 Subsidy 1597
E 179/172/416, /417; 179/256/7; 179/171/336 pt30 Poll Tax 1660
E 179/172/434, /441 Hearth Tax Exemptions 1670
E 179/256/11, /14, /16, /19 Hearth Tax 1664–5
E 310/23/128 Particulars for Leases
E 315/385 Rental, Possessions of Cecily Marchioness of Dorset, 15–17 Henry VIII [ff. 90–95d: Huntspill de la Haye]

LAND REVENUE, MISC. BOOKS

LR 2/191 Surveys of Compton, Tarnock, t. Eliz
LR 2/202 Survey of Moors and Low Grounds in Somerset 13 Chas I
LR 2/225 Survey of East Brent Manor, 4 James I

PROBATE

PROB 2 PCC, Inventories
PROB 4 PCC, Inventories
PROB 11 PCC, Register copy wills
PROB 28 PCC, Cause Papers, Early Series (1642–1722)

STATE PAPERS

SP 16/165, /169 Domestic, Charles I and Add. [Wedmore tithes]
SP 18 Domestic, Interregnum
SP 23 Committee for Compounding with Delinquents
SP 28 Commonwealth Exchequer Papers

SP 46 Supplementary

OTHER CLASSES

SC 6/HENVIII/3163 Minister's accounts: Glastonbury Abbey manors [S Brent, E Brent, Lympsham, Berrow, Withys in Huntspill]

SC 12/30/33 Surveys of manors, including Tarnock (t.Eliz)

ASSI 23/3 Gaol Book, Western Circuit, 1685

HO 67/2 Agricultural Returns, Somerset, 1801

REQ 2 Court of Requests, proceedings, Henry VII to James I

RG 31/7 General Register Office, Returns of Places of Worship

Somerset Heritage Centre, Taunton

RECORDS OF CLERK OF PEACE

Q/AWa Wage Assessments 1601–41

Q/SO/7 Quarter Sessions Order Book, 1676–1687

Q/SR Quarter Sessions Rolls, 1607–1688

RECORDS OF DIOCESE OF BATH AND WELLS

D\D/ct Wills and Inventories

D\D/pd Records of Peculiar of Dean of Wells

D\D/rg Glebe Terriers

D\D/cd Deposition books of ecclesiastical courts (Bishop's Consistory court unless stated) 1530–1694: vols 12, 15, 25, 28 (?Dean, 1596–1614), 36, 45, 51 (Dean, 1616–39), 54, 70–1, 76, 81 (Archdeacon, testamentary cases 1677–90), 129–31 (Dean and others, 1544–1675), 135 (Archdeacon 1661–70)

PARISH RECORDS

D\P\b.on.s/

- 23/4 Burnham-on-Sea parish rates, 1692–99, 1701
- 23/15 Burnham-in-Sea, survey of Mark moor with maps, 18th cent.

D\P\hun/

- 3/1/1 Huntspill, Court roll of Rectory manor, 1597–1617
- 3/2/1 Huntspill, Tithe book, 1693
- 3/2/2 Huntspill, Descriptions of tithes etc, 1697
- 3/2/3 Huntspill, Tithe cases and other material

D\P\w.st.c/17/1/1–2 Wells, St Cuthbert's, almshouse trust deeds

MANORIAL AND ESTATE RECORDS DEPOSITED BY CHURCH COMMISSIONERS

A. Bishop's Estate

DD\CC/A/13324 Fine book of bishop's manors, 1634

B. Chapter Estate

DD\CC/B/

- 110001 Parliamentary Surveys, 1649–50 2 vols
- 110002 Terriers of manors, 1570–71
- 110004 Proposal Book (*c.*1640)

111739 Reeve's Accounts 1545–7; Survey, late 17th cent.
114066–71 Books of Warrants, t.Eliz to Charles II

Composite Court Rolls, manors of Allerton, Biddisham, Burnham Rectory, 1506/7 to 1638/9
DD\CC/B/
131907/4, 6, 8, 12, 14, 15, 17, 19–21
131908/12
131909/15, 23
131910a/1, 2, 5
131911a/1, 2, 7
131913/2
131917
131920/10, 12
131921/2–4, 12, 13
131922/1, 2
131923/1–7
131924/1, 3–7
131925/2, 4–10
131925a/1–5, 7, 9, 10, 12, 13
131926/7

Composite Accounts, manors of Allerton, Biddisham, Burnham Rectory
DD\CC/B/
131907/3, 7, 11 1619, 1566/7, 1636/7
131909/14, 18 1605/6, 1661/2
131910a/3 1616/17
131911a/3 1581/2
131925/3 1617/18

Allerton Manor
DD\CC/B/
110574 Court Presentments 1641–1763
110565 Court rolls 1660–1690
DD\CC/T/10860 Map 1787
DD\CC/B/110563 Reference book for map

Biddisham manor
DD\CC/B/
110225 Court rolls, 1660–1690
110233 Presentments 1639–1700
110237 Accounts, bills etc. 1661–1700
131913a/2 Cancelled admissions
110300 Lease 1683
110232 Rent rolls 1701
110241 Lease 1658
110358–60 Leases 1617, 1661, 1691
110222 Survey of manor, 1787

DD\CC/T/10854 Map for 1787 Survey

Burnham Rectory manor (Parsonage)
DD\CC/B/
110480–1 Court rolls, 1660–1690
110488 Court papers, 1660–1700
110495 Lease 1664
110539 Lease of Parsonage 1633
110541 Lease of Parsonage 1660
110478 Map 1819

Cheddar Parsonage Manor
DD\CC/B/
131909/17 Estreat, 1539/40
176212 Court roll, 1629–1820
176214 Copy of customs of manor 1699

C. Wells Archdeaconry Estate
South Brent Parsonage (inc. land in Berrow)
DD\CC/C/
121812 Survey of manors of S. Brent Parsonage and Berrow, 1632
121651 S Brent, Parliamentary Survey 1650
121652 S. Brent, Rent rolls 1637–1690
DD\CC/T/11465 S. Brent, Map of parish, 1811 [no key]

F. Wells Deanery Estate
DD\CC/F/30900 Survey, Deanery estate inc. Mark and Wedmore, 1574

L. Wells Vicars Choral Cheddar
DD\CC/L/
116013 Parliamentary Survey 1649/50 [Vicars Choral]
115039 Deeds, 1590, 1731
115065 Deeds, 1601, 1701
275470a Lease of tithes, 1671
116008 Bounds of estate in Draycott, Rodney Stoke [?18th cent.]

O. Wells Sub Chantry Estate
DD\CC/O/
39493 a. Parliamentary survey of Sub-chantry estates, 1650 (Wedmore, Mark, Cheddar, Wellington)
30928 Survey 1650

P. Wells Prebendary Estate
DD\CC/P/
167286 Copies of surveys, 16th–18th centuries
114099 Parliamentary Survey of Compton Bishop, 1650
DD\CC/T/15874 Map of Compton Bishop, 1779

Principal deposited collections

DD\AB/22 MSS from Marquess of Ailesbury
DD\AH/11/9 Acland Hood family of Fairfax (Ct bk 1505–15, inc Huntspill Verney)
DD\ALN/6 Alletson & Partners
DD\ARN/12 Misc. Som Docs (Evered MSS)
DD\BD/99 Baker & Duke
DD\BRC/27 Bristol City Corporation deposit (will of Geo. Carde)
DD\CH/4–5 Channer & Channer (Recs of manor of Cheddar Parsonage,1651–1838)
DD\DN/2/19/4 Dickinson Family of Kingweston (Deeds)
DD\FD/2 Badgworth deeds
DD\FS/12/1/3 Foster (Solicitors) of Wells [will of Ric. Latcham 1677]
DD\GS/20 Glastonbury Antiquarian Society (Survey of Deanery estates [*c.*1610])
DD\PLE/40 Poole of S Petherton Collection (Deeds of Wedmore, Weare, Mark etc)
DD\PO/1, 9 Popham MSS (Cheddar Berkeley)
DD\SAS/ Somerset Archaeological Society
- C61/6 Batcombe deed
- C82/16 Huntspill deeds
- C795/FA/161 (Wills, etc, 1642–64)
- C795/PR/150 (Cheddar churchwardens presentments 1662–1701)
- C795/PR/462 (survey of Mudgley, Wedmore, 1558)
- C795/SE/30 (Wills register from bp's consistory ct)
- H143/4 Cheddar deeds etc.

DD\SE/17, 26, 59, 63–5 MSS of Hugh Sexey's Hospital, Bruton (Blackford manor; Cheddar)
DD\SFR 8/1–2 Society of Friends, Bristol & Som. Q.M.
DD\SFRw 1 Society of Friends, Som. M.M., Western Division
DD\SG/22 Strangways MSS (Glastonbury Customal, 1592)
DD\SH/18, 21, 23, 33, 35 Strachey of Sutton Court (Hodges and Wedmore MSS)
DD\WM/45 Miscellaneous Somerset deeds
DD\WO/49 Trevelyan MSS
DD\WY/70, /84 Wyndham MSS, and recent deposit of Orchard Wyndham MSS (unlisted).
(New cal. for DD/WY due for completion Autumn 2017.)
DD\S\GEO Map of Lympsham, 1803
DD\S\WH/209 Kemys-Tynte of Halswell (Mark manor 1591–1602, 1612–28)
DD\X\HKN Journal of Dr John Westover, 1685–*c.*1706
DD\X\HMD Blackford Court book, 1661–63
DD\X\MRD Plan of Wedmore, 1805

PHOTOCOPIES OF MSS DEPOSITED BY VCH SOMERSET
T\PH\vch/
- 11 Lands of John Rosse and Henry Sydenham (Survey of Mudgley and Stoughton 1609)
- 38 Rent roll of Edward Seymour, *c.*1540

British Library, Manuscripts

Add. Ch.
- 16336 Compoti, Sir Thos Gresham's manors, 1566–9
- 26507 Court rolls, Badgworth, Weare Burgus, 1602–4

Add. MS
    30077 Presentments of Rebels, 1685
    33828 Phelps MSS
    34012 Lists from Major-Gen. Disbrowe 1655
    41804 Middleton Papers, vol. II
Egerton MS 3034 Terrier of manors of Glastonbury Abbey 1515–17
Harley MS
    594 Bishops' Returns, 1563
    6845 no. 65, Papers re. Monmouth

Cathedral Library, Wells

Ledger Books, F, G, 1566–1681
Rental of manor of Biddisham, 1618
Books of Arrears, 1590–1631, 1531–43
Steward's Book, 1629–30
Communar's Cash Book (late 17th cent.)

Corpus Christi College, Oxford

Fn Records of manor of Northgrove, Somerset
Fn 1–4 Court rolls and books, 11 Hen. VII to 1729
Fn 12–14 Surveys, rentals
Fn 16 Notes and lists 16–18th cents, and early deeds
Fn 18 Correspondence, 17th cent.
Fn 000 Newlyn papers, including letters from steward, late 17th cent.
Calendar of MSS of Corpus Christi College, Oxford (photocopy by NRA), vols 27, 28, 30

Dorset History Centre

D-SHC/KG/2668 70 Sherborne Castle Estate (Burnham manor ct rolls, 1633–44)

Friends House, Euston Rd, London

Digests of births, marriages and burials for Bristol and Somerset Quarterly Meeting
Men's Minutes for North Somerset, 1667–1712
Photocopy of the register of Watchven, Burnham, Somerset

London Metropolitan Archives, London

CLA/044/05/042 Royal Contract Estates: John Norden's survey of manor of Lympsham, 1622

North Yorkshire Record Office

ZJX 3/19/105–110 Court rolls of manors of Lympsham Parva and Tarnock, 1558–61; 1583–1608 (Cunliffe-Lister MSS, formerly at Bradford Libr., W. Yorks)

Wiltshire & Swindon History Centre, Chippenham

161/57; 161/141 Lovell of Cole Park (MSS re. Huish in Burnham, E Brent)

Printed primary sources

Billingsley, John, *General View of the Agriculture of the County of Somerset* (2nd edn, Bath, 1798).

Bromwich, D. (ed.), *The Diary and Memoirs of John Allen Giles* (Somerset Record Society 86, 2000).

Brown, F. (ed.), *Abstracts of Somersetshire Wills*, 6 vols (privately printed for F.A. Crisp, 1887–90).

Calendar of Patent Rolls, Edward VI, vol. 1, 1547–8.

Calendar of State Papers Domestic, James II, vol. 2, Jan. 1686–May 1687 (1964).

Calendar of Treasury Books, vol. 8, *1685–9* (1923).

Camden, William, *Britannia* (1806 edn).

Colby, F.T. (ed.), *Visitation of the County of Somerset in the Year 1623* (Harleian Society 11, 1876).

Collier, Thomas, *A Confession of the Faith of Several Churches* (1656).

Collier, Thomas, *The heads and substance of a discourse... held at Axbridge, co. Somerset ... about the sixth of March 1650* (London, 1651).

Defoe, Daniel, *A Tour Thro' the Whole Island of Great Britain*, 2 vols (1927 edn).

Dwelly, E. (ed.), *Dwelly's National Records*, vol. 2, *Directory of Somerset* (Fleet, 1929).

Dwelly, E. (ed.), *Dwelly's Parish Records*, vol. 1, *Bishop's Transcripts at Wells* (Herne Bay, 1913).

Dyer, A.A. and Palliser, D.M. (eds), *The Diocesan Population Returns for 1563 and 1603* (British Academy, 2005).

Fussell, G.E. (ed.), *Robert Loder's Farm Accounts 1610–1620* (Camden Society 3rd ser. 53, 1936).

Green, E. (ed.), *Somerset Chantry Certificates* (Somerset Record Society 2, 1888).

Green, M.A.E. (ed.), *Calendar of State Papers, Domestic (Commonwealth)*, vol. 12, *1658–9* (1885).

Harbin, E.H. Bates (ed.), *Quarter Sessions Records for the County of Somerset*, vol. I, *James I, 1607–1625* (Somerset Record Society 23, 1907).

Harbin, E.H. Bates (ed.), *Quarter Sessions Records for the County of Somerset*, vol. III, *Commonwealth 1646–1660* (Somerset Record Society 28, 1912).

Harbin, S.W. Bates (ed.), *Somerset Enrolled Deeds* (Somerset Record Society 51, 1936).

Hawkins, M.J. (ed.), *Sales of Wards in Somerset, 1603–1641* (Somerset Record Society 67, 1965).

Hervey, S.H.A. (ed.), *Wedmore Parish Registers: Marriages 1561–1839* (Wells, 1888); *Baptisms, 1561–1812* (Wells, 1890); *Burials 1561–1860* (Wells, 1890).

Historical Manuscripts Commission, *Calendar of the Manuscripts of the Dean and Chapter of Wells*, 2 vols (1907–14).

Historical Manuscripts Commission, *Third Report*, Appendix (MSS of Corp. of Axbridge).

Hotten, J.C. (ed.), *Original Lists of persons of Quality; Emigrants; Religious Exiles; ... who went from Great Britain to the American Plantations 1600–1700* (New York, 1931).

Leadam, I.S. (ed.), *Select Cases in the Court of Requests AD 1497–1569* (Selden Society XII, 1898).

Legg, L.G. Wickham (ed.), 'A Relation of a short survey of the Western Counties ... in 1635', in *Camden Miscellany* 16 (Camden Society 3rd ser. 52, 1936).

Letters and Papers, foreign and domestic, of the reign of Henry VIII, 23 vols in 38 (London, 1862–1932).

Morland, S.C. (ed.), *Somersetshire Quarterly Meeting of the Society of Friends, 1668–1699* (Somerset Record Society 75, 1978).

Narrative of the proceedings of the General Assembly of divers pastors, and ministring brethren of the Baptized Churches, ... London, from Septemb. 3 to 12, 1689 (London, 1689).

Penney, N. (ed.), *Extracts from State Papers relating to Friends* (1913).

Rawlins, S.W. and Jones, I. Fitzroy (eds), *Somerset Wills from Exeter, 1529–1600* (Somerset Record Society 62, 1952).

Shilton, D.O. and Holworthy, R. (eds), *Medieval Wills from Wells* (Somerset Record Society 40, 1925).

Smith, L. Toulmin (ed.), *The Itinerary of John Leland in or about the years 1535–1543*, vol. I (parts I–III) (1907).

Straton, C.R. (ed.), *Survey of the Lands of William First Earl of Pembroke*, 2 vols (Oxford, 1909).

Taylor, John, 'The Carriers' Cosmography' (1637), in E. Arber (ed.), *An English Garner*, vol. I, 223–46 (1895).

Turner, G. Lyon (ed.), *Original Records of Early Nonconformity*, 3 vols (1911–14), vol. I (1911).

Vanes, J. (ed.), *Ledger of John Smythe, 1538–50* (Bristol Record Society 28, 1974).

Watkin, Dom A. (ed.), *The Great Chartulary of Glastonbury*, 2 vols (Somerset Record Society 63, 1952).

Weaver, F.W. (ed.), *Somerset Medieval Wills, 1501–30* (Somerset Record Society 19, 1903).

Weaver, F.W. (ed.), *Somerset Medieval Wills, 1531–58* (Somerset Record Society 21, 1905).

Weaver, F.W. (ed.), *Visitation of the County of Somerset, 1531, 1573, 1591* (Exeter, 1885).

Weaver, F.W. (ed.), *Wells Wills* (1890).

Whiteman, A. (ed.), *The Compton Census of 1676* (British Academy, 1986).

Whiting, John, *Persecution Expos'd, in some memoirs relating to the sufferings of J.W.* (1696).

Wigfield, W. McD., *The Monmouth Rebels 1685* (Gloucester, 1985).

Secondary sources

Acres, W.M., *A Brief History of Wedmore* (Wedmore, 1954).

Aggs, W.H., *Wharton's Law-Lexicon* (11th edn, 1911).

Allen, R.C., *Enclosure and the Yeoman: The Agricultural Development of the South Midlands 1450–1850* (Oxford, 1992).

Amussen, S.D., *An Ordered Society: Gender and Class in Early Modern England* (New York, 1988).

Appleby, A.B., *Famine in Tudor and Stuart England* (Liverpool, 1978).

Aston, M. and Gerrard, C., *Interpreting the English Village: Landscape and Community at Shapwick, Somerset* (Oxford, 2012).

Aston, T.H. and Philpin, C.H.E. (eds), *The Brenner Debate: Agrarian Class Structure and Economic Development in Pre-Industrial Europe* (Cambridge, 1985).

Aylmer, G.E. (ed.), *The Interregnum: The Quest for Settlement 1646–1660* (London, 1974).

Bailey, M., *The Decline of Serfdom in Late Medieval England: From Bondage to Freedom* (Woodbridge, 2014).

Bailey, M., 'The Transformation of Customary Tenures in Southern England, *c.*1350 to *c.*1500', *Agricultural History Review*, 62 (2014), pp. 210–30.

Baker, A.R.H. and Butlin, R.A. (eds), *Studies of Field Systems in the British Isles* (Cambridge, 1973).

Baker, J.H. (ed.), *Legal Records and the Historian* (London, 1978).

Barnes, T.G., 'County Politics and a Puritan Cause Celebre: Somerset Churchales, 1633', *Transactions of the Royal Historical Society*, 5th ser. 9 (1959), pp. 103–22.

Barnes, T.G., *Somerset 1625–1640: A County's Government During the 'Personal Rule'* (Oxford, 1961).

Beckett, J.V., 'The Peasant in England: A Case of Terminological Confusion?', *Agricultural History Review*, 32 (1984), pp. 113–23.

Bettey, J.H., 'Cultivation of Teazles in North Somerset', *Notes and Queries for Somerset and Dorset*, 34/348 (1998), pp. 235–6.

Britnell, R.H., *The Commercialisation of English Society, 1000–1500* (2nd edn, Manchester, 1996).

Broad, J., 'Alternate Husbandry and Permanent Pasture in the Midlands, 1650–1800', *Agricultural History Review*, 28 (1980), pp. 77–89.

Broad, J., 'Regional Perspectives and Variations in English Dairying, 1650–1850', in R.W. Hoyle (ed.), *People, Landscape and Alternative Agriculture: Essays for Joan Thirsk* (BAHS, 2004), pp. 93–112.

Brooks, C., 'The Agrarian Problem in Revolutionary England', in Whittle (ed.), *Landlords and Tenants*, pp. 183–99.

Campbell, B.M.S., *English Seigneurial Agriculture, 1250–1450* (Cambridge, 2000).

Campbell, M., *The English Yeoman: under Elizabeth and the Early Stuarts* (London, 1967).

Chambers, J.D. and Mingay, G.E., *The Agricultural Revolution 1750–1880* (London, 1966).

Chartres, J.A., 'Road Carrying in England in the Seventeenth Century: Myth and Reality', *Economic History Review*, 2nd ser. 30 (1977), pp. 73–94.

Clark, A., *Working Life of Women in the Seventeenth Century* (London, 1919).

Clay, C., 'Lifeleasehold in the Western Counties of England 1650–1750', *Agricultural History Review*, 29 (1981), pp. 83–96.

Coleman, D.C., *Industry in Tudor and Stuart England* (London, 1975).

Coleman, Prebendary, 'Manor of Allerton and its Tenants, 1530–1866', *Proceedings of the Somerset Archaeological Society*, 46 (1900), part II, pp. 65–108.

Collinson, J., *The History and Antiquities of the County of Somerset*, 3 vols (Bath, 1791).

Collinson, P., 'Cranbrook and the Fletchers: Popular and Unpopular Religion in the Kentish Weald', in P.N. Brooks (ed.), *Reformation Principles and Practice, Essays in Honour of A.G. Dickens* (London, 1980), pp. 173–202.

Cooper, J.P., 'Patterns of Inheritance and Settlement by Great Landowners from the Fifteenth to the Eighteenth centuries', in Goody *et al.*, *Family and Inheritance*, pp. 192–327.

Cornwall, J.C.K., *Wealth and Society in Early Sixteenth Century England* (London, 1988).

Coster, W., *Family and Kinship in England, 1450–1800* (London, 2001).

Croot, P.E.C., 'Aspects of Agrarian Society in Brent Marsh, Somerset, 1500–1700', PhD thesis (University of Leeds, 1981).

Croot, P. and Parker, D., 'Agrarian Class Structure and the Development of Capitalism: France and England Compared', in Aston and Philpin (eds), *The Brenner Debate*, pp. 79–90.

Cross, C., 'The Church in England, 1646–1660', in Aylmer (ed.), *The Interregnum*, pp. 99–120.

Cross, C., *The Puritan Earl: the Life of Henry Hastings Third Earl of Huntingdon, 1536–1595* (London, 1966).

Darby, H.C. (ed.), *A New Historical Geography of England Before 1600* (Cambridge, 1976).

Darby, H.C. and Finn, R.W. (eds), *The Domesday Geography of South-West England* (Cambridge, 1967).

de Vries, J., *Economy of Europe in an Age of Crisis: 1600–1750* (Cambridge, 1976).

Department of Health, *Manual of Nutrition* (12th edn, London, 2012).

Dobson, M.J., *Contours of Death and Disease in Early Modern England* (Cambridge, 1997).

Dowell, S., *A History of Taxation and Taxes in England* (London, 1888).

Dunning, R.W., *A History of Somerset* (Bridgwater, 1978).

Dunning, R.W. (ed.), *Victoria County History of Somerset*, vol. III (London, 1974); vol. VIII (London, 2004).

Dyer, C., *An Age of Transition? Economy and Society in England in the Later Middle Ages* (Oxford, 2007).

Dyer, C., 'The English Medieval Village Community and its Decline', *Journal of British Studies*, 33 (1994), pp. 407–29.

Earle, P., *Monmouth's Rebels: The Road to Sedgemoor 1685* (London, 1977).

Edwards, P., *The Horse Trade of Tudor and Stuart England* (Cambridge, 1988).

Ellis, F., *Peasant Economics: Farm Households and Agrarian Development* (2nd edn, Cambridge, 1993).

Erickson, A.L., *Women and Property in Early Modern England* (London, 1993).

Everitt, A., 'Nonconformity in Country Parishes', in Thirsk (ed.), *Land, Church and People*, pp. 178–99.

Foster, J., *Alumni Oxonienses: 1500–1714* [1892].

Foyle, A. and Pevsner, N., *Somerset: North and Bristol* (London, 2011).

French, H.R. and Hoyle, R.W., *The Character of English Rural Society: Earls Colne, 1550–1750* (Manchester, 2007).

Fussell, G.E., *The English Dairy Farmer, 1500–1900* (London, 1966).

Garrett-Goodyear, H., 'Common Law and Manor Courts: Lords, Copyholders and Doing Justice in Early Tudor England', in Whittle (ed.), *Landlords and Tenants*, pp. 35–51.

Gayton, J., 'Tenants, Tenures and Transfers: The Landholding Experience of Rural Customary Tenants in some Hampshire Downland Manors, 1645–1750', PhD thesis (University of Exeter, 2013).

Gibson, J.S.W., *Wills and Where to Find Them* (Chichester, 1974).

Goffin, R.J.R., *The Testamentary Executor in England and Elsewhere* (London, 1901).

Goody, J., Thirsk, J. and Thompson, E.P. (eds), *Family and Inheritance: Rural Society in Western Europe, 1200–1800* (Cambridge, 1976).

Gray, C.M., *Copyhold, Equity, and the Common Law* (Harvard Historical Monographs 53, Cambridge, MA, 1963).

Gray, H.L., *English Field Systems* (Cambridge, MA, 1915).

Gray, H.L., 'The Production and Exportation of English Woollens in the 14th Century', *English Historical Review*, 39 (1924), pp. 13–35.

Gritt, A.J., 'The Operation of Lifeleasehold in South-West Lancashire, 1649–97', *Agricultural History Review*, 53 (2005), pp. 1–23.

Guest, A.G., 'Family Provision and the *Legitima Portio*', *Law Quarterly Review*, 73 (1957), pp. 74–88.

Harrison, C.J., 'The Social and Political History of Cannock and Rugeley 1546–97', PhD thesis (University of Keele, 1974).

Hatcher, J. and Bailey, M., *Modelling the Middle Ages: The History and Theory of England's Economic Development* (Oxford, 2001).

Havinden, M., 'The Increase and Distribution of the Resident Gentry of Somerset, 1500–1623', *Southern History*, 20/21 (1999), pp. 68–107.

Helm, P.J., 'The Somerset Levels in the Middle Ages (1086–1539)', *Journal of the British Archaeological Association*, 3rd ser. 12 (1949), pp. 37–52.

Hembry, P., *The Bishops of Bath and Wells, 1540–1640* (London, 1967).

Hervey, S.H.A., *The Wedmore Chronicle*, 2 vols (1887, 1898).

Hey, D.G., *An English Rural Community: Myddle under the Tudors and Stuarts* (Leicester, 1974).

Hill, C., 'From Lollards to Levellers', in M. Cornforth (ed.), *Rebels and their Causes: Essays in Honour of A.L. Morton* (London, 1978), pp. 49–67.

Hilton, R.H., *The English Peasantry in the Later Middle Ages* (Oxford, 1975).

Hirst, D., *Representative of the People? Voters and Voting in England under the Early Stuarts* (Cambridge, 1975).

Holdsworth, W.S., *A History of English Law*, vol. III (3rd edn, 1923).

Horn, J.M. and Bailey, D.S. (eds), *Fasti Ecclesiae Anglicanae 1541–1857*, vol. V, *Bath & Wells Diocese* (London, 1979).

Hoskins, W.G., *Essays in Leicestershire History* (Liverpool, 1950).

Hoskins, W.G., *The Midland Peasant* (Chichester, 2008).

Hoskins, W.G., *Provincial England: Essays in Social and Economic History* (London, 1963).

Howell, C., 'Peasant Inheritance Customs in the Midlands, 1280–1700', in Goody *et al.*, *Family and Inheritance*, pp. 112–55.

Hoyle, R.W., 'Tenure and the Land Market in Early Modern England: or a Late Contribution to the Brenner Debate', *Economic History Review*, 2nd ser. 43/I (1990), pp. 1–20.

Hulbert, N.F., 'Survey of the Somerset Fairs', *Proceedings of the Somerset Archaeological Society*, 82 (1936), pp. 83–159.

Humphries, J., 'Enclosures, Common Rights, and Women: The Proletarianization of Families in the late Eighteenth and Early Nineteenth Centuries', *Journal of Economic History*, 50 (1990), pp. 17–42.

Hunt, T.J. and Dawe, P.N. (eds), *Notes and Queries for Somerset and Dorset*, 26 (1955).

Hunt, T.J. and Dawe, P.N. (eds), *Notes and Queries for Somerset and Dorset*, 29 (1968).

Hurwich, J.J., 'Social Origins of the Early Quakers', *Past and Present*, 48 (1970), pp. 156–62.

Jackman, D., *Baptists in the West Country* (Western Baptist Association, 1953).

Jones, I.F.H., 'Somerset Fairs', *Proceedings of the Somerset Archaeological Society*, 91 (1945), pp. 71–81.

Jones, J.R., *Country and Court: 1658–1714* (London, 1983 edn).

Keil, I.J.E., 'The Estates of the Abbey of Glastonbury in the Later Middle Ages', PhD thesis (University of Bristol, 1964).

Kerridge, E., *Agrarian Problems in the 16th Century and After* (London, 1969).

Kerridge, E., *The Agricultural Revolution* (London, 1967).

Kosminsky, E.A., *Studies in the Agrarian History of England in the Thirteenth Century* (London, 1956).

Laslett, P., *The World We Have Lost – further explored* (London, 1983 edn).

Locke, R., 'An Historical Account of the Marsh-Lands of the County of Somerset', *Letters and Papers of the Bath and West of England Society*, VIII (Bath, 1796), pp. 259–84.

Locke, R., 'A History of Brent Marsh', in *Letters and Papers of the Bath and West of England Society*, V (Bath, 1793), pp. 180–201.

Locke, R., *The Western Rebellion* (Taunton, 1912).

Macfarlane, A., *The Origins of English Individualism: The Family, Property and Social Transition* (Oxford, 1978).

Matthews, A.G., *Calamy Revised* (Oxford, 1934).

Matthews, A.G., *Walker Revised* (Oxford, 1948).

Mills, D.R., *Lord and Peasant in Nineteenth Century Britain* (London, 1980).

Morrill, J.S., *Cheshire 1630–1660* (Oxford, 1974).

Morrin, J., 'The Transfer to Leasehold on Durham Cathedral Estate, 1541–1626', in Whittle (ed.), *Landlords and Tenants*, pp. 117–32.

Muldrew, C., *Food, Energy and the Creation of Industriousness: Work and Material Culture in Agrarian England 1550–1780* (Cambridge, 2011).

Nair, G., *Highley: The Development of a Community, 1550–1880* (Oxford, 1988).

Netting, R. McC., *Smallholders, Householders: Farm Families and the Ecology of Intensive, Sustainable Agriculture* (Stanford, CA, 1993).

Notestein, W., 'The English Woman, 1580 to 1625', in J.H. Plumb (ed.), *Studies in Social History, presented to G.M. Trevelyan* (London, 1955), pp. 69–107.

Nuttall, G.F., 'The Western Baptist Association 1653–1658', *Journal of Ecclesiastical History*, 11 (1960), pp. 213–18.

O'Hara, D., *Courtship and Constraint: Rethinking the making of marriage in Tudor England* (Manchester, 2000).

Orbach, J. and Pevsner, N., *Somerset: South and West* (London, 2014).

Overton, M., *Agricultural Revolution in England: The Transformation of the Agrarian Economy 1500–1850* (Cambridge, 1996).

Overton, M., Whittle, J., Dean, D. and Hann, A., *Production and Consumption in English Households, 1600–1750* (Abingdon, 2012).

Page, W. (ed.), *Victoria County History of Somerset*, vol. II (London, 1911).

Pearl, V., 'London's Counter-Revolution', in Aylmer (ed.), *The Interregnum*, pp. 29–56.

Pollock, F. and Maitland, F.W., *The History of English Law before the Time of Edward I*, vol. 2 (2nd edn, Cambridge, 1911).

Ramsey, P., *Tudor Economic Problems* (London, 1968).

Rippon, S., *Landscape, Community and Colonisation: the North Somerset Levels* (York, 2007).

Rogers, J.E.T., *A History of Agriculture and Prices in England*, 7 vols (Oxford, 1866–92).

Scrase, T., *Somerset Towns: Changing Fortunes 800–1800* (Stroud, 2005).

Scriven, J., *Treatise on the Law of Copyholds* (6th edn, 1882).

Shaw, W.A., *The History of the English Church 1640–60*, 2 vols (1900).

Shaw-Taylor, L., 'The Management of Common Land in Lowlands England, *c.*1500 to *c.*1850', in M. de Moor, L. Shaw-Taylor and P. Warde (eds), *The Management of Common Land in North West Europe, 1500–1850* (Turnhout, Belgium, 2002).

Shaw-Taylor, L., 'The Rise of Agrarian Capitalism and the Decline of Family Farming in England', *Economic History Review*, 65 (2012), pp. 26–60.

Sheehan, M., *The Will in Medieval England* (Toronto, 1963).

Shepard, A., *Accounting for Oneself: Worth, Status and the Social Order in Early Modern England* (Oxford, 2015).

Simpson, A.W.B., *An Introduction to the History of Land Law* (Oxford, 1961).

Skipp, V., *Crisis and Development: An Ecological Case Study of the Forest of Arden 1570–1674* (Cambridge, 1978).

Speechley, H.V., 'Female and Child Agricultural Day Labourers in Somerset, *c.*1685–1870', PhD thesis (University of Exeter, 1999).

Spufford, M., *Contrasting Communities: English Villagers in the Sixteenth and Seventeenth Centuries* (Cambridge, 1974).

Spufford, M., 'Peasant Inheritance Customs and Land Distribution in Cambridgeshire from the Sixteenth to the Eighteenth centuries', in Goody *et al.*, *Family and Inheritance*, pp. 156–76.

Stenton, D.M., *The English Woman in History* (London, 1957).

Stretton, T., *Women Waging Law in Elizabethan England* (Cambridge, 1998).

Swainson, B.M., 'Rural Settlement in Somerset', *Geography*, 20 (1935), pp. 112–24.

Symonds, H., 'A By-Path of the Civil War', *Proceedings of the Somerset Archaeological Society*, 65 (1919), pp. 48–75.

Tate, W.E., *Somerset Enclosure Acts and Awards* (Frome, 1948).

Tawney, R.H., *The Agrarian Problem in the Sixteenth Century* (New York, 1967 reprint of 1912 edn).

The Compleat English Copyholder, 2 vols (1735).

Thirsk, J. (ed.), *The Agrarian History of England and Wales*, IV, *1500–1640* (Cambridge, 1967).

Thirsk, J. (ed.), *The Agrarian History of England and Wales*, V, *1640–1750*, 2 vols, i, *Regional Farming Systems* (Cambridge, 1984), ii, *Agrarian Change* (Cambridge, 1985).

Thirsk, J., *Agricultural Regions and Agrarian History in England, 1500–1750* (Basingstoke, 1987).

Thirsk, J., *Economic Policy and Projects: The Development of a Consumer Society in Early Modern England* (Oxford, 1978).

Thirsk, J., *English Peasant Farming: The Agrarian History of Lincolnshire from Tudor to Recent Times* (London, 1957).

Thirsk, J. (ed.), *Land, Church and People: Essays presented to Professor H.P.R. Finberg* (*Agricultural History Review*, 18, supplement, 1970)

Thirsk, J., *The Restoration* (London, 1976).

Thirsk, J., 'Seventeenth-Century Agriculture and Social Change', in *idem* (ed.), *Land, Church and People*, pp. 148–77.

Thirsk, J. and Cooper, J.P. (eds), 'Introduction of Excise, 1643', in *Seventeenth-Century Economic*

Documents (Oxford, 1972), pp. 631–4.
Thompson, E.P., 'The Grid of Inheritance: A Comment', in Goody *et al.*, *Family and Inheritance*, pp. 328–60.
Thompson, F.M.L., *English Landed Society in the Nineteenth Century* (London, 1971 edn).
Tomlins, T.E., *Law Dictionary*, vol. I (1835).
Trow-Smith, R., *A History of British Livestock Husbandry to 1700* (London, 1957).
Trow-Smith, R., *A History of British Livestock Husbandry, 1700–1900* (London, 1959).
Tyacke, N., 'Puritanism, Arminianism and Counter-Revolution', in C. Russell (ed.), *The Origins of the English Civil War* (London, 1973), pp. 119–43.
Underdown, D., 'The Ilchester Election, February 1646', *Proceedings of the Somerset Archaeological Society*, 110 (1966), pp. 40–51.
Underdown, D., 'The Problem of Popular Allegiance in the English Civil War', *Transactions of the Royal Historical Society*, 5th ser. 31 (1981), pp. 69–94.
Underdown, D., *Revel, Riot, and Rebellion: Popular Politics and Culture in England 1603–1660* (Oxford, 1985).
Underdown, D., *Somerset in the Civil War and Interregnum* (Newton Abbot, 1973).
Vann, R.T., 'Wills and the Family in an English Town: Banbury, 1550–1800', *Journal of Family History*, 4/4 (1979), pp. 346–67.
Verdon, N., '"... Subjects Deserving of the Highest Praise": Farmers' Wives and the Farm Economy in England, *c.*1700–1850', *Agricultural History Review*, 51/1 (2003), pp. 23–39.
Weaver, F.W., *Somerset Incumbents* (Bristol, 1889).
West, F.J., 'On the Ruins of Feudalism – Capitalism?' in E. Kamenka and R.S. Neale (eds), *Feudalism, Capitalism and Beyond* (London, 1975).
Whitley, W.T., *A History of British Baptists* (2nd edn, 1932).
Whittle, J., *The Development of Agrarian Capitalism: Land and Labour in Norfolk, 1440–1580* (Oxford, 2000).
Whittle, J., 'Enterprising Widows and Active Wives: Women's Unpaid Work in the Household Economy of Early Modern England', *The History of the Family*, 19/3 (2014), pp. 282–300.
Whittle, J., 'Housewives and Servants in Rural England, 1440–1650: Evidence of Women's Work from Probate Documents', *Transactions of the Royal Historical Society*, 15 (2005), pp. 51–74.
Whittle, J., 'Individualism and the Family–Land Bond: A Reassessment of Land Transfer Patterns among the English Peasantry', *Past and Present*, 160 (1998), pp. 25–63.
Whittle, J., 'Inheritance, Marriage, Widowhood and Remarriage: A Comparative Perspective on Women and Landholding in North-East Norfolk, 1440–1580', *Continuity and Change*, 13/1 (1998), pp. 33–72.
Whittle, J. (ed.), *Landlords and Tenants in Britain, 1440–1660: Tawney's Agrarian Problem Revisited* (Woodbridge, 2013).
Whittle, J., 'Leasehold Tenure in England c.1300–c.1600', in Bos van Bavel and Phillipp Schofield (eds), *The Development of Leasehold in Northwestern Europe, c.1200–1600* (Turnhout, 2009), pp. 139–54.
Whittle, J. and Griffiths, E., *Consumption and Gender in the Early Seventeenth-Century Household: The World of Alice Le Strange* (Oxford, 2012).
Williams, M., 'The 1801 Crop Returns for Somerset', *Proceedings of the Somerset Archaeological Society*, 113 (1969), pp. 69–85.
Williams, M., *The Draining of the Somerset Levels* (Cambridge, 1970).
Williamson, T., *Shaping Medieval Landscapes: Settlement, Society, Environment* (Macclesfield, 2003).

Wood, A., *Riot, Rebellion and Popular Politics in Early Modern England* (Basingstoke, 2002).
Wright, Joseph, *The English Dialect Dictionary* (Oxford, 1923).
Wrightson, K., *Earthly Necessities: Economic Lives in Early Modern Britain, 1470–1750* (London, 2002 edn).
Wrightson, K. and Levine, D., *Poverty and Piety in an English Village: Terling, 1525–1700* (London, 1979).

Index

Places are in Somerset unless otherwise stated